REVISITING "TORONTO THE GOOD":
VIOLENCE, RELIGION AND CULTURE
IN A LATE VICTORIAN CITY

D1596818

Abstract

Among historians of crime it is now almost universally held that, in Western contexts, interpersonal violence declined precipitously from the medieval period until the 1960s when it rapidly rose. This sharp decline follows the path of a U-shaped graph first identified by Ted Robert Gurr in 1981, following the theorizing of Norbert Elias and now popularized by Steven Pinker. This dissertation demonstrates the sharp decline in interpersonal violence in Toronto from 1880-1899 and argues that it is tightly correlated to the rise of a British evangelical Protestant (BEP) expression. For the decade from 1880-1889 I calculated the homicide rate at 2.6 per 100,000, while for 1890-1899 it dropped to 1.5 per 100,000. Historically, especially given the absence of trauma medicine, these are very low homicide rates. While recognizing that correlation does not conclusively prove causation, I use standard theory regarding causal inference to argue that communal BEP discourses and practices channelled the behavior of young males in nonviolent directions across Toronto's culture as a whole. Analysis of the Central Prison register for 1874-1889 demonstrates that BEP males listed as residents of Toronto were severely underrepresented for a range of offences that varied from drunkenness, to petty theft, to physical assault. Although class was a factor, I argue that religious ideology is the critical consideration in explaining the relative absence of BEP males in Central Prison, confirming previous studies by Oliver and by Darroch and Soltow. This absence appears even more pronouncedly when prisoners from Toronto are separated out and more pronouncedly still when violent offences are disaggregated. While declining violence in late Victorian Toronto was part of a process that had been underway for centuries in western societies, the rise of the BEP movement in Toronto shows how particular influence affected it. The cultural configuration of Toronto, which was saturated by BEP religion, coincide with very low levels of interpersonal violence as measured by homicide rates and thus points to the importance of ideology in shaping behaviour.

REVISITING "TORONTO THE GOOD": VIOLENCE, RELIGION AND CULTURE IN A LATE VICTORIAN CITY

William D. Reimer

GERHARD & CO.
2016

Revisiting Toronto the Good: Homicide Rates, Religion, and Culture
in a Late Victorian City
Copyright © 2016 William D. Reimer
E-mail: breimer074@gmail.com

Published 2016 by Gerhard & Company
212 Kingston Row
Winnipeg, MB
R2M 0T4

ISBN 978-1-57383-524-4

Cataloguing-in-Publication information is on file at Library and Archives
Canada.

Cover Image: Bird's-eye view, looking north from harbour to north of Bloor
St. and some points beyond, from Humber R. on the west to Victoria Park
Ave. on the east. Published by: Barclay, Clark & Co. Lithographers, 1893.
Image courtesy Toronto Public Library.

For Dorcas,
my love

CONTENTS

CONTENTS

CONTENTS

CONTENTS

CONTENTS

1

A PROBLEM IN SOCIAL HISTORY, HOW SCHOLARS HAVE APPROACHED IT, AND WHERE LATE NINETEENTH-CENTURY TORONTO FITS IN

Late Victorian Toronto was marked by sharply decreasing homicide rates that persisted in the following decades. At precisely the same time, British evangelical Protestantism became entrenched in the social and political fabric of the city. This thesis explores grounds for seeing a relationship between these two developments. It positions itself as an intervention in the major and ongoing debate over the decline of violence in world societies generally—a debate to which Steven Pinker's recent and much-discussed book, *The Better Angels of Our Nature*, has given fresh, vital, and controversy-inspiring life. It particularly locates itself in the phase of the debate that concerns causation, arguing, as it does, that the decline in domestic, interpersonal forms of violent behavior which Toronto witnessed was a function of social actors' internalization of the behavioural values and codes associated with a particular kind of Protestant Christian belief. Its relevance is thus to both the study of social behavior and to examination of the reasons why that behavior took the forms that it did. The thesis of this study, baldly stated, is that interpersonal violence declined in late nineteenth-century Toronto because of a prevalence of British evangelical Protestantism. I will accord sufficient nuance to this statement over the course of the study.

1.1 From Breslau to the British Library Reading Room

Any argument concerning a decline in violence must be placed in the broader context of the history of interpersonal violence and how it has been treated by investigators and commentators across several decades, in many countries, and through use of a wide variety of investigative tools. There is now a substantial body of historiography that provides evidence of downward paradigmatic shifts in interpersonal violence from the mid-sixteenth century and on into modern and late modern times.[1] The "discoverer" of this broad decline in violence was Norbert Elias (1897-1990). Like Marx from the previous century, Elias, a refugee from Nazi Germany, conducted his research in the Reading Room of the British Library over a three-year period beginning in 1936. His two-volume landmark work, *The Civilizing Process*, was published in German to little notice by a Swiss publisher, and, after the war, because of meagre sales, the publisher requested that remaining copies be pulped. Notwithstanding this unpropitious start, the theories of Elias increasingly gained currency among historians of crime, particularly following the publication of the first volume of *The Civilizing Process*[2] in English in 1978.

The core of Elias' thesis is that Western culture[3] underwent remarkable change due to increasing external and internal constraints exerted on the individual against the use of interpersonal violence. These increased restraints resulted from a "top-down" process whereby wars, feuds, brawls, and even bodily functions and table manners were increasingly regulated by elite-driven cultural prescriptions.

These cultural prescriptions were not teleological. The civilizing process Elias sees is rather the product of endless human interactions and agendas

---

[1] Violence and homicide have been a constant throughout the history of *Homo sapiens* both prior to and subsequent to the advent of written historical documents. For a summary of the evidence by a leading archaeologist see Barry Cunliffe, *Europe Between the Oceans: 9000 BC-AD 1000* (New Haven: Yale University Press, 2008), 81-85, 109-111, 484. See also Azar Gat, *War in Human Civilization* (Oxford: Oxford University Press, 2006), 6-10; Gregory Clark, *A Farewell to Alms: A Brief Economic History of the World* (Princeton: Princeton University Press, 2007), 124-128.

[2] The current one-volume edition is Norbert Elias, *The Civilizing Process* (Oxford: Blackwell Publishing), 1994.

[3] While Elias argues that the civilizing process is identified most closely with the West, he makes clear that this process is found everywhere. Its priority in the West came about because of certain thresholds being gained with respect to divisions of functions, monopolies, interdependencies, populations, and geography. Colonists and colonized intermingled gradually, with the resulting fusion producing new forms of civilization. Norbert Elias, *The Civilizing Process*, 379-387.

that give rise to an ordered pattern. It is "set in motion blindly" and is kept in motion by the web of human relations. Individuals are forced to "attune"[4] their conduct to that of others. With the consolidation of the state and the accompanying state monopoly on legitimate violence, "pacified spaces" are created within societies.[5] Longer chains of interdependence in a culture are accompanied by greater constraints on individuals in the exercising of compulsions and emotions. Societies with fewer divisions of function are more violent, while those with more divisions less so.[6]

Over time the battlefield increasingly came to be seen as situated *within* the individual and the controls inhibiting violence were viewed as partly conscious and partly habit. Human adaptability in this respect was thought to be due to the individual's possession of a "malleable psychological apparatus" that is socially shaped. According to Elias, the social "habitus" of a culture is the sets of characteristics that individuals share with other members of their social group. The order and direction that a society takes across time is not subject to individual control and is not produced by "rational" measures. Quantitative aspects of a given habitus can be accessed through empirical studies of social phenomena such as violent crime or automobile accidents.[7]

---

[4] This term is used in Norbert Elias, *The Civilizing Process*, 367, 403.

[5] Elias argues that stricter monogamy was a product of the process and that the social position of women was strengthened as a result. Norbert Elias, *The Civilizing Process*, 154-157.

[6] Norbert Elias, *The Civilizing Process*, 365-370. Here there is evidence of the influence of Freud. Roughly speaking, these changes came about from the sixteenth to the eighteenth century. Norbert Elias, *The Civilizing Process*, 89-91.

[7] For example, the number of vehicular fatalities per billion kilometers driven varies across countries. In Canada, the annual number of vehicular deaths can be ascertained with a fair amount of precision and does not vary significantly from year-to-year. On "habitus" see especially Norbert Elias, *The Civilizing Process*, 365-369. The thought of Elias in some ways resembles that of Foucault in that both were interested in how "power" functioned within the individual in relationship to culture and the state. Foucault translated for his own use Elias' *Loneliness of the Dying*. Of course, Elias was more interested in long-term changes in power. Foucault laid stress on top-down power while Elias accented the dynamic between individual and culture. See Petrus Spierenburg, "Punishment, Power, and History: Foucault and Elias" in *Social Science History*, 28, no. 4 (Winter 2004): 607-636. See also Andrea D. Buhrmann and Stefanie Ernst, eds., *Care or Control of the Self? Michel Foucault, Norbert Elias, and the Subject in the 21st Century* (Newcastle: Cambridge Scholars' Press, 2010). Jack Goody has critiqued thinkers such as Elias who, he argues, privilege a European line of development.

Decivilizing processes always remain a possibility and are accompanied by sharp increases in interpersonal violence.

1.2 Durkheim and Suicide

Elias' work, for all its originality, did have antecedents. Key among these was the work of the pioneering sociologist Emile Durkeim (1858-1917), which laid great stress on the unique dynamics or "collective realities" of cultures. Each culture, Durkheim argued, has unique characteristics that often can be empirically measured, as in the case of suicide. Central to Durkheim's thought is that "individual predispositions" are not alone in determining the occurrence of a suicide; a combination of factors is involved, including, most importantly, the social context. Different cultures produce different rates of suicide while *within* cultures different religious affiliations generate different suicide rates.[8]

Critical to Durkeim's thinking was the notion of *anomie*, that is, the displacement that resulted from living in the fluid, unstable, anonymous conditions of urban society.[9] Durkheim lays great stress on the need for informal structures of obligation in a cohesive society in order to minimize *anomie*. He says, for example, that married men have lower rates of suicide than single

---

According to Goody, Europeans have appropriated to themselves a variety of virtues and accomplishments that constitute a "theft of history". Jack Goody, *The Theft of History* (Cambridge: Cambridge University Press, 2006).

[8] Durkheim observed that as a rule the suicide rate for Protestants was higher than that for Catholics. The reverse was true with respect to homicide. However, England was an exception in that it had a lower suicide rate than other Protestant regions in Europe and it also had the lowest homicide rate of any European country whether Protestant or Catholic. Emile Durkheim, trans. by John A. Spaulding and George Simpson, *Suicide: A Study in Sociology* (New York: Free Press, 1951), 155, 160-161, 353-354.

[9] A condition of *anomie* existed for Durkheim when there is uncertainty with respect to norms and morals. Such uncertainty results in "passions" being less controlled by "a public opinion". Rapid urbanization and industrialization produce a "chronic state" of anomie and work against social integration. See Emile Durkheim, *Suicide* (New York: Free Press, 1951), 86, 170, 186, 202, 253-258. However, Durkheim did recognize that strong religious ties in a culture provided a protective function against acts of "passion" and used Britain as an example. Presumably Durkheim would have extended this function to Toronto and would not have been at odds with the general argument of this thesis. See Emile Durkheim, *Suicide*, 160-170.

men, not because married men are more moral, but because a "domestic society" provides reciprocal bonds that have a prophylactic effect against suicide. Larger families possess denser bonds and have correspondingly a lower suicide rate. With respect to religion, Durkheim does not attach any importance to specific beliefs but rather attributes religion's power to a "sufficiently intense collective life".[10] In this sense, insists Durkheim, religion fulfills an important function in a society.

1.3 The Enduring Legacy of Max Weber

A third social thinker closely allied to Elias and Durkheim is Max Weber (1864-1920). Both Elias and Weber share the idea that the state possesses a monopoly on legitimate violence. They differ, however, in that where Elias downplays the importance of religion[11] for Weber it is central. Weber was the earliest proponent of the classic, though much contested, argument that Calvinist Christianity brought a religious ascetic to the marketplace that molded the individual for a capitalist world. What is central in Weber's thought, so far as the present study is concerned, is his idea that Protestant asceticism, as seen particularly in the Calvinist, Methodist, and Baptist traditions, "bred" moral qualities in the individual. These qualities were required for membership within the "community circle". Within the circle a "continuous

---

[10] Emile Durkheim, *Suicide* (New York: Free Press, 1951), 169-170. He goes too far in dismissing the benefit of specific beliefs. I argue that a monogenesis doctrine with respect to human origins served to some degree as a protective against the polygenesis-type theories that underlay social Darwinism (as opposed to Darwin himself, whose theories stressed common origins). Durkheim's analysis of British religion is also flawed. He attributes the fact that England had the lowest rate of suicide among Protestant countries as due to an Anglican hierarchy. However by the 1870s, the decade represented in Durkheim's data, both Puritan and evangelical streams had reconfigured the religious landscape and it is more plausible to argue that the low suicide rate, if based on accurate data, could be the result of an evangelical disciplinary impulse that was not present to the same degree in the Protestant countries on the Continent. Emile Durkheim, trans. by John A. Spaulding and George Simpson, *Suicide: A Study in Sociology* (New York: Free Press, 1951), 160-161. Elsewhere, Durkheim argued that acts of individual violence were products of "a specific moral culture." See Manuel Eisner, "Long-Term Historical Trends in Violent Crime," *Crime and Justice; A Review of Research* 30 (2003), 131.

[11] For a critique of this neglect of religion by Elias see Keith Thomas, "The Rise of the Fork," *New York Review of Books*, May 9, 1978, 28-31.

and unobtrusive" ethical discipline took place with the accent being placed on ethical conduct rather than ethical doctrine.[12] The community member was required to morally prove him-or herself before other members of the community. This is in sharp contrast to membership in a state church to which one belongs simply by virtue of being born into the community.

Weber argues that ascetic Protestant cultures were resistant to an absolutist "Caesarism" as they were marked by a voluntarist principle,[13] the rejection of venality, and were characterized by relatively free institutions. These ascetic communities form the basis of a "modern individualism" that allowed for a break from authoritarianism and patriarchy.[14]

In summary, says Weber, *belonging* to a Protestant group brought with it communal benefits that entailed moral demands and intense scrutiny of personal conduct. These "psychological sanctions" gave direction to types of ethical conduct[15] that emphasized diligence, thrift, sobriety, and prudence,[16] all moral qualities that work towards restraining interpersonal violence.[17]

Contemporary theorists that overlap in important ways with the afore-mentioned trio of sociologists include Robert Putman and Philip Gorski. Putnam's ideas particularly share ground with Durkheim and Weber. Putnam has emphasized the concept of a "social capital". By this Putnam means the dense networks that tie individuals and groups together in reciprocal relationships that are mutually beneficial and produce norms of trustworthiness.[18]

---

[12] Max Weber, trans. H.H. Gerth and C. Wright Mills, *From Max Weber: Essays in Sociology* (New York: Oxford University Press, 1958), 320-321.

[13] Membership is voluntary and free but requires qualifications that are accepted by the other members of the community. See Max Weber, *From Max Weber*, 316.

[14] Max Weber, *From Max Weber*, 321.

[15] Max Weber, trans. Talcott Parsons, *The Protestant Ethic and the Spirit of Capitalism* (New York: Charles Scribner, 1958), 97.

[16] Max Weber, *The Protestant Ethic and the Spirit of Capitalism*, 3.

[17] Max Weber, *The Protestant Ethic and the Spirit of Capitalism* (London: Allen and Unwin, 1930). Especially formative for Weber's observations on the voluntarist principle was his trip to America in 1904. See especially Max Weber, *From Max Weber* (New York: Oxford University Press, 1958), 18-19, 304-307, 316-317, 320-321, 344-345.

[18] Robert Putnam, *Bowling Alone: The Collapse and Revival of American Community* (New York: Simon and Schuster, 2000), esp. 17-21. Putnam also connects Elias to social capital.

For example, according to Putnam—and here we see his debt to Durkheim particularly clearly—rates of suicide are sociologically determined according to the presence or absence of social networks that bond individuals to communities.[19] This notion, I will argue, has relevance to understanding the homicide rates of almost any given culture.

While stability and social order in a culture is not always easily measured, homicide rates do provide an index of interpersonal violence that gives considerable purchase on the matter.[20] Yale sociologist and neo-Weberian Philip S. Gorski uses such rates to considerable effect. According to Gorski, murder rates were dropping more quickly in England and the Netherlands than in surrounding European states during the post-Reformation era. In contrast to Elias, who emphasized a top-down disciplining power, Gorski argues that the disciplining impulse against violence came from below as well as from above. In parallel with Weber, Gorski sees the ascetic ethos produced by Protestantism, at the congregational level, as providing this disciplining power; it was generated collectively, by the group as a whole, and not simply imposed from above.[21]

The emphasis that Elias placed upon changes in interpersonal violence over time and the ability of the researcher to empirically[22] access these changes

---

See Robert Putman, *Democracies in Flux: The Evolution of Social Capital in Contemporary Society* (New York: Oxford University Press, 2002), 284-285.

[19] Robert Putnam, *Bowling Alone*, 326. See also Robert Putnam, *Democracies in Flux*, esp. 76-79. Durkheim's observation on the contagious effect of the news of suicide must surely in some way be related to the weakness of social networks and I would hypothesize that the same would apply to the news of homicide, and in particular, homicide involving handguns.

[20] Eisner cautiously accepts that homicide rates do coordinate with records of physical assault. Given that several hundred records from multiple localities and heterogeneous sources yield "coherent patterns", he concludes that the extant records are not "random noise". Given the ten to fifty-fold range of homicide decline over time, his conclusions hold even with uncertainty in the population estimates. Manuel Eisner, "Long-Term Historical Trends in Violent Crime", 93-94.

[21] Philip S. Gorski, *The Disciplinary Revolution: Calvinism and the Rise of the State in Early Modern Europe* (Chicago: University of Chicago Press, 2003), 31-33, 51-55. Foucault's disciplinary power worked from above and outside of the individual.

[22] Homicide rates per capita are most accessible but other rates such as armed bank robberies are obtainable within a range of reasonable certainty. Other empirical measurements for a

has been especially appealing to historians of crime. Although state officials and other observers were sometimes aware of changes in criminality within a limited time period,[23] the actual empirical study of such changes over extended periods of time did not fully arrive until the early 1970s.

With the upsurge in study of crime on both sides of the Atlantic by the late 1960s, and with generous government grants to study the phenomena of violence, both edited collections and monographs on the subject of violence began to appear in the 1970s.[24] British historical work on crime tended to be detailed local studies at the level of a county or city.[25] The quantitative work of V.A.C. Gatrell was particularly influential with its argument that, notwithstanding much-discussed current increases in crime rates, nineteenth-century statistics on larceny and violence painted a picture of crime in England over the course of the century that saw it decline. All forms of larceny and violent crimes known to the police, with the exception of sexual assault,[26] declined over the last half of the nineteenth-century. These decreases took place despite an increase in overall material prosperity, conditions usually equated with higher rates of property crime in particular. Increased staffing of police forces, Gatrell concludes, was important; normally this would mean an increase in the production of arrests rather than a decease.[27]

---

given habitus include road fatalities per billion vehicle-kilometers, stolen vehicles per capita, and lung cancer deaths per capita. See for example, OECD Organization for Economic Co-operation and Development, *Trends in the Transport Sector 2012 (International Transport Forum)* (Paris: OECD Publishing, 2012).

[23] See for example a report in 1897 from the inspector for Ontario of asylums and prisons, Thomas F. Chamberlain, in which he reported "a continued improvement in the diminution of crime as compared with former years." *Globe*, March 8, 1897: 8.

[24] This increase in the study of crime was in tandem with an increase in crime and violence in the 1960s and 1970s on both sides of the Atlantic.

[25] See for example the collection in J.S. Cockburn, ed., *Crime in England, 1550-1800* (Princeton: Princeton University Press, 1977). For an example of a monograph on crime in an industrial area see David Philips, *Crime and Authority in Victorian England: The Black Country, 1835-1860* (London: Croom Helm, 1977).

[26] The increase in cases involving sexual assault is consistent with a greater sensitization of crimes against women and with it a greater willingness to report and prosecute.

[27] V.A.C. Gatrell, "Theft and Violence in Victorian and Edwardian England" in *Crime and the Law: The Social History of Crime in Western Europe since 1500*, ed. V.A.C. Gatrell, Bruce

1.4 The Surprising U-Shaped Curve

In the midst of an increasing output of British literature on the history of crime an American scholar, Ted Robert Gurr, published a breakout essay on the long term trends of violent crime as seen in Britain, North America, and Europe. Making use of the British data that reached back to the medieval period, Gurr argued that homicide had dropped from up to 25 per 100,000 in the middle ages to approximately 0.7 per 100,000 in the 1950s. Then, using a graph of violent crime that begins with the much more reliable data produced in the nineteenth century, Gurr plotted a curve that drops over the course of the century, that continues to drop in the twentieth century reaching its nadir by the 1920s, that continues flat until about 1960 when it rises sharply, and that by 1970 reaches the levels of the early nineteenth-century.[28]

Significantly, Norbert Elias received a footnote in Gurr's landmark essay in the context of reference to a process of "civilization" that over time saw a decline in executions, the end of slavery, and various kinds of brutality that previously were a part of everyday life;[29] as Gurr's work continued, Elias moved from a footnote to the main body of Gurr's text.[30]

Lenman and Geoffrey Parker, (London: Europa, 1980), 238-338. One could argue that an increase in police officers would produce disincentives for criminal behaviour but Gatrell is arguing that an increase in officers would normally result in increased arrests.

[28] Ted Robert Gurr, "On the History of Violent Crime in History and America" in *Violence in America: Historical and Comparative Perspectives* rev. ed., ed. Hugh Davis Graham and Ted Robert Gurr (Beverley Hills: Sage Publications, 1979), 353-358. Gurr had also been assisted in gaining his insights through the local studies of American cities by scholars such as Theodore Ferdinand and Roger Lane. See for example Theodore N. Ferdinand, "The Criminal Patterns of Boston Since 1849," *American Journal of Sociology* 73 (July 1967): 688-698; Roger Lane, *Policing the City: Boston, 1822-1885* (Cambridge: Harvard University Press, 1967).

[29] Ted Robert Gurr, "On the History of Violent Crime in History and America", 355-356, 372 n. 7. This is the earliest reference that I can find of a historical thinker connecting Elias with the study of changes in rates of violence over time. Volume One of the *Civilizing Process* was published in English in 1978 while Volume Two in 1982. Elias uses the term "curve of development" with reference to the phases of the process from medieval times to modern. Norbert Elias, *The Civilizing Process*, 53, 71, 89-92, 152, 154.

[30] Ted Robert Gurr, "Historical Trends in Violent Crime: A Critical Review of the Evidence" in *Crime and Justice: An Annual Review of Research*, vol. 3, ed. N. Morris and M. Tonry (Chicago: University of Chicago Press, 1981), 342. In a massive 1977 collection, one year

The long-term graph of homicide in England that Gurr published in 1981 came to be called *the* "U-shaped curve". This label has stuck. It refers to the phenomenon of declining violence over a number of centuries followed by the sharp increase of violence that a variety of Western countries saw in the 1960s. Gurr, it should be noted, gives no special significance to the upturn of violence in the 1960s but rather sees it simply as another variation within the graph.[31]

The combination created by the new awareness of Elias and the revelation contained in Gurr's U-shaped graph quickly entered the scholarly debate on the history of violence. Lawrence Stone picked up on Gurr's analysis in an influential article. Agreeing that the issues were complex, not least that population numbers[32] from the past were tricky calculations, Stone did accept that homicide was a crime that was difficult to conceal and hence more likely to be recorded. He agreed that medicine was a factor, but the advances in medical care that came with the recognition of the importance of sterilization of medical equipment, did not really come until the end of the century and hence could not have been the reason for the decline in homicide rates prior to this point. Stone affirmed Gurr's interpretation, made use of Elias' theorizing, and called for more research that would explore causal relationships.[33]

Critiques of Gurr and Stone were hard-hitting and focused on population estimates, errors of fact, the assumption that policing did not deter violence, the notion coroners' reports were reliable, identification of "jurisdictional

---

before the Elias translation into English, the name "Elias" does not appear in any of the essays. Ted Robert Gurr, Peter N. Grabosky, Richard C. Hula, *The Politics of Crime and Conflict: A Comparative History of Four Cities* (Beverly Hills: Sage Publications, 1977).

[31] Ted Robert Gurr, "Historical Trends in Violent Crime: A Critical View of the Evidence," 296-298, 341-342. Gurr states that "no special, *sui generis* explanation is needed for the late increase in violent crime"; this was occasioned by the social turbulence of the 1960s and was simply a deviation from an underlying trend downwards. We now know, though, that the upturn lasted several decades and it remains unclear whether the U-shaped curve will change, despite some decline in the past two decades.

[32] Population numbers of course are important for the calculation of rates of crime which are usually expressed in units per 100,000 of population.

[33] Lawrence Stone, "Interpersonal Violence in English Society, 1300-1980," *Past and Present* 101, no. 1 (1983): 22-33.

peculiarities",[34] and the exclusion of infanticide from homicide rates. While the patchiness of the evidence was a common criticism levelled at the Gurr and Stone essays, it is extremely significant that their two strongest critics, J.A. Sharpe and J.S. Cockburn, actually *agreed* with the overall picture of the major decline in violence presented by Gurr and Stone and implicitly with the more detailed work of Gatrell.[35]

Since these early debates there has been an almost universal acceptance of the reality of the U-shaped curve and general acceptance of the theorizing of Norbert Elias.[36] Study of crime in historical context had been galvanized.

---

[34] J.S. Cockburn, "Patterns of Violence in English Society: Homicide in Kent, 1560-1985," *Past and Present* 130 no.1 (1991): 102. The term refers to the variability of juries and of conviction rates.

[35] J.A. Sharpe, "Debate: The History of Violence in England: Some Observations" *Past and Present* 108, no. 1 (1985): 205-215. For Cockburn see J.S. Cockburn, "Patterns of Violence in English Society", 70-106; J.S. Cockburn, "The Nature and Incidence of Crime in England, 1559-1625," in *Crime in England, 1550-1800*, J.S. Cockburn, ed. (Princeton: Princeton University Press, 1977), 49-71. In "Patterns of Violence" Cockburn argues that the upward swing of the curve beginning in the 1960s should be much steeper because, he estimates, homicide is actually 40% understated as the result of advances in medicine in the later half of the century as compared to the nineteenth century. See pp. 101-102. Sharpe in a 1995 essay accepts the U-shaped curve and makes no mention of Gurr and Stone but praises the work of Gatrell. See J.A. Sharpe, "Crime in England: Long-Term Trends and the Problem of Modernization" in *The Civilization of Crime: Violence in Town and Country Since the Middle Ages*, ed., Eric Johnson and Eric M. Monkkonen (Urbana: University of Illinois Press, 1996), 17-34. For a rejoinder to Sharpe see Lawrence Stone, "A Rejoinder," *Past and Present* 108, no. 1 (1985): 216-224. Stone, in response to Sharpe's agnosticism about how different societies actually experience violence, argues that homicide rates are related at some level to the amount of violence in a society and that a population is sensitive to its presence and makes adjustments accordingly.

[36] The editors of one collection were representative in their guarded, but approving, comments on Elias' impact:

> Some of the essays in this collection may seem to be inattentive to customary social theory. Where are the classical social thinkers who address the centuries-long transformations of the West? Durkheim, Weber and Marx are underplayed, as is even Michel Foucault. Instead, a shadowy figure, Norbert Elias, appears, his presence announced by the English historian James Sharpe's reference to the "civilizing process".

Eric Johnson and Eric M. Monkkonen, eds., *The Civilization of Crime*, 2. Elias himself was influenced by Durkheim, Weber, and Freud. A sampling of more recent works that make use of the U-shaped curve and usually make reference to Elias, include: Roger Lane, *Murder in America: A History* (Columbus: Ohio State University Press, 1997), 297-298; Eric H.

There was general agreement among students of the matter that violent crime had, in Western contexts, dropped steadily from the medieval period through the twentieth century before rising sharply beginning around 1960. This major historical finding continued, however, to be under recognized.[37]

1.5 Steven Pinker on the Curve

In the past two years, the situation has changed. Gurr's largely unknown work has been taken up and popularized by academic "rock star" and

---

Monkkonen, *Murder in New York City* (Berkeley: University of California Press, 2001), 154-158; Julius R. Ruff, *Violence in Early Modern Europe, 1588-1800* (Cambridge: Cambridge University Press, 2001), 7-9; Manuel Eisner, "Long-Term Historical Trends in Violent Crime," 83-142; Martin J. Wiener, *Men of Blood: Violence, Manliness and Criminal Justice in Victorian England* (Cambridge: Cambridge University Press, 2004), 2-3, 11-13; J. Carter Wood, *Violence and Crime in Nineteenth-Century England: The Shadow of Our Refinement* (London: Routledge, 2004), 15-25, 145-159; Clive Emsley, *Hard Men: The English and Violence Since 1750* (London: Hambledon and London, 2005), 10-13, 23-25, 42-43; Mike Maguire, Rod Morgan, Robert Reiner, *Oxford Handbook of Criminology* (Oxford: Oxford University Press, 2007), 116-117, 369-370; Pieter Spierenburg, *A History of Murder: Personal Violence in Europe from the Middle Ages to Present* (Cambridge: Polity, 2008), 2-7.

[37] Since Gurr's article additional empirical, long-term studies of homicide in Finland, Norway, Sweden, and Netherlands have overwhelming supported Gurr's earlier conclusions. For a survey of these studies see Manuel Eisner, "Long-Term Historical Trends in Violent Crime," 86-87. J. Carter Wood finds it surprising that the history of violence was such a "late bloomer". He attributes this to an earlier focus on property crime that I would argue was due to a concentration on material interests as seen in the early work of Douglas Hay. See J. Carter Wood, "Criminal Violence in Modern Britain" in *History Compass*, 4, no. 1 (January, 2006): 77. For work critical of the U-shaped curve emphasis, see Howard Taylor, "Rationing Crime: The Political Economy of Criminal Statistics Since the 1850s" in *Economic History Review* 51(3), 1998, 569-590; John E. Archer, "The Violence We Have Lost? Body Counts, Historians and Interpersonal Violence in England," *Memoria y Civilizacion* 2 (1999): 171-190; Mary Beth Emmerichs, "Getting Away With Murder? Homicide and the Coroners in Nineteenth-Century London," *Social Science History* 25, no. 1 (March 1, 2001): 93-100; Jeffrey S. Adler, *First in Violence, Deepest in Dirt: Homicide in Chicago, 1875-1920* (Cambridge, MA: Harvard University Press, 2006); John E. Archer, *The Monster Evil: Policing and Violence in Victorian Liverpool* (University of Liverpool Press, 2011). Each of the above are local studies that quite helpfully point out anomalies such as murders "missed" by coroners and those that were not pursued by the justice system. Adler, for example, found the official records very accurate but questions how Chicago's high homicide rate at the time fits Elias' civilizing process thesis. However, no scholar has attempted to refute the U-shaped curve with a large coordinated study.

Harvard-based social psychologist, Steven Pinker.[38] Aided by the book jacket blurbs of fellow "rock stars" Richard Dawkins and Niall Ferguson, the theories of Elias and Gurr have been elevated, in a symbiotic relationship with the media, to the "blogosphere" by the op-ed columns of national newspapers[39] and by Amazon.com; they have now reached astronomical numbers of readers relative to the numbers in touch with the academic journals and monographs that had previously served to channel the same basic idea.[40] Regardless of how durable Pinker's book proves to be, the idea of an historical decline in violence has been disseminated in ways that were not previously possible.

Victor Gatrell, more than thirty years before Pinker, labelled the unmistakable drop in violence during the Victorian and Edwardian periods as an event that was "extraordinary". Using Durkheim-like language, Gatrell proclaimed that this dramatic drop in violence ~~has been rapid~~ly "must strike as

[38] For references to Gurr in Pinker see Steven Pinker, *The Better Angels of Our Nature: Why Violence Has Declined* (New York: Viking, 2011), 60-61, 78, 389. Pinker states he was "stunned" when he first saw Gurr's U-shaped graph and that it became the "seed" for his book. Elias is referenced throughout the book but see especially the chapter entitled "The Civilizing Process", 59-128.

[39] Pinker hit #14 on the non-fiction hardcover bestseller list of the *Sunday Book Review* of the *New York Times* for October 30, 2011.

[40] Gurr's early work (1969) in conjunction with a Presidential commission on violent crime was certainly widely read. From 1969-1977 there are 11 articles in the *New York Times* that make mention of Gurr; mainly with respect to his work on various aspects of violence in America. However from 1978 (Gurr published his U-shaped graph in 1981) and on, there are only 3 mentions of Gurr and only one briefly alludes to a decline in violence in the past. The *Times Literary Supplement* has no reference to Gurr, the *Globe and Mail*, has no reference to Gurr, while *The Times* has one brief reference to Gurr in a broad op-ed essay on violence. In contrast, in the first five months after the release of *Better Angels*, the *New York Times* had 10 articles that mentioned the book, *The Times* published a 750-word review, and in the *Globe and Mail* it was listed as "Book of the Year" by two contributors. Op-ed article writers that mention Pinker included Stanley Fish and David Brooks; both with large readerships. A Google search (April, 2012) using the combined terms, "better angels of our nature" "steven pinker" yielded 163,000 results while, "robert ted gurr" "violence in america" yielded 16,000 and combinations of "robert ted gurr" "u-shape" and "u-shaped" yielded a total of 750 results. Clearly Pinker has propelled into new territory the idea of declining rates of violence over time. Even the combination of "steven pinker" "gurr" had 3,800 results which points towards the phenomenon of Gurr's ideas "hitching on" to Pinker, a full 30 years after Gurr's first putting forward his U-shaped graph.

a great social fact, and one worth investigating."[41] Likewise, Steven Pinker asserts at the beginning of *Better Angels* that the overall decline in human violence, since antiquity, "may be the most important thing that has happened in human history."[42]

1.6 Manuel Eisner and the "Moral Individualism" Hypothesis

While there is now general agreement that interpersonal violence has undergone "staggering"[43] rates of decline—Robert Muchembled can categorically claim that "all specialists" have concurred with these findings—[44] there remains the question: why has there has been such a decline? Manuel Eisner in 2003 posed this question, enumerated the explanations given to date, and pointed out that criminologists had utterly failed to supply explanations for the phenomenon. According to Eisner, the "stock" theories of criminologists (and historians, no doubt) might explain why violence should *rise* in the face of rapid urbanization and industrialization, but they had not been helpful in explaining why rates of violence should *fall*. Eisner rejected Gurr's explanation that this decline was due to an increasing "sensitization" to violence: this, he said, simply amounted to a restatement of the finding itself.[45]

Eisner accepts that the theories of Elias do provide some broad explanations for the decline of violence but points out the need for more contextual studies that will enable a refining of the broader theories.[46] Furthermore,

---

[41] V.A.C. Gatrell, Bruce Lenman, and Geoffrey Parker, eds., *Crime and the Law*, 341.

[42] Steven Pinker, *The Better Angels of Our Nature*, xxi.

[43] Eisner uses adjectives and adverbs such as "staggering", "massive", and "remarkably" because of the magnitude of the shifts involved. Manuel Eisner, "Long-Term Historical Trends in Violent Crime," 86, 101, 83.

[44] Robert Muchembled, *A History of Violence: From the End of the Middle Ages to the Present* (Cambridge: Polity, 2012), 306.

[45] Manuel Eisner, "Long-Term Historical Trends in Violent Crime," 87, 122. To be fair to Gurr it should be pointed out that the "sensitizing process" hypothesized by him included increased policing, better access to education for all, and the new religious force represented by Methodism. Ted Robert Gurr, "Historical Trends in Violent Crime: Europe and the United States" in *Violence in America*, vol. 1, third ed., ed., Ted Robert Gurr (Newbury Park: Sage Publications, 1989), 46.

[46] Manuel Eisner, "Long-Term Historical Trends in Violent Crime," 108.

Eisner doubts that broad, social control explanations that involve changes in the state can explain the scale of the declines in interpersonal violence. While the Low Countries with decentralized governments experienced sharp declines in interpersonal violence, Italian cities, with relatively large police forces, did not experience similar declines. Eisner posits a sociological dimension to the decline in violence that involves high levels of "trust" between the state and its citizenry, with, he continues, that trust arising out of a mindset related to Protestant Christianity.[47]

In seeking a cultural explanation for the decline in violence, Eisner thus reaches back to the theories of Max Weber. The Protestant ethic according to Weber was inner-directed and involved one "giant disciplining project" that brought about within the individual an intense scrutiny of one's moral behaviour. With both the Protestant Reformation and even to a degree with the Catholic Counter Reformation, there came increased clerical intrusion into the private sphere. Accompanying these changes in religiosity was much greater emphasis on literacy and education.

With respect to possible reasons for the decline of violence in Sweden in the seventeenth-century, Eisner offers the hypothesis that the new teachings of the Lutheran church concerning the expiation of sin[48] combined with an increased concern for "issues of human dignity" and "empathy for the weak". Similarly, he suggests that the decline in serious crime in seventeenth and eighteenth-century Britain resulted from a cultural shift brought about by a Protestant emphasis on "individual responsibility". A new rhetoric of interpersonal violence was disseminated through a pervasive culture of Protestantism that made use of "cheap print". Closely entwined with these Weberian developments was the eventual emergence of a modern individualism that spread throughout European culture.[49]

Eisner concludes his discussion by appealing to criminologists to

---

[47] Manuel Eisner, "Long-Term Historical Trends in Violent Crime," 128-130.

[48] Lutheran theology tended to teach that "salvation" was obtained directly by the individual from God whereas Roman Catholic theology emphasized that it was mediated by the Church and the Sacraments.

[49] Manuel Eisner, "Long-Term Historical Trends in Violent Crime," 130-132.

embrace the rise of "moral individualism" as being a "plausible candidate for explaining the fall in criminal violence."[50] It is this approach that has been taken in the present study. A moral individualism[51] brought about by the presence of British Protestant evangelicalism beckons as an obvious path of exploration in a study of the decline in interpersonal violence in late nineteenth-century Toronto. Eisner has set out the line of questions to be posed in such a study.

1.7 Additional Hypotheses Explaining the Great Decline

Eisner has not been the only scholar to implicate religion in the decline of interpersonal violence during the nineteenth century. Victor Gatrell, Clive Emsley, and Martin Wiener have all written highly influential studies on the "English miracle" of declining interpersonal violence over the course of the nineteenth century. They further suggest that religion was involved in this decline.

Gatrell, in a consideration of the broad decline in violence in late Victorian England, cites steep declines in homicide, in trials for assaulting police officers, and in assault involving serious wounding as indicative of actual decline in, as opposed to simple changes in attitudes to, crime. Given that between 1850 and 1914 the population of England doubled and urban populations tripled while average annual prosecutions in England dropped from 98,000 in the 1870s to less than half that number in the years immediately before 1914, Gatrell finds it "unthinkable" that this was merely a culture's changing attitude to prosecution. He is in agreement with the Criminal Registrar who at the time concluded that there had been "substitution of words without blows for blows with or without words". According to Gatrell, this situation

---

[50] Manuel Eisner, "Long-Term Historical Trends in Violent Crime," 131-132. While Pinker is dependent on Eisner's work at a key point, he does not refer to Eisner's suggestions concerning the role of Protestant rhetoric and a decline in violence.

[51] Here Eisner appears to echo Weber on "modern individualism". While an "individualism" may be the end result, I would prefer not to use the term "moral individualism" in the context of BEP Toronto, but rather would argue that the "individual" was "morally" shaped by religious discourses of Christian communities. Weber speaks of the development of a "modern individualism" but always in the context of a disciplining, voluntarist community.

had been brought about by a "variety of educative, religious, and disciplinary agencies of which the police were only one."[52]

Emsley likewise accepts the thesis that there were sharp declines in violence in England over the course of the nineteenth century. The stereotypical English male had evolved from being violent and uncouth to functioning as a being typified by the English gentleman who by the later part of the century was known for reserve, restraint, and "fair play". Furthermore, according to Emsley, this image came to be emulated by the workingman. As well, women were expected to refrain from anything "physical" beyond bearing children.[53] Linked to this image of the gentleman, Emsley suggests, were the "Victorian virtues" of "morality and probity" combined "with good works and service to others" to reduce violence and drunkenness. Victorian Britain had undergone a "moralisation" process.[54]

A "Victorian civilizing offensive" brought about sharply reduced violence, particularly that directed against women, according to Martin Wiener. Following Callum Brown, Wiener argues that the "Evangelical movement" did much to shape Victorian Britain and also went "far beyond the middle class alone" to transform wider aspects of British culture, including the whole of British Christianity itself. Male behaviour was increasingly problematized. The "moral task" facing the nation was not merely to reform the nation's institutions but also to reform Britain's males. High on the agenda was the need to protect women from "unreformed" men. Evangelicals and

---

[52] V.A.C. Gatrell, "Theft and Violence in Victorian and Edwardian England", 292-295. The sociologist Christie Davies builds on the work of Gatrell and ties declines in crime and violence in Britain to the growth of Sunday Schools and religion during the nineteenth-century. Christie Davies, *The Strange Death of Moral Britain* (New Brunswick, New Jersey: Transaction Publishers, 2004), 1-62.

[53] Clive Emsley, *Hard Men: The English and Violence Since 1750*, 11-13; obviously this statement about women is highly rhetorical. See below for reference to Callum Brown. Jonathan Rose argues that the working class take-up of middle-class values was not primarily an "aping" of such values, but a "grass-roots working-class struggle for mutual improvement". Jonathan Rose, *The Intellectual Life of the British Working Classes* (New Haven: Yale University Press, 2001), 63.

[54] Clive Emsley, *Crime and Society in England, 1750-1900*, 2nd ed. (London: Longman, 1996), 48-49.

Utilitarians together propagated, both at home and abroad, a reform program that stressed civility as against a still too prevalent barbarity. The "civilizing offensive" was successful in democratizing itself and transferring its values to working class and lower working class men who were known for brutalizing "their" women, behavior that changed as such action was increasingly brought before the courts. This cult of respectability was to last until the 1960s when new forces of violence were unleashed, according to Wiener, against both women and men.[55]

A complex explanation for the decline in violence is proposed by Randolph Roth in a major study of the history of homicide in the U.S. Roth's overarching argument is that a low homicide rate is the product of a trust in government on the part of the general populace. When there is a strong, stable government and the grievances of the populace are addressed, homicide rates can drop down to the range of 6-10 per 100,000. When confidence in government is strong and there are also dense social networks, then it is possible for rates to fall to 1-2 per 100,000. Particularly critical are:

1. The belief that government is stable and that its legal and judicial institutions are unbiased and will redress wrongs and protect lives and property.
2. A feeling of trust in government and the officials who run it, and a belief in their legitimacy.
3. Patriotism, empathy, and fellow feeling arising from racial, religious, or political solidarity.
4. The belief that social hierarchy is legitimate, that one's position in

---

[55] Martin J. Wiener, *Men of Blood*, 13, 29-31, 35-37, 152, 228, 289-291. Ted Robert Gurr suggests that the decline in violence in England was due to a "sensitizing process" brought about through the new police forces, public schools, and Methodist churches. For a similar explanation see Ted Robert Gurr, "Historical Trends in Violent Crime: Europe and the United States," 46. Gertrude Himmelfarb ties the drop in homicide in Victorian Britain to the growing influence of British evangelical Protestantism. The evangelical "moral reformation" was merged into British society to produce the "Victorian virtues". Gertrude Himmelfarb, *The De-Moralization of Society: From Victorian Virtues to Modern Values* (New York: Vintage, 1994), 7-13.

society is or can be satisfactory and that one can command the respect of others without resorting to violence.[56]

In a brief survey of the history of homicide in Canada, Roth suggests that it is the development of "responsible government" at a relatively early stage that explains the much lower Canadian homicide rates in its "core provinces"; this bred a feeling that government was, in fact, linked to the people, concerned with their interests, and virtually certain to behave in a way consistent with the fashion in which they had voted.[57] Jeffrey McNairn makes a related point concerning political culture in Upper Canada.[58]

Steven Pinker, as against all this, dismisses religion as a causal factor

[56] Randolph Roth, *American Homicide* (Cambridge, MA: Harvard University Press, 2009), 17-18. Of course, the linkage of responsible government to declines in violence is highly contestable; it is perhaps the only consideration of Canada in a broad study of interpersonal violence and seems to overlap in some ways with the importance that Jeffrey McNairn attaches to "deliberative democracy" (see below). See also Amy E. Nivette, "Cross National Predictors of Crime: A Meta Analysis", *Homicide Studies* 15, no. 2 (2011): 103-131 and Manuel Eisner and Amy E. Nivette, "Does Low Legitimacy Cause Crime? A Review of the Evidence" in *Legitimacy and Criminal Justice: An International Exploration*, ed. by Justin Tankebe and and Alison Liebling (Oxford: Oxford University Press, 2014), 308-325.

[57] Randolph Roth, *American Homicide*, 244-246, 297-298. With the exception of Roth's treatment of Puritanism, religion is strangely absent from his work even though it underlies key developments in American culture. Furthermore Roth's criteria tend to be descriptive of the macro level as opposed to the moral, cultural field that individuals negotiate in the daily interactions of urban life.

[58] Jeffrey L. McNairn, *The Capacity to Judge: Public Opinion and Deliberative Democracy in Upper Canada, 1791-1854* (Toronto: University of Toronto Press, 2000). Upper Canada, according to McNairn, was characterized by a "deliberative democracy" in which public opinion was formed in a "classical" fashion in the exchange of information and arguments that shaped the politics of the era. At the centre of this information exchange were the wide variety of voluntary associations and the numerous newspapers that had sprung up and whose readerships effectively were types of voluntary associations. Membership in voluntary agencies was disproportionately made up of evangelicals who were part of a democratic religious movement. In the end, says McNairn, responsible government came about as the product of voluntary societies and was itself a kind of voluntary society. This process, says McNairn, demonstrated that Upper Canada was not a colonial backwater but was open to a wide range of Western cultural influences. These influences resulted in a society where people had close relations with each other, prejudice was "worn off", manners learned, and there was strong desire for knowledge, and 'good' behavior ensued.

with respect to the long-term decline of violence in the world. Although, he concedes, religion in particular circumstances has worked on behalf of peace—Martin Luther King, Desmond Tutu, and a few Quaker abolitionists show this—religion has been epiphenomenal to the general culture across time and generally has been more involved in promoting violence and oppression than reducing it. According to Pinker, it was the Enlightenment that eventually brought about the abolition of slavery as well as the increased levels of human empathy that served to depress levels of interpersonal violence.[59]

The influence of the Enlightenment on humanitarian movements broadly fits within the thesis of this study. This thesis is not monocausal but relies on developments within the culture of a Western Europe that saw violence already declining in the medieval period. These developments predated Protestantism and certainly the Enlightenment. The argument in this study is that a *particular* Protestant religious expression *further* depressed interpersonal violence in late Victorian Toronto. I argue that the BEP expression mirrored a substantial amount of Enlightenment thought, that there were multiple European enlightenments all growing out of Christian seedbeds, and that the British Enlightenment shared many common concerns with the BEP movement.[60] This is a point to which I will return in Chapter Two.

[59] Steven Pinker, *The Better Angels of Our Nature*, 184-188, 676-678.

[60] For an argument that evangelicalism was closely allied with the Enlightenment in Britain see David Bebbington, *Evangelicalism in Modern Britain*, 19, 48-104, 141-153. On the influence of evangelicalism on the British Enlightenment see Gertrude Himmelfarb, *The Roads to Modernity: The British, French, and American Enlightenments* (New York: Knopf, 2004). For example, Himmelfarb views John Wesley as a key figure of the Enlightenment, p. 6. Wesley certainly would not make Pinker's list. On the Continent, Immanuel (changed from Emmanuel) Kant, who looms large for Pinker, was raised in a Pietist Prussian household. Pinker himself implicitly distinguishes between the Enlightenments when he privileges the American Revolution, as opposed to the French Revolution, as it was built on the English Civilizing Process, p. 185. Pinker's most vociferous critic is the political thinker John Gray, who argues that the liberal humanism of Pinker and others is a secularized Christian "faith" and political action is a "surrogate for salvation." Like Pinker, Gray is a non-theist. Gray does not critique Pinker's use of statistics but rather his Long Peace. See John Gray, "Delusions of Peace" *Prospect* (September 21, 2011), accessed May 19, 2013, http://www.prospectmagazine.co.uk/magazine/john-gray-steven-pinker-violence-review/#.UZmm_Bzxa68. See also John Gray, *Straw Dogs* (New York: Farrar, Straus and Giroux, 2007). On humanism as "faith" see pp. xi-xv, 1-34.

A PROBLEM IN SOCIAL HISTORY

1.8 Max Weber at the University of Paris

In a recent work on the history of violence in Europe, the eminent French social historian Robert Muchembled has argued that *all* specialists accept that interpersonal violence declined sharply from the thirteenth century until the last third of the twentieth century and that European culture operated as a "factory" to drastically modify the behaviour of young males.[61]

While Muchembled does not deny that the state had imposed top-down pressure against interpersonal violence (here he follows Elias), he emphasizes the cultural constraints that were placed on male violence through morality and religion. In this his proposals closely resemble Eisner's. The earliest drops in violence took place in Protestant areas and followed Weberian pathways.[62] The Protestant ethic that fostered capitalism also provided young men with an increased respect for the value of life in general and the lives of others. This ethic was "inculcated" through the churches and socializing institutions. Muchembled cites Gurr's U-shaped curve as evidence of the impact of the European "factory" on the behaviour of young males and, indeed, argues that the curve should be drawn much more sharply.[63]

In summary, there is widespread agreement that Western Europe underwent massive declines in interpersonal violence over centuries reaching a nadir that extended somewhat past 1950. The reasons for this decline remain, however, subject to some disagreement. Two of the ranking scholars in the field, Eisner and Muchembled, do make a strong case for what happened as a result of the moral and religious shaping of the individual. That case, as I will argue, can also be advanced in respect of Toronto: the city in fact offers considerable confirmation for the Eisner-Muchembled line of argument, and, because of the richness of the data it makes available to the student, deserves a principal place in the critically important arguments that have been unfolding.

---

[61] Robert Muchembled, *A History of Violence*, 1-2, 306 n. 1.

[62] "Weberian pathways" is shorthand for processes that result in outcomes that are seemingly original or unique to Protestant cultures. These identifications are defensible but can be highly contestable. "Weberian" I use to describe the ascetic practices of Protestant "sects" that Weber described as culturally shaping.

[63] Robert Muchembled, *A History of Violence*, 24-25, 38-44.

1.9 Interpersonal Violence in the City of Churches

Little has been written on the topic of the dynamic of religion, violence, and culture in industrializing, late Victorian Toronto. However, census data on religious affiliation in Canada during the period under study provide unparalleled opportunity for investigation of that topic when they are coupled with the available records of homicide. At present, research on homicide in nineteenth-century Canada has been meager and data are fragmentary.[64] The homicide data for late nineteenth-century Toronto are entirely original to this study. They allow it to add a new dimension to the investigation of Canada's nineteenth-century social history. They also contribute importantly to argument concerning the causes of the decline in interpersonal violence more generally.

Investigators have done some preliminary work on the issue. Using census data and prisoner data in a study of inequality in Ontario circa 1870, Peter Oliver, Gordon Darroch, and Lee Soltow concluded that there were religious dimensions to crime based on the overrepresentation of Anglicans and Roman Catholics in Ontario prisons and the underrepresentation of Baptists, Methodists, and Presbyterians.[65] "Arresting" was the term that historian John Weaver used to describe the findings of Darroch and Soltow on the relationship between crime and religion.[66] Weaver's comment, however, is the only ripple of response that Darroch and Soltow's work has provoked in the years following its publication in 1994. Peter Oliver made similar observations concerning the relation between crime and religious affiliation in a 1998 study and these too went largely unnoticed.[67]

---

[64] This is evident in the data that Roth relies on to plot homicide rates in nineteenth-century Canada. See the sources that he relies on in, Randolph Roth, *American Homicide*, 244-246, 297-298.

[65] Gordon Darroch and Lee Soltow, *Property and Inequality in Victorian Ontario: Structural Patterns and Cultural Communities in the 1871 Census* (Toronto: University of Toronto Press, 1994), 109-110.

[66] John Weaver, "Review of Property and Inequality in Victorian Ontario," *Ontario History* LXXXVII, no. 1 (1995): 87-88.

[67] Peter Oliver, *'Terror to Evil Doers': Prison and Punishments in Nineteenth Century Ontario* (Toronto: University of Toronto Press, 1998), 449-450. While Oliver was published four years later he does not acknowledge the earlier work of Darroch and Soltow.

A PROBLEM IN SOCIAL HISTORY

Helen Boritch's work on policing in Toronto bears most directly on the issue of interpersonal violence in late nineteenth-century Toronto, though it is concerned with that of violence's decline rather than the reasons for the decline. In keeping with parallel developments in the U.S. and Europe, Boritch affirms an "unmistakable" drop in Toronto crime from 1859 to 1955 with the steepest fall-off in the years 1891-1920. Arrest rates for violent crime dropped sharply from 1891-1920, while homicide arrest rates remained stable. The decline in violence in the 1890s took place in the face of severe economic depression. Further declines of arrests for violent crime continued from 1920-1955 but did not match the steep rate of decline in the late nineteenth century.[68] Significantly, female arrest rates declined following the male pattern, a development pointing to a general downward trend rather than selective policing based on gender.[69]

While Boritch considers the role of urban moral reformers in late nineteenth- century Toronto,[70] the work of Desmond Morton on Mayor William

[68] Helen Boritch, "The Making of Toronto the Good: The Organization of Policing and Production and Production of Arrests, 1859-1959" (PhD diss., University of Toronto, 1985), 208-219. It is important to note that Boritch only measured rates of arrest. The calculations I have made are based on homicides as opposed to arrests for homicide. Initial homicide charges for vehicular deaths were increasing during the period with, for example, the coming of the electric streetcar and unduly influenced homicide arrests. These homicide charges were then almost invariably dropped skewing homicide arrest rates. The key finding of Boritch's work is that policing shifted from a function of class control in the nineteenth century to that of crime control in the twentieth century. See also Helen Boritch and John Hagen. "Crime and the Changing Forms of Class Control: Policing Public Order in "Toronto the Good," 1859-1955," *Social Forces* 66, 2 (December 1987): 307-335.

[69] Helen Boritch and John Hagen. "Crime and the Changing Forms of Class Control," 574-576. John Weaver, at least in 1996, was still questioning the long-term decline in homicide, the U-shaped curve, the inconsistencies of crime reporting, and the phrase "known to the police". Notwithstanding the lack of absolute precision of homicide numbers, dissenters such as Weaver have still to explain the persistent long-term patterns across multiple localities in the more recent and highly-detailed work of Manuel Eisner. See Manuel Eisner, "Long-Term Historical Trends in Violent Crime," 83-142.

[70] Helen Boritch, *The Making of Toronto the Good*, 122-127. Boritch does point out that during the temperance campaigns of the 1890s there were decreasing arrests for drunkenness and that this correlated with decreasing arrests for assaults (pp. 254-258). However, I will point out in Chapter Three that these decreases in arrests were part of an evolving philosophy of the reformers concerning arrests for drunkenness.

Howland and that of Christopher Armstrong and H.V. Nelles on the controversy over Sunday streetcars deal most directly with the religious ideology
of the moral reform movements, underscore its impact, and suggest, though
they do not indicate directly, that temperance orientations influenced rates of
violence—a point I will take up.

The argument I make in the chapters that follow moves through three
stages. I will first indicate the character of the vigorous, and vigorously-ex-
pressed, British Evangelical Protestant (BEP) ideology that circulated in
Toronto in the last decades of the nineteenth century. I will then consider
the institutional and other machinery—journals, public addresses, educa-
tional frameworks, women's organizations, the systems set up and run by
the churches themselves—used in disseminating that ideology, giving it its
very wide reach, and making it the critically important element in the city's
ideological apparatus that it was. Finally, I will lay out the vitally important
relationships that census data, prison records, and other materials allow us to
see between religious affiliation and key types of criminal behavior, especially
criminal behavior involving interpersonal violence. The existence of clear
correlations between exposure to BEP ideology and engagement or distance
from certain types of behavior will be demonstrated. The meaning of these
correlations, and their demonstration of causal links, will be explored through
use of standard causal inference theory. The support the Toronto data give to
the Muchembled-Eisner line of argument will be especially emphasized. The
Toronto experience will, indeed, be cited as centrally relevant to propositions
citing the role of religious as opposed to secular determinants in violence's
decline generally. That experience will thus emerge, not simply as a phenomenon the study of which allows an additional and important contribution to
examination of religion in Canadian history—an examination that both has
strong roots and a vital current existence in Canadian historical writing[71]—

---

[71] As much work clearly demonstrates; see, in particular, S.D. Clark, *Church and Sect in
Canada* (Toronto: University of Toronto Press, 1948); S.D. Clark, *The Developing Canadian
Community*, 2nd ed. (Toronto: University of Toronto Press, 1968); John Webster Grant, *A
Profusion of Spires: Religion in Nineteenth-Century Ontario* (Toronto: University of Toronto
Press, 1988); Goldwin French, "The Evangelical Creed in Canada" in W.L. Morton, ed.,
The Shield of Achilles (Toronto: University of Toronto Press, 1968); Michael Gauvreau, *The*

but also as a phenomenon whose investigation has considerable relevance for elucidation of a major problem in social history generally. Offering up a particularly rich, focused, and revealing body of evidence for that investigation, it—and study of it—stands to shed much additional light on what continues to be a basic issue in a broad, much-considered, and still problem-filled field of inquiry.

Evangelical Century: College and Creed in English Canada from the Great Revival to the Great Depression (Montreal and Kingston: McGill-Queens University Press); Marguerite Van Die, "The "Double Vision": Evangelical Piety as Derivative and Indigenous in Victorian English Canada" in Mark Noll, George Rawlyk, and David Bebbington, eds., *Evangelicalism: Comparative Studies in North America, the British Isles, and Beyond, 1700-1900* (New York: Oxford University Press, 1994); George Rawlyk, ed., *The Canadian Protestant Experience, 1760-1990* (Montreal and Kingston: McGill-Queen's University Press, 1990); George Rawlyk, ed., *Aspects of the Canadian Evangelical Experience* (Montreal and Kingston: McGill-Queen's University Press, 1997; William Westfall, *Two Worlds: The Protestant Culture of Nineteenth-Century Ontario* (Kingston and Montreal, 1989); John Webster Grant, *A Profusion of Spires: Religion in Nineteenth-Century Ontario* (Toronto: University of Toronto Press, 1988); Nancy Christie and Michael Gauvreau, *Christian Churches and Their Peoples, 1840-1965* (Toronto: University of Toronto Press, 2010); Michael Gauvreau and Ollivier Hubert, eds., *The Churches and Social Order in Nineteenth-and Twentieth-Century Canada* (Montreal and Kingston: McGill Queen's University Press, 2006); Nancy Christie and Michael Gauvreau, "Modalities of Social Authority: Suggesting an Interface for Religious and Social History", *Histoire sociale / Social History* 36, no. 71 (Mai-May, 2003); Marguerite Van Die, *Religion, Family, and Community in Victorian Canada: The Colbys of Carrollcroft* (Montreal and Kingston: McGill-Queens's University Press, 2005); Sharon Cook, *"Through Sunshine and Shadow": The Woman's Christian Temperance Union, Evangelicalism and Reform in Ontario, 1874-1930* (Montreal and Kingston: McGill-Queen's University Press, 1995); Maria Valverde, *The Age of Light, Soap, and Water: Moral Reform In English Canada, 1885-1925*, 2nd ed. (Toronto: University of Toronto Press, 2008).

2

EVANGELICAL IDEOLOGY AND
THE DECLINE OF VIOLENCE

Overview

In Chapter One I have mentioned scholars who have hypothesized that there is a link between *religious* change and declining violence One must also ask whether there have been other studies that have suggested a link between *evangelicalism* and declining interpersonal violence. In Chapter Two I will first identify previous studies that have attached declining violence to an evangelical religious ideology. I will then define my use of the term "ideology" and will then seek to outline the contours of British evangelical Protestantism in late nineteenth-century Toronto. If it is the BEP factor that is all important for an explanation of sharply declining interpersonal violence, then it is necessary to describe the nature and roots of Toronto evangelicalism.

2.1 Previous Research Linking Evangelicalism and Declining Violence

In tandem with England, Toronto by 1880 was experiencing a steep decline in interpersonal violence. For the years 1880 to 1900 this decline became precipitous. While a relationship between a religious moralizing process and declining levels of interpersonal violence has been broadly hypothesized by scholars such as Eisner, Muchembled, and Gorski, as outlined in the Introduction, no detailed study of such a relationship exists.

Gertrude Himmelfarb and Christie Davies have claimed that a sharp decline in crime and violence in late nineteenth-century England was due to a surging evangelicalism. Himmelfarb argues for an evangelical "moral

reformation" that shaped "Victorian virtues".[1] Sociologist Davies has proposed that the rise and fall of religion in British society best explains the
parallel fall and rise of crime over the nineteenth and twentieth centuries.
Davies argues that the Protestant Sunday School was the primary carrier of
these religious values.[2] E.P. Thompson, too, contends that the work-discipline shaping of working-class England was the product of Methodism and
the Sunday School.[3]

The most detailed study linking nineteenth-century Protestant evangelicalism to declines in violence is that of David J.V. Jones in *Crime in
Nineteenth-Century Wales*. For Jones, claims that late nineteenth-century
Wales had low levels of violence due to its largely BEP commitments were
essentially accurate. "Moral tuition", "temperance pioneers", and a sense of
"self-respect" combined with "ideas of reverence and decorum" to do important work.[4]

In the far-removed context of 1980s Columbia, the anthropologist
Elizabeth Brusco has argued a broadly similar thesis. Pentecostal evangelical
religion, appropriated by women as a form of collective action, has domesti-
cated males. Males are detached from the cult of machismo. They are urged to
renounce drinking, smoking, and extramarital sex. Monies formerly spent in
the tavern and the brothel, often amounting to 20-40% of a family's income,
are to be channeled back into the household budget. Sexuality within the
marital relationship is emphasized, as opposed to the traditional sexual configuration that stressed the reproductive function of the wife and the sexual

---

[1] Gertrude Himmelfarb, *The De-Moralization of Society: From Victorian Virtues to Modern
Values* (New York: Vintage, 1994), 7-13.

[2] Christie Davies, *The Strange Death of Moral Britain*, 44-47.

[3] Of course, Thompson, as outlined earlier, was critical of the Sunday School but acknowledged that it shaped working class behaviour. While large numbers of Thompson's working
class were skilled, Thompson emphasizes that large numbers of Methodist workers *"were* the
poor." E.P. Thompson, *Making of the English Working Class*, 337.

[4] As quoted in David J.V. Jones, *Crime in Nineteenth-Century Wales* (Cardiff: University of
Wales Press, 1992), 64. For relevant passages see Jones, 47-48, 61-64, 68-69, 72, 102-104,
241-251. Jones does not focus on the relationship of religion and crime but does discuss the
subject, particularly in the above passages. He does make qualifications for some urban areas.

role of the "other woman".[5]

Similar processes, says Brusco, are occurring among aboriginal evangelical converts in Papua, New Guinea. As in Columbia, male domestic responsibilities are taking precedence over old ways; behaviour is changing under the influence of religious ideas.[6]

The worlds of evangelical minorities in 1980s Columbia and Papua are far-removed from the world of late Victorian Toronto; one can nonetheless hypothesize parallel processes of male domestication and lowered rates of interpersonal violence. The industrial world of Toronto contained many of the broad social processes that Brusco observes in the societies she investigates. There was a wage-labour frontier. Migrant families and single men and women steadily flowed into the city. Life was often tenuous. Women with children were dependent on breadwinners. Religious influence entered and life was ordered in such a way that males were disciplined and interpersonal violence plunged to new lows.

In *The Better Angels of Our Nature: Why Violence Has Declined*, Steven Pinker considers violence in the history of *Homo sapiens*. Pinker, like Norbert Elias, Robert Ted Gurr and Manuel Eisner, argues that in Western cultures, violence has undergone a massive decline since the medieval era. Pinker marshals data to argue that this decline has broadened in the post-World War II period. Pinker's claim that the spread of Enlightenment thought, preceded by the Civilization Process, is central to the decline of violence has much to be said for it.

However, he does concede considerable territory in his consideration of these *"particular* religious movements", that through their use of "parlayed Enlightenment arguments", have contributed to a decline in violence. These efforts included the anti-slavery movements, the pacifying of the "wild

---

[5] Elisabeth E. Brusco, *The Reformation of Machismo: Evangelical Conversion and Gender in Columbia* (Austin: University of Texas, 1995), 1-5, 17, 22, 37-38, 75-78, 120-123. For a similar argument to Brusco see David Martin, *Pentecostalism: The World Their Parish* (Oxford: Blackwell Publishing, 2002), 73-75.

[6] Brusco, *The Reformation of Machismo*, 141. Brusco self-identifies as writing from a Marxist-feminist perspective and successfully resisted the efforts of her subjects to "convert" her. Pp. 136, 166.

frontier" in the American South and West,[7] and the temperance campaigns of the Women's Christian Temperance Union and the Salvation Army "who were responding to the very real catastrophe of alcohol-fueled bloodbaths in male-dominated enclaves."[8]

That ideology rather than material progress is responsible for the remarkable decline of violence in Western culture and the coming of a Humanitarian Revolution is a highly defensible proposition. Book production and widespread literacy, central to the argument of this thesis, brought "an expansion of people's minds" and "added a dose of humanitarianism to their emotions and their beliefs."[9] "The empathy circle" enlarged. This in turn increased the human capacity for extending "compassion" toward the "stranger" and the "foreigner".[10] Likewise, an emphasis on general cleanliness impacted moral sensibilities; empathy was also more easily expressed to a previously despised "other".[11]

Pinker's sense of morality as resting on the "universality of reason" is also to be supported. He sees a "humanism" that places the accent on all that makes for "the flourishing of humans" developing.[12] Other factors too are in play. Self-control, alcohol use and its neurobiological consequences, the presence of women in the lives of males all count for much in giving human behaviour its forms.[13]

Monogamy and marriage have critical role. These reduce male testosterone and "tend to drain the swamps where violent male-male competition proliferates." This "feminization" of males allows for the investing of time in the children that they have "sired".[14] The importance of these can be seen in its absence; with the 1960s loss of social connectedness in the American

---

[7] Steven Pinker, *Better Angels*, 677-678.

[8] Steven Pinker, *Better Angels*, 107-108.

[9] Steven Pinker, *Better Angels*, 172-174.

[10] Steven Pinker, *Better Angels*, 175-173.

[11] Steven Pinker, *Better Angels*, 170.

[12] Steven Pinker, *Better Angels*, 182-183.

[13] Steven Pinker, *Better Angels*, 105-106.

[14] Steven Pinker, *Better Angels*, 687.

inner city, women lost "the bargaining power to force the men into a civilized lifestyle." The result was high levels of interpersonal violence that continue down to the present.[15]

Pinker is generally opposed to the hypothesis that religion, as traditionally defined, has contributed to the decline of violence. While the influence of the Enlightenment on humanitarian movements is highly contested terrain, Pinker's argument broadly fits within the thesis of this study.

Turning to the Canadian context, with the advent of social history in the 1970s came the blossoming of studies on nineteenth-century evangelical social reform movements. These included monographs by Mariana Valverde on evangelical "social purity", Phyllis Airhart on revivalism and progressivism in the Methodist tradition, Sharon Cook on the reform efforts of the Woman's Christian Temperance Union in Ontario, and an essay by J.I. Little on the "moral engine" of temperance reform. While each of these studies highlight the discourse of evangelical reform there are few hints that this discourse brought about actual behavioural changes in the broader community such as a decline in public drunkenness, petty crime, or interpersonal violence.[16]

Several writers do drop hints of changes in behavior brought about by evangelical discourse. J.I. Little, using a quote from the time, describes temperance reform in the Eastern Townships of Quebec, as "a moral engine of such incalculable power". However Little is highly ambivalent about the results of the early decades of temperance activism ending at the middle of the nineteenth century. Marguerite Van Die, in a monograph on the Colby family of the Eastern Townships, argues that evangelical religion "shaped and reshaped" the family, as well as community life in general.[17] Furthermore, using the work of Boyd Hilton, Van Die maintains that even economic life was shaped by evangelical discourse.[18] Concerning the topic of violence, Van

---

[15] Steven Pinker, *Better Angels*, 115-116.

[16] There is however acknowledgement of high church attendance rates within the evangelical tradition. Similarly education reform brought significantly higher rates of school attendance.

[17] Marguerite Van Die, *Religion, Family, and Community in Victorian Canada: The Colbys of Carrollcroft* (Montreal and Kingston: McGill-Queens's University Press, 2005), 13.

[18] Marguerite Van Die, *Religion, Family, and Community in Victorian Canada*, 38, 99.

EVANGELICAL IDEOLOGY

Die, without elaboration, favourably quotes Daniel Walker Howe maintaining that "politeness and evangelical moral reform helped reshape the world into a place where violent behavior was discouraged and commercial relations between strangers would be facilitated."[19]

Sharon Cook, in her evaluation of the impact of the WCTU, points to "hundreds of thousands of children" having been "reached" through the activities of both WCTU groups and Sunday schools such that their lives were aligned in "healthy" directions. Furthermore, men were "convinced to act more responsibly and less violently to their wives and families".[20] Cook points out that by the 1990s, the White Ribbon that had been the symbol of the WCTU had been appropriated by *men* in a campaign condemning violence against women.[21]

Several recent studies of Canadian evangelicalism have centred on the nineteenth-century urban context of evangelicalism,[22] although there remains no major work on evangelical social reform in late nineteenth-century Toronto. Nancy Christie and Michael Gauvreau have most importantly, for the present thesis, emphasized that nineteenth-century Canadian evangelicalism cannot be reduced to a surrogate nomenclature for "middle-class".

Where Canadian urbanization has been viewed as part of a secularizing narrative, Christie and Gauvreau instead see Christianity as having "infiltrated the pathways of urban culture", at least during the late nineteenth-century. This process was true for both the Roman Catholic and the Protestant expressions of Christianity.[23] The large Gothic church buildings that lined city streets

[19] Marguerite Van Die, *Religion, Family, and Community in Victorian Canada*, 144.

[20] Sharon Cook, *"Through Sunshine and Shadow": The Woman's Christian Temperance Union, Evangelicalism and Reform in Ontario, 1874-1930* (Montreal and Kingston: McGill-Queen's University Press, 1995), 207.

[21] Sharon Cook, *"Through Sunshine and Shadow"*, 207. Mariana Valverde mentions that family violence was a concern of the Salvation Army but does not elaborate. See Maria Valverde, *The Age of Light, Soap, and Water: Moral Reform In English Canada, 1885-1925*, 2nd ed. (Toronto: University of Toronto Press, 2008), 66.

[22] See for example Eric R. Crouse, *Revival in the City: The Impact of American Evangelists in Canada, 1884-1914* (Montreal and Kingston: McGill-Queens University Press, 2005).

[23] Nancy Christie and Michael Gauvreau, *Christian Churches and Their Peoples, 1840-1965* (Toronto: University of Toronto Press, 2010), 62; Michael Gauvreau and Ollivier Hubert,

31

were not middle-class enclaves but rather were socially mixed with working class members contributing financially to their construction.[24] Within a rapidly urbanizing Canada, religious ideology functioned as a "protean force" that cut across class and this remained true until at least the 1960s.[25]

As far as I can identify, the above references are the closest that a Canadian historian comes to putting forward an argument that nineteenth-century evangelicals imprinted a moral code upon the community such that behavior was changed and interpersonal violence suppressed. Certainly, the discourse of evangelical "purity" and temperance reform movements has been closely examined. But any detailed evaluation of the impact of this discourse on behavior is lacking. I will seek to close this major gap in the history of nineteenth-century Canadian evangelicalism.[26]

---

eds., *The Churches and Social Order in Nineteenth-and Twentieth-Century Canada* (Montreal and Kingston: McGill Queen's University Press, 2006), 5-15.

[24] Nancy Christie and Michael Gauvreau, *Christian Churches and Their Peoples*, 71. Christie and Gauvreau critique Lynne Marks's emphasis on the middle-class makeup of evangelicalism as due to her focus on small town evangelicalism and upon membership rates instead of the broader attendance rates. Rather, they argue that it is when the focus is shifted to urban areas, where there was a developing working class, that one finds a strong representation of workers in churches. See Nancy Christie and Michael Gauvreau, "Modalities of Social Authority: Suggesting an Interface for Religious and Social History", *Histoire sociale / Social History* 36, no. 71 (Mai-May, 2003): 5-9. See also Kenneth L. Draper, "A People's Religion: P.W. Philpott and the Hamilton Christian Workers' Church", *Histoire sociale / Social History* 36, no. 71 (Mai-May, 2003): 99-121; Edward Smith, "Working-Class Anglicans: Religion and Identity in Victorian and Edwardian Hamilton, Ontario", *Histoire sociale / Social History* 36, no. 71 (Mai-May, 2003): 123-144; Nancy Christie, ""On the Threshold of Manhood": Working-Class Religion and Domesticity in Victorian Britain and Canada", *Histoire sociale / Social History* 36, no. 71 (Mai-May, 2003): 145-174.

[25] Nancy Christie and Michael Gauvreau, "Modalities of Social Authority", 3.

[26] Helen Boritch in a study of policing and the "production" of arrests in Toronto, does point out that decreases in arrests for drunkenness correlates with decreases in arrests for assault during the period from 1891 to 1920 and suggests that this could be due to temperance reform. However there is not an extended discussion of the possibility that evangelical ideology depressed interpersonal violence. See Helen Boritch, "The Making of Toronto the Good: The Organization of Policing and Production and Production of Arrests, 1859-1959" (PhD diss., University of Toronto, 1985), 120, 125-135, 142, 254-255, 312. Callum Brown also hints that in Britain, violence had decreased under a withering evangelical onslaught from which "[t]here was no escape. Through this vast machinery of Christian 'agency', the discourses on personal religiosity were circulated." Callum Brown, *The Death of Christian*

2.2 BEP Ideology

In late Victorian Toronto, a pervasive British evangelical Protestant ideology placed enormous constraints on males and essentially removed interpersonal violence. This process in turn created conditions amenable to a liberal democracy.[27] In Chapter Three I will identify and describe the distinctive characteristics of British evangelical Protestant ideology, including behavioural prescriptions that served to restrain physical aggression. For the remainder of the present chapter I will introduce my use of "ideology" and briefly account for the presence of British evangelical Protestantism in late Victorian Ontario.

The period 1880-1900 marks the emergence of a forceful religious ideology within the culture of Toronto. By "culture" I refer to a concrete, bounded "world" with a population that has a set of beliefs, customs, practices, tendencies, and values. The boundary is semi-permeable and is resistant but not impervious to change.[28] The rise of BEP ideology during this period demonstrates this semi-permeable nature of the boundary of a culture and the way that human actors possessing a powerful ideology are capable of accomplishing significant cultural change.

"Ideology" denotes a system of ideas that underlies and informs the political and social activity that exists within a culture. Ideology is entwined in a vastly complex web of relations and so it both "constructs" and "reflects" the culture that it is part of. All dominant social viewpoints are ideological, are ubiquitous, and have aspects that are empirically accessible. While "ideology" often carries Marxist connotations, it need not always do this and can be used

---

Britain, 55-57.

[27] Not all liberal democracies have low levels of interpersonal violence, and liberal democratic cultures are still capable of high levels of lethal violence directed outside of its borders, i.e. warfare by nation states. I am asserting that high levels of interpersonal violence within a culture tips the balance of power toward "warlords" and away from leaders elected by democratic process.

[28] This corresponds with Muchembled's conception of culture as plastic and malleable with respect to violence. See also William H. Sewell Jr., *Logics of History: Social Theory and Social Transformation* (Chicago: University of Chicago Press, 2005), 168-171.

in ways that are not simply epiphenomenal to material processes.[29] In this study, I use "BEP ideology" to denote an increasingly powerful BEP social agenda that sought to impose a temperance stance, aimed at improving the economics of the household while inhibiting the "rough" male behaviour that was perceived to be centred on the tavern. Ideology, in a nutshell, is that set of social and behavioural ideas that gets woven into a culture and shapes the actions of its members. Evangelical anti-slavery ideology is a prime example of this.

Conceptualizing the ways that ideology is taken up by a culture can be difficult. The history of anti-smoking in Canada is illustrative. Laws were introduced as early as 1908 that made it illegal to sell cigarettes to those under the age of sixteen. BEP prescriptions against problematic male behaviour were certainly a factor in this. Over time, anti-smoking took on a public health dimension. While individual human actors had placed restrictions on smoking all along, increasingly broader cultural forces came into play making the constraints placed on smoking highly complex and difficult to map. In this sense, the human limitations of the interpreter force one to speak in terms of the "constraints" placed on individuals by an anti-smoking ideology.[30] Following this line of reasoning, I will speak of a BEP ideology that "constrained" interpersonal violence.

Violence, for the purposes of this study, can broadly be defined as the intentional application of physical force to another person contrary to his-or her wishes. In late nineteenth-century Canada, an assault causing bodily harm was an indictable offence while such an assault causing death was culpable homicide.[31] Violence is of course a much broader cultural issue and cannot

[29] See Michael Freeden, "Ideology" in *Routledge Encyclopedia of Philosophy*, vol. 4, ed. E. Craig (London: Routledge, 1998), 681-685. But note that in neo-Gramscian conceptions of hegemony there is allowance for human aspirations that are not reducible to economic activity.

[30] Likewise one can use similar reasoning when speaking of the gradual spread of the wearing of auto seatbelts and the cultural pressure and laws mandating their use. Interestingly, these laws appear to follow Weberian pathways; i.e. they tended to be adopted first in cultures heavily influenced by Protestantism.

[31] For expanded definitions of assault and homicide see Henri Taschereau, *The Criminal*

be confined to physical assault. The topic can be easily expanded to include violence of psychological, economic, racial, age-based, and gender-based types. However, the level of physical assault in a culture is determinative[32] and to a degree is quantifiable. It is within the context of cultures that are marked by lowered levels of physical violence that other forms of violence have come to be identified. Violence appears to have sharply declined in Toronto during the period from 1880-1900, at precisely the time when a British evangelical Protestantism was peaking in strength. This makes late Victorian Toronto an ideal location to test a hypothesis concerning the relation between a highly moralistic religious ideology and the depression of interpersonal violence.

In probing the religious ideology of nineteenth-century Toronto, I rely heavily on statistical analysis. While never neutral, quantitative data can shed light on the way BEP culture was taken up by the broader culture. The religious categories of the decennial Canada Census allow for tracking of the numerical strength of the BEP movement in the period under study. In addition, detailed data on the religious affiliation of prisoners allow the interpreter to formulate hypotheses concerning indices of the strength of the religious and social bonds formed in individual communities in Toronto. Here I am claiming that one can quantitatively measure the social controls that regulate both individual church attendance and individual behaviour with respect to the law.[33] The present study will be an elaboration of this claim. (But note

---

Code of the Dominion of Canada As Amended in 1893 (Toronto: Carswell, 1893), 210-211, 252-267. For purposes of this study I have not counted as homicides women who died as a result of undergoing an abortion procedure or those persons who died in construction, train or vehicle accidents even when there was a finding of culpable homicide. These instances did not involve deliberate attempts to commit bodily harm on the person named as the victim in a finding of homicide. For example, two street car employees, John Gilroy and Frank Kane, were convicted of manslaughter in the street car death of Harry Flood and received one-year sentences to Central Prison. According to my definition for purposes of the present study, this was not an example of violent assault whatever the negligence involved. *Globe*, July 15, 1889: 8; October 26, 1889: 16.

[32] Eisner points out that the relation between homicide and other types of violent crime are comparable in a number of cross-national studies. See Eisner, "Long-Term Historical Trends in Violent Crime," 93-94.

[33] At this point I am in close alignment with the claims that Hugh McLeod has made regarding church attendance data. Hugh McLeod, "Class, Community and Religion: The

that the actual uptake of this ideology with the development of a BEP infra-structure will not be described until Chapter Four.)

At the outset of this study, no claim is made for the absolute uniqueness of British evangelical Protestant Toronto. In England, the towns of Bristol, Leicester, and Hull were all BEP centres with very high attendance in the 1881 newspaper church censuses.[34] These cities could provide opportuni-ties for promising comparative studies with Toronto in the area of violence and denominational affiliation. However, the lack of official census data on religious affiliation for British cities after 1851 would make this task more difficult. The present study of Toronto allows for the possibility of additional highly detailed comparative work that lies outside the range of this study.

2.2.1 Defining Evangelicalism

While evangelicalism is marked by distinctive religious beliefs, in seeking to account for a BEP culture in Toronto, one can map its contours by first outlining its social vision and then moving to a consideration of belief. From its very beginning, York (later named Toronto) was subjected to a nascent evangelical ideology. In the 1790s, Lieutenant Governor John Graves Simcoe foisted an abolitionist viewpoint upon an unwilling Council and general pop-ulace that resulted in the eventual elimination of slavery in Upper Canada.[35]

Religious Geography of Nineteenth-Century England" in *A Sociological Yearbook of Religion in Britain* 6, ed., Michael Hill (London: SCM Press, 1973), 30.

[34] Hugh McLeod, "Class, Community and Religion", 43-48.

[35] Simcoe's abolitionist beliefs are understudied and therefore obscure but seem to stem from a religious conversion that he underwent while convalescing in England following imprisonment during the American Revolutionary War. Elected to the House of Commons in 1790, he had a very brief parliamentary career that went almost unrecorded. However, he seems to have come within the circle of the evangelical abolitionist, William Wilberforce, as there is an apparent record of Simcoe speaking out in favour of a motion to abolish slavery. See S.R. Mealing, "John Graves Simcoe" in *Canadian Dictionary of Biography*. See also Mary Beacock Fryer and Christopher Dracott, *John Graves Simcoe, 1752-1806: A Biography* (Toronto: Dundurn Press, 1998), 112. Simcoe is listed as a subscriber to the memoir by Equiano, the ex-slave, evangelical abolitionist. This inclusion places Simcoe squarely within early evangelical abolitionist circles. See Olaudah Equiano, "The Interesting Narrative of The Life of Olaudah Equiano, or Gustavus Vassa, The African, Written by Myself" in *Slave Narratives*," ed., William L. Andrews and Henry Louis Gates Jr. (New York: Library of America, 2002), pp. 39-46.

EVANGELICAL IDEOLOGY

By his one action Simcoe removed the culture of violence associated with slavery that was to plague numerous sectors of the Americas in subsequent decades. In Britain and its Empire, antislavery was the first successful evangelical foray into politics, with an eventual abolitionism continuing on as an engine of reform for the upstart BEP movement. It is no coincidence that the "econocide"[36] of abolition was accompanied by steep drops in violence in British culture as a whole.

In the years after Simcoe, evangelical reformist impulses were increasingly important and in Toronto had spun a vast web of voluntary associations by 1880. Close analogues to abolitionism included the temperance movement and the Bible societies. Temperance, beginning in Britain in 1828, had in common with anti-slavery, "the same friends—women, Quakers, and evangelicals; and the same enemies—cockfighters, swearers, gamblers, tyrannical husbands, irresponsible drinksellers, and Sabbath-breakers."[37] Without the finely honed organizational skills of the British abolitionists whose early leaders were aristocrats,[38] the subsequent temperance movement would have failed to gain momentum.

Writing in 1829, Thomas Carlyle, no friend of abolition, bemoaned the social reform paradigm that had been laid down in the anti-slavery cause:

> Has any man, or a society of men a truth to speak, or a piece of spiritual work to do, they can nowise proceed at once and with the mere natural organs, but must first call a public meeting, appoint committees, issue

---

[36] Econocide is the term used by Seymour Drescher whereby Britain turned sharply against its economic self-interest by moving to abolish slavery. Seymour Drescher, *Econocide: British Slavery in the Era of Abolition* (Pittsburg: University of Pittsburg Press, 1977).

[37] Brian Harrison, *Drink and the Victorians: The Temperance Question in England, 1815-1872*, 2nd ed. (Staffordshire: Keele University Press, 1994), 91. Harrison was able to examine memoirs and obituaries of 382 teetotalers finding that prohibition and anti-slavery along with the Anti-Corn Law League, in that order, were the three most common reforming activities of teetotalers. Anti-slavery continued into the 1860s and beyond. Brian Harrison, *Drink and the Victorians*, 139-166.

[38] But note that while the leadership was aristocratic, Jan Noel has found that in Toronto the rank and file was from the artisan and working class. Jan Noel, *Canada Dry: Temperance Crusades before Confederation* (Toronto: University of Toronto Press, 1995), 105-106.

prospectuses, and in a word, construct or borrow machinery wherewith to do and speak it. Then every machine must have its moving power in some of the great currents of society.[39]

This paradigm is clearly present in the reform efforts of evangelicals in the English-speaking world throughout the nineteenth century and was almost entirely absent on the Continent despite the presence there of Enlightenment networks. The English-speaking world was to hold proprietary rights on the voluntary society for a century and when, for example, abolitionist societies existed on the Continent they were inevitably a British "export". Why the "post" of slavery, a key economic support of Empire, should be allowed to be "kicked out" by elements within is in ways imponderable but, following Drescher, no doubt was due to a powerful BEP ideology.[40]

The beginnings of temperance societies in Canada, like Britain, also date to 1828 when a temperance sermon was preached in a Montreal pulpit by a transplanted American Presbyterian minister, Joseph Christmas.[41] The formation of societies followed in the same year in Montreal while in Toronto the evangelical reformer, Jesse Ketchum, led in establishing the Toronto Temperance Society in 1829.[42] In the temperance movement there is evidence of a "North Atlantic Triangle" in operation, with societies being founded in the U.S., British North America, and in Great Britain within the space of three years.[43] Once again there are imponderables, but the movement is one

---

[39] Thomas Carlyle in *Edinburgh Review* (June 1829), 442-443. Eventually Carlyle himself was caught up in the fervour of temperance although he retained a deep antipathy towards abolitionism.

[40] See for example Seymour Drescher, *Abolition: A History of Slavery and Antislavery* (Cambridge: Cambridge University Press, 2009), 276-293. On the evangelical "benevolent empire" in the U.S. see Daniel Walker Howe, *What Hath God Wrought: The Transformation of America, 1815-1848* (New York: Oxford University Press, 2007), 186-195.

[41] John G. Wooley and William E. Johnson, *Temperance Progress in the Century* (London, Toronto, Philadelphia: Linscott Publishing, 1903), 249-250. See also Jan Noel, *Canada Dry*, 58-62.

[42] See Jan Noel, *Canada Dry*, 105-108.

[43] While U.S. temperance had begun as early as 1808, the national American Temperance Society was organized in 1826 and was transplanted to Canada almost immediately. See

of "resistance" from large numbers mainly of women who possessed a BEP bent. Significantly Canada was to be the only sector of Empire to embrace prohibition, and this is the measure of a powerful discourse.[44]

The Upper Canada Bible Society was founded in 1816. Transplanted from Britain, it served as an umbrella organization for a variety of evangelical reformist causes. Agitation for "responsible government" emerged largely from this base of temperance societies, the Upper Canada Bible Society and a multitude of reform movements.[45] In the drive to "responsible government", a preponderance of Reformers was from nonconformist religious backgrounds. With a government that was increasingly accepted by the general populace came increased potential for less violent cultural configurations, in line with the hypothesis of Randolph Roth.[46]

With the BEP drive to abolish slavery and the broad cultural acceptance of temperance, constraints on male interpersonal violence continued to tighten. The institution of slavery had generated deep animosities and preserved

---

Craig Heron, *Booze: A Distilled History* (Toronto: Between the Lines, 2003), 53.

[44] Here it can be argued that Prohibition in Canada was heavily influenced by the United States albeit with the rhetoric of Canadian Prohibition having a more evangelical flavour. But most of Scandinavia, under the influence of evangelicalism, had forms of prohibition or increased regulation. For example, Norway prohibited the sale of liquor from 1917-1927. See Per Ole Johansen, "The Norwegian Alcohol Prohibition; A Failure", *Journal of Scandinavian Studies in Criminology and Crime Prevention* 14, no. S1 (2013): 46-63.

[45] The Toronto based Anti-Slavery Society of Canada was formed in 1851 in the aftermath of the Fugitive Slave Law and its members disproportionately came from the ranks of temperance societies and voluntary groups such as the Bible Society. See my unpublished paper "A Genealogy of Reform in Victorian Toronto." Board members who appear in the present study include George Brown, John McMurrich, and Oliver Mowat. Daniel Wilson was also a member of the Society.

[46] Using the appendix in J.K. Johnson, I compared the political affiliation with the religious affiliation of the 283 men who were elected to the Upper Canadian House of Assembly. In those cases where both designations are given, 50 of 75 Conservatives were Anglican. Of 48 Reformers only twelve were Anglican, whereas thirteen were Presbyterian, and fourteen were Methodist, with the remaining spread among five other denominations. One cannot conclude too much from these statistics but they do point to Reformers tending to come from Nonconformist religious backgrounds. See J.K. Johnson, *Becoming Prominent: Regional Leadership in Upper Canada, 1791-1841* (Montreal and Kingston: McGill-Queen's University Press, 1989). On Roth's hypothesis that utilizes "responsible government" see Randolph Roth, *American Homicide*, 244-246, 297-298.

cultures of heightened violence wherever it had become widely established, as in the American South and in Brazil. Similarly, the unrestrained use of alcohol accelerated all manner of violence, including interpersonal and group violence, as well as the vehicular fatalities that were to increase after the introduction of the automobile in the twentieth century.

The argument here is that declines in violence is attached to the take-up of an evangelical ideology within British culture that includes Toronto. However one defines "evangelical", it concerns a Protestant religious movement that centres on transformative change, both communally and individually. The BEP culture, with roots in the Evangelical Revival but also going back to Puritanism and to the Reformation, was a call to behavioural seriousness.[47] The term "evangelical" is an unassailable identity marker in the British context, beginning with the Evangelical Revival of the 1730s.[48] Over the course of the century, the term was used increasingly of the distinct beliefs and the personalities attached to this revivalist movement. While all religious expressions of the era became tinged by evangelicalism,[49] there remained a distinct BEP religious expression.[50]

By 1851 Nonconformity was controlled by what the historian of Dissent,

---

[47] W.R. Ward, *Christianity Under the Ancien Regime* (Cambridge: Cambridge University Press, 1999), 132-146. The Pietist movement in Halle, under the leadership of Phillip Spener (1635-1705) pioneered the class meeting and the Protestant voluntary association. Placing an emphasis on a mystical, "heart" religion, Pietism emphasized personal accountability toward other members of "small groups". There are linkages between Continental Pietism and the young John Wesley and George Whitefield, key leaders in the Evangelical Revival that began in Britain in the 1730s. See also W.R. Ward, *Early Evangelicalism: A Global Intellectual History, 1670-1789* (Cambridge: Cambridge University Press, 2006), 24-39. For the emphasis on "seriousness" see Ian Bradley, *Call to Seriousness: The Evangelical Impact on the Victorians* (New York: Macmillan, 1976).

[48] On the Continent "evangelical" of course became a label associated broadly with Lutheranism. The use of "evangelical" beginning in eighteenth-century Britain is a more specific term and crosses denominational boundaries as will be discussed throughout this chapter.

[49] Evangelicalism with a strong doctrine of Providence blended well with the "superstitious" beliefs of popular folk religion. Michael Watts, *The Dissenters*, vol. two, *The Expansion of Evangelical Nonconformity* (Oxford: Oxford University Press, 1995), 106-110.

[50] David Bebbington, *Evangelicalism in Modern Britain: A History from the 1730s to the 1980s* (London: Routledge, 1989), 2-4.

Michael Watts, has termed the "three great Evangelical movements": Congregationalism,[51] the Baptist churches, and Methodism.[52] The British Census of 1851 gave evidence that evangelical Nonconformity shaped millions, and according to Watts, found its main support "among the poor, the ignorant, and the unsophisticated." The chapel was more influential among the poor than any kind of political or trade union movement and perhaps was only rivaled by the "public house",[53] a rivalry that will loom throughout the present study.

Evangelicalism permeated the Church of England as well. William Wilberforce (1759-1833), George Whitefield (1714-1770), John Wesley (1707-1788), John Newton (1725-1807), John Venn (1759-1813), Hannah More (1745-1833), and Charles Simeon (1759-1836) were prominent early evangelical Anglican leaders. As Boyd Hilton has established, key British political leaders such as Canning, Peel, and Gladstone were all infected by the evangelical idea even if they were not in fact strictly evangelical. The novels of Jane Austen and George Eliot include an abundance of evangelical characters. In addition, the two prominent Roman Catholic cardinals from the era, the converts John Henry Newman (1801-1890) and Henry Edward Manning (1808-1892), had evangelical sojourns as young men.[54]

Boyd Hilton argues that by the generation following Wesley and Whitefield evangelicals had achieved a measure of intellectual respectability in national debates, including those on the British economy. With the outbreak of the French Revolution and the Napoleonic wars, the "mind" of middle and upper class England became unhinged as British culture entered a time of turmoil. During this period evangelicalism became a powerful influence with its emphasis on both biblicism and "heart" religion. While it was a time of

---

[51] Congregationalists believed in the independence of the local congregation and date to the time of Elizabeth. Baptists, with roots in early seventh-century Netherlands, shared similar beliefs with Congregationalism but rejected the baptism of infants.

[52] Michael Watts, *The Dissenters*, vol. two, 3.

[53] Michael Watts, *The Dissenters*, vol. two, 3.

[54] See David Newsome, *The Parting of Friends: The Wilberforces and Henry Manning* (Cambridge, MA: Harvard University Press, 1966).

conflicting ideas, Hilton maintains that evangelicalism came to be the dominant influence on the middle and upper classes.

In the evangelical doctrine of the Atonement, it was the death of Christ on the cross that purchased redemption for the sins of all humankind. Evangelicalism's system of rewards and punishments, according to Hilton, came to be applied to the economic sphere and conditioned people to think in terms of revolutionary cycles.[55] While evangelicals remained a minority, their morality came to be imposed on the general population through a powerful discourse. Furthermore, in neo-Weberian fashion, Hilton argues that it was this evangelical theology of Atonement that came to shape economic relations in nineteenth-century Britain. Acknowledging that evangelicalism and Bentham's "deontology"[56] were parallel developments that cannot be easily disentangled, Hilton reasons that the writings of both Bentham and the Enlightenment philosophers were actually read by very few. In contrast, evangelicalism exercised a distinct "sway" on the middle class.[57] Over time it succeeded in imposing an intense time consciousness that was revealed by scrupulously kept daily diaries.

The importance of Hilton for understanding the Canadian context is that first, if evangelicalism as a minority religion held "sway" at the centre, then at the periphery in Ontario where the established church had lost official status, one could expect evangelicalism to be the ascendant ideology. This was in fact the case, as I will argue in what follows. Second, if evangelicalism exerted a powerful force at the heart of Westminster, then one could expect an echo

---

[55] For example, the evangelical theologian T.R. Birks speaks of "transfers" and "payments" with respect to the Atonement. T.R. Birks, *The Victory of Divine Goodness* (London, Oxford, and Cambridge: Rivingtons, 1867), 151, 153, 164. To be fair, Hilton is much more mechanical in his explication of the doctrine than Birks, who is always careful to emphasize the "personal".

[56] This refers to an ethical system that is duty or "rule"-based as opposed to that which is pragmatic-based.

[57] While not accepting E.P. Thompson's oscillating theory that matches upswings in evangelical fervour with economic downturns, his tying of an increased emphasis on time and punctuality in nineteenth-century British culture to evangelical discourse is a compelling argument. See E.P. Thompson, *The Making of the English Working Class* (New York: Vintage, 1966), 380-400.

in Ottawa and at Queen's Park. Again this was the case, with evangelical power extending out far beyond the metropole and into the colonial political corridors of Ontario. Third, in Britain if evangelicals such as the prominent Scottish divine and economist, Thomas Chalmers, espoused a mechanistic Free Trade, then one could expect this principle to be picked up and carried into Canadian politics. This principle was picked up by Reformers such as the Scottish evangelicals George Brown and Alexander Mackenzie, one a Presbyterian and the other a Baptist, and was implemented with varying success.[58]

While the emphasis on Free Trade is congruent with a liberal economic ordering, evangelicalism carried with it a moral and spiritual fervour that cannot be easily collapsed into mere economics. Hilton traces a development from an Age of Atonement in the first half of the century to an increased emphasis on the Incarnation in the second half. With its accent on the life of Jesus in contrast to his death, Incarnational Christianity emphasized social service.[59] The evangelical Cambridge theologian T.R. Birks reflected this new emphasis in his espousal of the "higher science" of "Moral Chrematics" in contrast to "Natural Chrematics":

> [W]e must create and develop a higher science of Natural Chrematics, or the laws of social duty by which man is bound both to God and his fellowmen in the right use, social adaptation, and religious consecration, of all outward and visible things. It is not universal free trade, least of all its freedom from moral restraints, but universal uprightness, integrity, and brotherly kindness, in trade, labour, commerce, and all social relations, which is the true and effectual remedy for these threatening evils. The whole system of trade, the manifold treasures which human

---

[58] On Peter Brown's liberalism see By Libertas [Peter Brown], *The Fame and Glory of England Vindicated Being an Answer to "The Glory and Shame of England"* (New York and London: Wiley and Putnam, 1842. Brown's liberalism will be discussed in Chapter Three.

[59] Boyd Hilton, *The Age of Atonement: The Influence of Evangelicalism on Social and Economic Thought, 1795-1865* (Oxford: Clarendon Press, 1988), 255-285. But the Atonement continued to loom large in evangelical thought despite the increasing importance of the Incarnation.

skill and industry derive from their parent earth, when once they break loose from the great law of love, may soon lose themselves in outer darkness. But when they learn to submit reverently to this higher law, they revolve harmoniously in their own orbit, and are bathed in a light and beauty which shines on them from above.[60]

Birks, at least in theory and without jettisoning the Atonement, embraced an Incarnational principle that rejected unrestricted Free Trade. While liberal social order proponents could argue that Birks's words were mere rhetoric, they reveal an ideology that sought to abolish slavery and increasingly advocated temperance, movements that went counter to economic interests. I will argue that it is precisely the discourse that we see in the above passage on "a law of love" that was also shaping male behaviour and depressing interpersonal violence.

Callum Brown has been the most articulate advocate of a "discursive Christianity". This discursive Christianity operated in addition to the institutional, intellectual, functional, and diffusive forms of Christianity that were present in the Christian culture of Britain during the nineteenth century and into the twentieth century. By discursive Christianity, Brown means "the people's subscription to protocols of personal identity that derive from Christian expectations, or discourses, evident in their own time and place."[61] Christian discourses emanated from pulpits, lecterns, media, and from private individuals whether in the home, the workplace, or places of leisure. There was a uniformity to these discourses that produced protocols of behaviour, speech, and appearance, as well as varied activities such as church-going or family devotional exercises. Most importantly for this study, "rough" behaviour associated with the drinking of alcohol was condemned.[62] Self-identities were shaped

[60] T.R. Birks, *First Principles of Moral Science: A Course of Lectures* (London: Macmillan, 1873), 162. For a discussion of this passage and Birks see Boyd Hilton, *The Age of Atonement*, 365-367. "Chrematic" is apparently derived from *chrema*, the Greek word for "thing".

[61] Callum Brown, *The Death of Christian Britain: Understanding Secularisation, 1800-2000* (London: Routledge, 2001), 12.

[62] Callum Brown, *The Death of Christian Britain*, 90, 98, 125-126, 154.

through the adoption of BEP protocols. These nineteenth-century evangelical discourses can be accessed in newspapers, religious tracts, sermons, obituaries, and in oral history collections that were gathered in the 1970s and 1980s.[63]

Denominational statistics produced during the last half of the nineteenth century are also a product of Christian discourse. Rich data on church membership and attendance, as well as sermons published *verbatim* and reports of voluntary associations, preserve some of the "noise" of the evangelical movement that becomes less accessible later in the twentieth century when such reporting gradually fades. Gross citywide church attendance figures are thus accessible at points both for cities in Britain and in the Empire, perhaps uniquely in Toronto. Comparative quantitative analysis potentially allows for crude measurements of the strength of Christian discourses and the protocols that were products of such discourse. I will argue that it is the strength of a given discourse that determines aggregate denominational attendance in a place of worship. On the flip side, it was the strength of a religious discourse that determined how few males of a given denomination were incarcerated in prisons.[64]

Based on the strength of the institutional base of the BEP movement,[65] one can make a judgment that it spawned a controlling ideology capable of producing a set of normative beliefs and behaviours. In the case of Toronto, this dominant ideology produced a cultural configuration that led to depressed levels of interpersonal violence across the *entire* community. This process is made up of innumerable personal interactions and incalculable swirling eddies of communal activity. It is in this sense that one portrays "ideology" as shaping behaviour. Inevitably, historical conceptualizing involves "black box" elements

---

[63] See Callum Brown, *The Death of Christian Britain*, 12-15.

[64] Hugh McLeod marshals evidence from the oral history study, referred to above, of participants born in late nineteenth-century and early twentieth-century Britain that demonstrates that 33% of non-churchgoing fathers spent most of their free time in taverns while only 7% of churchgoing fathers spent a similar amount of time in such establishments. Hugh McLeod, *Religion and Society in England, 1850-1914* (New York: St. Martin's Press, 1996), 125-126.

[65] This institutional base will be described in Chapter Four.

and resists schematization.[66]

2.3 BEP Toronto

Ultimately the culture of Toronto was heavily influenced by BEP ideology, including all non-BEP sectors. Toronto did not remain a BEP culture. But it did remain a religious culture for decades, and it was capable of absorbing and pacifying young males from a variety of cultures, even cultures with much higher rates of interpersonal violence than Canada, such that homicide rates remained low for decades.

Nineteenth-century evangelicalism in Toronto was in direct continuity with British evangelicalism and hence my label 'BEP'. I regard the movement as an outlook or spirit that was Protestant and assumed the central place of the Bible in life and practice. It was a "religion of the heart" in that it emphasized the role of religious experience, including prayer and devotional practices in communal contexts. An inward, somewhat mystical focus on the life and death of Christ was central.[67] Evangelism, including overseas missions, was stressed such that one historian can speak of a "salvation industry".[68]

Evangelicals certainly had denominational loyalties but these were readily dispensed with for efforts at outreach and for associational purposes. Prominent BEP organizations had board members that usually included Methodist, Presbyterian, Congregationalist, Baptist, and evangelical Anglican

[66] On the complexity of historical explanation see T.J. Jackson Lears, "The Concept of Cultural Hegemony: Problems and Possibilities," *American Historical Review*, 90 (June 1985): 567-593.

[67] For an overview of some of these categories see John Webster Grant, *A Profusion of Spires: Religion in Nineteenth-Century Ontario* (Toronto: University of Toronto Press, 1988), 52-67 and William Westfall, *Two Worlds: The Protestant Culture of Nineteenth-Century Ontario* (Kingston and Montreal, 1989), 50-81. The Canadian percentages are taken from the Canada decennial census. There are continuities between nineteenth-century evangelicals and the early modern Protestants or "evangelicals". Alec Ryrie helpfully describes the movement as "a restless, progressive religion which was nourished by crisis and starved by routine... [t]his four-cornered dance, with intensity and dynamism facing off against hypocrisy and idleness". Ryrie rejects Weber's characterization of the movement as "bleak" and marked by the "unprecedented inner loneliness of the single individual." See Alec Ryrie, *Being Protestant in Reformation England* (Oxford: Oxford University Press, 2013), 3-4, 104.

[68] Callum Brown, *Death of Christian Britain*, 43-57.

clergy and laymen. While there were core evangelical beliefs, the movement can also be tracked in a phenomenological manner by a noting of who sympathized openly with an evangelical icon such as the American evangelist, D.L. Moody. A perusal of the newspaper reports of the massive Moody meetings in Toronto in 1884 and in 1894 lists prominent BEP ministers and laymen and serve to give one a sense of the range of whom functionally was an evangelical in this period.[69] When the Anglican W.H. Howland died in 1893, the *Globe* obituary emphasized that his "Christian sympathies were not narrowed by any sectarian lines."[70] It was said that there was hardly a Methodist pulpit in Toronto that Howland had not preached in.

Although evangelicalism in Canada closely resembled its counterpart in the British Isles, it was modified in important ways by the colonial setting in North America. A comparison of the Protestant religious composition of Ontario in 1871 with England and Wales in 1851[71] reveals significant differences:

Table 2.1 Denominational comparison of Ontario with England and Wales, 1871 and 1851

Ontario 1871	% of population	Toronto 1871 % of population	England and Wales 1851	% of population
Methodist	28.5%	17%	Methodist	25%
Presbyterian	22%	16.3%	Presbyterian	2.2%
Anglican	20.4%	37%	Anglican	48.6%
Baptist	5.5%	4%	Baptist	8.5%

[69] See *Globe* Dec. 1, 1884:3-4; 2:2; 3:2,5; 4:5; 5:5; *Globe* Nov. 10, 1894:1-2; 12:2; 23:5; 26:8. Prominent church leaders who sat on the platform and led in prayers, or served on organizational committees, included Methodists, Congregationalists, Presbyterians, and evangelical Anglicans such as Howland and Blake. The first rally in 1884 was held in the Metropolitan Methodist Church while in 1894 it was in Massey Hall.

[70] *Globe*, Dec. 13, 1893: 2.

[71] This was the final year that religion was included in the British census. However, the percentage figures are estimates. Only church attendance was part of the census. These estimates for England and Wales are based on the estimates made by Currie, *et al*, and by Watts. See Robert Currie, Alan Gilbert, and Lee Horsley, *Churches and Church-Goers* (Oxford: Oxford University Press, 1977), 21-45; Watts, *The Dissenters,* vol. two, 22-29.

| Roman Catholic | 16.9% | 21% | Roman Catholic | 3.5% |
| Other | 6.9% | 4.8% | Independent | 11.1% |

These differences reflect an Ontario population mix that was taken from the British Isles at large, with the key difference being the greater number of Irish Catholics and Scottish Presbyterians in Ontario and the resulting smaller percentage of Anglicans, although in Toronto itself, the percentage of Anglicans resembles more closely that of England and Wales.

The presence of large numbers of Ontario residents from the "Celtic fringe" of Great Britain had major implications for the political development of both Ontario and Toronto. Evangelical Protestants with roots in Ireland and Scotland were disproportionately involved in the fight for "responsible government", the assault on clergy reserves, and the drive for church disestablishment.[72] This British Protestant and dissident political persuasion was given a boost by its close proximity to a fledgling Republic, when in the aftermath of rebellion, Lord Durham counselled responsible government.

While certainly influenced by the large geographical expanse of North America and the blend of revivalism and republicanism to the south, Toronto's British evangelical Protestantism was distinguished by a decidedly British tilt. A birthplace analysis of the biographical profiles of fifty-seven prominent Toronto clergymen in 1891 yields the following:

Table 2.2 Birthplace analysis of prominent Toronto clergymen, 1891

Birthplace	Number	
Canada	26	(UC 18, LC 3, NB 3, NS 2)
England	8	
Scotland	7	
Ireland	5	
United States	4	
India	2	

[72] For a lucid essay outlining the influence of a transplanted Irish Whig ideology see John McLaren, "The Rule of Law and Irish Whig Constitutionalism in Upper Canada: William

West Indies	1
Wales	1
Unknown	3

UC=Upper Canada, LC=Lower Canada, NB=New Brunswick, NS=Nova Scotia.

Of the 26 Canadian-born clergy, nine seem to have been first-generation Canadian, (e.g. "of sturdy British stock" or "Scottish parentage.")[73]

While American ideas were certainly in circulation, as evidenced by the sale of American books and magazines, as well as the sermons of the Brooklyn preacher Thomas Dewitt Talmage that were printed weekly for a time in the *Globe*, the channelling of British ideas by telegraph, steamship, and through the flow of immigrants tended to offset the cultural influence from the United States.[74] English-speaking Canadians identified closely with the British Empire but simultaneously with a Canadian twist.[75]

The evangelical E.H. Dewart, in compiling Canada's first collection of poetry, argued for a distinctly *Canadian* poetry.[76] While recognizing the political advantage of Empire, he pleaded for a "national literature" that would help cut against the grain of a situation that saw Canada's "mental wants provided by the brains of the Mother Country". Clearly, from Dewart's vantage point as a prominent Methodist editor-minister in Toronto, the prime cultural mover in Canada remained the "Old Country".[77]

Warren Baldwin, the 'Irish Opposition,' and the Volunteer Connection" in *Essays in the History of Canadian Law*, Volume Ten, *A Tribute to Peter Oliver*, ed. Jim Phillips, Roy McMurtry, and John T. Saywell, (Toronto: University of Toronto Press, 2008), 320-350.

[73] G. Mercer Adam, *Toronto, Old and New: Historical, Descriptive and Pictorial* (Toronto: The Mail Printing Company, 1891), 71-88.

[74] Careless, J.M.S. ""Mid-Victorian Liberalism in Central Canadian Newspapers, 1850-67," *Canadian Historical Review*, XXXI, no. 3 (September 1950): 221-236.

[75] See for example Carl Berger, *The Sense of Power: Studies in the Ideas of Canadian Imperialism, 1867-1914* (Toronto: University of Toronto Press, 1970).

[76] Note that Dewart's collection was not narrowly sectarian but also included, for example, the writing of poet-politician D'Arcy McGee, a Catholic.

[77] Edward Hartley Dewart, *Selections From Canadian Poets* (Montreal: John Lovell, 1864), VII-XIV. For the pervasive influence of American publishing on Canada see Allan C. L. Smith, "The Imported Image: American Publications and American Ideas in the Evolution of

Dewart was a product of a Canadian evangelical revivalism that had introduced a BEP understanding of life to a large percentage of Ontario residents at mid-century. By 1880 this evangelicalism had been largely institutionalized, as will be outlined in the next chapter. At its core BEP messages were religious in nature, but these messages were linked to prescriptions for behaviour. Protestant behavioural prescriptions would be inconsequential if they simply emanated from the beliefs of a small religious minority. However, these messages amounted to a controlling ideology in the case of Toronto's British evangelical Protestants, given the size into which the movement had evolved. The previously Tory and Anglican world of Toronto had been seriously challenged.

---

the English Canadian Mind, 1820-1900" (PhD diss., University of Toronto, 1972).

3

BRITISH EVANGELICAL PROTESTANT DISCOURSE

Overview

The central argument of Chapter Three is that Protestant messages were linked to prescriptions for human behaviour. These messages, when combined with the scope of the movement, amounted to a controlling ideology. British evangelical Protestantism was a highly gendered religious expression. BEP messages were disproportionately aimed at shaping male behaviour, especially that of young males. Furthermore the BEP movement produced increased opportunity for the expression of human empathy. In summary, BEP discourse succeeded in largely blunting interpersonal violence.

Introduction

Teachings on the Christian family and "true manliness" were prominent in messages from BEP pulpits and lecterns and were heavily influenced by female concerns for increased levels of male domesticity. Men were disproportionately the targets of Christian moral teaching, a reflection of the fact that women formed a large majority of church members and attendees. Although many males did not regularly attend church services, Protestant messages were carried by women into households and into the culture of Toronto at large.[1]

As had the abolitionism of a previous generation, the new evangelical ideology of temperance collided with prevailing cultural norms and, in particular, with a traditional male culture in which the tavern was a centre

---

[1] The disproportionately high BEP female membership will be accounted for in Chapter Four.

of life. Evangelical teachings on temperance and manliness were closely entwined. Intemperance came to be seen as a "road to the gallows". "Rough" male behaviour, whether gambling, dog baiting, cock fighting or boxing was condemned. Over time, the legitimacy of male involvement in violent altercations decreased.

Providing for one's wife and children became a central BEP virtue; negligence in this area also created the risk of an appearance before the Police Magistrate. Male sexuality was greatly constrained by BEP ideology with births outside of marriage becoming more infrequent, even after accounting for pre-nuptial conceptions. While this type of familial configuration was ideal for maintaining a stable work force in an industrializing economy, critically for this study, it also decreased the violence caused by the jealousies of overlapping sexual rivalries and relationships.[2]

The researcher who takes on the task of trying to make sense of Toronto's BEP discourse is faced with a deeply layered past that runs through all manner of writings, including bulging volumes of City Council Minutes, the hundreds of thousands of pages from the many daily newspapers of the period, the steady stream of periodicals and books that circulated from offices of religious denominations located in Toronto, and in the records of a vast network of voluntary associations whose workers sought to reform and shape an urban frontier. Sermon collections remain from the pulpits of stone edifices, for which Toronto was dubbed "City of Churches". Thousands of meters of microfilm in denominational archives record the births, baptisms, mundane activities, and deaths of congregants. Diaries always have the potential to allow the interpreter to explore inner sanctuaries.[3] Inscriptions

[2] Steven Pinker argues that in cultural configurations marked by polygyny, poor men are forced into desperate and violent competition for women while Christian cultures have enabled poor males to remain in the marriage "game". See Steven Pinker, *How the Mind Works* (New York: W.W. Norton, 1997), 475-479.

[3] Max Weber emphasized the Calvinist habit of taking one's "own pulse" and methodically monitoring one's own behaviour and the behaviour of God in the details of the individual life. Max Weber, *The Protestant Ethic and the Spirit of Capitalism* (Abingdon, Oxford: Routledge, 2001), 76-77.

on memorials[4] and obituaries are overlaid with religious language and point to an underlying common religious lingua. Manuscript census data provide a wealth of material on the extent of Toronto's religious communities that is not duplicated elsewhere.

I will probe BEP discourse, firstly, through the writings and records of activities of evangelical elites. These will be accessed using texts such as the daily newspapers the *Globe* and *Evening Telegram, The Shaftesbury Hall Weekly Bulletin,* the *Report of the Royal Commission of the Liquor Traffic*, mayoral speeches as published in the *City Council Minutes*, the records of voluntary associations as recorded in their minutes and publications, as well as sermons. Secondly, I will argue that religious demographic changes, as evidenced in census documents, were brought about primarily as the result of religious discourse rather than strictly material causes. These data show that distinctive religious identities were claimed by virtually all of Toronto's population. [The 1901 Canada Census is a rich source of data on religious communities and to date, there has been no extensive use of it to map the religious contours of Toronto's neighbourhoods.]

All cultures of course contain a multitude of discourses. The central argument of this study is that the behaviour of young males in late nine-teenth-century Toronto was being shaped in new and even radical ways that were unique to BEP cultures. The fact that such large-scale cultures are now extinct adds a "lost cause" dimension to the study. It is extremely difficult to imagine a scenario whereby the prohibition of alcohol, for example, could be repristinated in a Western culture. While the interpreter's perspective is never neutral, there is a measure of objectivity in the study of a lost cause such as prohibition since this "cause" no longer has a large constituency.

The BEP moral shaping of males in late nineteenth-century Toronto was a "package deal". There can be no sharp separation of temperance, sexual reg-ulation, and strictures against male violence. This ordering of male behaviour

---

[4] For example a bronze sculpture by Sir Thomas Brock of Robert Raikes, the Gloucestershire founder of the Sunday School, stands at Queen's Park to the side of the legislature building. Duplicate copies stand in Bristol and London, attesting to the Atlantic nature of BEP.

paradoxically led to greater freedom in terms of the universal franchise for women and working-class men, as well as a multitude of everyday freedoms that evolved once male violence was effectively reduced.[5]

3.1 Male Behaviour

A broad reading of Toronto's BEP primary sources impresses one with the fact that although the BEP movement might have possessed an individualistic message, this message was transmitted within a communal context. Much was at stake. On an industrial frontier any disruption in the income of a family produced immediate hardship. With the upsurge in evangelicalism in the nineteenth century, the "rough" behaviour that typified males became the primary target for BEP behavioural codes. Although these codes generally had their origins in certain interpretations of biblical injunctions, they can be tied to the pragmatic concerns of women.

BEP sermons and lectures regularly reiterated themes of "true manhood," "honest manhood," and the search for "A Man".[6] Teaching on true manliness was often contained within narratives of "salvation" or "death". Drink, a constant topic, was said to lead in a downward spiral beginning with "waste of time, neglect of business, to slovenly habits, ...almshouse...to brutality, to murder, to prison, to the gallows..."[7] Narratives of young men were usually set within familial contexts rather than being strictly individualistic. The emphasis on "sobriety" is consistent with the religious asceticism of

---

[5] Here I am in agreement with Robert Muchembled, who argues that the emerging new world of "self control" was one in which young males faced a cluster of constraints on violent and sexual activities which amounted to a Western "factory" that processed young men and rendered them much less violent. Robert Muchembled, *A History of Violence*, 1-3, 40-42, 204-211. See also Gary A. Haughen and Victor Boutros, *The Locust Effect: Why the End of Poverty Requires the End of Violence* (New York: Oxford University Press, 2014).

[6] See for example the *Globe*, April 22, 1880: 6; April 9, 1883: 6; *Globe*, June 9, 1883: 5; *Shaftesbury Hall Weekly Bulletin*, March 8, 1884: 3. The young historian to-be and ex-president of the University YMCA, George Wrong, in a talk on Christian "work", underlined the need for "men to do the work." "They must be <u>men</u>-true men. If there is anything a student dislikes and readily detects, it is a sham. But they like a true man. So a true man, one sincere, faithful, humble, will never fail to secure a hearing." *Shaftesbury Hall Weekly Bulletin*, March 8, 1884: 6.

[7] *Shaftesbury Hall Weekly Bulletin*, July 17, 1880.

the Protestant "sects" that Weber saw as underlying the moral ordering of Protestant cultures.[8]

Male declension inevitably had implications for other family members. An article in a YMCA publication, entitled "A Young Man's History in Brief," tells the story of a young partygoer who took a glass of wine "at the urgent solicitation of a young lady[9] to whom he had been introduced". The narrator then fast forwards to the young man's funeral procession and sketches a picture of "hearts cast down", a father's grey hairs "going to the grave with sorrow" and a mother weeping "that she had given birth to such a child."[10]

Narratives of salvation were at least as numerous. The weekly bulletin of Toronto's YMCA recounts the story of a young man who had "taken to drink" and had bought a revolver with the implication that he intended to take his life. Instead he checked into a room at the YMCA, received assistance in finding a job, and then, in a letter, informed the members that he was on the road to recovery.[11] Another letter received at Toronto's YMCA, written by a prisoner at Central Prison, tells a story of his "conversion" as the result of visits from a YMCA worker.[12] These narratives were printed and distributed as new print media served to propagate BEP moral codes.

Public policy on alcohol proved to be a point of generally respectful but deep division within BEP churches and voluntary associations. A range of attitudes existed, from the minority who argued for the responsible use of alcohol with a restriction on liquor licenses, to the majority who advocated the prohibition of all alcoholic beverages including beer. Generally Methodists and Baptists were prohibitionists, while Presbyterians and evangelical Anglicans were advocates of temperance.[13] Again, the argument taking shape here is

---

[8] Max Weber, *From Max Weber*, 320-322.

[9] Note this was not the conventional route, as it was the male who generally was portrayed as leading to the "ruin" of the female.

[10] *Shaftesbury Hall Weekly Bulletin*, May 6, 1882: 2.

[11] *Shaftesbury Hall Weekly Bulletin*, June 9, 1883: 3.

[12] *Shaftesbury Hall Weekly Bulletin*, March 8, 1884: 3.

[13] But certainly there were major exceptions, such as the Anglicans S.H. Blake and William H. Howland, who were major figures in the prohibition movement, and Casimir Gzowski, a temperance supporter who was active in the coffee house movement and was known to host

that the temperance was critical for declining rates of interpersonal violence; at least in the urban frontier of late nineteenth-century Toronto.

3.2 Sexuality, Courtship and Marriage

Male behaviour increasingly was under scrutiny in the BEP world, beginning in the family as adolescence approached and then within courtship and marriage. Frequent, if often veiled, references were made to men, women and sexuality within BEP discourse. Women were generally given the benefit of the doubt with respect to "virtue", while men were usually seen as having the potential to lead a young woman astray or to "ruin" a marriage.[14] A Presbyterian pastoral in 1883, read to all the Presbyterian churches in Toronto, proclaimed that family worship was the best protection for the family while the family itself was the best "safeguard" of "virtue" and "happiness" for males.[15]

Similarly, a *Globe* commentary on a joint YMCA-Ministerial Association directive that called for special sermons to be preached for young men affirmed that, "Young men are peculiarly sensitive to all the tides of thought". Given that more young men were now living in the city and facing temptations not known in the "quiet" countryside, many a young man found in the clamour for "wealth and fame" that with "his moral anchor gone, there [wa]s but little to prevent him drifting to ruin." The reporter, perhaps paraphrasing one of the "special sermons", saw it as the duty of ministers to "slay the dragons" that "beset" the early years of "manhood". The reporter concluded:

---

large social functions that included alcohol. Peter Oliver, *The Conventional Man: The Diaries of Ontario Chief Justice Robert A. Harrison 1856-1878* (Toronto: University of Toronto Press, 2003), 296. Gzowski could have changed his view by the 1880s. Numerous ministers and temperance workers (as well as vigorous opponents of prohibition) were called to testify at the Royal Commission on the Liquor Traffic in Canada in 1892. I will refer to testimony from key witnesses such as William H. Howland later in the thesis.

[14] See for example the sermon of Rev. J.P. Lewis of Grace [Anglican] Church entitled "Temptations to Young Men". Women are pictured as "faithfully working at home" with men all too often being "unfaithful to every vow." *Globe*, April 16, 1883: 6.

[15] Pastoral by Dr. King, Moderator of the Presbyterian Church in Canada. *Globe*, October 8, 1883: 5. King was the pastor of George Brown, Oliver Mowat, and other members of the Presbyterian ruling elite.

The minister who wraps himself up in his ecclesiastical garments and does not mingle in the throng and keep his finger on the pulse of the great world's heart around him is unfitted for the task of aiding young men. They must be met by whole-souled, enthusiastic, but not gushy men, whom they instinctively endorse as "sensible" and free from cant and ecclesiastical mannerisms. Such ministers, fortunately, are not uncommon in Toronto, and are found in all denominations. They rally around them the young men of the day in striking vigorous blows at evil.[16]

When it is kept in mind that this is BEP commentary from a large daily newspaper, one can see that the distinction between "secular" and "religious" was significantly blurred.

Church youth associations, as well as the pulpit, also served to regulate courtship. Rev. Dr. W.J. Hunter, the popular Methodist minister, addressed a newly established Queen St. Methodist Young People's Association in 1881 just prior to Christmas. In flowery Victorian language, he proclaimed that "Woman…was designed to make the full complement of men." The Male "stands" in the midst of an "inferior tribe" while "woman stands between her husband and her God, and is the glory of man and all the earth besides." Nonetheless, even though morally superior to the man, woman is doomed to second best because of being deceived in Eden. Hunter went on to opine that all should marry and that vows of celibacy were "wicked". Women were warned to avoid men who indulged in the "flowing bowl" while "flirts" were the "most contemptible of creatures". The marks of a BEP sexual regulatory regime were plain.[17]

---

[16] *Globe*, Nov. 14, 1881: 9.

[17] *Globe*, Dec. 14, 1881: 10. Note that it is in this period that the seduction law sponsored by the BEP MP, John Charleton, was passed. Whether this law is a vestige of patriarchy or is driven by concerns of women is a matter for debate. For a report on the law see *Globe* April 28, 1883: 4. While one can detect a passing swipe at Roman Catholicism with respect to "vows of celibacy", the emphasis is clearly on the fact that "all" should marry (a Pauline allusion from 1 Corinthians), no doubt for the purposes of controlling sexuality. For a diary account of the inward sexual restraints imposed by BEP culture in an earlier period see Peter

3.2.1 BEP Discourse Concerning Sexual Regulation

While much is often made of Victorian hypocrisy with respect to sexual restraint, BEP sexual regulation was apparent even in the daily business of a "respectable" hotel. Under the heading, "Honeymoon Vicissitudes," the *Globe* reported the story of a newly married couple from the country that, before breakfast, was ejected from a Toronto hotel because of their inability to produce a marriage license. During the evening the "landlord" had for some reason come to suspect that the couple were not married and in the morning took it upon himself to discuss with them the "rather delicate subject." The pastor of the humiliated couple travelled to Toronto to obtain an apology from the hotel owner who refused to give it. In the end, court action was threatened.[18] This story, when combined with the regular reporting of cases of bigamy[19] no doubt brought about by the difficulty of obtaining a divorce, points to the exalted view of the marriage contract on the part of Toronto's BEP culture and the great lengths to which hotel keepers and clergymen would go to uphold its force.

In parallel with social developments in Britain,[20] rhetoric concerning prostitution increasingly came into the foreground in the 1880s. Beginning in November of 1881, the Ministerial Association, dominated by BEP clergymen, took up the question of "The Social Evil." In the initial meeting, there was vigorous debate as to whether brothels should be licensed. Most concurred that a licensing system for the estimated 50-150 houses in Toronto was unacceptable. Sympathy was expressed for the young women caught up in the trade, and the need for "refuges" for the women was voiced at the meeting. The difficulties of prosecuting were acknowledged, although a letter

---

Oliver, *The Conventional Man: The Diaries of Ontario Chief Justice Robert A. Harrison 1856-1878* (Toronto: University of Toronto Press, 2003), 151-171.

[18] *Globe*, April 23, 1881: 14.

[19] On the cultural concern with respect to bigamy see *Globe* Jan. 10, 1890: 2.

[20] See for example Lisa Severine Nolland and Clyde Binfield, *A Victorian Feminist Christian: Josephine Butler, the Prostitutes and God* (Carlisle: Paternoster Publishing, 2004). For an argument that the British moral regulation movement was driven by feminist concerns see Alan Hunt, *Governing Morals: A Social History of Moral Regulation* (Cambridge: Cambridge University Press, 1999), 140-191.

from Premier Mowat offered additional legal power in the effort "to put down such houses." An unidentified reporter from the *Globe*, who had tried to gain attendance, criticized the Association for excluding all newspaper reporters from a meeting that had been publicly announced through the distribution of printed fliers. Ministers simply did not want their names associated with what was said on such a delicate topic as prostitution.[21]

Guests of the Association in subsequent weeks featured Police Magistrate Denison[22] and Judge Mackenzie, who both were subjected to withering critique for lack of enforcement of existing laws by a deputation that included Crown Attorney Fenton. In the reportage, one detects a shift away from an opposition led by clergy to one led primarily by prominent lay leaders such as William H. Howland, Clark Gamble, and William McMaster. After a flurry of negotiation, public letters between Crown Attorney Fenton and Chief Constable Draper, ostensibly at the request of Police Magistrate Denison, communicated to the public that the laws regarding prostitution would be enforced.[23] These events form some of the background in the lead-up to the mayoralty of William H. Howland, beginning in 1886, which will be described in Chapter Four.

3.2.2 BEP Discourse Against "Immoral" and "Blasphemous" Literature

Novel-reading could receive criticism from some BEP quarters with

---

[21] *Globe*, Nov. 19, 1881. These meetings were held at Shaftesbury Hall. Owned by the YMCA and located on Queen St. where the Eaton's Centre is today, the hall featured an 800-seat auditorium and served as a venue for a wide variety of BEP activities. It was replaced by a larger facility in 1885.

[22] Denison estimated 40 houses in Toronto.

[23] *Globe*, Nov. 30, 1881: 9; Jan. 14, 1882: 15; Jan. 26, 1882: 11; Feb. 14, 1882: 8; Feb. 15, 1882: 2. One could argue that BEP rhetoric about prostitution cancels out a presumption of female "virtue." That prostitution is merely an anomaly is borne out by a YMCA publication that argues, "the greatest cause of all for the ruin of so many young women is man's own shameful cruelty towards them." John Ferguson, *Social Purity* (Toronto: Toronto YMCA, 1891), 12. William Howland argued that poor wages and even the threat of "starvation" caused young women to become prostitutes, although he did not discount "laziness" as at times being a factor. See Howland's testimony in *Royal Commission on the Relation of Labor and Capital: Evidence-Ontario* (Ottawa: Queen's Printer, 1889), 168.

respect to frivolity,[24] but on at least one occasion public controversy flared up when a shipment of books was seized by the local Collector of Customs on the apparent instructions of a mandate from Ottawa. The aggrieved bookseller complained that the books, by Paine and Voltaire, were "theistical" and not "atheistical" and threatened to take the matter to court. He recounted in response being told by a government official, "My good man, let me advise you for your eternal welfare not to try to sell any such books."[25]

On the Sunday following the seizure, in the pulpit of the Metropolitan Methodist Church, Dr. Potts supported the Collector and railed against the literature:

> If these works are not immoral, indecent, and blasphemous, then there is nothing immoral, indecent, blasphemous in literature. The Pocket Theology [Voltaire] is reeking with the obscene and the blasphemous. In these days of peril to young people from the infidel and indecent literature which is becoming more common, the Collector of Customs in this city is worthy of the thanks of the community for his action in this case. We cannot too earnestly protest against the incoming of the moral poison, and we should do all in our power to suppress what must be socially and morally destructive to the young people of the land.[26]

The Customs Officer received a *pro forma* commendation by the Ministerial Association,[27] but no doubt the incident was a "tempest in a teapot" in that many of the educated BEP clergy and academics would surely have been familiar with the writings in question. Still, the seizure illustrates the outer range of BEP ideology.[28]

---

[24] See for example *Shaftesbury Hall Weekly Bulletin* (February 2, 1885): 2.

[25] *Globe*, Oct. 10, 1881: 8.

[26] *Globe*, Oct. 17, 1881: 8.

[27] *Globe*, Oct. 25, 1881: 9.

[28] During Howland's mayoralty, there was also an attempt, supported by the majority of Council, to "suppress questionable photographs and pictures" displayed in the windows of cigar stores. See "Morals of the City" in *Globe*, June 24, 1886: 8.

3.2.3 BEP Discourse: Sabbath Regulation

"Desecration of the Sabbath" was a constant BEP rallying cry in the lead-up to Toronto's "street car wars" of the 1890s. From a century on, this theme has a highly individualistic, minority religious ring to it, but at the time the defence of the concept of "Sabbath" was a communal response to encroaching modernity. Enforcement of *Lord's Day* laws could descend to the level of arresting children for playing cards on a vacant lot on a Sunday.[29] Likewise newsboys were threatened with arrest by Crown Attorney Fenton because of the involvement with newspapers that were printed on Saturday night but distributed Sunday morning. Fenton publicly attacked Chief Constable Draper in letters printed in the *Globe*, threatened to take the issue of Draper's inaction to the police commissioners and admonished "that it was the duty of all Christian people to prevent others from buying Sunday newspapers." A Rev. Gregg remarked that surely the people who bought the newspapers were greater offenders than these boys who sold them.[30]

3.2.4 BEP Discourse: "Rough" Male Behaviour

Strictures against "rough" male behaviour were directed against boys at an early age in BEP Toronto and were seen as a communal responsibility within the BEP sector. Young males were warned of the dangers of alcohol and smoking: cigarette smoking led to the cigar, the glass of lager and then the pool hall. The Toronto YMCA publication *Our Boys* claimed that an early smoker generally became a man lacking in physical and mental "energy". Adolescents were warned to avoid associating with those—"profane boys"—with a "cruel disposition who take pleasure in sporting with and maiming animals and insects, and robbing birds of their young."[31]

Regular reports of young men throwing stones and occasionally snowballs appeared in the city's daily newspapers.[32] One incident of "serious snowball-

---

[29] *Globe*, Jan. 17, 1880: 4. While his companion escaped, newsboy Charles Helsey had the misfortune of being taken to #2 Station.

[30] *Globe*, April 23, 1885: 6.

[31] *Our Boys*, Feb. 1885: 2.

[32] *Globe*, June 4, 1880: 6; April 23, 1880. Mayor Howland banned firecrackers for the May

ing" involved a group of boys, "including one big fellow named Higgins, the biggest of the lot", who "stalked off" leaving "Willie ---d of Adelaide" lying on the ground and bleeding profusely from the face.[33] Here we have a clear example of a highly literate culture, using a new mass media to police societal norms. A more serious case involved the death an eleven-year-old after being struck by a stone thrown by a fourteen-year-old youth. The accused, William McKechnie, was jailed and charged with murder. McKechnie was discharged by a Coroner's jury but not before gaining notoriety on the pages of the newspaper for himself and his mother.[34] While the regulatory system was not without empathy that was often expressed in newspaper accounts, an obsession with male violence was demonstrated in the mass media of BEP Toronto.

The ready availability of handguns inevitably led to incidents of accidental wounding involving youths. A Toronto newspaper report on one such accident in Montreal moralistically described the shooter as a "small boy addicted to the pistol habit." The implication is that the "habit" is too common and that it needs to be controlled. William Lyon Mackenzie King, as a university student, spoke of two friends firing a revolver at a target on the door of a room in their university house.[35] These occurrences raise the question of why the criminal use of handguns was not more prevalent in Toronto.[36] One answer, to be explored in subsequent sections of this study, is that increasingly religious ideology with its discourses of non-violence produced non-violent males within a BEP world.

Heightened rhetoric on the subject of cruelty to animals and children can be discerned in BEP writings over the course of the 1880s. In 1886, a letter was received at the *World* concerning an old "worn-out" white horse that was

---

24 festivities in 1886. *Globe* May 24, 1886: 1,8.

[33] *Globe*, Feb. 22, 1882: 8.

[34] *Globe*, June 23, 1886: 8; June 25, 1886:1,8. See also another death involving stone throwing, *Globe*, June 9, 1887: 8; June 24, 1887: 8. In this case "no bill" was found.

[35] *Diaries of William Lyon Mackenzie King*, Tuesday, December 12, 1893.

[36] Compare the use of handguns in Chicago at a contemporaneous time, Jeffrey S. Adler, *First in Violence*, 33. Chicago was a much larger city. For the ready availability of handguns in Toronto see *T.E. Eaton Catalogue, 1901.*

daily to be seen on the streets of Toronto. A reporter picked up the drum and started a "relief fund" with a notice that was regularly listed in the paper, acknowledging gifts to the cause of "prevention of cruelty." Eventually a meeting was called at Shaftesbury Hall, which resulted in the establishment of the Humane and Children's Aid Movement. The Executive bristled with BEP representatives. Arguments were made for the provision of drinking troughs for horses. Agitation against de-horning was a feature of the new Humane Movement. Simultaneously, the Children's Fresh Air Fund was launched that allowed for summer excursions from the city. The first Juvenile Court Law was passed in 1888. Prison reform was also advocated and legislated.[37] A 10,000 copy run of a hardcover compendium of the Movement's teachings went to press and was sold for $15 per 100 copies.[38] In commending the Humane Society, Rev. Arthur H. Baldwin (nephew of the hero of responsible government—Robert Baldwin) attached the notion of Christian manhood to the defence of helpless animals. In attacking the "wanton destruction" of birds and small animals in Muskoka and even the practice of caging birds, he could "not conceive of a Christian man being guilty of cruelty, as love and kindness were the fundamental principles in Christianity."[39]

3.3 BEP Activist Discourse: An Engine of Reform

The appeal to "love and kindness" fits in with a broad and pervasive BEP discourse on the unity of all the "nations of earth" and the "equality of rights and privileges of all."[40] Although this theme has deep roots in Christian tra-

---

[37] J.J. Kelso. *Early History of the Humane and Children's Aid Movement, 1886-1893* (Toronto: L.K. Cameron, 1911).

[38] J. George Hodgins, ed., *Aims and Objects of the Toronto Humane Society* (Toronto: William Briggs, 1888). For a city of less than 200,000, a print run of 10,000 copies was ambitious. I will develop this further in the next chapter. The officers of the society were predominantly prominent BEP figures and include: the evangelical Anglican William Howland, the Presbyterian Rev. D.J. MacDonnell, the Baptist Rev. John Castle, the Congregationalist Rev. Joseph Wild, and the Methodist Rev. William Briggs.

[39] *Globe*, May 18, 1891: 8. See also G.G.S. Wallace, *Globe*, Oct. 12:8.

[40] *Globe*, Jan. 12, 1880: 2, in a report on meetings of the Evangelical Alliance. See also George M. Grant on the "idea of the unity of the race" in *Globe*, Dec. 9, 1893: 13.

dition,[41] the rise of a North Atlantic evangelical movement in the eighteenth century with abolition of slavery serving as a prime focus, gave it particular force. While the structures of BEP voluntarism will be examined in detail in Chapter Four, any discussion of the moralistic discourse that saturated the movement should point out that there are readily apparent vertical linkages between Late Victorian voluntary and philanthropic reform groups and earlier antislavery societies. In Britain as soon as reforming, humane principles were articulated in abolition, this "reforming dynamic" moved on to encompass a variety of causes from chimney-climbing boys, to prostitutes, vivisection, temperance, to persecuted Bulgarians, and even to prisoners. Libertarian principles that were allied to this movement led to Catholic[42] and Jewish emancipation and to the incipient enfranchisement of women. The dynamic of reform in a continuous process uncovered additional areas of perceived evil throughout the nineteenth century and beyond.[43]

The 1830s and 1840s saw the arrival from Scotland and Ireland of a number of Anglican and Presbyterian families whose sons eventually became BEP leaders of late Victorian Toronto. The "fathers" included the Scottish Peter Brown, and the Irish William Hume Blake, W.W. Baldwin, and Benjamin Cronyn.[44] Each possessed a spirit of dissent from a Tory Anglicanism that included opposition to clergy reserves, despite the fact that the latter three were Anglicans. Both Brown and Cronyn were ardent abolitionists. This group formed the nucleus of the Reformers in Canada West and in turn passed on the mantle of leadership to its sons (the sons were George Brown,

---

[41] Here the teaching of the common origins of all humans known as monogenesis is a factor. For a BEP "scientific" espousal of monogenesis see Daniel Wilson "On the Supposed Prevalence of One Cranial Type Throughout the American Aborigines," *Edinburgh Philosophical Society Journal*, New Series (January 1858), text-fiche, CIHM 63246.

[42] This does not preclude a very deep-seated Anti-Catholicism.

[43] See for example Brian Harrison, "A Genealogy of Reform," in *Anti-Slavery, Religion and Reform: Essays in Memory of Roger Anstey*, ed. Christine Bolt and Seymour Drescher (Folkestone, Kent: Wm Dawson and Sons), 1980.

[44] For an essay by on the Irish background of the political and religious beliefs of W.W. Baldwin see John McClaren, "The Rule of Law and Irish Whig Constitutionalism in Upper Canada," 320-350.

Edward Blake, Samuel H. Blake,[45] and Robert Baldwin, while Cronyn became father-in-law to the Blake brothers).[46] The fact that they were members of the Anglican and Presbyterian BEP elite gave the group clout of a sort that Methodists and Baptists did not possess.[47]

Because this group was primarily activist in outlook, access to its religio-political BEP philosophy can be gained through speeches, editorial slants of newspapers, and in the records of the activities of voluntary societies. Peter Brown is an exception to this rule, having written a political tract in 1842 that put forward a radical political agenda. As an abolitionist from Scotland, he had seen radical evangelical views such as abolition forced upon Parliament in Westminster. Brown's liberal agenda, based on religious values, argued for the "protection of person and property", individual rights, and the "majesty of the law". In Brown's view, "liberty" needed four important supports: "Liberty of speech, right of petition, trial by jury, and a free press."[48]

To what is now seen as conventional liberal philosophy, Brown added what he labelled the "law of love":

> Liberty has three great stages. The first is a desire for national independence; the second is to add to national independence, the enjoyment of personal freedom, and of such social and political privileges as are necessary for an enlightened community. The third, in addition to the other two, arises when the nation is so enlightened as fully to estimate all the advantages of these high privileges, and to desire to see them extended to all nations less favorably situated. In short, it is the progress of that law of love which makes a man love his neighbour as himself.[49]

[45] In the case of Cronyn the link is his son-in-laws Edward and Samuel Blake.

[46] Robert Baldwin had died early in 1858. However, even though Anglican, he had been an ardent opponent of establishment which paved a path for other BEP Anglican dissidents.

[47] The Methodist clergyman, Egerton Ryerson, and the Baptist stonecutter, Alexander Mackenzie, are obvious exceptions.

[48] By Libertas [Peter Brown], *The Fame and Glory of England Vindicated Being an Answer to "The Glory and Shame of England"* (New York and London: Wiley and Putnam, 1842), 260.

[49] Peter Brown, *The Fame and Glory of England*, 262-263.

This progress of liberty allowed for state intervention in "protecting the weak". All of this was obtainable under the flexible English constitution, as opposed to an American republic that still harboured "evil" slaveholders.[50] Initially Brown advocated a "plural establishment" and eventually, consistent with the other Reformers, a complete voluntarism principle. The antislavery movement remained the paradigm for BEP religio-political involvement, and it was this organizational principle that carried on in BEP Toronto.[51]

Similarly, later in the century, a young twenty-year-old William Lyon Mackenzie King was able to start a workingman's class at the Presbyterian St. Andrew's Institute. One night after an evening of singing songs and drinking coffee with a group of working class males, King confided to his diary that he truly loved "those who have not had as many opportunities as myself but who are my fellowmen."[52]

In line with the earlier Peter Brown, King mirrored the BEP emphasis on monogenesis that saw humankind as one, and in turn was linked to a belief that all human beings were created in the Image of God. Despite a wavering in the face of the onslaught of social Darwinism, this doctrine continued to energize BEP outlooks such that the movement could not simply be defined in the negative by the terms of "constraint", "compulsion" or "control". An empathy that produced individual and communal forms of compassion is difficult to evaluate given analysis's domination by economic and class considerations. Liberal-communal impulses, whether of an antislavery or a

---

[50] Peter Brown, *The Fame and Glory of England*, 262-263.

[51] See also Michael Gauvreau, "Reluctant Voluntaries: Peter and George Brown; The Scottish Disruption and the Politics of Church and State in Canada" *The Journal of Religious History* 25, no. 2 (June 2001): 134-157. Antislavery continued to be mentioned not least because slavery carried on in numerous parts of the world well into the period under study. See for example *Globe*, July 9, 1893: 3; Oct. 21, 1887; June 29, 1888: 3; Nov. 17, 1888; June 1, 1889; Aug. 13, 1892. In an address to "young men" Samuel H. Blake mentions three spiritual exemplars that evangelical young men should aspire to: the abolitionists William Wilberforce and Thomas Fowell Buxton, and the prison reformer John Howard. Samuel H. Blake, *The Young Men of Canada: A Lecture* (Toronto: B.J. Hill, 1876), 11, 40. Blake's father-in-law was Bishop Benjamin Cronyn, an abolitionist. The Blake and Cronyn families had traveled to Canada together from Ireland in 1832. The overlap of families would have provided Blake ample opportunity to become acquainted with the abolitionist paradigm.

[52] October 14, 1895.

prison reform nature, nonetheless shaped political ideas and agendas. One can follow this follow this BEP doctrine of monogenesis as BEP ideas increasingly moved into the political arena.

3.3.1 BEP Activist Discourse: The Political Rhetoric of William Holmes Howland

In the following section, I will examine the BEP discourse of William H. Howland as it manifested itself in a speech Howland gave upon his mayoral victory in 1886. The rhetoric of a relatively short-term mayor would be inconsequential apart from the fact that it is hitched to a non-violent discourse that emphasized the dangers of an uncontrolled trade in alcohol and the need to protect women and children from male violence. Both of these emphases, assuming that they were taken-up by Toronto culture as a whole, which is the argument of this thesis, go far in explaining the decline of interpersonal violence.

Howland, the son of "Father of Confederation" William P. Howland, was a prominent evangelical Anglican reformer and humanitarian elected mayor of Toronto by a wide majority. In an unexpected upset, Howland rode to victory on the coattails of a newly eligible women's vote and the labour vote. While he was pro-temperance and reform-minded, his incumbent opponent was outspokenly opposed to the Scott Act and was Anglican Tory. Soon after being elected Howland announced that henceforth all City Council meetings would be opened with prayer. A *Globe* reporter who interviewed ten of 36 aldermen on the subject found general support for Council prayers, although one stated caustically that Council had "heavier work to do than [pray]."[53]

On January 18th, newly elected Mayor Howland entered Council chambers to cheers. The meeting was opened with prayers delivered by the Bishop of Toronto "that lasted some minutes".[54] Of the mayor's inaugural performance, the *Globe* reported that attendees were "much impressed with the business-like manner" of Howland.[55]

---

[53] *Globe*, Jan. 18, 1886: 1,8.
[54] *Globe*, Jan. 19, 1886: 5.
[55] *Globe*, Jan. 19, 1886: 5.

The "illegal sale of liquor" ranked first on the agenda he presented in his inaugural speech. His second priority was sewage and sanitation, followed by an emphasis on the expanded rail lines that the city needed in order to attract new industries. The final part moved into sermonic mode as Howland made a plea for greater police action for the "protection of women and children." He spoke of several children who had recently been admitted to the hospital with broken bones, including one who "had its limbs broken, through the grossest cruelty of some one." He ended by voicing strong opposition to granting "bonuses" to industrialists for locating in the city.[56] His was not an entirely unique agenda, but it was laid out with unprecedented moral fervor and constitutes a telling example of the BEP creed in political action.[57] Lines had been clearly drawn, BEP rhetoric and proposals were in play, and the stage was set for BEP-influenced action in the coming decade.

After stepping down from the mayoralty, Howland continued his wide-ranging efforts to influence the public sphere. Sometimes this got negative reaction. The moral tone of a Howland letter pleading clemency for a young prisoner condemned to death[58] brought a sharp response from an opinion letter in *Toronto Life*. An author using the pen name of "Golan" wrote:

> If the object is to kill two dogs with one stone as it were, and, while appealing to the Minister, keep Mr. Howland's name before the public; why the open letter plan is perhaps not altogether a bad one. But there will be people who will think that a notoriety hunt might be conducted with less offence to good taste. This open letter has too much of the praying on the house tops and standing in the street flavor about it.[59]

That Howland's positions were having an effect on public debate is nonetheless very clear.

---

[56] *City Council Minutes*, Appendix: 1-6 (1886).

[57] *Globe*, Nov. 4, 1887: 8.

[58] *Globe*, Feb. 21, 1888: 8. I will discuss the circumstances of the prisoner, Robert Neil, in Chapter Six.

[59] *Toronto Life*, 1, no. 1 (1888), text-fiche, p. 147, CIMH 05994078.

An example of that effect is the book by C.S. Clark, *Of Toronto the Good: The Queen City as it is: A Social Study*.[60] Written ostensibly in response to Howland-like remarks made by Toronto delegates in 1897 at the Social Purity Conference in Baltimore and in world meetings of the W.C.T.U. in Toronto, the tract is a withering critique of BEP morality in general. Laying the blame for the "Puritanical rule exercised in Toronto" directly at the feet of the then-dead Howland, Clark argued that Howland had come to power through a "combination"[61] of newspapers, temperance, and labour circles. Howland had been able to "expose" a municipal fraud scheme, and this "exposure became the lever that triggered the idea of a strictly moral city."[62]

BEP women also have an important place in Clark's attack. He attributes a new, unintended, sexual forthrightness on the part of young women to the agitation of "present day moralists" who promote "fads" such as "Prohibition and Woman's Enfranchisement."

> With the progress in religion that has been made within the past few years and the agitation of the right of women to vote together with the interest displayed on the part of women to prohibit other women's husbands and brothers from drinking, it is not to be wondered at that young girls consider themselves to be relieved from the necessity of an introduction to a boy or young man whose acquaintanceship they desire to make, presuming doubtless, that this is one of the fundamental principles which women are striving for, and which the evolutionary process under way at the present time will render quite unnecessary.[63]

An anti-BEP discourse can also be detected in the *Trip Hammer*, the

---

[60] C.S. Clark, *Of Toronto the Good: The Queen City as it is: A Social Study* (Toronto and Montreal: The Toronto Publishing Company, 1898). Who exactly was Clark seems to be an open question. Oft-quoted, Clark apparently worked as a newspaper reporter. Was he "Golan"?

[61] This is the equivalent of the BEP "machine" that I describe in Chapter Four.

[62] C.S. Clark, *Of Toronto the Good*, 8-9.

[63] C.S. Clark, *Of Toronto the Good*, 114.

employee journal of the Massey Manufacturing Company. Taking concern over Chinese labour as its point of departure, the *Trip Hammer* had this to say:

> We have heard over and over again that it is unchristian—that that it is sinful to exclude the Chinaman from our shores if he wants to come— that the Chinese make good servants, are inoffensive, peaceful, and well-behaved, and that we ought to hail the opportunity their coming would afford to Christianize them and bring them under the influence of civilization.[64]

Criticism, though, was a testament to influence and a mark of the fact that BEP ideas were deeply entrenched, including the all-important thinking on non-violence.

3.4 BEP Discourse: "Toronto, the City of Churches"

"Christ I hate to leave Paris for Toronto the City of Churches."[65]

-Ernest Hemingway

When Hemingway arrived in Toronto as a writer for the *Toronto Star* in the early 1920s, the city had a decades-old reputation for being densely churched. Toronto was typically portrayed in the media as a peaceful, churchgoing and orderly city in sharp contrast to cities to the south.

Chief Constable Grasett, son of the evangelical Arthur Grasett, longtime dean of St. James Cathedral, could write in 1895 in his Annual Report on Crime that the city had a right to continue to claim its title of "Toronto the Good" as there was "no other city in America of equal population that has but one case of murder to charge up against the past year."[66] Similarly in the previous year, he reported that it "is a matter for sincere congratulations that

[64] *Trip Hammer*, vol. 1, no. 8 (September 1885): 106.

[65] Letter from Ernest Hemingway to Isabel Simmons, June 24, 1923. Ernest Hemingway, Carlos Baker, ed. *Ernest Hemingway Selected Letters* (New York: Scribner, 2003), 84.

[66] *Globe*, February 16, 1895: 3.

murder, the darkest crime of all, has almost disappeared from the records".[67] The alert reader no doubt would have read these comments in context, as the "City News" page had not a few headers that read, "Wife Beater".

A trip to Chicago in 1884 by a *Globe* reporter resulted in the headline, "Sunday in Chicago: City Where Vice Walks Openly and is Unpunished." The story describes a city where the comparative number of saloons was much higher than in Toronto, while disproportionately there were only one-sixth the churches. The writer closes with an admonishment that if readers were to visit Chicago they would "return to their homes determined that if their votes will prevent it, Ontario's cities [would] run no risk."[68]

Later that same year, the *Globe* declared, "there is not in all of Christendom a city in which church going is so much the fashion as it is in <u>this</u> city." But more cautiously the same article quoted a Methodist leader as saying that the churches had become "too respectable" and that they were losing "their saving power." The editorial called for a system of "free pews".[69]

Globe coverage of city churches was not uncritical. By the 1880s, there existed an undercurrent of lament that churchgoing had become a fashionable activity. In 1884, an undercover *Globe* reporter set out to gauge the reception when he arrived at church "considerably underdressed." In prestigious Methodist, Anglican and Presbyterian churches, he had "cold" and "not

[67] *Globe*, January 31, 1894: 3.

[68] *Globe*, May 17, 1884: 12. See also the evidence given by William H. Howland to the Royal Commission. In a discussion of prohibition in Maine he was asked to make a comparison with Canada: "Would a comparison with Canada be a fair one?— Canada is also very similar. Canada only consumes something over 4 gallons of liquor per head of the population, and the United States something like 17 gallons. Canada is a singularly temperate country." *Royal Commission on the Liquor Traffic: Minutes of Evidence*, vol. IV, part II (Ottawa: Queen's Printer, 1895), 904. For Howland's comparison of Toronto with other cities in North America see *Globe*, December 21, 1887: 4.

[69] *Globe*, August 2, 1884: 3. Numerous visitors and writers comment on the large numbers of churchgoers on the sidewalks of Toronto on their way to Sunday night services. An *Evening Telegram* reporter in the 1880s wrote that "no other city on the American continent presents such a spectacle as is seen every Sunday evening on the streets of Toronto. Thousands of people walk the avenues and thoroughfares on their way to church. It is the real "live" hour of the day." John Ross Robertson, *Landmarks of Toronto*, Fourth Series (Toronto: Evening Telegram, 1904), 373. See also *Globe*, March 3, 1887: 8; *Globe*, September 6, 1887: 4.

warm" welcomes, while at a Baptist and a Congregationalist church he was treated "just like a well-dressed person". In a similar vein, the *Globe* in 1888 editorialized on the way "strangers", especially if "shabby", were sometimes poorly welcomed in Toronto's churches, but nevertheless concluded that most were welcomed. Certainly contemporary evidence points to churchgoers as "well-dressed" and fashion conscious. But it would be a mistake to infer that the presence of fashion conveys the absence of the working-class population from city churches. By the late nineteenth century, "respectable" middle-class habits permeated British culture on both sides of the Atlantic.

BEP churchgoers mirrored the progressive culture that surrounded them. Confident, exuberant BEP entrepreneurs set the tone with their leadership in both church and civic matters. Outlets in the public sphere for upper and middle-class BEP women were plentiful. In contrast to an earlier Puritanism that sought to erect a utopia, British evangelical Protestant enterprise in Toronto saw Providence as constantly adapting rather than fixed.[70]

But offsetting this progressive spirit, there remained a deeply ingrained sense of human fallibility and sinfulness. Perhaps it is this emphasis that explains the almost distinctive BEP discourse on the need to visit prisoners and to ameliorate the dreadful conditions of prisons. Speaking from the pulpit of Central Presbyterian Church in 1888, the Rev. P. Macleod declared, "God forgive us if we have forgotten the prisoners and that they are our brothers." Christian principles are to be applied in prison rather than "the coldness of brutality." These principles include not imprisoning individuals for "drunk and disorderly" conduct but rather "caring" for them. For the "startlingly" high one-fifth of prisoners who are illiterate, they should be given the tools of literacy before being liberated.[71]

In the above sermon, there is the positive outlook of a BEP reforming emphasis that is transformative, that emphasizes BEP literacy regimes, and that advocates the need to treat drunkenness as a condition requiring

---

[70] See for example the Methodist Albert Carman's "philosophy of history" and views on Providence in E.H. Dewart et al., *Centennial of Canadian Methodism* (Toronto: William Briggs, 1891), 230.

[71] John Ross Robertson, *Landmarks of Toronto*, Fourth Series, 260-261.

intervention at ⬛ both the individual level and the societal level. Several years after Macleod's sermon, *Telegram* editor John Ross Robertson commented on the progress that had been brought about by BEP penal reform:

> The preceding portion of this sketch as can be seen by the reader, describes a past state of affairs; since it was written many changes have taken place, none though of a retrograde description. The whole of the working machinery of the church remains as effective in 1896 as it was in 1888—all the alterations have been in the direction of improvement.[72]

It is noteworthy that a highly placed newspaper owner with BEP affinities is arguing that a BEP "*working machinery*" [emphasis mine] remains intact as late as 1896, and that it is continuing to churn out needed reforms.

Samuel H. Blake likewise summed up his address to a Prisoners' Aid conference in 1896:

> In conclusion, I would solemnly ask that each one consider what criminals we ourselves are; how much we have been forgiven; and, in this same spirit of love and forgiveness, proceed to do our best for other criminals in our land.[73]

Whether in an earlier abolitionist drive or in the contemporary temperance movements, BEP discourse presented a progressive spirit tempered by traditional outlooks on human fallenness. It was this BEP discourse that continually produced movements of reform.

---

[72] John Ross Robertson, *Landmarks of Toronto*, Fourth Series, 262.

[73] Samuel H. Blake, *Our Faulty Gaol System* (Toronto: Methodist Magazine and Review, 1897), 7. But note that in the early 1890s BEP prison reformers, including Blake, debated and even advocated the use of the "lash" as an alternative to the brutal prison system. The deep contradictions and ambiguity of this development are heightened considering that BEP reformer George Brown lobbied for the abolition of whipping as early as 1849. See for example J.M.S. Careless, *Brown of the Globe*, vol. 1, *The Voice of Upper Canada, 1818-1859* (Toronto, Macmillan, 1959), 78-87.

3.5 BEP Empathetic Discourse

It would be a distortion to over-emphasize BEP discourse as fixated on sexuality and "rough" male behaviour. A New Year's Eve tragedy provides the occasion for tracking how a BEP empathetic discourse on quite a different subject was produced by a young William Lyon Mackenzie King, writing as a new journalist. On the afternoon of New Year's Eve, King visited the Orphan's Home and wrote in the *Globe* of the "joy and gladness" experienced by the boys and girls at the home on the appearance of Santa Claus. Appended to the article were the names of the seventeen female "managers" of the institute.[74]

Immediately after writing the article at the *Globe* office King, as he records in his diary, went off to Union station to meet an arrival, and while there he saw the body of a man, one James Read, who had died after having been struck by a train some minutes before. King's diary gives no further details of the accident other than a comment on the tragedy of such an event occurring on the eve of the New Year and how uncertain life is. Towards midnight he wrote:

> Would to Heaven that all the evil of the world might pass with it. May God pardon the sins of all, may he make his kingdom more hastened during the coming year...Bless those I love and know,—be with every heart who would know of thee–especially the poor.[75]

The viewing of the body of James Read had cast a shadow on King, but the diary does not reveal the entire story. Identification had been found on Read's body and a reporter had gone off to locate the man's family. The reporter[76] had found the family in their home on Symington Avenue, where Read's wife was "anxiously awaiting" his return. When the reporter informed Mrs. Read

[74] *Globe*, January 1, 1896: 6.

[75] December 31, 1895.

[76] King may have been involved in some of the writing of the article but he must have returned home by the time Read was identified according to the chronological account given in the *Daily Mail and Empire*, January 1, 1898: 6.

of the news the reaction "was pitiable to observe".

The *Globe* devoted almost half of the article to the financial straits of the Read family:

> Read had been out of employment nearly all the year, only working about six weeks since last winter, and as soon as the snow came he intended going into the country to seek a job. As a necessary consequence of his lack of employment the family are in very destitute circumstances. There are twelve children living out of a family of seventeen; ten of these are at home: the oldest girl, 23 years old, is an epileptic and unable to work; the eldest boy at home is seventeen, but he had his right arm cut off in a railroad accident, at the Junction two years ago and he can do little or nothing, and yet another child is a cripple. The family is absolutely without means of support. There is scarcely a bit of food or fuel in the house and the case is as pitiful and distressing as can well be imagined. Deceased was a member of the Bricklayers' Union and of the Portsmouth Lodge. S.O.K.B.S. for many years, but since he had been out of work had fallen behind in his dues and his family are not entitled to any relief from either. He was a native of Tunbridge Wells, Kent England, was 49 years of age and had been in Toronto about ten years. He was a steady, industrious workman when able to get employment and a good father and husband. One son, William, is married and lives at 156 Gladstone avenue. He is a moulder in the employ of the Bertram Engine Co.[77]

This extended passage on the predicament of a working class family is revealing at multiple levels. The reporter, seeing deep human need, carefully crafted an appeal to *Globe* readers. The children are enumerated, disabilities are listed, and the acute material needs of the family are laid out. The good work habits and moral qualities of the late husband and father as well as his

---

[77] *Globe*, January 1, 1896: 6. The *Daily Mail and Empire* had an initial article on the accident but devoted much less space to the predicament of the family. Likewise with the coverage of the *World*.

British origins are all emphasized. By naming the trade union to which Read belonged, the article implicitly appealed to it for relief.

At another level the description of the family, only known to us because of the tragedy that caused the circumstances to be recorded, points to the precariousness of working-class life in late Victorian Toronto. A mother such as Mrs. Read, with a clutch of children, was highly dependent on a stable breadwinner. Having given birth to what appear to have been fifteen children, she would be poorly positioned to deal with unemployment or any diversion of her husband's income to the purchase of alcohol. In this context the BEP emphasis on sobriety and respectability meshed with the concerns and agendas of women.

The *Globe* was not finished with the Read family. A follow-up story the next day again emphasized the moral qualities of the late James Read, describing him as "steady, sober, and industrious". The writer reported how their small collection of furniture had been diminished in order to buy bread. Some of the children were without boots, and "without money, food or fuel, their pitiable condition could scarcely be more desperate."[78]

In classic BEP fashion a "Read Fund" spontaneously arose out of the dogged reporting. Updates on growth of the fund were printed every few days. On January 3 there was mention that the "ladies" of the Bond Street Congregational Church Bible Class were taking a "warm interest" in the family and were gathering clothing.[79] A reporter was travelling across town almost daily to visit the family. In summary, a carefully written discourse couched in BEP rhetoric generated a wide-ranging communal response that highlighted the ongoing work of the women of a church Bible class as well as a BEP presence in the community that could be appealed to.[80] Part of a

---

[78] *Globe*, January 2, 1896: 10. A report on funeral arrangements mentioned that members of Portsmouth Lodge, Sons of England would be in attendance. *Globe*, January 3, 1896: 8. On the 4th it was reported that the Bricklayers' Union had paid for internment of the remains for which the family was grateful. The inclusion of the street number of the family residence resulted in direct assistance from "citizens" visiting the Read household. *Globe*, January 4, 1896: 20.

[79] *Globe*, January 3, 1896: 8.

[80] See also *Globe*, January 6, 1896: 10; January 7: 10; January 8: 10; January 9: 10 (The

general humanizing impulse, this communal response generated increased, largely female-created, social capital; Toronto was assisted towards social improvement on yet another front.

A reading of a daily newspaper such as the *Globe* displays a broad BEP discourse as seen in the James Read story. When the reader turns to the religious press—the *Christian Guardian*, in particular—one unsurprisingly uncovers an even thicker BEP discourse.

3.6 E.H. Dewart and the Christian Guardian

By 1851, Methodism was the largest religious affiliation in Ontario. At the time of the 1871 Canada Census, it was also the largest Protestant denomination in Canada. Its growth had been explosive. Methodism, with roots in the Evangelical Revival in England during the 1730s and 1740s, was a movement from within the Church of England that was marked by an intensely personal religious experience that was accompanied by a strict moral code and was expressed communally, both in the family and in the church. At its origins the bulk of its membership came from the poor and the working class, particularly in places where the Anglican Church lacked strength. From within the established British church and culture, the early Methodists faced significant discrimination that extended well into the nineteenth century. Still, the Methodist outlook was expansive and sought to transform culture rather than to remain "cloistered".[81]

While alcohol was never prohibited within Methodism during its first decades, beginning in the 1820s temperance gained a foothold in Canadian Methodist circles. By the 1840s it was becoming increasingly associated with Methodism even though Canadian drinking habits had still not been seriously impacted at mid-century. Moral suasion rather than political

inquest reported the death as "accidental" with crossing gates recommended at the location of the fatality.); January 13: 10; January 15: 10; January 16: 12; January 28: 8 (The son with the "disabled" arm had been provided funds with which to attend school. I did not track the fund past January by which time it was well over $100. This includes only the funds that were channeled through the *Globe*).

[81] See Neil Semple, *The Lord's Dominion: The History of Canadian Methodism* (Montreal and Kingston: McGill-Queen's University Press, 1996), 53-70.

activism held sway as the social change agent. Women, seen as the defenders of family morality and as morally superior to men, were presented as prime examples of temperance and were deeply involved in the battle against intemperance.[82]

At the time of the Union of 1833, which united the major streams of Methodism in Upper Canada, membership stood at 16,000. From its beginnings, Methodism was a movement that emphasized reading and the publishing and selling of books, tracts, and periodicals. The denominational weekly newspaper, the *Christian Guardian*, was founded in Toronto in 1829. Its first editor was Egerton Ryerson who went on to become Canada's leading Methodist, a pioneering educator, and a prominent politician. By 1831, the *Guardian* was spending more on postage costs than all other periodicals in Upper Canada *combined*, reaching a circulation of 3,000 by 1832.[83] The *Guardian* remained the largest Canadian Methodist journal serving the largest Ontario denomination. E.H. Dewart, its long-term populist editor (as opposed to academic) thus serves as a representative BEP writer. Given the circulation of the *Guardian*, one can reasonably argue that Dewart's editorials had the broadest readership among religious periodicals in Canada.

Rev. Edward Hartley Dewart became editor of the *Guardian* in 1869, serving until he was forced out of the position in 1894. Born in Ireland in 1828, Dewart came to Upper Canada at the age of six with his family. They settled near what is now Peterborough and converted to Methodism. A teacher, preacher, and a poet, Dewart was also active in the Liberal party. Already in 1864, Dewart had edited Canada's first poetry collection. Both the spirit of Dewart's drive and the outward look of the Methodist movement can be captured in a sampling of his early verse:

Christian Work

"Inasmuch as ye have done it to one of the least of these my brethren, ye have done it unto me."   Matt. Xxv. 40

[82] Semple, *The Lord's Dominion*, 66-70.

[83] Lorne Pierce, ed., *The Chronicle of a Century: The Record of One Hundred Years of Progress*

Go while the light is beaming,
Ere the evening shadow fall;
Rest not in idle dreaming,
While want and suffering call.
Gloom and gladness here are blended—
Earth has many a dreary lot—
Rise and work till life be ended—
Hearts are bleeding—linger not.
Go where poverty and sickness
Shroud the poor in lonely grief;
Wake the sleeping pulse of gladness,
Bring the fainting hearts relief.
Tho' their fate be dark and lonely,
God still watches o'er the poor;
And, to those who kindly aid them,
Heaven's sweet promises are sure…[84]

By generating editorials and overseeing a newspaper, E.H. Dewart was following a Methodist tradition of writing that, as these lines make clear, was consciously seeking to mold character rather than to sell copy. Reading, books, and education, according to Dewart, were to be at the heart of Christian formation that took place in the home. Books in the home were a requirement, and parents simply did not have "a right to bring up children without furnishing them with good reading."[85] In 1890, Dewart called on the provincial government to enforce school attendance between the ages of seven and thirteen years and require 100 days in the classroom per year.[86] Furthermore, with reference to a young man condemned to be hanged, Robert Neil (see Chapter Six), Dewart wrote that it was the government's

---

in the Publishing Concerns of the Methodist, Presbyterian and Congregational Churches in Canada (Toronto: Ryerson Press, 1929), 13.

[84] Edward Hartley Dewart, *Songs of Life* (Toronto: Dudley and Burns, Printer, 1869), 119-121.

[85] *Christian Guardian*, Nov. 7, 1883: 348.

[86] *Christian Guardian*, Oct. 22, 1890: 680.

responsibility to "educate and uplift" young criminals.[87]

Within the extensive editorial writing of E.H. Dewart, one can track a discourse that, first, emphasized the importance of temperance in promoting peaceful familial and societal relationships. Second, his writing displays an obsession with violence and the need for nations and societies to suppress it in all its variations. Third, increasingly Dewart recognized that the new industrial city called for a "social" response by the church. The "Social Gospel" that eventually emerged in early twentieth-century North American Protestantism has often been attributed to a developing liberal Christianity, but the editorial writings of E.H. Dewart give evidence of a nascent social gospel from within the BEP mainstream. From this stream came a humanizing impulse that served to reduce the violence that is often associated with urban frontiers.[88] I will focus on the writing of Dewart from 1880-1894 and then briefly on that of his successor, Andrew Courtice, for the years 1894-1899.

3.6.1 Dewart on Temperance

While at the helm of the *Guardian*, Dewart constantly advocated both temperance and the legal prohibition of alcohol. Opposed to the licensing system that sought to regulate purchases of alcohol by restricting outlets,[89] he was incensed by drunkenness among "boys and young men" and promoted laws that would make the sale of alcohol to minors punishable by imprisonment.[90] However, Dewart shrewdly recognized that it was more prudent to pursue a strategy of gradual change that prioritized plebiscites in rural counties rather than cities, where they were doomed to fail in the short run.[91] The election of Howland in 1886 was seen as an event of more than "ordinary significance". Dewart applauded Howland's tightening of alcohol regulation,

---

[87] *Christian Guardian*, Feb. 29, 1888: 136.

[88] It is important to emphasize that no doubt all religious traditions in Toronto at the time served to blunt violence and had been doing so broadly over several centuries within Western contexts, despite the warfare with religious overtones that had erupted at points.

[89] *Guardian*, Dec. 21, 1881: 406; Feb. 7, 1882: 44.

[90] *Guardian*, Dec. 13, 1883: 393.

[91] *Guardian*, Sept. 10, 1884: 302.

predicting that this would help protect "women and children from the vicious habits of husbands and fathers".[92]

Dewart frequently connected violence to alcohol in his editorials. In at least two instances, he recounted the story of homicides that involved young men of "good character" and "sober habits" who were victims of assailants under the influence of drink.[93] U.S. prison statistics were used by Dewart to argue that evangelicals were greatly underrepresented in prison populations. He reasoned, firstly, that evangelical religion was the "most potent factor" behind a virtuous and orderly society; secondly, that education was the "handmaid of religion" in safeguarding the nation; and thirdly, that if intemperance was not the primary cause of crime, then it was associated with crime in three-quarters of cases.[94]

Temperance instruction, he wrote, should be given in public schools (a curriculum was in place by the 1890s) and it should be a "scientific temperance", complete with a textbook. Clearly, boys were the targets of such teaching: "Give a boy such knowledge, and, as a rule, he will be in favor from youth to manhood." Often, boys would respond to warnings from teachers more than "the voice of parents." [95] Predictably, Dewart viewed the Sunday School as a "temperance training school".[96] Similarly, with respect to tobacco, Dewart reprinted an article that revealed BEP moral aims:

A boy once gotten beyond this unripe age, so succulent of moral malaria, without the habit, finds nothing in its appeal to his growing judgment and experience.[97]

---

[92] *Guardian*, Jan. 6, 1886: 24; Feb. 10, 1886: 89.

[93] *Guardian*, July 26: 236. Aug. 15, 1883: 236.

[94] *Guardian*, Feb. 24, 1886. Dewart used published statistics for the state prison in Joliet, Illinois. Religious affiliation was listed in at least some prison registers in the U.S. and in England. However, government census data did not include religious affiliation in both countries. Nineteenth-century British criminal statistics are accessible on-line. See for example: www.nationalarchives.gov.uk.

[95] *Guardian*, Sept. 6, 1893: 568. See also Oct. 18, 1893: 665.

[96] *Guardian*, March 21, 1888:184; Dec. 18, 1889: 809.

[97] *Guardian*, Feb. 2, 1887: 65.

Once a young man, he would have avoided the expense of the "habit" and thus, in classic Weberian fashion, would exercise the "wise economy" needed for "success".[98]

Dewart envisioned saloons being supplanted by successful coffee houses.[99] Shortly before being forced out as editor of the *Guardian*,[100] Dewart was able to trumpet the resounding victory for pro-prohibition forces in the Toronto Scott Act plebiscite of 1894. The total vote was 56% in favour of prohibition, and while Dewart was dismayed that 28% of eligible women voted against the measure, a larger proportion of women than men had been solidly in favour; female support was critical to its success.[101]

3.6.2 Dewart on Violence

Predictably, in step with BEP codes of morality, anti-violence was a common theme throughout Dewart's editorial columns. Although Dewart emphasized a common thread in alcohol-induced violence, his pronouncements went beyond temperance concerns to the violence implicit in sport, sectarian conflict and pogroms, lynching, world slavery, and cruelty towards animals.

Boxing was consistently condemned even when "respectable people" were in attendance. In January 1884, with the Toronto Chief of Police and members of the legislature present, a boxing match took place at a skating rink in Toronto. Although boxing gloves were used, the "blood flowed freely" in a "demoralizing exhibition". Dewart asked, "Can any intelligent Christian wish his sons to become adept in the boxing art?"[102]

Besides criticizing the Chief of Police, Dewart went much further when he chastised the Prince of Wales for having received and commended the

---

[98] *Guardian*, Feb. 2, 1887: 65.

[99] *Guardian*, May 10, 1882: 150; March 25, 1891: 185; Sept. 9, 1891: 568.

[100] Dewart's ouster concerned his unbending theological positions rather than temperance. See Pierce, *Chronicle of a Century*, 48-56.

[101] *Guardian*, Jan. 3, 1894: 8. One can also speculate that a portion of the male vote for prohibition was due to the persuasive voice of women within the household.

[102] *Guardian*, Jan. 28, 1882: 137.

famous boxer, John L. Sullivan, "the American bully."[103] Some months later, after the death of a Toronto boxer in Dakota, Dewart called for the "law" to impose heavy penalties on boxing in order "to stamp it out".[104] Even lacrosse, Canada's "national game", came under Dewart's critical gaze after a match between Toronto and Montreal degenerated "into fierce assault in the form of violent blows".[105]

Turning toward Mexico, Dewart condemned bull-fighting particularly in view of the way crowds erupted in cheers after the killing of a matador by the bull, action that arose from, and encouraged, "the indolence and vice of the people".[106] He soundly condemned a "disgraceful", violent, assault upon the Irish Republican William O'Brien during his visit to Toronto in 1887. "Mob law" could not be defended. "The right of freedom of speech is a sacred thing, which must be sacredly protected."[107]

Lynching received particular opprobrium from Dewart's pen.[108] Dueling in France and Germany was labelled as "barbarism".[109] Discrimination against Jews in Germany[110] and pogroms in Russia were condemned.[111] Dewart joined the chorus of BEP protest against "Armenian atrocities".[112] However, he supported capital punishment, writing to this effect in the context of the

---

[103] *Guardian*, Dec. 28, 1887: 823.

[104] *Guardian*, Oct. 3, 1888: 633.

[105] *Guardian*, Sept. 14, 1892: 585. See also Oct. 4, 1893: 532-533. In both cases, Dewart blamed the excessive violence on gambling. Following 5 fatalities in the U.S. and 26 in Britain during football, Dewart wrote: "Any game that imperils life and limb, and gives occasion to rowdyism is a positive wrong, and our colleges ought to be the first to find it out and condemn it." Dec. 6, 1893: 776.

[106] *Guardian*, Aug. 3, 1892: 488.

[107] *Guardian*, May 18, 1887: 313.

[108] *Guardian*, June 15, 1892: 377; May 24, 1893: 354; Sept. 27, 1893: 617; Nov. 29, 1893: 761; July 4, 1894: 424-425.

[109] *Guardian*, April 23, 1890: 265.

[110] *Guardian*, Jan. 11, 1893: 25.

[111] *Guardian*, Feb. 8, 1882: 44; March 22, 1882: 89.

[112] *Guardian*, April 3, 1895: 209. See also an Andrew Courtice editorial. *Guardian*, Feb. 13, 1896: 104; Sept. 23, 1896: 616.

Haymarket bombing in Chicago[113] and a Chinese rebellion in 1891.[114]

Anti-slavery remained part of the heart of the BEP movement, and from 1880 through 1894, slavery was the subject of at least seventeen Dewart editorials. His coverage ranged from Brazil to Cuba, to West Africa, Egypt, and around the horn to East Africa. With the end of Spanish slavery in 1886, Dewart over-optimistically commented that its abolition was "a striking evidence of the rapid development of ideas more in harmony with the Christian civilization of the age."[115] In the end, he was disappointed with European and British attempts to eradicate the abuse, for it still endured in too many places.

Dewart and Courtice were also consistently outspoken in defence of Chinese living in Canada. As early as 1882, when anti-Chinese laws were introduced in the U.S., Dewart argued that such laws were "a subversion of republican principles" and "unchristian". He believed that the "moral character and the cruel government of San Francisco" had contributed to poor standards of living among its Chinese population. Dewart proposed that the solution was to give Chinese labourers full citizenship so that they could have families.[116]

With respect to the Chinese in Canada, Dewart reprinted an article that defended them on the grounds they had been misrepresented by "demagogues", "sandlot orators", and politicians who were anxious to get the working class and "the Irish vote". In the article's estimation, there was "no class of foreigners coming to our shores" who were "more peaceable, industrious, honest and frugal than the Chinese." The author stated that they suffered from "ruffians and cowards of our own race" and were never in court unless

---

[113] *Guardian*, Nov. 16, 1892: 729.

[114] Dec. 16, 1891: 792. Dewart did express the opinion that more "humane" forms of capital punishment needed to be found and expressed hope for electricity, but he eventually turned against the electric chair. Feb. 29, 1888: 136; Sept. 11, 1889: 585; July 22, 1891: 457.

[115] *Guardian*, Oct. 13, 1886: 648. See also *Guardian*, March 15, 1882: 81; Aug. 1, 1883: 244; July 15, 1885: 441; Feb. 13, 1889: 105; Jan. 15, 1890: 40; July 30, 1890: 489; Jan. 31, 1894: 73.

[116] *Guardian*, April 5, 1882: 108. However, Dewart was ambivalent about large-scale Chinese immigration. *Guardian*, March 19, 1884.

"seeking redress that they seldom get."[117]

Courtice, Dewart's successor, likewise called for Chinese living in Canada to be granted citizenship. In the aftermath of riots and near pogroms in British Columbia, Courtice found ludicrous the argument that the Chinese were incapable of adapting to Canadian customs. Even though "intermarriage" might be deemed "undesirable", there should be no "interference" with it. As to a Chinese propensity to wish to "return home", Courtice was dismissive, writing that "in BC everyone does" [desire to return home].[118]

For Dewart and Courtice, both of whom still possessed deep streaks of racialism and paternalism, pro-Chinese sentiment had its roots in the BEP doctrine of monogenesis. While this was not enough to halt Chinese exclusion laws in Canada, it did work to abate racial violence and large-scale pogroms. The beginnings of an anti-racist discourse that was nurtured in BEP quarters spread elsewhere;[119] BEP influence was, indeed, of some considerable importance in denying racist discourse legitimacy.

3.6.3 Urban Christianity and the Roots of the Social Gospel

The developing industrial city was recognized by Dewart to be the centre of intellectual and social influence. Toronto had become the Protestant capital of Canada and now housed the Methodist and Presbyterian central offices. The entrepreneurial BEP church and associational infrastructure sought to transform the "evils" associated with late nineteenth-century urban experience. BEP writings gave evidence of the view that urban poverty was not simply the product of "personal sin" but rather that it had "social" roots within urban culture. Dewart's editorials increasingly reflected this perspective; first, in his

---

[117] *Guardian*, March 3, 1886: 134. See also July 26, 1886: 489; June 6, 1888: 361; Sept. 20, 1893: 601.

[118] *Guardian*, Dec. 14, 1898: 785.

[119] On this general process see, Colin Kidd, *The Forging of Races: Race and Scripture in the Protestant Atlantic World, 1600-2000* (Cambridge: Cambridge University Press, 2006). Anti-racist sentiment could also exist in the sliver of the Canadian population that was the successors of the Benthamites. Of course, some evangelicals could also harbour racist attitudes, but British evangelicals were the only large sector of the population that had been committed abolitionists.

prescriptions for the improvement of housing for workers; second, in his reasoning on the proper relationship between capital and labour; and thirdly, in
his analysis of urban crime.[120]

"Dissipated habits" was cited by Dewart as a major cause of many urban
families living in one room. Although the situation had improved through
the work of city missionaries, Dewart held that over one-quarter of the wages
of "denizens of the slums" was spent in bars. However, the "gross" neglect by
landlords combined with the shortage of housing, rapid increases in population, and extreme poverty were major contributing factors behind widespread
urban poverty.[121]

In typical BEP fashion, Dewart called for both legislative and social reform
to work "side by side" with religious reform. Landlords were to be compelled
to keep dwellings in better condition. Government or chartered companies
should provide cheap cottages at reasonable rent or affordable terms of pay-
ment. The churches would seek to prevent the poorer classes from growing
up without religion.[122]

In the 1880s, the Salvation Army emerged as an urban Christian movement in England, North American, and Europe. The Army caught the
attention of Dewart, and he frequently defended it in his editorials.[123] Already
in 1884, Dewart reported that large numbers of the "non-church attending
class" were present in the Army gatherings.[124] Likewise, Dewart advocated
that Methodism, in order to attract more of the working class, needed to be

[120] For the developed social gospel of twentieth-century Methodism, social salvation preceded individual salvation. Dewart always emphasized the priority of personal salvation. On
the twentieth-century social gospel see Semple, *The Lord's Dominion*, 350-356.

[121] *Guardian*, Feb. 6, 1884: 44.

[122] *Guardian*, Feb. 6, 1884: 44.

[123] See for example *Guardian*, April 12, 1882: 116; May 3, 1882: 140; July 26, 1882: 234;
April 16, 1884: 124; April 30, 1884: 148; Oct. 29, 1890: 696; Nov. 12, 1890: 728; Jan. 14,
1891: 24; Sept. 9, 1891: 569; Jan. 13, 1892: 24; April 25, 1893: 216. In particular Dewart
decried physical violence being used against Army members in Britain and elsewhere. He
lauded Army work among the poor and held it up as exemplary for the wider church.

[124] *Guardian*, Feb. 6, 1884: 44. Dewart maintained that many Methodists had once been
poor but had been "lifted up". *Guardian*, Sept. 17, 1984. In 1892 Dewart remarked that the
growth of the Salvation Army had been "remarkable". *Guardian*, Dec. 28, 1892: 825.

adaptable and tolerant rather than rigid and dogmatic.[125]

The reality of wage labour and family economics in an urban centre such as Toronto slowly widened the world of women. In tandem, an outward looking and adaptive BEP ideology encouraged increased social opportunity in both the Church and the public square. Dewart's editorials reflect this fact. By 1883, Dewart increasingly accepted that women should be allowed employment in professions that previously only allowed males. In supporting the establishment of the Women's Medical College in Toronto, he wrote that women possessed "a special fitness for carrying to the homes of ignorance and suffering the message of life and hope."[126] Traditional roles were assumed, but new possibilities were raised.

While from a certain angle it is possible to interpret Dewart's pronouncements on women as a concession and simply an extension of the "separate sphere", there is a more radical dimension to Dewart's position. He argued that "the barbarous and false ideas of woman's inferiority and subjection which prevails in Eastern lands, still lingers, even in the most civilized countries of the world."[127] Here there is implied the need for a sharp break with tradition. One can speculate that its source is an egalitarian BEP ideology existing within the context of a rapidly changing urban setting. The biblical text that there is "neither Jew nor Greek, male or female" was marshaled by Dewart to argue for the equality of women.[128]

Concerning the topic of women's work and women's wages, Dewart lashed out against the industrial practices of "scanty wages" and "long hours". Because of a "natural timidity and aversion to public discussion", women had not been vocal concerning their plight. Against the argument that women's wages were lower because they lacked the physical strength of males, Dewart reasoned that women's employment often did not require "unusual strength". He voiced "hearty sympathy" with any labour movement that sought higher

[125] *Guardian*, Sept. 8, 1886: 568.

[126] *Guardian*, April 18, 1883: 124.

[127] *Guardian*, April 18, 1883: 124. See also his argument that in Brazil the sequestering of women impeded their ability to meet "eligible men". July 26, 1886: 486.

[128] *Guardian*, June 3, 1885: 344.

remuneration for women workers.[129]

On the topic of "women in business", Dewart saw no contradiction between the life of a woman "in the home" and in the business sphere. While such public work had previously been "deemed foreign to her sphere", this was an "injustice" that was to be remedied by a greater appreciation and demand for women taking on jobs in the business world.[130]

Within the Church, the gifts of all members "should be brought forward" and women should be provided with the opportunity of "systematic employment" in an "opening up of new spheres of usefulness for women".[131] While, according to Dewart, large numbers of women such as "Mrs. Youmans", the temperance worker, were exercising gifts in the broader sphere, even "timid women" could exercise gifts in the prayer meetings, love feasts, and in the class meetings of churches.[132]

This increased importance of women in the church was reflected in the "newly-felt power" of women in the municipal and political realms. Dewart stressed the importance of moving quickly to bring change, as Protestantism had lost much in the past by not according the ministry of women its "true place". He supported a formal Methodist deaconess program[133] that would:

[R]elieve the wants of the needy, whether they be physical or moral; to instruct the ignorant, visit the sick, to comfort the sorrowing, to relieve the destitute, to look after neglected children...[134]

Likewise, granting the franchise to women would bring the public sphere

[129] *Guardian*, July 27, 1887: 473. See also *Guardian*, Aug. 24, 1887: 536.

[130] *Guardian*, Sept. 26, 1888: 616.

[131] *Guardian*, April 4, 1894: 216; *Guardian*, Oct. 15, 1890: 664. This was a "recovery" of past history, as ordained women preachers were not uncommon in the early decades of Methodism. Here Dewart does not seem to be openly advocating the full ordination of women.

[132] *Guardian*, Feb. 25, 1891: 120. "Mrs. Youmans" refers to Letitia Youmans, the Canadian Methodist temperance activist.

[133] *Guardian*, March 22, 1893: 185.

[134] *Guardian*, April 4, 1894: 216.

to a "higher plane intellectually". In Dewart's words the operative phrase was "Loose her and let her go." As women were elevated, children would become "wiser and better".[135] Dewart, in short, favoured a type of "New Womanhood":

It is an indisputable fact that within the memory of people not much past middle life, women have taken a place among the intellectual, industrial and social forces of society greatly in advance of the position they formerly occupied.[136]

Dewart consistently held that throughout the world, it was Christianity that had improved the position of women. In the context of changing "intellectual and social forces", cited in the above quotation, Dewart is anticipating the emphases of the developing "social gospel". The eventual legislation of Prohibition, which became a central plank of the social gospel, is inexplicable apart from the significant involvement of women in the public sphere. While Prohibition did not last, and no major Canadian interest group would support it today, it ranks as the most radical piece of social legislation in Canadian history.

As the century wound down, the "question of labour" increasingly loomed large for Dewart and for the developing social gospel. In keeping with Wesleyan social tradition, Dewart was a consistent defender of private property. Rejecting Henry George's "single tax" on the values of land, he did argue that the relation between "Labor and Capital" needed to be "grappled" with and "settled". However, from 1880 he increasingly sided with a developing labour movement. Dewart warned of a "communist revolution" if rich owners were allowed to keep the "lion's share of the profits".[137]

Dewart was a supporter of the D.L. Moody evangelistic meeting in Toronto in 1884, but he also wrote that evangelistic methods were "inadequate" with

---

[135] *Guardian*, April 19, 1893: 249.

[136] *Guardian*, Jan. 2, 1895: 8.

[137] *Guardian*, April 30, 1884: 140.

respect to the improvement of urban social conditions.[138] Going beyond the message of Moody, Dewart called for a "Christian Socialism" that would carry "one another's burden" and so "alleviate" the evils of society.[139] Still, Dewart insisted that any solutions to poverty must also include the "individuality and independence of man" and that "industry, economy, and sobriety" were obligatory.[140]

By 1890, Dewart was a supporter of the "Eight Hours Movement" and a right to strike.[141] Profits, he maintained, were to be distributed between the employer and workers with the percentage to be decided by an "independent authority".[142] Because the development of labour-saving machinery benefited the employer, capitalists would be "greedy and short-sighted" if the labourer were not given a portion of the savings. By rewarding the worker, "It would make the manual laborer more of a man and less of a working animal."[143]

Late in his career, Dewart admitted to the overwhelming nature of the problems of inequality that confronted Toronto. He feared the transfer of "Old World" poverty to Toronto. The roots of the problem he believed resulted from the conditions of the "social environment". In contrast to Europe with its "feudal aristocracy", Dewart saw an emergent "plutocracy" grasping an "industrial power". In the face of such change, "[o]ld remedies" were of no use while "solutions were not yet understood". The only certainty was that they were "on the eve of momentous changes, and these are sure to be more radical than any which have hitherto marked the path of progress."[144]

The concern of Dewart over urban sanitation, the quality of drinking water, and the prevalence of disease, cannot be subsumed under the trope of "purity". As late as 1885, a smallpox epidemic in Montreal had claimed

---

[138] *Guardian*, Dec. 3, 1894: 400; Dec. 10, 1894: 410.

[139] *Guardian*, March 24, 1886: 185. This would include the respecting of both property and labour. See also Oct. 12, 1892: 648.

[140] *Guardian*, June 29, 1887: 408; *Guardian*, July 20, 1887: 457.

[141] *Guardian*, Aug. 30, 1890: 536.

[142] *Guardian*, Nov. 19, 1890: 744.

[143] *Guardian*, April 22, 1891: 248-249. See also *Guardian*, April 26, 1893: 264.

[144] *Guardian*, March 15, 1893: 168.

the lives of over 3,000.[145] Dewart blamed smallpox and a variety of fevers on unsanitary housing conditions. Landlords who installed defective plumbing were labeled "murderous" by Dewart and, he wrote, should be treated as criminals.[146] After seeing positive advances in public health during a visit to Washington, Dewart warned that better sanitation was needed in Toronto. Cases of typhoid and diphtheria had increased and he urged that Toronto could learn from techniques used in other cities.[147]

Through the "science of statistics" many of the "diseases of society" could be discovered, Dewart proposed. With a growing standard of living came "greater sensitiveness and restlessness". Dewart pointed to rising suicide rates as a "fact" that demonstrated weakness in the "social framework". These social weaknesses called for a "practical Christianity" to "awake and clothe" itself "in the spirit of knowledge as well as love." The Church and the "saving agencies" were to "understand the social and industrial, as well as the spiritual needs of the time."[148] Dewart proved also to be an advocate of penal reform, in the BEP drive to ameliorate conditions in Ontario's prisons.[149]

Broadly, Dewart's social teaching was consistent with that of the social gospel that developed in the first decades of the twentieth century.[150] However, he refused to prioritize the need to change urban social conditions over the urgency of the need to change the individual. In this, he was in continuity with the traditional Methodist and BEP "religion of the heart" that imparted "moral principles" and controlled the "affections".[151] The "peace

---

[145] See Michael Bliss, *Plague: A Story of Smallpox in Montreal* (Toronto: Harper Collins, 1992).

[146] *Guardian*, Oct. 3, 1888: 633. See also *Guardian*, Oct. 6, 1886: 632.

[147] *Guardian*, Nov. 4, 1891: 697.

[148] *Guardian*, May 10, 1893: 296.

[149] See for example *Guardian*, Dec. 21, 1881: 388; Dec. 12, 1888: 793; March 20, 1889: 184; July 3, 1889: 424; July 17, 1889: 457; Dec. 7, 1889: 776-777; Nov. 5, 1890: 713.

[150] On the Canadian Social Gospel see Richard Allen, *The Social Passion: Religion and Social Reform in Canada, 1914-1928* (Toronto: University of Toronto Press, 1971). By the 1890s Dewart was viewed by as a conservative by the progressive Methodist elites and so it can be argued that Dewart's social views were representative of many traditional Methodists; a religious movement that had radical roots and had espoused the abolition of slavery.

[151] *Guardian*, March 12, 1884: 82.

and consolation" of an inward faith "brightened the lot of the lowly", and Methodism had lifted up "many thousands".[152]

While Dewart affirmed the importance of "organized machinery" [Dewart's terminology] in all Church work, this machinery needed to be subordinated:

> As the power that moves any machinery is more important than the machinery, so in Church work spiritual life and power are of far greater importance than the organization.[153]

Furthermore, he warned that too often church finances, agencies, societies, and church buildings became the ends rather than the means. "Numbers", Dewart admonished, were lower in importance. What was needed was "a larger measure of the love of Christ to counteract our natural selfishness."[154]

In 1895, Dewart was replaced as editor of the *Guardian* by Methodist clergyman, Andrew Courtice. Coutice's wife, Ada Mary Brown Courtice, was to be the more prominent social reformer;[155] Courtice, moreover, lacked the flair and editorial range and energy of Dewart. He was, nonetheless, more open to a liberalizing theology that later came to be linked with the social gospel. He proved to be a strong advocate of temperance. He opposed the Spanish-American War of 1898,[156] seemed to oppose capital punishment,[157] and continued Dewart's advocacy of prison reform.[158]

Courtice, like Dewart, insisted that social reform could not consist of "mere committee work" and "hireling agents". Rather, there must be "personal

---

[152] *Guardian*, Aug. 18, 1886: 504.

[153] *Guardian*, Sept. 1, 1886: 552.

[154] *Guardian*, Sept. 1, 1886: 552. Perhaps Dewart was prescient in this analysis, given that the greatly expanded infrastructure of early twentieth-century Methodism was followed by the sharpest decline of any Canadian denomination.

[155] See Lorne Pierce, *Chronicle of the Century*, 59-62.

[156] *Guardian*, April 27, 1898: 264.

[157] *Guardian*, Feb. 16, 1898: 97.

[158] *Guardian*, Jan. 13, 1896: 17.

work among the poor" by "men and women whose hearts God has touched" and who were willing to visit "desolate homes".[159] It is, he wrote, "individual regeneration" that drives "the machinery of social reconstruction."[160]

In the editorials of Dewart and Courtice, the themes of a broad anti-violence outlook were present, specific male violent behaviours were targeted, and the opening up of women's spheres were advocated so that there was allowance for the concerns of women to be expressed, particularly that of temperance. Their work epitomized BEP concerns; it stands as a principal statement of what those concerns were. The link between BEP texts, literacy and declining interpersonal violence will be evaluated in Chapter Six.

3.7 BEP Discourse: A Summary

The central argument of this chapter has been that a BEP discourse aimed at shaping moral behaviour was pervasive within the context of the urban environment of late nineteenth-century Toronto. BEP moral prescriptions were a "package" and were aimed at "rough" male behaviour in particular. These prescriptions emanated from multiple sources that included institutional churches, voluntary associations, media, and the political arena. They also served to "humanize" the city, such that the treatment of children, prisoners, and even animals became perceptibly more humane. At minimum, the abuse of alcohol was become much more problematized and with it male violence.

Not all discourse is of course equal. Smaller social movements may have a strong discourse but lack the infrastructure needed to infuse a culture. There is a "tipping point", where a given discourse amounts to a controlling ideology that one community seeks to impose on a larger culture. In Chapter Four, I will examine the development of the BEP "machine" in the BEP Toronto used to further this goal. The size and strength of this machine is statistically quantifiable; one can follow its increase in political traction and discern the political reaction to its growth. Most important for this thesis, the imposition

---

[159] *Guardian*, May 20, 1896: 328.
[160] *Guardian*, July 29, 1896: 488.

of a BEP ideology corresponds with a decline in male interpersonal violence that is statistically tracked in Chapter Seven.

4

THE BRITISH EVANGELICAL PROTESTANT MACHINE

Overview

A grid of churches had been laid down in Toronto by 1880. At this time the ideologies of the BEP movement had the "machine" and personnel sufficient to affect the character of the city overall to such an extent that its rhetoric and values suffused the public sphere and significantly shaped it. The BEP sector was undergoing rapid growth as measured by new buildings, rates of church-going, and numbers of voluntary associations. This growth in turn resulted in increased diffusion of BEP political power. By following the election of William Howland to the Toronto mayoralty in 1886, it is possible to identify the key institutions and associations that comprised the BEP "machine". This machine, and the ideas it diffused, shaped the behavioural norms of late nineteenth-century Toronto to such an extent that, as Chapters Five and Six will show, interpersonal violence declined, human interdependence increased, church attendance grew, and a large percentage of the Toronto population became situated within the orbit of BEP religion. However imprecise the measurement, the pressure of BEP ideology, diffused by the BEP machine, sharply depressed interpersonal violence in Toronto by the 1890s.

Introduction

By 1880, BEP ideologies possessed the "machinery" needed to control much of the discourse in both the public and private spheres. Politics, business, and the media were heavily influenced by evangelicals who succeeded in reshaping Toronto's social landscapes. "Machine", in political and cultural contexts, has over the past century been laden with mechanistic and disembodied meanings. However, in the nineteenth century "machine" could still evoke feelings of wonder, beauty, and progress; hence, it is an appropriate term to attach to a movement that envisioned cooperation with a God who actively shaped urbanscapes on industrial frontiers.[1] The Victorians used "machinery" in an expansive sense; it suggested, for them, that society and culture were organically linked to the mechanical.[2] In contrast, the "mechanical" in the twentieth century increasingly came to be viewed as deterministic with respect to the social.[3]

4.1 The Toronto Church Grid

A flurry of church building construction in the period 1880-1900, resulting in a grid of at least 90 churches in what is now the inner core of Toronto, demonstrated the ability of religious communities to construct an extensive visible presence.[4] Furthermore, moving out from this core to the boundary of the city, turn-of-the-century Toronto had a total in excess of 150 church

[1] This is not to say that "machine" could not have pejorative connotations when applied by, say, Toronto Tories to the Ontario Liberal Party. For the Victorian romantic-mechanic dynamic on "machine" see Herbert Sussman, "Machine Dreams: The Culture of Technology," *Victorian Literature and Culture* 28, no. 1 (2000): 197-204.

[2] In a two-month analysis of *The Times* (of London), from January 1, 1880 to February 28, 1880, approximately 25% of occurrences of "machine" are in an organic sense rather than an electrical or mechanical one, when excluding want ads. "Machine" is used when referring to the "nervous system" that is the "immediate power of the human machine" (January 2, 1880: 2); to the Church in the sense that by removing one of its parts (worship, schools, etc.) "it [wa]s like removing a wheel from a machine" (January 7, 1880: 5); to the "labour machine" with reference to strikes (January 9, 1880: 8); to an Irish politician who was referred to as a "machine-man" of "Parliamentary obstruction" (January 13, 1880: 9); to the army when in "proportion to its perfection" it becomes a "simple machine" (January 23, 1880: 9); and to the post office wherein the individual postman is described as the "escapement wheel" of the "mighty machine" (February 2, 1880: 11). Note that I have not attempted to paraphrase the Victorian language in the above quotations.

[3] Herbert Sussman, *Victorian Technology: Technology, Innovation and the Rise of the Machine* (Santa Barbara: Praeger, 2009), 1-7. E.P. Thompson uses the term "moral machinery" in a derogatory fashion with respect to moral suasion of Nonconformity in general and Methodism specifically. E.P. Thompson, *The Making of the English Working Class* (New York: Vintage, 1966), 350, 365.

[4] For the geographical and historical mapping of these core churches see Jon Caulfield, "The Growth of the Industrial City and Inner Toronto's Vanished Church Buildings", *Urban History Review/Revue d'histoire urbaine* XXIII, no. 2 (March 1995 mars), 3-43.

buildings. This sharp increase in largely Protestant church construction provided the entire Toronto population with a church structure within an easy walk of any family domicile.

At the heart of the city core stood imposing church buildings that served as key instruments in pushing a largely BEP message out into the neighbourhoods. In 1853, a newly reconstructed St. James Cathedral opened on King Street. With a seating capacity of 1200, its Gothic structure signaled a change in architecture that was to be followed in the design of most large Protestant edifices in the decades that led into the twentieth century.[5] Farther down King Street, New St. Andrew's Presbyterian, with a capacity of 1800, opened in 1875. To the north on Queen Street, Metropolitan Methodist, the "cathedral" of Methodism, opened in 1870 with a seating capacity of 2500. To the east on Queen stood Cooke's Presbyterian, also with a capacity of 2500. Not to be outdone, the Baptists constructed the remarkable Gothic building, Jarvis Street Baptist, which opened in 1874 and seated 2000 in an amphitheatre arrangement.

While church buildings that stood farther out in the neighbourhoods tended not to be such fine architectural achievements, these often large, downtown functional buildings were centres of BEP propagation and community activity. The evangelical Grace Anglican Church, built for the poor, stood in "The Ward" and had a capacity of 1000. By the 1890s, no less than nineteen Methodist churches had seating for 1000 or more congregants. Trinity Methodist Church, at Bloor Street and Robert Street, seated 2000 worshippers in a Romanesque building that still stands today. Likewise, Broadway Methodist Tabernacle on College at Spadina had accommodation for 2000. Along with the majority of these nineteenth-century churches, the Tabernacle was demolished in 1930 to make room for an office building, effectively airbrushing away a major chapter of Toronto's social history.

---

[5] On Gothic church design in Ontario see William Westfall, *Two Worlds: The Protestant Culture of Nineteenth-Century Ontario* (Toronto: University of Toronto Press, 1989), 126-158. See also Barry Magrill, *A Commerce of Taste: Church Architecture in Canada, 1867-1914* (Montreal and Kingston: McGill-Queen's University Press, 2012).

4.2 Protestant Sunday Schools

Sunday Schools were primary vehicles for incorporating children into churches through indoctrination into Protestant faith and practice. The reading of religious texts was close to the heart of Protestantism, hence the BEP emphasis on a universal literacy. A Protestant analogue, universal elementary education, was an outcome of this literacy drive and came into force in Ontario in 1871. Here the argument is in-line with that of Darroch and Soltow who maintain that the evangelical emphasis on literacy and education in general produced a "moral order" and was part of an ongoing "civilizing process" that, as in Weber, was specific to Protestant cultures.[6]

In 1880 there were 19,200 scholars enrolled in Toronto's Sunday Schools, with girls outnumbering boys 56% to 44%, reflecting the gendered nature of the BEP movement. With 1,900 teachers, combined Sunday School participants accounted for more than 25% of Toronto's population. The Protestant Sunday School allowed for standardized Protestant messages about behaviour to be transmitted to a large percentage of the city's children, often even in cases where parents did not attend church.

Victorian church authorities were self-aware and deliberate in the way in which they sought to mold behavioural norms in children and "young people". The language of an 1882 article on Toronto Sunday School statistics echoes churchly moralistic language. In this piece of *Globe* reportage entitled "The Churches Nurseries", the writer proclaims that it is in the Sunday School that "the moral tone and bias given to the nascent mind, with the reiterated urging of ethical commands and prohibitions, cannot but have a salutary effect and a certain restraining influence through life."[7]

Evangelicalism was a highly gendered form of religious expression, as discussed in Chapter Three. Although teachers had rough gender parity in Toronto in 1880 (1094 "ladies" and 904 "gentlemen"), the available evidence points to a wider disparity among general churchgoers. In St. Stephen, New Brunswick, in 1861, approximately two-thirds of evangelical church members

---

[6] Gordon Darroch and Lee Soltow, *Property and Inequality in Victorian Ontario*, 111-147.
[7] *Globe*, September 2, 1882: 5.

were women. Of the men, the majority were married and very few were single (for Presbyterians 6%), whereas 39-42% of women were single.[8] The Toronto worship censuses[9] did not record the gender of attendees but, tantalizingly, in 1888, according to a *Telegram* report, the raw, unpublished records did include a breakdown by gender that showed the percentage of male attendance was "very small". Exceptions were Roman Catholic attendance, which was 25% male, and Jewish attendance, which was 66% male.[10]

4.3 The Religious Demography of Late Victorian Toronto

The propagation of BEP ideas, including non-violence, was dependent on personnel. Fortunately, the emergence of a powerful religious impulse in late Victorian Toronto coincides with a wealth of census data on religion that is unmatched for any other time period. Since this study relies heavily on census data, a discussion of the Canadian federal census and the Toronto newspaper church censuses is appropriate and can be found in APPENDIX C. Certainly, my calculations regarding crime and denominational affiliation are heavily dependent on census data. The denominational changes in Toronto from 1881-1891 are as follows:

Table 4.1 Denomination Changes in Toronto, 1881-1901

	1881	%	1891	%	1901	%	% Change 1881-1901
C of Eng	30,913	36%	46,084	32%	46,442	30%	50.2%
RC	15,716	18%	21,830	15%	23,699	15%	50.7%
Meth	16,357	19%	32,505	23%	35,130	23%	114.7%
Pres	14,612	17%	27,449	19%	30,812	20%	108.6%

---

[8] Hannah M. Lane, "Tribalism, Proselytism, and Pluralism: Protestants, Family, and Denominational Identity in Mid-Nineteenth-Century St. Stephen, New Brunswick" in *Households of Faith: Family, Gender, and Community in Canada, 1760-1969*, ed. Nancy Christie (Montreal and Kingston: McGill-Queen's University Press, 2002), 123-125.

[9] These newspaper church censuses will be more fully discussed below.

[10] *Evening Telegram*, December 22, 1888: 6.

	1881	%	1891	%	1901	%	% Change 1881-1901
Bap	3,667	4%	6,909	5%	8,148	5%	122.2%
Other	5,150	6%	9,246	6%	11,867	7%	130.4%
Totals	86,415	100%	144,023	100%	156,098	100%	

The above data show unmistakably the strength of the BEP discourse. Methodists, Presbyterians, Baptists, and Other denominations experienced explosive growth, while Anglican and Roman Catholic growth did not match population growth. While a lack of absolute precision certainly exists with respect to census data and religious identities, the overall patterns of religious identity, as laid down in the decennial census, hold up with remarkable consistency when compared to newspaper church censuses. The pattern of BEP diffusion is also congruent with the 1882, 1888, and 1896 newspaper church census data that are summarized in APPENDIX C. Weberian pathways are highlighted in these data. The church census data for Toronto, when combined with the Canada Census religious data, give researchers unsurpassed and previously under recognized denominational data for Toronto. These prove invaluable for the analysis of Central Prison prisoner data later in the study.

4.4 The Reach of BEP Associational Life

If industrialization was the engine of the Victorian city then philanthropic voluntarism would be its heartbeat, serving to humanize life on a capitalist frontier. Frank Prochaska argues that Anglo-Saxon Protestantism provides a powerful expression of "public spirit" that filled the "moral space" between rulers and ruled. As Victorian cities expanded, charities and other communal forms acted as "schools of citizenship" for both political insiders and outsiders.[11] All-importantly, activist and BEP-inspired philanthropy carried

---

[11] Frank Prochaska, *Christianity and Social Services in Modern Britain* (Oxford: Oxford University Press, 2006), 5. See also Frank Procahska, "Philanthropy" in F.M.L. Thompson, *Cambridge Social History of Britain, 1750-1950*, vol. 3, *Social Agencies and Institutions* (Cambridge: Cambridge University Press, 1990), 357.

with it a discourse of non-violence. While many Victorian Protestant church buildings still stand, with their pronounced pulpits and gallery seating, the traces of the vast network of voluntary agencies, except for scattered archival documents, have all but disappeared.

The maze of Victorian social agencies is difficult to fathom or reconstruct; historians have tended to conflate nineteenth-century Victorian charities with twentieth-century government social services.[12] In the Victorian city, associational philanthropy "saturated people's lives."[13] The extent of it is staggering; in the 1890s, the charitable receipts for London alone were greater than the total budgets of several European countries.[14] Toronto conformed to this pattern. Writing in 1891, G. Mercer Adam listed a sampling of charitable associations including: the Home for Incurables, the House of Industry, the Infants Home and Infirmary, the Prisoners' Aid, the Haven for Discharged Female Prisoners, and the Newboys' Lodging and Industrial Home.[15] While corporate boardrooms and government chambers were strictly male preserves, a high percentage of charitable association volunteers were female. These associations, combined with church and Sunday Schools, provided a wide public sphere of influence for entrepreneurial and activist women as well as men.[16] A discourse of non-violence was carried by these religious messengers whose activities fanned out at the neighbourhood level beyond the Gothic

---

[12] Ibid, pp. 17-23.

[13] Ibid, p. 23.

[14] *The Times* reported in 1885 that charitable receipts in London alone exceeded the entire national budgets of Denmark and Portugal, and were twice that of the Swiss Federation, while they were slightly less than that of the Netherlands and Belgium. *The Times*, January 9, 1885: 5. See also Frank Prochaska, *Women and Philanthropy in Nineteenth-Century England* (Oxford: Oxford University Press, 1980), 21-22; Frank Prochaska, *The Voluntary Impulse: Philanthropy in Modern Britain* (London: Faber and Faber, 1988), 60; David Owen, *English Philanthropy, 1660-1960* (Cambridge: Harvard University Press, 1964), 469-499.

[15] G. Mercer Adam, *Toronto, Old and New*, 114.

[16] Even in death this remarkable charitable activity continued, although among women of means the charitable portion of estates was significantly larger than that of men. The *Daily Telegram* in the 1890s listed the details of 466 estates. Of these 150 were the estates of women who left an average of 25.8% to charity in contrast to men who left 11.3% of their estates to charity. See Frank Prochaska, *Women and Philanthropy*, 35-36.

edifices on Toronto main streets. This Protestant activism of course follows the typing of Protestant "sectarians" by Weber.

The diary of the young William Lyon Mackenzie King is a portal into this BEP world of entrepreneurial activity. The BEP propensity to seek out dangerous places[17] was a habit picked up by King. Beginning in 1894 he sought especially to reform young working women who were perhaps casual prostitutes or at least "fast" women, as King described them. One night in the fall of 1894, he and a friend visited the residence of Edna and Jennie, two prostitutes on King Street, one of whom had been a nurse at the hospital. For hours King and his friend listened to their "story", King stayed on when his friend left, prayed with the women, and tried to persuade them to leave a life of "degradation".

The inward faith of the young nineteen-year-old seemed to grow in relation to the outward risks that he took.[18] After leaving the two young women, King returned to his room and made the following entry:

> I left them crying but my heart is bigger now than it ever was. I needed to be working again to get nearer to the dear Saviour from whose loving grasp I seem to have fallen to some degree. I could sing hymns with joy. May God hear my prayer when I ask him that I may live to see the day when both these girls are serving Him.[19]

[17] The danger of physical abuse was regularly faced by evangelicals. Particularly in Britain, there were frequent newspaper reports of members of the Salvation Army being physically assaulted. The Methodist Adam Clarke described young men of the Methodist Society in Manchester as being "not afraid to look death in the face". He urged that poverty be alleviated in all quarters of the city and "to take the dangerous labour on themselves of visiting the wretches in cellars and garrets…and where the most virulent contagion had dwelt for many years with increasing, because undisturbed malignity." Robert F. Wearmouth, *Methodism and the Common people of the Eighteenth Century* (London: Epworth Press, 1945), 213. The danger of overseas missionary endeavours was also a common theme. Of course, evangelicals would have viewed quarters of the city that housed taverns and brothels as symbolically "dangerous" as well.

[18] When advising a fellow student, Davy Duncan, who had doubts about the existence of God, King told him that "good Christian <u>work</u> is [the] best mode" for resolving doubt. October 22-23, 1894.

[19] Friday, October 4, 1894. Interestingly, in passing, King mentions the hazing of freshmen

THE BRITISH EVANGELICAL PROTESTANT MACHINE

Over the next few days King continued to visit Jennie and Edna[20] and eventually Edna agreed to move into the Haven, a BEP home for prostitutes and women who had been released from the Mercer Reformatory.[21]

It is through King's diary that we catch glimpses of Mrs. Harvie, the long-time president of the Haven, and an example of the place women had in this sort of activity. While Harvie served on the committee of the Haven for at least 31 years and was president for 17 of these years, her activities are only hinted at in the annual reports of the various BEP associations. In King's diary, however, Harvie is a figure consulted every few days in his efforts to reform a number of young women. She becomes a much more substantial being. From the diary's pages we learn that Harvie paid home visits to these

---

at Massey Hall earlier the same evening, when he "had a fight" with Registrar Brebner (the Canadian historian's father) and "threw him down three times". On the 7th he visited Brebner's home to apologize. In the apology, whatever the motives for it, one can detect BEP protocols and constraints on violence. King makes numerous comments on university faculty, especially Professors Wrong and Mavor.

[20] Etta (Emily Bliss) is listed in the 1891 census as 20 years old, Anglican and English-born, with the occupation of housemaid. Edna's name is transcribed as Etta in places in the on-line diary. Unlike C.S. Clark, King's diary can be checked for accuracy at innumerable points.

[21] See October 5, 10, 14, 19, 20, 21, 23, 28, 1894; November 20, 26 1894. C.P. Stacey argues that King consorted sexually at times with the various prostitutes that he befriended. While this is possible, the diary evidence does not seem to indicate this at least at this point in King's life. His periods of deep guilt over sin do not coordinate with his meetings with prostitutes but rather seem to be more conventional "sins" of missed Bible reading, missed church, or perhaps those of a masturbatory or voyeuristic nature.

See C.P. Stacey, *A Very Double Life: The Private World of Mackenzie King* (Toronto: Macmillan, 1976). For a different and more plausible interpretation of these passages see Joy E. Esberey, *Knight of the Holy Spirit: A Study of William Lyon Mackenzie King* (Toronto: University of Toronto Press, 1980), 26-32 and esp. 46. See entry of July 16, 1896 where King mentions Ezekiel 16:16, particularly the phrase, "played the harlot" and 1 Corinthians 10:13 concerning "temptation". On August 2, 1896 King writes, "Some good angel has watched me again this week & though I had been walking on a ledge & slipped many times yet has kept me from falling." The nature of "falling" remains ambiguous. See also August 20, 1896. For the most recent interpretation of these passages, one that is similar to Esberey and contra Stacey, see Allan Levine, *King: William Lyon Mackenzie King, A Life Guided by the Hand of Destiny* (Vancouver and Toronto: Douglas and McIntyre, 2011), 42-45. King's interpreters entirely overlook the standard BEP tradition of working in pairs, walking the "streets" and seeking to dissuade prostitutes in their places of solicitation and praying for them in their rooms. See Frank Prochaska, *Women and Philanthropy in Nineteenth-Century England* (Oxford: Oxford University Press, 1980), 182-221.

women and in another case arranged for a "woman" doctor to visit one who was sick.[22]

Although only a volunteer, Harvie was obviously readily available during the day and was constantly present at the Haven. She was the daughter of a Methodist minister and in addition served as president of the ladies' committee of the Hospital for Sick Children for five years. As well, she founded the Y.W.C. Guild for Working Women, was the "inspiration" behind the Neglected and Dependent Children, was active in the W.C.T.U., and was the first secretary of the Presbyterian Board of Woman's Foreign Missionary Society, in which capacity she visited India, and assisted in the founding of the Woman's Medical College in Toronto.[23] Harvie represents that group of BEP volunteer women who expended Herculean and deeply empathetic efforts on behalf of destitute women. As King's diary shows, there are only fleeting images of this vast volunteer force of women; their role was nonetheless vital

[22] See for example October 19, 20, 23; December 8, 10, 16. On the Haven see John R. Graham, "The Haven, 1878-1930: A Toronto Charity's Transition from a Religious to a Professional Ethos" in *Histoire sociale-Social History* XXV, no. 50 (novembre-November 1992): 283-306. The Haven was the only Toronto institution to accept women with venereal disease. See also John R. Graham, "William Lyon Mackenzie King, Elizabeth Harvie, and Edna: A prostitute rescuing initiative in late Victorian Toronto," *Canadian Journal of Human Sexuality* 8.1 (Spring 1999): 47-60. In 1893 the Haven had a capacity of approximately 60 residents and over the course of the year housed a total of 741. Of these 578 were Protestant and 163 Roman Catholic. Since the percentage of Catholics was higher than that in the general Toronto population, there was no obvious exclusion on the basis of religion. See Ontario Legislative Assembly, *Ontario Sessional Papers,* vol. XXVII—part III (Toronto: Queen's Printer, 1895), 83.

[23] See the entry for Elizabeth J. Harvie in Henry J. Morgan, *The Canadian Men and Women of the Time* (Toronto: William Briggs, 1912), 511-512. In 1896 Harvie became a full-time employee of the provincial Neglected Children's Office and retired with the rank of Inspector in 1912. She annually travelled thousands of miles visiting the homes where orphans had been placed by the Office. For an example of one of her reports see Ontario Legislative Assembly, *Ontario Sessional Papers,* vol. xxxii—part x (Toronto: Queen's Printer, 1900), 27-32. The reports hint at a religious motivation behind her activities. For example, she reports handing out "over 50 well-bound Bibles" in her visits (p. 32). The historian Donald Creighton was the grandson of Harvie. See Philip Creighton, "Lizzie Creighton", *York Pioneer* 98 (2003): 53-60. In personal correspondence with the family I ascertained that there is no substantial collection of personal writing by Harvie. Likewise, I have not found any record of substantial personal writings of any Toronto female activist for the period under study. The King diaries remain the richest primary source for the topic.

in shaping what was done.

At university, King had an abundance of male and female friends and certainly took notice of young women. His BEP evangelistic efforts were not restricted to prostitutes and young girls at Sick Kids'. In the fall of 1894 King organized a newsboys' association, and soon there were over 200 boys in attendance at the meetings. He found the newsboys "intelligent and clever" and obviously had a rapport with them.[24] Likewise, a twenty-year-old King was able to start a workingman's class at the St. Andrew's Institute, singing songs with them and chatting over coffee. He reflected later that he truly loved "those who have not had as many opportunities as myself but who are my fellowmen."[25]

King mirrors the BEP emphasis on monogenesis, which saw humankind as one and in turn was linked to a belief that all human beings were created in the Image of God. Despite a wavering in the face of an onslaught of social Darwinism, this doctrine continued to energize BEP outlooks, such that the movement could not simply be defined in negative terms such as "constraint", "compulsion" or "control".

This energy can be seen in the way that King's social philosophy was developing. As his graduation approached he confided in his diary:

I felt in a very philosophical mood tonight especially while walking along Queen St. I was trying to understand the different types of faces, what people were thinking about, whither were they trending [?] etc. I always feel the fact of their [sic] being such great inequalities in the happiness and lots of different people, is almost sufficient proof of a better world to come when we shall all have been made equal in the sight of God.[26]

[24] *Diaries*: November 4, 11, 18, 1894; December 23, 25, 1894; January 13, 1895; February 24, 1895. I was not systematic in tracking all the meetings. Beginning in Richmond Hall, King needed the large Temperance Hall by the time of the Christmas meeting, when 350 boys were present.

[25] October 14, 1895.

[26] March 23, 1895.

The yearning for equality led to his increasing involvement in meetings of the Socialist Labour Party. While he strongly endorsed a movement of society towards equality, he rejected social evolutionary schemas that left out the religious dimension. In an address to workingmen on the "labour question" he expressed doubt that, in the short run, socialism or co-operative commonwealths could bring about equality; it would take education and the "enlightenment of the masses" to do this. With respect to the latter he closed with a "strong reference to religion [and] the poor man in the sight of God."[27]

The importance of King as a source is in the wide-ranging commentary he gives on the BEP movement, both with respect to his inward life and his observations on BEP associational life. As a student his observations included Sick Kids' Hospital (largely BEP in its roots), the Haven, the YMCA, and St. Andrew's Church[28] where he was a member. King is quite revealing with respect to religious activity; for another kind of light on that activity, let us now turn to Samuel Hume Blake and William H. Howland, in whom BEP entrepreneurialism is writ large. At one time or other, each of these men served as a board member for many key Toronto charitable associations. Blake, a lawyer, and Howland, a businessman, both practiced their vocations as a virtual sideline while frenetically overseeing an empire of BEP voluntary societies. The following is a table listing some of the BEP associations and the most "usual suspects" who served on boards of directors:

[27] December 8, 1895. For King's involvement with the Socialist Labour Party including an address that King gave to a meeting of the movement see July 13, 1895; October 6, 20, 1895; November 3, 1895; December 15, 1895. Certainly not all evangelicals espoused socialist ideas, but the BEP emphasis on universal humanity pushed King in this direction for a time. Here are seen ideas that are undoubtedly connected with a "Social Gospel" that more fully develops within early twentieth-century Canadian Christianity.

[28] The popular D.J. Macdonnell was pastor of St. Andrew's and can fairly comfortably be placed within the BEP orbit even if a dissenter on prohibition. One of Macdonnell's published sermons can be coordinated with a King diary entry. See the diary entry for September 10, 1893 and J.F. McCurdy ed. *Life and Work of D.J. Macdonnell* (Toronto: William Briggs, 1897), 490-495. King also regularly heard George Grant in the pulpit of St. Andrew's.

Table 4.2 Membership in BEP Associations

	William Howland	S.H. Blake	Daniel Wilson	C.S. Gzowski	John Macd.	Henry O'Brien
Evangelical Alliance	x	x	x	x		
Newsboys' Home	x	x	x	x		
Prisoners' Aid	x	x				
Boys' Home	x	x	x	x		x
House of Industry (not BEP)	x					
Mission Union	x	x		x	x	x
Wycliffe College	x	x	x	x		
Home Sick Kids	x					
Coffee House Association	x			x	x	
Upper Canada Bible Society	x	x		x	x	
Magdalen Asylum	x	x				
West End Temperance Society	x	x				
Infants' Home	x	x				
Prison Gate/Haven	x	x				
Home For The Aged	x					
Toronto General Hospital	x					
Hillcrest Convalescent Hospital	x					
Mimico School For Boys	x					
Home For Incurables	x					
Dominion Alliance	x	x				
Willard Tract Depository	x	x				
YMCA	x	x				
Children's Aid Society	x	x				
Humane Society	x	x				
Shaftesbury Hall	x	x				

Howland and Blake, and their equivalents in Montreal, London, and

Edinburgh, represent an assertive[29] and newly emergent group of BEP businessmen and professionals. Not to be pushed about by clergymen, these powerful laymen, used to having their own way, had ample opportunity for entrepreneurial activity in the wide variety of BEP organizations and churches that the hierarchical High Church Anglican, traditional Presbyterian (but not the Free Church tradition), and Roman Catholic traditions did not afford.

These two BEP entrepreneurs must be seen within the expanding evangelical movement, acting in relation to a receptive culture that spawned a network of voluntary associations that cut across denominational lines. These religious voluntary associations oversaw the "safety net" in Toronto that ranged from hospitals to old age homes. There was a web of civic, national and international religious connections that offered paradigms of reform that could be adapted for the Toronto context. Howland and Blake were usually found at the centre of these reforming activities.

The YMCA housed Shaftesbury Hall, where a variety of inter-Protestant events were held. Named after the British social reformer and patterned as a smaller version of Exeter Hall, London, it seated 1,700 and hosted speakers, temperance rallies and political campaigns by Protestant reformers. The pattern for these reform rallies had been laid down by the earlier abolitionist movement which had sought to impose evangelical abolitionist views. With the passage of the Canada Temperance Act of 1878, the BEP machine gained momentum and was able to rally significant, widespread support behind a cause. Buildings and a street took on the "Temperance" name. Ontario prisoners were listed in official registers as "temperate" or "intemperate." The Ontario Board of Education began to offer "temperance education" in the classroom. This slow march of temperance reform can be followed in *The Canada Year Book* annual listings of counties that had passed referenda under the Canada Temperance Act.

---

[29] For Howland's assertiveness, as well as his eagerness to reconcile opposing groups, see *Globe*, September 13, 1882: 10; *Globe*, March 27, 1883. For a scathing critique of the character of Edward and Samuel Blake see Charles Durant, *Reminiscences of Charles Durant, Barrister* (Toronto: Hunter, Rose, 1897), 487-488. He describes Edward as "proud", "conceited", "unprincipled", and both presenting a "foxy look" and a "sneer".

THE BRITISH EVANGELICAL PROTESTANT MACHINE

Evangelicals were adept at using print media to disseminate their ideology that included its discourse on non-violence. Common religious assumptions that were shared across a variety of churches and voluntary associations effectively streamlined religious propaganda aimed at an increasingly democratic popular culture. Denominational periodicals such as the Methodist *Christian Guardian*, as discussed earlier, had a wide circulation. *The Shaftesbury Hall Bulletin* was a weekly publication that highlighted the activities of the YMCA as well as BEP churches. Its pages also featured inspirational sermonettes on topics such as temperance and the "dangers" that faced young men in the city. Both Blake and Howland served on the board of the YMCA for many years. Sermons from local pulpits appeared in daily newspapers alongside the weekly sermons of C.H. Spurgeon of London, England. "True Manliness" was a not-infrequent sermon topic that was captured in the headers of sermons published in newspapers such as *The Globe* and the *Evening Telegram*.

The memoir of one long-time resident who experienced over five decades of Toronto's first century, Conyngham Crawford Taylor, is a fascinating source that illustrates multiple aspects of the BEP machine. Taylor emigrated to Canada from Ireland in 1847, entered the dry goods business and eventually worked as an officer in the Customs House. At the time of his arrival, mail was delivered from Britain every two weeks while news via telegraph was printed as "extras" in the daily newspaper. He lived to see the city transformed.

A reading of Taylor's memoir reveals observations about the entrepreneurial business climate of the Toronto of the time, the perceived impact of newspapers, and the ordering of a culture through a constellation of religious organizations. Writing in 1888, Taylor boasts of having visited every "large churchgoing" city on either side of the Atlantic and finding no equal to Toronto, "a City of Churches", in terms of the number of churches or their seating capacity given the size of the population. On Sunday evenings, as the churches emptied at the services close, sidewalks were "blocked with the throngs returning to their homes."

Taylor then breaks into prose that drips with sentiment as he describes congregations across the city coming together for Sunday worship:

The ringing of bells is at an end, the rumbling of the carriage has ceased, the pattering of feet is heard no more, the flocks are folded in the numerous churches. For a time everything is hushed, but soon is heard the deep pervading sound of the organ, rolling and vibrating through the buildings and out into the streets. The sweet chanting of the choirs makes them resound with melody and praise, while it is poured forth like a river of joy through the recesses of the city, elevating and baring the soul on a tide of triumphant harmony to heaven.[30]

One can hear the "noise" of assemblies and see the religious shaping of a culture through the religious leaders that Taylor describes as "educating" the religious populace up to the "present high standard of churchgoing in Toronto."[31] The preachers he lists, and claims to have heard, come from a cross-spectrum of denominations ranging from Baptist to Salvation Army and are generally BEP in outlook. He, as a Methodist, could retain his identity but still strongly identify with the religious culture as a whole, though it, revealingly, was not seen by him as including Roman Catholics; none are on his list of preachers and their denominations—though no anti-Catholic discourse is present either.

The ubiquitous presence of newspapers and their power to shape opinion

---

[30] Conyngham Crawford Taylor, *Toronto Called Back* (Toronto: William Briggs, 1892), 163.

[31] Conyngham Taylor, *Toronto Called Back*, 162-163. Numerous visitors to the city commented on the number and on the pride of place for Toronto churches. For the comments of a visitor from Lancashire see *Globe*, April 6, 1883: 6. Rev. Dr. Crafts of New York sent out a survey across the U.S. and elsewhere asking, "Where in your travels had you seen the Sabbath best observed?" The "great majority" answered Toronto while second was Edinburgh. *Globe*, March 3, 1887: 8. Rev. A.T. Wolf of Alton, Illinois served as pulpit supply in a Presbyterian church in Toronto during the summer of 1887. Of this experience he later wrote in a U.S. religious periodical, "Toronto is a standing example of what a great city can do to maintain law and order." Describing a Toronto summer Sunday morning he wrote a caption for a pen drawing: "it seems as if the houses have literally emptied themselves upon the streets; old and young, men, women and children, orderly, clean, well-dressed, they are on the way to church." *Globe*, September 6: 4. Similarly, with the opening of the Bloor Street Presbyterian Church, the headline states, "A Magnificent Building: The City of Churches Fully Sustaining her Reputation". The article, in excess of one-half page with illustrations, concludes by describing the $100,000 building as "substantial, handsome, and perhaps more modern" than any other church building in the city. *Globe*, August 30, 1890: 3.

is seen in Taylor's description of the "daily" as the great "educator" of all. Lamenting that there were no longer book-readers, he describes the newspaper as that "'flying role' of the Apocalypse": that is "book, pulpit, and platform" all rolled together. The person that does not "take" the newspaper is a "curiosity".[32] Taylor quite rightly recognized the religious instrument that the paper was, in contrast to twentieth-century interpreters of the history of the Toronto newspaper. Next in influence to the Bible: "it is swift-winged and everywhere present, flying over fences, shoved under the door, tossed into counting-houses, laid on the work bench, read by all".[33]

Taylor gives no hint of religious or moral declension in the Toronto of 1890. His writing has a millennialist flavour in its claims for Toronto religiosity. The centre point of the Dominion, a "city set on a hill", "Toronto" was now "the synonym of order, morality, temperance, and religion." According to Taylor, charitable associations had transformed the lives of the poor and sick; all needs were provided for. Crime itself was on the verge of abolition in the face of the temperance movement. The Fleming licensing bylaw (under the Howland administration) had made great progress, further license activity would accomplish a "total prohibition" in Taylor's opinion.[34]

---

[32] Taylor, *Toronto Called Back*, 220-224. Here Taylor is extensively quoting the Brooklyn, New York preacher, Thomas De Witt Talmage.

[33] For example, Paul Rutherford transposes the nineteenth-century century Canadian newspaper into a secularization narrative. Rutherford interprets the 1882 *Globe* church census as meaning that less than 50% of Toronto's population were churchgoers, when in reality it meant that 45% of Toronto's population was in church on a *particular* Sunday in February and is evidence of an extremely high percentage of churchgoing. See Paul Rutherford, *A Victorian Authority: The Daily Press in Late Nineteenth-Century Canada* (Toronto: University of Toronto Press, 1982), esp. 17, 197-204. But see pp. 171-172 for an acknowledgment of an underlying religious "utility". Maurice Careless in his major work on George Brown is sensitive to his subject's religious motivations and yet does not demonstrate how the *Globe* was a religious instrument that significantly shaped Ontario's culture. See, nonetheless, J.M.S. Careless, *Brown of the Globe*, vol. two, *Statesman of Confederation, 1860-1880* (Toronto: Macmillan, 1863), 357-358.

[34] Taylor, *Toronto Called Back*, 249-250. William H. Pearson, a city resident from 1835-1920 and also a Methodist, wrote a memoir published in 1914, after the period of this study. Like Taylor, Pearson has a progressive reading of Toronto but he demurs on the labelling of the city as "Toronto the Good", given the "evil" that was present (p. 362). Pearson, who converted to abstinence in 1849 (p. 235), recollected the widespread use of alcohol

The *Globe* was a key instrument of both Liberal and evangelical reform, and its contents, like Taylor's memoir, reveals no separation between the religious and the secular. The daily newspaper was a Victorian "authority"[35] that was the first "mass media", allowing for a wide circulation of religious news and ideas with daily print runs in the tens of thousands. By 1900, the *Globe* had the highest circulation in Toronto at a daily 69,000 copies (compare to 323,000 today) and had surpassed the Conservative *Mail and Empire* in the final decade of the century during the city's reformist era.[36]

Widespread literacy was critical for the broad dissemination of BEP propaganda. The campaign for literacy itself was a longstanding activity that continued into the period under study, most obviously in the person of Methodist minister and longtime Ontario Superintendent of Education,

---

at mid-century; gentlemen commonly got drunk after dinner, and even beer drinking was usual among Methodists. "Treating" of cabmen was routine. He recounts the drop in taverns from 1 per 127 inhabitants to 1 per 4,091 in 1911, an astounding change. Regardless of the amount of illegal alcohol, surely Pearson is correct in his assessment of steep declines in consumption (pp. 233-239). His memory included the public executions, earlier in the century, that saw large numbers of people, out of "curiosity", pour in from the surrounding towns and countryside (p. 199). In his conclusion, the well-travelled Pearson observes that compared to Toronto, there are few cities that are its equal in terms of caring for the "indigent, helpless, and sick". Church attendance was relatively high, and more males were in attendance than in most U.S. cities. He judged that there was relatively little graft in business, and his position as manager of the Consumers' Gas Company would have given him a ringside seat in this respect. In contrast to Taylor he is much more sanguine, recognizing the existence of "slums", the need for better housing, more playgrounds, the abolition of bars, and the "Canadianization" of "the multitudes of "foreigners"; a task which had devolved to the schools and churches. His ending note is a wish, that flows out of his progressive BEP outlook, for the diminution of poverty (pp. 362-365). William H. Pearson, *Recollections and Records of Toronto of Old: With Reference to Brantford, Kingston, and Other Canadian Towns* (Toronto: William Briggs, 1914). Charles Durand, a lawyer writing in 1905, recalled how "thousands were rescued from drunkenness" through membership in divisions of Sons of Temperance. Furthermore, membership fees were used for a benefit fund in case of sickness. See Charles Durand, *Reminiscences of Charles Durand of Toronto, Barrister* (Toronto: Hunter, Rose Co., 1897), 470. For a valuable but much later recollection of Toronto's "crowded by thousands" Sunday streets by a non-BEP book publisher see George H. Doran, *Chronicles of Barabbas, 1884-1934* (Toronto: George J. McLeod, 1935), 4-13. A revealing and unparalleled inside look at Samuel Blake, William Gooderham, and BEP activists associated with the Willard Tract Depository.

[35] To use Paul Rutherford's designation.

[36] Paul Rutherford, *A Victorian Authority*, 238-239.

Egerton Ryerson. By 1880 Ontario had one of the highest literacy rates in the world.[37] While caution needs to be employed at this point, the dramatic rise in literacy within Ontario's population in the nineteenth century is at least consistent with the rise of a religious culture that emphasized the reading of religious texts.[38]

Whatever the exact relationship between literacy and Protestantism, it is possible to analyze BEP literacy activism by focusing on literacy efforts directed towards a small group of Chinese men by members of the YMCA. Again, we see an important female role. In 1882, a *Globe* article, written in a context of anti-Chinese agitation in British Columbia and anti-Chinese laws in the U.S. that had sent a trickle of immigrants to Toronto, featured the small Chinese male community in the city. In highly racially charged language, the headers read:

THE CELESTIALS
John Chinaman as he Lives and
Works in Toronto

WASHEE-WASHEES BUSY AND CONTENT
Kept out of the Flowery King-
dom by American Laws
Y.M.C.A. INSTRUCTION CLASS

---

[37] See Michael B. Katz and Paul H. Mattingly, *Education and Social Change: Themes from Ontario's Past* (New York: New York University Press, 1975), 265-268.

[38] For a cautious recognition of the role of Protestantism in the rise of literacy see Carl F. Kaestle et al., *Literacy in the United States: Readers and Reading Since 1880* (New Haven: Yale University Press, 1991), 3-32. It is fascinating to follow the decline of illiteracy along the lines of Philip Gorski's Calvinist disciplining thesis. In 1880, Prussia, Scotland, Netherlands and England, in that order, clearly had the lowest rates of illiteracy with France not far behind. See David Vincent, *The Rise of Mass Literacy: Reading and Writing in Modern Europe* (Cambridge: Polity, 2000), 9. One could reverse the argument and maintain that it was the high levels of literacy that allowed for the diffusion of the BEP expression. However, a literacy discourse seems to be at the centre of BEP propaganda, and there is no other non-Protestant culture with literacy rates approaching that of the Protestant cultures mentioned above.

The main body of the article, employing less racist language but still laced with a deep paternalism, highlights the YMCA's literacy efforts with the 16 students, who collectively made up three-quarters of the Chinese community in Toronto. Each of the students had his own teacher. All of the teachers were "ladies" as the "Chinamen" had "the good sense to prefer young ladies as teachers". BEP men, according to the writer, were "impatient", "business-like", and "unsympathetic". Several of the students were described as having made good progress, with a new lesson book shortly anticipated. The purpose of the class was twofold: both to teach English and "to induce [the pupils] to embrace Christianity"; hence, students were required to kneel for prayer prior to lessons.[39] The prominence of women in this activity was not an exception; repeatedly in the minutes of the annual meetings of voluntary associations, one observes the following: the reports of the associations' activities, after the details of the voting on male officers, the activities themselves are reported as being carried out largely by women. Furthermore, if one reads between the lines, as in the report on Chinese language students, one is led to hypothesize that it is the concerns of women that are largely manifest in associational activities. Religious women seem to have expressed greater empathy towards the "stranger" than did males. One can also hypothesize that many of the BEP males, active in voluntary associations, were motivated by the influence of women in their lives. I will apply this hypothesis below to BEP temperance activities and the way that the BEP "machine" was employed.

4.5 British Evangelical Protestantism and the Ontario Liberal Party

Politics show BEP ideas reaching into the community. George Brown, Alexander Mackenzie, Edward Blake, and Oliver Mowat, all important members of the Liberal party, all possessed BEP identities. Mowat, "The Christian Politician", was Premier of Ontario for 24 consecutive years while serving concurrently as president of the Evangelical Alliance.

Though, however, this group of Liberal politicians broadly shared a religious outlook, each was pragmatic and they were not above infighting.

---

[39] *Globe*, October 23, 1882: 8.

THE BRITISH EVANGELICAL PROTESTANT MACHINE

The first Liberal Prime Minister of Canada, Alexander Mackenzie, a strict teetotal Baptist, took a cautious approach to temperance in the political realm, resisting calls for legislated Sunday and temperance laws while finally seeing through passage of the Scott Act in 1878 that gave a municipality and county the option to ban the sale of alcohol by plebiscite.[40] Although a weak compromise, the "local option" was a rallying call for increased temperance agitation. The BEP temperance agenda was an overt political move that had broad appeal, even if there was not unanimity concerning the details of the advocated reform. Oliver Mowat managed the issue well.

Mowat inherited a Liberal party that has been described as a "semi-organized 'tendency'".[41] Under Mowat's organizational genius the Ontario Liberal machine became a powerful force at the local level despite the influence of John A. MacDonald's Tory party. Mowat's riding officers tended to be progressive, representative of the newly arrived elites whose political power came from their Liberal party connections rather than longstanding community ties. This made for a party that was centrally controlled and an electoral machine that was "without peer."[42]

While the Liberal Party was a locus of political power and patronage, a heavy dose of BEP morality shielded Mowat and his government from the conventional corruption that typically accompanies machine politics. Mowat himself, like Alexander Mackenzie, was never tarred by any serious corruption scandal, directly or indirectly.[43]

---

[40] Dale C. Thomson, *Alexander Mackenzie: Clear Grit* (Toronto: Macmillan, 1960), 261-262, 326-327. For Mackenzie on George Brown and the *Globe*'s temperance advocacy see Alexander Mackenzie, *The Life and Speeches of Hon. George Brown* (Toronto: Globe Printing, 1882), 153. In 1887, Edward Blake, claiming to be an abstainer, played both sides by stating that he was against "emasculating" the Temperance Act and then equivocated by going on to say that, "I am for a full and fair trial of the Act in the localities in which it is in force, with all the aid that executive action can properly afford." *Globe*, January 11, 1887: 5.

[41] S.J.R. Noel, "Oliver Mowat, Patronage, and Party Building" in *Ontario Since Confederation: A Reader*, ed., Edgar-Andre Montigny and Lori Chambers (Toronto: University of Toronto Press, 2000), 96.

[42] I am dependent here on S.J.R. Noel, "Oliver Mowat, Patronage, and Party Building", 98-100.

[43] S.J.R. Noel, "Oliver Mowat, Patronage, and Party Building", 102-103. A. Margaret

The Liberal machine was fired by BEP ideology on the tricky terrain of alcohol regulation. While carefully avoiding the extreme periphery of the temperance movement, Mowat, acting in line with the Crooks Act of 1876, succeeded in removing liquor licensing from the jurisdiction of municipalities and assigning these responsibilities to three provincially appointed officials in each city, town, and district in the province. In one fell swoop he managed to placate much of the temperance movement (at least for a time) while establishing a political network of party officials in each locality. Thus, the rise of Mowat and the Liberal machine coincides almost precisely with the rise of the BEP machine in Toronto.[44]

4.6 The BEP Temperance and Prohibition Dynamic

Howland's election as mayor of Toronto in 1886, seemingly out of the blue, was part of the growth of a broad-based BEP infrastructure. Loose-knit and with multiple power bases, this religious machine contrasted sharply with the top-heavy, centrally controlled, Liberal Party. Although no written record exists of Howland's path to power, a close reading of newspapers, including the *Globe*, allows one to approximate the route[45] and by following this route to identify the measure in which this activity formed part of the BEP machine. Given that there are strong arguments linking the control of the sale of alcohol to rates of interpersonal violence, a careful accounting of Howland's temperance agenda is of relevance to this study.

Evans, *Oliver Mowat* (Toronto: University of Toronto Press, 1992), 342-345.

[44] Note that although there is a close association between support for prohibition and the Liberal Party, it is not necessarily consistent. This is seen in the strong anti-prohibitionism of Prescott and Russell counties. Strong prohibition sentiment was seen in southern Ontario in close proximity to urban areas even if it was lower in the city limits. Peel County, near Toronto, gave prohibition an 88% vote in 1894. See Graeme Decarie, "Something Old, Something New…: Aspects of Prohibitionism in Ontario in the 1890s", in *Oliver Mowat's Ontario*, ed, Donald Swainson, (Toronto: Macmillan, 1972), 155-156. Mowat was an abstainer. For Mowat's political handling of the temperance question see A. Margaret Evans, *Oliver Mowat* (Toronto: University of Toronto Press, 1992), 106-109.

[45] Desmond Morton narrates the election of Howland but does not examine the several years run-up to it. See Desmond Morton, *Mayor Howland: The Citizens' Candidate* (Toronto: Hakkert), 1973.

THE BRITISH EVANGELICAL PROTESTANT MACHINE

A powerful and energetic individual, Howland was a representative of a movement that was cresting in the 1880s. Combining substantial political pedigree with business acumen, Howland possessed an expansive gregariousness that energized him in public settings, making him an ideal political candidate. Furthermore, a freshly acquired religious zeal seems to have given him a compulsion to constantly spend time with poor people; whether in The Ward (St. John's Ward), a short distance from his comfortable residence at Blythe Cottage, Queen's Park, or on the periphery, in the forsaken Central Prison. All these ingredients came together to make Howland the ideal populist candidate.[46]

Temperance had become a cause that interlocked with a cluster of BEP voluntary movements. Howland had, according to his obituary, been converted to teetotalism when the Dunkin Act, which allowed a "local option", was put to the vote in Toronto in 1877. At that time, Howland "carefully examined the whole question, came to the conclusion that the arguments against the liquor traffic were sound and wise, accepted the situation, became both a total abstainer and a prohibitionist, and at once threw his energies into the organized temperance and prohibition work in which he played so prominent part."[47] Temperance, according to BEP ideology, was an entirely rational viewpoint. Howland was relentless in pursuing the logic of this position, and by tracking his activities it is possible to roughly sketch an important phase of the BEP machine's work over the 1880s and into the 1890s.

[46] This evaluation of his personality and character is shared even by his religious antagonists. The obituary in the High Church *Canadian Churchman* described Howland in the following manner: "His nature was a curious study, as most people would probably agree—exhibiting an abnormal kindness of heart, leading the man to apparent or real extravagancies of action….So excessive in the element of generosity as to be a rarity, his character was both example and warning." As quoted in "William Holmes Howland," *Dictionary of Canadian Biography*.

[47] The *Globe*, December 13, 1893: 2. Leonard Tilley, one-time Reform premier of New Brunswick and later the architect of the National Policy in a Macdonald government, was married to the sister of Howland's wife. Tilley, a long-time temperance and prohibition advocate, undoubtedly had considerable influence on Howland's evolving views on temperance and perhaps his political aspirations. Interestingly Howland was a supporter of Mowat's Liberal government as well as, federally, the National Policy. The Tilley family papers could provide additional Howland material.

While Howland may have been convinced of the general analysis of the liquor problem put forward by the Dunkinites in the summer of 1877, he seems to have wavered on the advisability of legislative action. In January of 1878, Howland chaired a temperance meeting that featured as speaker the American temperance activist and recovered alcoholic, D.I.K. Rine. An opponent of the Dunkinites' agenda, Rine was an advocate of a "gospel temperance" that relied on moral suasion as opposed to prohibition.[48]

In his introductory remarks as chair of that meeting, Howland referred to himself as only an "armour bearer". (The *Globe* writer at this point injected an editorial aside that Howland was "a pretty heavy one, some of them would say, and able to carry a heavy weight of armour.") Howland went on to mention his recent appointment as Chairman of the Board of Trustees of Toronto General Hospital, and the fact that in this capacity he had come to see the need to restore the "drunkard" through "proper care" and the application of "proper methods" in combination with the offering of "hope". He commended Rine for having adopted "a right plan" and lauded him for "coming forward and acknowledging the errors of the past." Howland's "heart went out" to those who could confess that, "I was a brute, but now I am a man." As for the temperance movement itself, such strides were being made that, in Howland's estimation, "whiskey and even intemperance would be quietly pushed out of the land". This would be gradually accomplished through the "moral strength of the community" and without the use of "force".[49]

This occasion marks the beginning of Howland's path as a moral reformer. Already we see a BEP machine with its web of influence able to take a new and "heavyweight" convert such as Howland and catapult him to the public

[48] See *Globe*, June 1, 1877: 4. Rine ridiculed efforts that relied on lectures peppered with statistics and medical evidence in order to gather votes from propertied elites. Elsewhere Rine, speaking from his experience, passionately recounted that, "I have felt sometimes that if a man would just speak to me as he ought to speak, would speak like a brother, I might struggle up again. I have no faith at all in society—so-called society…But until society bends from its iron rule of etiquette, speaks to the fallen, and not at them, and grasps them by the hand, there will never be a man lifted…to happiness and life. *Ottawa Free Press*, October 1, 1877: 4. As quoted in A.J. Birrell, "D.I.K. Rine and the Gospel Temperance Movement in Canada," *Canadian Historical Review* 58, no. 1, (1977): 28.
[49] The *Globe*, January 8, 1878: 4.

forefront in the context of a temperance campaign. The bulk of the text of this *Globe* report was devoted to Howland's introductory comments, with only a few lines on Rine's temperance sermon. The Rine campaign itself covered several months in Toronto, moving seamlessly among Temperance Hall, Elm St. Methodist Church, Shaftesbury Hall, and Carleton St. Primitive Methodist Church,[50] and it clearly had the support of the *Globe*, a key organ of BEP propaganda.[51]

The introductory remarks delivered by Howland betray an ambivalence towards legislative prohibition that also marked the BEP movement. Shortly after the Rine meeting, Howland became the chair of the Toronto chapter of the Dominion Alliance for the Total Suppression of the Liquor Traffic. In this capacity he was committed to the prohibition and "suppression" of all aspects of the manufacture and distribution of alcohol. In Howland the Alliance possessed the ideal networker who, by the beginning of the 1880s, was a board member of most of the BEP voluntary agencies as well as the broader House of Industry.

Howland's temperance efforts were not restricted to the non-sectarian Alliance, but extended to his position as Second Vice-President of the Toronto and Yorkville Christian Temperance Mission. Chaired by A.T. McCord, a founding board member of the Anti-Slavery Society of Canada in the 1850s, the organization was founded in 1879 to reach those persons who "could not be reached by existing organizations," and in this has the marks of a machine that was all pervasive even to the point of multiple redundancies.[52]

Evidence of these redundancies can be seen in a letter to the *Globe* from an observer who had recently attended an organizational meeting at Metropolitan Methodist for yet another temperance society.[53] The writer, estimating that there were over two dozen temperance organizations in the

---

[50] See The *Globe* May 28, 1877: 4; June 1, 1877: 2; June 15, 1877: 4; January 8, 1878: 4. Clearly it is the Methodists who are most comfortable with the temperance movement.

[51] See especially the *Globe* editorial comments on Rine on June 1, 1877: 2.

[52] *Globe*, November 18, 1879.

[53] This perhaps may have been a follow-up to the organizational meeting at Shaftesbury Hall of the Toronto and Yorkville Christian Temperance Mission.

city, advocated an amalgamation under "one great banner", which, though it would be difficult, "could be accomplished by such men as Dr. Potts [then the current minister of Metropolitan Methodist], Vice-Chancellor [Sam] Blake, Mr. W.H. Howland, and others". Importantly, the letter points out that it was the women of the Ladies Union who were carrying out the bulk of the temperance work on the ground, whether that of establishing coffee houses, attending prayer meetings, or, at their own expense, having "victualied and clothed" the families of "poor drunkards". Here again, there is very strong evidence that the daily work of organizations of the type overseen by the likes of Howland or Blake was carried out by an army of women on the ground.[54]

By 1878, Howland was also serving as Chairman of the Board of both the Toronto General Hospital and the Manufacturers' Association, giving him enormous leverage in civic affairs as well as ready access to the editors and reporters of the *Globe*.[55] Genuinely averse to politics, preferring instead a

---

[54] Letter dated December 24 on the editorial page in *Globe*, January 2, 1880: 2. "Ellis" mentions being present at a recent prayer temperance meeting in the West End Coffee house, and that the only participants present were a "few" women from the Ladies' Union and West End Temperance Society.

[55] The *Globe* pages strongly supported temperance and Howland, scion of a key political ally of George Brown, almost invariably received laudable coverage. For an exception see a somewhat congenial condemnation of Howland's support of the National Policy, in the *Globe*, November 16, 1878: 4. Coming one month after the federal Liberal defeat, the opening line of the editorial states that, "Mr. Howland is a pleasant man, one whom his friends like, and whom his enemies, if he have any, cannot hate very vigorously." Then with a Brownite fuselage the editorial goes on to state that Howland "has not been noticeable for any great vigour of thought or any great power of utterance" and does not "love to meddle with politics" but "goes strongly for Prohibition". However, according to the writer, Howland is trumping the National Policy as a "potent wand to conjure with" such that NP would be "carried to the benefit of all and the injury of none." The writer goes on to reason that if the end result of the National Policy is independence from Britain, Howland is then prepared to cover even this result with religious piety and quotes Howland as stating that, "all these things—the rise and fall of nations—were in the hands of God, and that it was not, by any puny efforts of ours that his unalterable will be changed." The comeback from the writer to this is that, "Mr. Howland has great faith in Providence, but he has great faith also in helping forward the ways of Providence in certain directions." Coming from the *Globe*, generally an ally of the Howland that is emerging as an urban reformer, the above does give insight into the dynamic of Howland's public persona. It also casts light on the assertive and optimistic outlook of BEP ideology, as exemplified by Howland, as well as the presence of an inner tension with a lingering quiescent piety within the movement. In the approach of Brown (whether or

role as an activist Christian social reformer and humanitarian, Howland was slowly drawn into municipal politics through his new involvement in the Dominion Alliance. Temperance activism cut across denominations, being most attractive to evangelicals, reinforcing the BEP linkages that existed already through voluntary associations and chiselling away at denominational particularities.[56] The Ministerial Association, organized in 1878 on the basis of the Evangelical Alliance, became an important point of connection for temperance activism with the BEP machine.[57]

The winter of 1878 saw Howland attend a meeting at City Hall with a group of largely BEP leaders, including the politicians George Brown and G.W. Allan, to consider whether to re-open the Old Gaol as a "Shelter for the Homeless". There was general support for the idea, although Howland and others urged priority be given to providing for the unemployed of Toronto ahead of the inevitable "wandering tramps from all over the country" who would be attracted to Toronto by the scheme. Significantly, George Brown urged "a grand system of Christian charity" whereby all the benevolent associations would unite for the purpose of administering relief for those in need. This proposal resulted in formation of a United Charities grouping in the early 1880s although Brown did not live to see its full fruition.[58]

This continued "discovery" of poverty, and the expansion of a charitable

---

not he wrote the editorial), one sees an evangelicalism that is more cautious with respect to Providence and more reliant on Scottish Common Sense philosophy.

[56] For example, Jarvis St. Baptist, later home to the fiery fundamentalist T.T. Shields, hosted a WCTU meeting with Frances Willard. See *Globe*, October 24, 1878: 4. The Dominion Alliance sought broad linkages including those with non-abstainers. It made use of the BEP web of influence using agents, print media, conventions, and meetings in both churches and halls. *Globe*, January 9, 1879.

[57] For the announcement of its organization and its constitution see *Globe*, November 19, 1878: 4.

[58] See *Globe*, December 7, 1878: 8. No doubt Brown was influenced in some sense by Thomas Chalmers, who had attempted the large-scale voluntary relief of poverty in Glasgow earlier in the century. More directly he would have been influenced by the Whig-evangelical views of his father, Peter, who argued for a combination of government intervention and voluntary relief. See Michael Gauvreau, "Reluctant Voluntaries: Peter and George Brown; The Scottish Disruption and the Politics of Church and State in Canada" in *The Journal of Religious History* 25, no. 2 (June 2001): 146-147.

empire to deal with it were part of a BEP attempt to alleviate poverty and to address the underlying conditions that BEP actors saw producing it. The abuse of alcohol was seen as a prime reason for violent crime and poverty. BEP efforts to promote temperance alternatives to the tavern, rather than simply engage in rhetorical suasion, were central features of the activity being promoted.

The period of the early 1880s saw Howland increasingly involved with the running of the fledgling Coffee House Association. Following the British original, the organization sought to offer an alternative to the public house while at the same time providing shelter for "cabmen", and even overnight accommodation for farmers, at the St. Lawrence Market. The prime officers in the organization included Howland, Sam Blake, and Casimir Gzowski.[59]

The first major coffee "tavern" opened at St. Lawrence Market in February of 1882. Although this was a BEP organization, the Catholic Archbishop Lynch made the opening speech at City Hall while the presence of the Mayor[60] and the Lieutenant Governor gave the events a secular, 'public' character. The Archbishop stressed that the coffee house was aimed at workingmen, "the bone and sinew of the country", with the intent to make coffee a replacement for the liquor that was having such negative effects. It was the "duty of the higher class" to keep workingmen from the "temptations of liquor". His Grace declared that he would instruct the pulpits of the city to recommend the coffee houses. Dr. Castle of Jarvis St. Baptist, the Presbyterian D.J. Macdonnell, and the Catholic Bishop O'Mahony all addressed the City Hall audience, giving a sense of the range of support for this BEP venture.[61] Here

[59] *Globe*, December 16, 1878: 4. Sir Casimir Gzowski was a Polish Russian émigré, a prominent engineer, and an active evangelical Anglican who was involved in multiple BEP causes. Peter Gzowski was his great-great grandson.

[60] Note that the two-term mayor for 1881-1882 was William B. McMurrich, a lawyer and BEP Presbyterian layman. McMurrich served with Blake and Howland on the board of the Prisoners' Aid Society. See *Globe* December 21, 1880:8; December 20, 1881: 10. McMurrich is an example of the broad base of BEP power. Several mayors during the period of 1880-1900 were of BEP persuasion. Most took different paths to political power. The BEP "machine" had no centre of control, as Howland's path is beginning to demonstrate. This is not to say that the activities of key personages did not overlap.

[61] *Globe*, February 17, 1882: 8. But note that some smaller coffee houses were already

one sees a clear manifestation of the BEP networks that attempted to shape male culture, whether through the organizational activities of male elites or in the day-to-day activism of women.

By 1882 a second coffee house, large enough to accommodate temperance meetings, was in operation at Shaftesbury Hall. The original St. Lawrence house was in the process of relocating to larger facilities on King St. near St. James's Cathedral. The example of the coffee house movement in Liverpool was consciously followed as a model for the fledgling Toronto society. Plans were made to scatter smaller coffee houses around the city such that when prohibition was finally in place, according to Howland, there would be provision for "houses of refreshment and entertainment without the temptation of taverns." Liberal MP G.W. Allan, speaking at the annual meeting of the Association, praised the "growing interest in the coffee house movement all over the world" and recognized the new strategies as a "factor of immense importance in the onward march of the temperance cause." Importantly, too, the statistical breakdown of customers on a single day showed an unmistakable mixing of the social classes and hint at the ability of a BEP discourse to cross divisions of class. [62]

---

present in 1879. See note 59 above. The presence of Archbishop Lynch and Bishop O'Mahony at a temperance event is an indicator of BEP ideology permeating the broader Toronto culture. There was some vocal Catholic support for temperance but much less so for prohibition. Elsewhere, in the Ontario hinterlands, Roman Catholic Church leaders were more reticent to symbolically support Protestant initiatives such as the "Ross Bible". Lynch, for some reason, felt the need to cooperate publicly at select BEP functions.

[62] *Globe*, October 6, 1882: 6. These "coffee houses" were sizeable operations. In 1884 at the annual meeting the statistic of 370,000 meals served was announced, as compared to 290,000 in 1883. *Globe*, November 28, 1884: 6. In 1883 the customer breakdown at the St. Lawrence location for a typical day was as follows:

Merchants, lawyers, bankers, etc.	125
Clerks in stores and offices	200
Ladies, "supposed to be shopping"	40
Mechanics and labourers	225
People from the country	70
Girls from stores	40
Lads under 15 years of age	45

See *The Coffee Public-House News and Temperance Hotel Journal* (London, November 1, 1883) 128.

Having already served on the board of the Prisoners' Aid Society for a number of years, Howland established in 1880 a Sunday School for women at the Mercer Reformatory. It was in the context of its work in prisons that the Prisoners' Aid Society, led by Blake and Howland, began to advocate political action to separate young and first-time offenders from repeat offenders. In this they worked closely with prison and provincial government officials. Warden James Massie of Central Prison, who on occasion attended Prisoners' Aid Meetings, pledged to separate young offenders from older prisoners in an effort to prevent prison from becoming a "school of crime". Furthermore, at the December 1883 meeting, Massie agreed to "breaking down and removing the barrier between Roman Catholic and Protestant prisoners." That an organization whose president was an Irish Protestant (Sam Blake) should agitate against sectarian divisions is noteworthy.[63]

The board of the Prisoners' Aid Association was top-heavy with lawyers and politicians. (Howland as a businessman was an exception.) The motivations for the involvement of lawyers no doubt came through their everyday work with prisoners and the criminal justice system. The presence of Vice-Chancellor (Samuel) Blake and Ontario Deputy Minister of Education J.G. Hodgins gave the Association a voice in the Ontario government, while Liberal politicians Edward Blake and John Macdonald (the Methodist Toronto businessman) represented their interests in Ottawa.[64] This group influenced legislation at both levels of government.

In the area of the perceived need to treat juveniles separately, the Prisoners' Aid Society deputized a delegation to visit Mowat, who at the time, served as both Premier and Attorney General. Howland addressed Mowat on the need for an industrial school for "young criminals". Outlining how the concept had developed in England, where 200 such schools existed, and how large numbers of juvenile offenders there had been "reclaimed" and were leading

---

[63] *Globe*, December 21, 1880: 8. The presence of the choir of the West End Temperance Society at the meetings illustrates how temperance causes overlapped with the Association. But note that a cell block for Roman Catholics still existed in 1885. *Globe*, March 19, 1885: 3. Of course Blake wanted Catholic prisoners to have the option of attending Protestant meetings.

[64] See for example the board members elected for 1881 in *Globe*, December 21, 1880: 8.

productive lives, Howland made the case for a Toronto school. Mowat promised that the recommendation would receive "earnest consideration."[65] That it was Howland, a businessman, who led a delegation made up largely of lawyers and politicians is indicative of Howland's emergence as a recognized leader within the BEP community. The initiative eventually resulted in the founding in 1887 of the Mimico Boys' Industrial School[66] with Howland as its chairman.[67]

The Society's work, too, involved in advocating the founding of an "asylum" for "inebriates". This was a reflection of the temperance movement conviction that alcohol use was the root cause of most crime; certainly a large percentage of convicts were in prison for alcohol-related offences. Already in 1880 a delegation of BEP clergy and physicians from the Toronto and Yorkville Christian Temperance Mission had met with Mowat concerning provincial backing for an asylum that would serve "for the care, and if possible cure, of inebriates." The delegation argued that it was to the advantage of the "community" to "reclaim" the inebriate. They urged consideration of U.S. models that were heavily funded by the government sector. The argument, which was elaborated much further after Howland became mayor, was based on viewing alcoholism as a disease and not strictly as moral failure. Furthermore,

---

[65] *Globe*, May 17, 1883: 8.

[66] Later renamed Victoria Industrial School.

[67] While Howland and the lawyer Beverley Jones eventually organized the school, the BEP lawyer and eventual mayor, W.B. McMurrich, had lobbied for the concept in the 1870s. See Paul W. Bennett, "Turning 'Bad Boys' into 'Good Citizens': The Reforming Impulse of Toronto's Industrial School Movement, 1883 to the 1920s" in *Ontario History* Vol. LXXVII, No. 3 (September 1886), 209-232. The industrial school system itself developed into a highly disciplined, oppressive, and abusive system and eventually was dismantled in the later part of the twentieth century. Ever the optimist, Howland had envisioned schools with "firm but gentle" discipline. However, the industrial school "system", as envisioned by Howland, did function to separate young, often pre-teen, "waifs" from the adult criminal system. On the development of the industrial (reform) school system in Ontario see Brian Hogeveen, "Accounting for Violence at the Victoria Industrial School" in *Histoire Social/Social History* 43, no. 82 (May 2009): 147-176. In the end, Ontario opted for a foster home model, as opposed to an institutional model that went beyond those in the rest of the English-speaking world in its integration of the federal provincial and private charitable realms. See A. Margaret Evans, *Sir Oliver Mowat*, 287-288.

a communal responsibility was affirmed, and, by extension, a state obligation to seek to assist those who were victimized by the "traffic".

Mowat's response to the delegation was conditioned by the political delicacies of temperance. He recalled that in previous years the government spent $100,000 on a similar plan for the city of Hamilton but that the temperance backers lost interest and moved on to prohibition causes, with the result that the building became a conventional "lunatic asylum". There should, said Mowat, be more private funding. The counter from the committee was that the expense would then fall on the "righteous part of the community" when it was the "general purse" of the "liquor dealers and saloon keepers" that should be required to bear the cost of the "destruction" of "young men".[68]

While Howland was increasingly an advocate of strict prohibition, he was not representative of the BEP movement, which included more moderate approaches to the question of temperance. The prominent Presbyterian minister D.J. Macdonnell, an opponent of prohibition, served as president of the Society for the Prevention and Suppression of Intemperance (S.S.I.). Committed to a pledge of not drinking any beverage stronger than beer or wine, the society held its second annual meeting in the new Shaftesbury Hall Coffee House just prior to the 1883 mayoral election. The meeting heard that whereas just two years previous there had been no coffee houses in the city, there were now two and that "workingmen" were holding their meetings there and "they were better off" than in the pubs. The meeting was also told that the elected officers, who included Sam Blake, Casimir Gzowski, and outgoing mayor William McMurrich, had recently deputized a committee to meet with the alcohol Licensing Committee of the city in an effort to restrict drinking establishments.[69]

---

[68] *Globe*, November 15, 1880: 2. A letter to the *Globe*, signed "Humanity", lays out the case for an inebriate asylum in familial terms. Arguing for intervention by the "commonwealth", the writer states that, "there are families suffering beyond endurance—sufferings worse and harder to bear than bereavement or even lunacy—more families so afflicted than those who are not "behind the scenes" suspect." The writer is "behind the scenes" and could very well be Howland or an associate. *Globe*, January 2, 1880: 2.

[69] *Globe*, December 15, 1882: 6. Interestingly, Howland is not mentioned in the report although Blake and numerous others of the Howland circle are. Perhaps Howland's role

The next month a "large and influential deputation" of the S.S.I., led by Macdonnell, addressed City Council. Arguing for a bylaw that would reduce the number of tavern licenses from 216 to 150, and proposing that the number of liquor sales licenses for shops be cut from 100 to 50, the Hon. G.W. Allan emphasized that the S.S.I. included both abstainers and non-abstainers and their purpose was not one of "enforcing prohibition."[70]

The increased BEP political activism at the municipal level became apparent in the annual mayoral contest. With Howland's nomination for mayor by the BEP supporting Methodist John Withrow, the tempo of reform sharply increased in the January 1883 election. Running on a platform including the strict regulation of liquor licenses, the Liberal Withrow stunned the traditionally Tory electorate of Toronto by losing to the Conservative Arthur Boswell by a hairbreadth three votes. Though the next year Withrow's loss was by a greater margin—145 votes—his candidacy still showed the strength of the BEP cause.[71]

Withrow's defeat was in fact only a minor setback in the BEP effort to regulate alcohol in Toronto. In a "crowded to the doors" December 1883 meeting at St. Andrew's Hall just prior to the 1884 municipal election, "ratepayers" made known their displeasure with City Council equivocation over the banning of the sale of alcohol in grocery stores. Howland moved the adoption of a resolution that was in line with the recent Dominion License Act and the Ontario Liquor License Act (Crooks Act) and advocated that City Council ban the sale of alcohol in grocery stores. In a blistering attack, Howland decried that he had observed children being sent by mothers on

---

in the Dominion Alliance posed political complications for a role in Suppression of Intemperance.

[70] *Globe*, January 30, 1883: 6.

[71] It was a tradition to give the incumbent a bye in the following year's election, hence Boswell's uncontested win in 1884. For a brief summary of the 1883-1885 elections see Desmond Morton, *Mayor Howland*, 3-10. Alcohol regulation did not register on the initial platforms of Manning or Withrow but was present as an issue during the campaign. As chair of a Manning rally, Goldwin Smith made the statement that he "was there not as a representative of any creed or party." In this Smith was telegraphing his later involvement as a formidable opponent of municipal alcohol legislation. *Globe*, January 3, 1885: 2. It was alleged that many "corpses" voted for Manning, but Withrow did not call for a recount.

a shopping errand to these "nurseries of drunkenness" which included the obligatory "bottle of whiskey".[72]

The evangelical N.W. Hoyles, representing the Church of England Temperance Society that allowed for the right of individuals to drink "moderately", argued that grocery stores distributing alcohol were particular dangers to women, the "mothers of the future people of the Dominion". The Presbyterian minister John M. Cameron added that his wife, "in company with other ladies", had canvassed grocers along Queen St., and in "every case the grocer was willing to give up the sale of liquor if the other grocers were obliged also to give it up."[73] Again, women appear as the "foot soldiers" in day-to-day BEP activities.

After debate on a Howland motion to ban the sale of alcohol in grocery stores, and after it had become clear that the motion did have City Council support, it was decided to allow the question to be voted upon by the municipal electorate. The Salvation Army, which was "present in a body", concluded the meeting with an "amen in three volleys" that was followed by a round of applause.[74] The stage was set for a February 25 popular vote on the question of grocery store sales of alcohol.[75]

On the eve of the vote, the Rev. Hugh Johnston[76] thundered from within the cavernous Metropolitan Methodist Church on Queen St. that the liquor

---

[72] *Globe*, December 12, 1883: 6.

[73] *Globe*, December 12, 1883: 6. The previous year during an Anglican temperance mission that Hoyles had addressed, the opinion was expressed that "ladies", who had more leisure, were in certain ways "better qualified for the work than men." *Globe*, December 6, 1882: 5. The following day a report of a meeting held at the BEP St. Peter's Anglican Church contained an announcement of the formation of the Church of England Temperance Association. Howland, described as an "extreme temperance man", was the final speaker at the meeting. *Globe*, December 7, 1882: 6.

[74] *Globe*, December 12, 1883: 6.

[75] Additional BEP public temperance meetings were held at Shaftesbury Hall in the run-up to the vote. See *Globe* January 11, 1884: 6; February 15, 1884: 6.

[76] Johnston was the clergyman who served with Howland as spiritual advisor to a condemned man, Robert Neil, in 1889. See Chapter Six. For the summary of a sermon preached at Central Methodist Church entitled, "The Kind of Men Wanted for Our City Council: Men of Honour and Honesty", see *Globe*, December 29, 1884: 6.

traffic was a "Niagara of intemperance" that was "sweeping away" the "vital and financial resources" of Canada and that the "duty of the hour" was to "dry up the river of intemperance." City Council had shirked its duty in not passing a by-law because of the "power of the liquor dealers". But whether the trade was overturned in twenty-four hours or whether it took longer, victory would eventually come because of the "immense power of the Presbyterian and Baptist churches, and the Methodist churches with not a liquor dealer among its members from one end of the land to the other."[77]

With the temperature hovering at freezing, and a two- inch snowfall over the course of the day, "the largest vote ever polled in the city" resulted in the "separation" of grocery and liquor sales. With the announcement of victory, a celebration capped the night at Shaftesbury Hall. A litany of BEP self-congratulatory speeches emanated from a lineup of politicians, clergymen, and lay leaders. An eager committee was instructed to "apprise" the Mayor at 10 am next day of the desires of the electorate and to request that a by-law be passed at the "earliest possible moment."[78]

Agitation for temperance extended from Shaftesbury Hall at Queen and Yonge to the university campus several blocks north. In the fall term of 1883, in the midst of the grocery store campaign, the University College Temperance League was formed. By March 10 it numbered 203, with 32 registered as "moderate drinkers" and 171 as "total abstainers." Speaking at a gathering on that date, Dr. W.T. Aikins, Dean of Toronto School of Medicine, argued that alcoholism was a disease whose "only true cure was obtained by embracing Christianity." Ontario Minister of Education and prohibitionist G. W. Ross followed, urging that it was the obligation of the state to be the "guardian of the morals of the community" and to impose prohibition as "affirmed" by the Dunkin Act and "reaffirmed" by the Scott Act in 1878. The lawyer and Howland colleague, Henry O'Brien, rounded out the evening. Speaking as the founder of the Toronto Argonaut Rowing Club, O'Brien maintained that

---

[77] *Globe*, February 25, 1884: 6. On the same page, a letter was printed from the BEP Anglican lawyer, N.W. Hoyles, with the backing of the Bishop, advocating support for the by-law.

[78] *Globe*, February 26, 1884: 6.

total abstinence was needed to distinguish oneself in athletics and, further-more, this was "the Scriptural standpoint."[79]

On March 10, 1885 at Shaftesbury Hall, Howland took the chair of a meeting of the Toronto Temperance Electoral Union. Discussion followed on the advisability of organizing petitions in the city and then submitting the Scott Act to the Toronto electorate in November. A motion to follow this direction was rejected, as evidently the majority felt that the city was not ready to vote on the question. A defeat in Toronto could have jeopardized the movement, although the secretary of the organization opined that many of the ward organizations were "at death's door" due to a lack of activity. Somewhat surprisingly, no comments by Howland were reported in a *Globe* article on this meeting, an article that, appropriately, carried the headline, "Making Haste Quite Slowly".[80]

No doubt Howland had been mulling his next step. In those counties where the Scott Act was in place, there was lack of enforcement. There were even reports of Dominion License Commissioners issuing druggist licenses to hotel-keepers for the purposes of "dispensing" alcohol. In an effort to spur the government toward a policy of enforcement, Howland as part of a deputation of temperance advocates visited Premier Mowat in May 1885. They were politely received but left the meeting with little apparent resolution.[81]

Throughout 1885, discussions concerning the Scott Act topped the agenda for organizations such as the W.C.T.U., the Dominion Alliance, and denominational temperance organizations.[82] The Scott Act allowed for a

---

[79] *Globe*, March 11, 1884: 2. By November of 1885 the number of University College stu-dent members of the League had increased to 287 of a total student body of 400, with 267 listed as "total abstainers". Regardless of a "fudge" factor the numbers are remarkable, and combined with the fact of the meeting hall being "nearly filled" amounts to a very powerful BEP discourse. *Globe*, November 27, 1885: 8.

[80] *Globe*, March 11, 1885: 6. Certainly members of the Union would have vivid memories of the defeat of the Dunkin Act in Toronto in 1877 and the 10,000 strong celebratory torchlight parade of the victors. See *The Yeas and Nays Polled in the Dunkin Act Campaign in Toronto*. Howland's name is included in the list of those voting "yea".

[81] *Globe*, May 6, 1885: 6.

[82] For example the St. James's Cathedral Church of England Temperance Society had 460 persons signed up for the abstinence pledge while 82 took a more moderate pledge. BEP

vote if 25% of the electorate signed a petition to force a plebiscite on the prohibition of the retail sale of "intoxicating liquor".[83] Across the province small platoons of workers, predominantly in rural settings, diligently gathered names in the slow march of prohibition, village by village and county by county. Embedded in this grassroots political activism was continued and insidious pressure against male violence. This pressure was maintained in the Howland mayoral campaign.

4.7 The 1886 Mayoral Campaign

The mayoral election of 1886 proved to be a "barnburner". On November 17, 1885 at Temperance Hall, the Temperance Electoral Union met to plot strategy for the upcoming municipal election. Rumours were swirling about three potential mayoral candidates, with only one an identifiable temperance advocate. While Howland's name was not mentioned in the article, in retrospect it can be inferred that he was this candidate. The chair for the evening, J.J. Maclaren, Q.C., was described as having "an onerous job in the extreme" as the events of the meeting progressed. Maclaren mentioned the presence of "ladies" at the meeting, who for the first time would be voting in a municipal election. He went on to express the hope that women would also soon be able to vote in provincial and federal elections and in doing so would "thus purify the political air."[84]

The meeting produced deep fissures between those who advocated beginning a "third" temperance party and those who felt that individual candidates should be supported through activity at the ward level. In the heat of the evening it was proposed by "an old worker for the cause" that one should "vote for no man unless he was a total abstainer." In the end a broad motion was adopted; municipal candidates whose views were "in harmony" with the

---

Canon Dumoulin decried the fact that the cause of temperance had been besmirched "by indiscriminate abuse heaped upon those persons who partook of alcoholic beverages in moderation." Here is additional evidence of a less than univocal BEP voice. *Globe*, November 10, 1885: 6.

[83] George E. Foster, *The Canada Temperance Manual and Prohibitionist's Handbook* (Toronto: Hunter, Rose, and Co., 1881), 10.

[84] *Globe*, November 19, 1885: 5.

principles of the Electoral Union should be supported.[85]

Despite "unfavourable weather", the following night the city's Reformers (Liberals) met in the same Temperance Hall to consider ways to end the Conservative's thirty-year stranglehold on the city. Until then the policy of the party had been to not present a slate of official Reform candidates for municipal elections. This policy was reversed, with the decision being made that candidates would be selected at the ward level, and that a Reform platform would be presented to the electorate.[86]

The Reformers' new approach was in some measure upended by a Howland entry into the mayoralty contest. That entry injected a "nonparty" civic reform platform into the municipal campaign, which, though actually quite congruent with the aims of the Reformers, stood apart from the earlier Reform platform that had been laid out by the Liberal *Globe*. Both, however, supported provisions for clean water, improvements in sewage and sanitation, and an increase in liquor license fees as well as the reduction of the number of licenses.[87]

A mock election of sorts took place at the Toronto Board of Trade the week before the official Howland announcement of candidacy. Rumours had been reported on the street that "the brewers and liquor men" would attempt to "blackball" Howland because of his strong views on alcohol. As a result, the "temperance men" were present in "strong force" and "elected" Howland by a wide margin. The *Globe* commented on this highly unusual occurrence as proof of the hostility in some quarters towards Howland's "temperance principles". Usually a businessman would only be denied election to the Board for moral reasons.[88]

The following week, Howland's official candidacy was announced at a

[85] *Globe*, November 19, 1885: 5.

[86] *Globe*, November 19, 1885: 5.

[87] *Globe*, November 16, 1885: 4. Clean water went hand-in-hand with temperance, as alcoholic beverages, having often been boiled and made with the cleanest municipal water, were perceived as being healthier than normal city water.

[88] *Globe*, November 28, 1885: 13. See also *News*, November 28, 1885: 12. The *News* makes no mention of the attempted blackballing of Howland in its report of the meeting.

gathering in Shaftesbury Hall that was "crowded to the doors." The "requisition" requesting his candidacy was handed to Howland accompanied by the obligatory speeches and ovations. Up in the gallery "were large numbers of ladies", some of whom were eligible for the first time to vote in a Canadian municipal election. According to the *Globe* reporter:

> Th[e] requisition contained the names of gentlemen of EVERY POLITICAL PARTY and every nationality. They had all united in requesting the man who had the confidence of the citizens of Toronto, and from his position as a mercantile man, would be able to represent the mercantile city of Toronto to be their candidate for the Mayoralty. (Cheers) He was a man of progressive ideas, a man who was prepared to look at Toronto as it would be 50 years hence, and not as it may be two or three years hence.[89]

The "mercantile" interests of the city were certainly well represented on the Shaftesbury Hall platform. But when one does an analysis of this platform party, one is also struck by the BEP flavour of the group. A total of 29 "prominent supporters" were on the platform. These included the following: Henry O'Brien, the BEP Anglican lawyer and associational activist; A.M. Smith, a Presbyterian lawyer with an independent, liberal streak; William G. Storm, the Methodist architect and later BEP Anglican; Edward Gurney Jr., the Methodist industrialist; A.M. Rosebrugh, a BEP physician, scientist, and Prisoners' Aid Association board member; J.W. Bengough, sometime BEP Anglican writer, cartoonist and prohibitionist; George McLean Rose, Liberal political leader, journalist, Coffee House Association board member and Unitarian temperance advocate; R.J. Fleming, the Methodist prohibitionist Liberal municipal politician who was to become a four-term mayor in the 1890s; J.J. Maclaren, Q.C. and temperance worker; Thomas Thompson a King St. merchant; and Stapleton Caldecott, a BEP Anglican dry goods merchant.[90]

---

[89] *Globe*, December 2, 1885: 8.
[90] *Globe*, December 2, 1885: 8.

Howland was presented as an independent candidate who was simply a "philanthropist" and "a private citizen". In his acceptance speech, Howland reinforced his supposed independence by describing himself as an advocate of the Conservatives' National Policy while simultaneously a solid supporter of Oliver Mowat. He promised his cheering audience that if he were successful it would be a victory for the "citizen's party". Thus, while brilliantly appealing to both the industrialist Tory and to the Liberal, Howland distanced himself from the Scott Act, pledging that he would avoid "extreme views on temperance". Vowing to oppose the liquor men who controlled the city, Howland put forward the moderate temperance platform of the Presbyterian Rev. D.J. Macdonnell that called for the enforcing of existing laws and the reduction of licenses.[91]

The *Globe* initially gave barely tepid support to a Howland candidacy. Criticizing him for his support of the National Policy, it did however commend him for years of service in "ameliorating and improving the condition of the poor" and in particular the condition of poor children, "irrespective of creed or nationality". But the editorial stopped short of endorsement, presumably reflecting the views of the editor, who, though a temperance advocate, was also a Liberal. There was no unified BEP voice.[92] BEP power remained diverse, with multiple centres.

While the presence of industrialists and businessmen added necessary capitalist brawn to the Howland drive to City Hall, the temperance bent of the supporters of the Howland candidacy was obvious. The Liberal journalist Goldwin Smith was quick to make this recognition, as were the industrialists and brewers who had attempted to blackball Howland only days earlier at the Toronto Board of Trade. Howland was seen, quite rightly, as a prohibitionist threat.

As president of the Liberal Temperance Union, Smith sought clarity from

[91] *Globe*, December 2, 1885: 8.

[92] *Globe*, December 3, 1885: 4. The *World* argued that the *Globe* covertly supported Howland throughout the campaign. The apparent hesitancy for openly supporting him was attributed to Howland's abandonment of Alexander Mackenzie in "his hour of need" during the 1878 federal election. *World*, January 2, 1886: 2.

the Toronto Temperance Electoral Union as to their intentions with respect to the Scott Act. Smith, in a public letter, urged an immediate vote, no doubt in the aftermath of the Act's recent difficulties in urban areas, and he argued that prolonged agitation for prohibition negatively affected the values of certain properties and securities. With Howland's candidacy in mind, he labelled such ongoing agitation a "manifestly unrighteous policy" and one that was inadmissible by "any one pretending to the name of a moral reformer." G.M. Rose,[93] James Thomson, and J.J. Maclaren, all prominent "platform" supporters at Howland's recent nomination, responded strongly to Smith's missive. Howland's recent resignation as President of the Electoral Union, due to potential conflict of interest if he were elected as mayor, was alluded to as proof of his morality and rectitude.[94]

The sight of the Liberal Goldwin Smith chairing the nomination meeting to re-elect the Tory incumbent Mayor Manning was a function of the ongoing liquor wars. Smith, as leader of the Liberal Temperance Union, advocated the current licensing system as the way to properly control the sale of alcohol, itself, he thought, a legitimate enterprise. According to Smith, if the liquor licenses were abolished, illicit alcohol would flow freely and there would be no practical means to limit its presence.[95]

The public opposition of Smith stimulated the broader BEP machine to attempt to outflank him by appealing directly to Manning prior to the election. A large committee of the more moderate and prominent BEP professionals and clergymen requested a public meeting of ratepayers for the purpose of considering the reduction of liquor licenses in the city.[96] That

---

[93] G.M. Rose is yet another example of the gravitational pull of the BEP orbit. A publisher and temperance worker, Rose was a staunch Unitarian who regularly taught a Sunday afternoon Bible class at the First Unitarian Church. See his entry in *Dictionary of Canadian Biography*.

[94] Globe, December 9, 1885: 8.

[95] *The Week*, January 7, 1886: 88.

[96] *Globe*, December 12, 1885: 12. These ranged across the BEP spectrum from N.W. Hoyles, the Anglican lawyer, to D.J. Macdonnell the Presbyterian minister, and on to the Methodist magnate Timothy Eaton, and Methodist ministers John Potts and E.H. Dewart. The requisition meeting was held on December 18 and ended up being dominated by the brewers and other members of the "trade". Manning prevailed, and that resulted in a watered

same week a far more strident response came from Methodist quarters. Rev. D.V. Lewis responded directly and forcefully to Smith's "public utterances:

> We dare not stand still and let this terrible traffic go on. God has laid the burden on us. You only make our work the harder but you do not discourage us into inactivity, and indifference and you cannot defeat us, for we know that you and those with you are fighting against God. For there never was upon this earth any other thing which offered so many insults to God and His Son, or put so many hindrances in the way of his cause...Ask us to license it. We dare no more to consent to license Pandora to open her box; than we dare to license men to turn loose in our streets the
>
> WILD BEASTS OF THE JUNGLES.

A challenge to Howland's decision to work within the constraints of the licensing system can also be seen in this statement. Followed up by a lecture by the same Rev. Lewis the following night at Metropolitan Methodist Church, it points to the fashion in which responses to the liquor question on the eve of the 1886 mayoral election indicate multiple, overlapping, and significant manifestations of BEP power.[97]

In the midst of the mayoral campaign, on December 17, the Judicial Committee of the Privy Council in London rendered its decision on the federal "Dominion License Act" of 1878 in a decision that reinforced provincial rights and played directly into the hands of temperance activists. Headlines in the *Globe* spelled out the implications of the decision in bold lines: "The Crowning Victory"; "The Dominion License Act Slaughtered"; "Sir John Not Even Allowed to Issue Wholesale and Vessel Licenses—His Paws Must be Kept Off the Liquor Trade". In a stunning put-down of a Canadian Supreme

---

down general statement "that the city council should exercise its discretionary power to reduce the number of hotel and shop licenses." *World*, December 19, 1885: 1. The *World* obviously saw the mayoral contest as making good copy and thus carried the debates on the front page.

[97] *Globe*, December 10, 1885: 2.

Court decision to grant the federal government major licensing powers, all such powers were proclaimed to belong to the provinces. Fresh momentum was added to BEP efforts at the local and provincial level to limit the easy availability of alcohol.[98]

Howland continued to be viewed by the Manning camp as an upstart and not a threat. In a campaign speech Manning, confident of victory, proclaimed that he "had not intended to deal much with Mr. Howland" but had been forced to, as Howland was "LED BY THE LADIES and a number of voting men of the Christian Association [YMCA]". Howland's lack of steadiness was also targeted; he had, said Manning, jumped between churches, and in the public sphere had left the Board of Trade only to rejoin it again. With respect to municipal politics Howland was a novice.[99] But the heart of Manning's critique was the involvement of women in Howland's campaign and their meddling in the politics of the liquor question. According to Manning, women "had other duties to perform"; there was "nothing so beautiful or becoming as the character of a modest woman" and this had to be maintained. For both Goldwin Smith and Alexander Manning, concerns of overenthusiastic women were behind the deeply troublesome and wrongheaded temperance movement and these had to be kept under control.[100]

Whatever the initial hesitancy in the editorial room of the *Globe* so far

---

[98] *Globe*, December 18, 1885: 1, 4. However anti-Scott proponents argued that if the Scott Act itself were tested at the highest court it would be termed *ultra vires* and tossed out altogether. See for example the *World*, December 25, 1885. Although cagey on prohibition, Mowat was entirely in favour of temperance and of provincial licensing control.

[99] The *World* provided a withering, almost daily front-page critique of Howland. Howland had a "disposition to either rule or ruin" and worked "assiduously" to become the president of every association he joined before moving on to the next. Wanting always to "lead the procession" Howland "will fight in no cause except as a brigadier-general." *World*, December 22, 1885: 2.

[100] *Globe*, December 18, 1885: 8. Women were not simply "courted" but were organized in preparation for the vote. The *World* reported a WCTU campaign meeting at Shaftesbury Hall for which printed circulars were distributed. Ward committees were formed, presumably to persuade women to vote. While the meeting was planned exclusively for women, a few of the "sterner sex" were in attendance including Howland who was described as the "Scott act candidate" who "wore his most pleasant smile and did a heap of handshaking." *World*, December 12, 1885: 1. See also *Mail*, December 18, 1885: 6.

as supporting Howland's candidacy was concerned, by mid-December the paper was fully engaged in an effort to unseat Manning. Howland's views on alcohol joined with BEP activity to tip the balance. Daily half-page sections polled prominent Torontonians as to their opinions on the liquor license question.[101] The majority strongly favoured license reductions. In an editorial, two weeks before the election, the *Globe* compared the "liquor interest" to the "slave interest" and predicted its sure demise.[102]

At a Howland meeting at Mission Hall in St. John's Ward, two days before Christmas, G.M. Rose declared that attendees were not present at a "political meeting" but at "A FIGHT BETWEEN VIRTUE AND VICE" and in opposition to "the devil [who stood] against all that was good." For too long the people of Toronto had been governed by "party and pocket". Manning, with $70,000 invested in the liquor industry, was, said Rose, a liquor party man. Howland, in contrast, was Independent and led a coalition that combined "working Grit and Tory" who were "running now like young colts, quite free and side by side."[103]

The Howland campaign continued to gain momentum and sought the vote of the workingman with the pledge to not raise his taxes despite a reduction in liquor licenses. Howland assured his audiences that larger tax revenues could be obtained from gas and water works companies. Meeting at the Massey Manufacturers Works, owned by the prominent Massey—and Methodist— family, Howland stressed the need to reduce the number of licenses but promised not to move towards prohibition. Attention, too, was given the need for a new sewage system and clean water; nor, he said, should

[101] See for example *Globe*, December 22, 1885: 8.

[102] *Globe*, December 21, 1885: 4. The *World* in particular reacted strongly to attacks on Manning. A maverick, populist paper with increasingly Tory leanings, its attack went along the lines of the following anti-BEP script: "There is but one man in all Toronto who is truly good and honest and God-fearing, and he is William H. Howland; and G. Maclean Rose, the Creaking Grip, Henry O'Brien, J.J. MacLaren and that ilk are his prophets...These self-righteous citizens..." The editorial predicted that unless Howland addressed the important questions he would lose the election by "thousands" of votes rather than "hundreds". *World*, December 26, 1885: 2. Also *World*, December 28, 1885: 2.

[103] *Globe*, December 24, 1885: 8. Howland was downplaying the largely Liberal sympathies that he shared with a large number of key supporters.

workingmen be forced to compete with unjustly cheap labour; a many-dimensional platform was clearly on offer.

The most important fact about the meeting was that it was chaired by the company superintendent and no doubt organized by company ownership. Employees had also been brought to sign a document in support of Howland's candidacy, only one refusing to do so. A large BEP-owned company was exerting enormous leverage on workingmen. The BEP machine had a quite, though not always apparent, coercive aspect.[104]

This was, of course, not the only ground for workingmen's support; labour leadership was active too.[105] The Toronto Typographical Union, long in a simmering labour dispute with the *Mail*, called for a boycott by labour unions of all municipal candidates endorsed by the *Mail*.[106] A large ad on Election Day morning in the *Globe*, taken out by the TTU, called on "all workingmen" to "vote against Manning".[107]

Temperance remained central. Election rhetoric was heavily coloured by temperance issues, whether in newspaper articles, church and association meetings, or reports of women election canvassers. A week before the election Manning complained that "Willie" Howland sought election for reasons of "religion" and had no interest in the city itself. He had even "neglected his business for religion". Manning himself could complain that he was

---

[104] *Globe*, December 21, 1885: 8. Likewise Edward Gurney, the Methodist president of a stove manufacturing company, boasted that only one employee of a hundred in his employ did not sign Howland's requisition. Gurney, a Liberal, chaired Howland's nomination meeting. See *World*, December 22, 1885: 2.

[105] Gregory Kealey argues, contra Desmond Morton, that it was the labour vote that propelled Howland to power. In this reading, the signing of the requisition for a Howland candidacy by Massey employees was a function of labour rather than management. While labour was a factor, I argue below that the labour vote is not the primary explanation of a Howland mayoralty. Gregory S. Kealey, *Toronto Workers Respond to Industrial Capitalism, 1867-1892* (Toronto: University of Toronto Press, 1980), 211, 234-236, 387 n. 183.

[106] *Globe*, December 8, 1885: 8.

[107] *Globe*, January 4, 1888:5. The *Globe* also carried a report on a January 2 meeting of the TTU, in which a list of suitable aldermanic candidates was presented and another list of those to be voted down. Of the 31 candidates that the union supported, 17 were elected while 7 of the ten that they opposed were elected. No incumbent opposed by the TTU was unseated.

not respected as mayor but instead was "denounced as a brewer" and that the municipal election had been reduced to a contest between "vice" and "virtue"—in response to which a voice in the audience called out "We will have vice and Mr. Manning."[108] The lines were drawn for the January 4th contest. Sewage, clean water, and labour issues remained, but feelings ran deepest over the sale of alcohol in the city. Manning, in final words to his supporters, warned "that the women would be out to vote and that his supporters should be up bright and early on Monday morning."[109]

Election morning brought a "pitiless January rain" that kept up all day. For the first time women voted in an election and over 1,000 of them were reported to have turned out to cast their votes. There were claims that many women were harassed by Manning supporters demanding that they be sworn in; in at least one case, one was asked to kiss a "greasy" Bible. At the end of the day, Howland had achieved an overwhelming victory with a majority in excess of 1,600 votes.[110]

Significantly, a number of women and labour leaders were on the platform at the Howland victory celebration at Shaftesbury Hall. Swarming around Howland, both women and men waved brooms over his head. Addressing the crowd, he attributed his victory to the labour vote. He also thanked the "ladies" and vented his anger at the way women had been "ill-treated" at some of the polls. Thomas Tracey, President of the Trades and Labour Council,

---

[108] Here, of course, is a deftly written piece of editorial opinion on the part of a *Globe* reporter who was marching to a BEP drumbeat. *Globe*, December 29, 1885: 8. At this point Manning's supporters were confidently predicting victory. The opening words of one of the closing election editorials of the *World* stated matter-of-factly that, "Mayor Manning will have a second term. The rousing meeting of last night in the opera house, the returns of the ward organizations, and the weakenings and defections in the Howland ranks, all go to establish this without a doubt." *World*, December 31, 1885: 2.

[109] *Globe*, December 30, 1885: 8. It must be kept in mind that headlines concerning the Scott Act controversy across the country were a constant in the city newspapers. The judgment of the Privy Council had amplified the temperance issue in the midst of the campaign, and the full text of the decision was printed in the week prior to the election. This judgment reinforced the power of Provincial legislatures to license the liquor trade and downplayed Dominion liquor laws making Ontario a fertile ground for temperance and prohibition activism. *Globe*, December 31, 1885: 2.

[110] *Globe*, January 5, 1886: 8.

addressed the gathering. Tracey proclaimed that organized labour could no longer be ignored, and that Howland would enforce the bylaws of the city with integrity.[111]

Any attempt to account for the Howland victory on the basis of BEP influence needs to address the way that contemporary observers and participants explained the upset. Goldwin Smith, clearly agitated by the result, argued that the Trade Unions had voted in a "sectional" fashion in order to punish the *News* over the ongoing labour dispute. Smith estimated that Howland had received close to 2,000 labour votes as a result. Secondly, he acknowledged that the "female vote" was determined by the "influence of Shaftesbury Hall" rather than any desire to vote for the most-qualified candidate.[112]

According to the *Daily Mail*, the women's vote was Howland's "tower of strength." The day after the election, the Conservative newspaper reported that each temperance lodge in the city had appointed two or three "ladies" to canvas the female vote. In the case of one woman, four different women had brought a carriage around to her residence, offering transport to the polling station.[113] Manning himself, prior to the election, recognized that the female

---

[111] Typical quotes from the day before the election: "An old lady in the East End remarked yesterday:—"I am 80 years old; I have been steeped up to my neck in taxes for a long time but I thank God that I have lived to get a vote.'" "Ten thousand married women in this city," said an enthusiastic Howland supporter yesterday, "are saying if we were widows for half an hour there would be no doubt about Manning's defeat." *Globe*, January 5, 1886: 8. Note however that the *World* makes mention of box seating being full of "ladies" at Manning's final rally at the Grand Opera House, where a reported 3,000 supporters were in attendance. *World*, December 31, 1885: 1.

[112] *The Week*, January 14, 1886: 104. For Smith, women's suffrage was a threat to Canadian society. According to Smith, women were easily manipulated by the pulpit such that whatever cause advocated by the preacher was equated with the cause of "Christ" while any opposition was deemed to be siding with "Barabbas", the criminal in the biblical crucifixion story. When women legislate, law inevitably breaks down because males will not abide by female enactments, as all law rests on the "force of the community", and this "force" is male. According to Smith, the root cause of the attempted "forced imposition" of prohibition on the general population was Methodism. He insisted that he was not opposed to the practice of Methodism but rather its attempt to impose its beliefs on other religious bodies. *The Week*, January 14, 1886: 104; February 11, 1886: 168.

[113] *Daily Mail*, January 5, 1886: 1.

vote was one to be reckoned with.[114]

The *Globe* also had a clear vision of its importance:

The vote of the women has been gratifyingly large all over the Province. Next year it will be much more so. And when in this way and by these means whiskey is pretty well cleaned out, as by-and-bye it will be, it will be found that at the same time a very large amount of bad and questionable politics has also received decided notice to quit.[115]

Arguable, the female vote was the decisive factor in Howland's victory.

Given that a record 13,500 voted in the election, with perhaps close to 2,000 being labour votes and well over 1,000 the votes of women, and observing a Howland plurality of 1,700, it is difficult to argue that the labour vote alone made the difference. Up until two nights before the election, the Trades and Labour Council had not given their membership firm instructions on how to vote.[116] It is thus difficult to be certain that an overwhelming percentage of union members actually did place a vote for Howland, especially given a presumed workingman bias against temperance.

The evidence of the vote of women, combined with the temperance influence, points to their action as central in the result produced. Election rhetoric was heavily coloured by temperance newspapers such as the *News* or *World*, or Goldwin Smith's essays in the *Week*, both of which zeroed in on Howland's views on temperance and identified him as a subversive Scott Act candidate. BEP rhetoric and influence were such that even Manning and Smith identified themselves as "temperance" advocates in their support of a licensing system. Women's support for all this was vital.

The BEP machine generally was, of course, also important. Shaftesbury Hall and temperance halls and lodges provided assembly points for rallies. Churches, some seating up to 2,500, provided pulpits from which BEP

---

[114] *Mail*, December 18, 1885: 6.

[115] *Globe*, January 6, 1886: 4.

[116] On election morning the *World*, which proclaimed itself the workingman's paper, stated that the workingman should be left to vote on his own. *World*, January 4, 1886: 1.

rhetoric emanated virtually seven days a week. Likewise, pan-evangelical associations such as the YMCA, YWCA, the WCTU, the University College Temperance League and other temperance associations all backed the Howland candidacy. Women were active, and they certainly influenced the way that eligible male voters in their households voted, but they were one of a number of factors engaged.

4.8 The BEP Machine: A Summary

The election of William Howland as mayor in 1886 on a platform that included both temperance and sabbatarian laws reflects the ideological power of activist Protestants, who now had the power to swing mayoral elections in a previously Tory Toronto. The Presbyterian, Methodist, and Baptist populations had grown most rapidly during the 1880s and 1890s, and it was this religious base that furnished the votes needed to elect a reformist, evangelical mayor.

Howland came to power as the result of the votes of women, the labour movement, the temperance vote, and members of the middle class. He proved to be very popular.[117] During his mayoral terms, the temperance lobby succeeded in cutting back the number of tavern licenses while increasing license fees.[118] Throughout the 1880s and 1890s, Howland and his coreligionists served as mayors for a total of ten years, reflecting a new reformist and evangelical bent to the city's electorate.[119] This in itself demonstrates the power of

[117] In his second election in 1887, Howland considerably widened his majority and could probably have run uncontested for a third term, but he stepped down ostensibly to continue his work with the poor (which he did), and to help run the businesses of his aging father. However his giving to charitable causes apparently kept him in debt, and the small mayoral stipend of $2,000 combined had stretched his means. He had the popularity and charisma to pursue a grander political career but chose not to, seemingly out of religious compulsion.

[118] It was Howland who appointed Detective David Archibald to head up a "morality squad". Archibald was known for his efforts to suppress vice, but preventing the abuse of children was also part of Archibald's mandate. I have chosen not to dwell on the details of Howland's mayoral years. This has been covered in Desmond Morton, *Mayor Howland*.

[119] Despite large population increases, by 1890 tavern licenses had been cut to 150 while shop licenses were reduced to 50. See Edward Clarke and William Roaf, *By-laws of the city of Toronto* (Toronto: Rowsell, 1890), 124. For Howland's description of his efforts at license reduction see *Report of the Royal Commission on the Liquor Traffic*, 889-890.

a BEP discourse to shape the contours of political culture in late Victorian Toronto. BEP activists were able to place restrictions on the sale of alcohol and worked to prevent persons detained for drunkenness from being committed to prison.[120] Once in power, Howland argued strongly that chronic drunkenness be treated as a disease rather than a crime. Over the following years, the city council developed a policy of not arresting persons solely for drunkenness, either allowing them to return home or accommodating them at the police station overnight for their own safety.[121]

Temperance was the defining issue for the Howland mayoral campaign, but the BEP agenda he represented was much broader. The poor, prison work, particularly among youthful prisoners, and improving the position of women received much attention. Each of these issues contributed to an increasing humanitarian impulse and a ratcheting up of strictures on interpersonal violence.

The details of William H. Howland's rise to power offer one a good understanding of the workings of the various parts of the BEP machine; examining them, one gets a clear idea of concerns, objectives, purposes, and means of getting ideas into practice. How the machine might work, and what it might do to accomplish its ends, stands forth with great clarity. A central phase in BEP history is illuminated and its central elements underscored.

While I have tracked Howland as a "marker", the same could be done with Methodist Robert J. "The People's Bob" Fleming. Fleming was first elected alderman in 1886 and was responsible for introducing the bylaw that restricted liquor licenses. In the 1890s he was elected mayor four times. Marguerite Van Die is currently at work on a major study of the Fleming family.

[120] For example see the report on the annual meeting of the Christian Temperance Mission. *World*, November 23, 1887: 1. "Reformation homes" were recommended where persons convicted as well as vagrants could receive moral and employment training. Prisons in such cases were deemed "agencies and nurseries of crime" and "seminaries of Satan."

[121] *Report of the Royal Commission on the Liquor Traffic*, 889-890.

5

THE TAKE-UP OF BEP IDEAS IN LATE VICTORIAN TORONTO

Introduction

It has been argued in Chapter Three and Chapter Four that BEP teachings were strongly present and widely disseminated in the Toronto community. These teachings were present in church, ethnic, neighbourhood, family, and personal discourses. They were adopted and promoted in pronounced ways by women who were disproportionately represented in BEP religious communities and who exerted their influence not only through familial structures but also through BEP associational activities.

By 1880, the evangelical infrastructure allowed a crossing of a threshold of power that made it effectively supplant a Tory-Anglican moral hegemony. An examination of behaviour in the community offers evidence that BEP ideas were actually present in the thinking of its residents and, more, that those ideas were affecting behaviours that include church and Sunday School attendance, rates of petty larceny, attitudes towards alcohol, and incidences of interpersonal violence. Homicide rates were especially important. These sharply declined in Toronto during the period from 1880 to 1900, a decline, I will argue, that was due to the increasing dominance of a British evangelical Protestant religious expression (BEP), the "take-up" of these ideas by individuals, and the changes in "civility" that it produced.

Chapter Five's main concern is with the measure in which BEP ideas were adapted in Toronto and can be seen influencing behavior. While Chapter Four argues that church and Sunday School data demonstrate disproportionate church building construction, high Sunday School attendance rates, and substantial financial giving to churches, Chapter Five, Part 1 will examine church census data from the point of view of individual religious compulsion as seen in financial giving. Secondly, the rapid growth of the Salvation Army during the 1880s and 1890s is indicative of an increased, BEP-driven focus on the poor. Finally, the overwhelming take-up of BEP religious identities by Toronto's small Chinese population, points to the power the belief system had.

Chapter Five, Part 2, will return to the young Mackenzie King's diary as an indication of how a religious ideology was received in the mind and then expressed in behaviour. In King we have a "deep" account that allows the interpreter to enter into the world of BEP Toronto. Within this world we also encounter Eliza (Lizzie) Harvie and in doing so catch a glimpse of a female BEP activist. We see BEP protocols inflecting outlook and behavior alike.

5.1 The Toronto Religious Census Data and BEP Take-Up

Toronto church census data have been previously introduced and are evaluated in APPENDIX C. The following section will return to these data examining them from a new angle. By using them to "follow the money" one gains another angle of vison on BEP take-up. This concerns the ability of a given denomination to compel individuals to contribute monetarily to the expansion of seating capacity and for ministerial salaries. These data carry one further into the material dimension of churchgoing in late nineteenth-century Toronto. One would predict that Anglican elites would have the greatest capacity for financial giving.

BEP diffusion and a resulting personal religious compulsion can be measured in the increased building of churches and in the increase of total seating capacity. Newspaper data[1] prove invaluable in that they show seating capacities for all church buildings and the denominational seating totals; increases in seating can be measured over a 14-year period, a very helpful feature lacking in the similar London, England newspaper censuses.[2] The picture given

---

[1] These data are derived from three church censuses conducted by Toronto newspapers for the years 1882, 1888, and 1896. See *Globe*, February 2, 1882: 7; *Evening Telegram*, December 22, 1888: 6; *Evening Telegram*, May 4, 1896. For a *Globe* summary of the 1896 census see *Globe*, May 5, 1896: 4.

is dramatic in its implications:

Table 5.1 Toronto church seating capacity according to the church censuses

	1882 capacity	1888 capacity	1896 capacity	% Growth
C of En	11220	16785	20676	84.3%
Bap	3300	8625	9920	200.1%
Meth	12880	27675	32770	154.4%
Pres	10320	17290	22749	120.4%
RC	4250	7610	8332	96%
Other	7890	19025	18405	133.3%
Totals	49,860	97,010	112,852	126.3%

All denominations show substantial growth in seating capacity over a period of fourteen years, but it is the BEP denominations that outstrip the Anglican and Roman Catholic churches. One would expect the Church of England, to which moneyed elites had the most affinity, to be most capable of expanding seating capacity. But this example of what took place in the "seat wars", shows ideology trumping personal wealth.

What the census material reveals concerning annual church revenues is also significant. I estimate Protestant Toronto annual church receipts in the 1890s to have been considerably more than $0.5 million as compared to total Toronto municipal government receipts of $7.3 million for 1896 and $3.9 million[3] for the Ontario provincial government in 1891. Combined with the well over $0.5 million in largely religious voluntary association revenues, these receipts indicate a substantial ecclesiastical infrastructure, one operating on the basis of voluntary giving and with largely voluntary time commitments.[4] Given that much charitable aid, given from religious motives,

---

[2] On the English newspaper church censuses see APENDIX C.

[3] For 1891, total expenditures by the Province of Ontario were $3.9 million. See Ontario Legislative Assembly, *Ontario Sessional Papers*, vol. xxxiii—part v (Toronto: Queen's Printer, 1891) 301.

[4] See the appendices on individual church annual budgets, seating capacity, and on voluntary associations.

went unrecorded, the importance of this may be even greater.[5] Ministers' salaries were also reported, along with church bonded debt.[6] The data in dollars for the year 1888 are as follows:

Table 5.2 Toronto church financial data for 1888 as derived from the church census

	#Churches	Annual Revenue	% Total	Ministers' Salaries	Church Debt	Building & Prop. Values
C of Eng	35	125,970	25	35,620	282,900	985,600
Bap	13	42,000	8.3	16,050	59,850	339,000
Meth	27	127,510	25	42,300	400,610	1,042,815
Pres	24	133,420	26	43,070	285,567	735,860
RC	9	-----		-------	61,000	634,690
Other	38	77,240	15	25,497	161,530	544,940
Totals	146	506,144		162,537	1,251,657	4,282,305[7]

BEP ministers' salaries were higher, at least in the aggregate.[8] Methodist and Baptist denominations, and also the Presbyterians, far outstripped the Anglicans in per capita giving for buildings and ministerial salaries. Thus, in the important realm of religion the propertied class lost "turf", at least for a number of pivotal decades.[9] In summary, the BEP denominations show

[5] Nancy Christie and Michael Gauvreau, *Christian Churches and Their Peoples*, 54-56.

[6] Total debt was estimated to be double the bonded debt. See Appendix B.

[7] *Evening Telegram*, December 22, 1888: 6.

[8] This does not mean that the average BEP church minister had a higher salary; rather it refers to the aggregate budget for ministerial salaries.

[9] *Evening Telegram*, December 22, 1888: 6. Here the "facts" are that the weather masked normal check attendance on Sundays that were not inclement. Note that the 1896 census covered several suburbs not included in 1886 but the additional population is insignificant in comparison to the aggregate. It is important to point out here that overall Roman Catholic attendance rates were much higher than the Anglican rates in all 3 censuses. The resemblance is that in the 1888 church census both denominations dropped sharply in attendance and both were losing "market share" in the period from 1881 to 1901 as per the decennial census. At an aggregate of 62% attendance in the 1896 church census, Toronto had a slightly higher attendance than the BEP strongholds of Scarborough, Peterborough, and

strong growth from 1881 to 1901.

Certainly, disproportionate BEP growth took place in Toronto in the last two decades of the century. This growth includes especially the "Other" denominational category that encompassed Congregationalists, Plymouth Brethren, the Salvation Army and other smaller groupings that were heavily influenced by evangelicalism. Furthermore, approximately 40% of Anglican churches had BEP outlooks and presumably the actual percentage of laity influenced by evangelicalism was much higher.[10] The extremely high BEP churchgoing rates reflect the measure in which BEP discourse produced a compulsion on the part of individuals to attend church and make ~~and make~~ a public commitment to BEP principles and teaching.

The same growth pattern occurred in the Protestant Sunday School in Toronto (see APPENDIX C). The growth in attendance of the BEP Sunday School far outstripped that of the Anglican Sunday School, a measure of comparative strength in take-up including familial take-up regardless of whether or not parents attended church. (The Roman Catholic Church did not have a comparable Sunday School.) No doubt the Sunday School had varying degrees of behavioural influence; there was generally only one

---

Bristol. Only Bristol had a comparable population. The largely Church of England, Bath, had similar attendance but was much smaller than Toronto. For England and Scotland see Hugh McLeod, "Class, Community and Region: The Religious Geography of Nineteenth-Century England" *A Sociological Yearbook of Religion in Britain,* 6, ed. Michael Hill (London: SCM, 1973), 29-72. For New Zealand see Alison Clarke, "Churchgoing in New Zealand, 1874-1926, a Re-evaluation" (lecture and accompanying slides presented at the New Zealand Historical Association Conference, Hamilton, November 2011). See also Hugh Jackson, "Churchgoing in Nineteenth-Century New Zealand," *New Zealand Journal of History* 17 (1983): 43-59. There does not appear to be complete data on Australian churchgoing.

[10] This presumes that laity were more susceptible to popular, evangelical movements in the church while clergy were less so. Fascinatingly, All Saints' Anglican Church on one hand, whose rector Arthur H. Baldwin (nephew of Robert Baldwin) is a clearly identifiable evangelical and known for his public-speaking abilities, had an attendance of 800 in 1882, 1033 in 1888, and 1620 in 1896. Grace Church on the other hand, which had been founded as an evangelical parish for the poor in 1875 and had in 1884 undergone a shift to a higher church liturgy and with it the forcing out of Howland and Blake, had dropped from an attendance of 996 in 1882 to 450 in 1888. Again, these data are entirely congruent with the thesis that the strength of a BEP discourse can be measured by church attendance, even in inclement weather. My estimate of 40% of Toronto Anglican churches as BEP is based on descriptions of individual churches in J. Ross Robertson, *Landmarks of Toronto,* Fourth Series.

hour of classroom time a week with voluntary teachers of different levels of teaching competence. But attendance at Sunday School was nonetheless one more indication of the BEP capacity to influence behavior and marshal clear types of response. The *Globe* writer even claimed that in Toronto the aggregate number of Sunday School students outnumbered that of the city Public Schools, 15,032 to 12,462.[11]

The Sunday School intersected with the lives of thousands of working class children who otherwise did not have contact with church life. The historian E.P. Thompson argued that the Sunday School was a form of "psychic exploitation" that helped to shape pupils in such a way that they developed the "work-discipline" needed for the British factory system.[12] And if the Sunday School could shape the industrial work force of the nation then it would certainly enforce other BEP behavioural norms.

While I do not have an extensive account of a Toronto Sunday School teacher working with children of the poor, there is such an account by city missionary, John G. Paton, working in Glasgow in the 1850s. This account sheds some light on what was undoubtedly taking place in Toronto. Paton, who later went on to become a foreign missionary hero of many a Toronto pupil, was expected, as part of his urban work, to spend four hours daily visiting house-to-house in a "very degraded" district. He began by visiting the homes whose occupants had not been in church in a decade or more. After one year of visits he had succeeded in persuading only a handful of young students to attend meetings. Slowly he attracted to an early Sunday morning class a group of mostly the "poorest young women" who would come in everyday clothes, "some without shoes". Paton then describes a fascinating process:

[11] *Globe*, September 2, 1882: 5. This statistic appears not to include private schools and neglects to mention that Sunday Schools counted scholars through age 18. The reporter does accurately quote the official public school statistics of 12,465 enrolled with average daily attendance of 8,215. See *Annual Report of the Inspector of the Public Schools of the City of Toronto for the Year Ending December 31, 1880* (Toronto: Patterson and Company, 1881), 1-11.

[12] Here Thompson is critiquing the Sunday School but also arguing that it was behaviourly formative. E.P. Thompson, "Time, Work-Discipline and Industrial Capitalism" in *Customs in Common*, E.P. Thompson (London: Penguin, 1991), 387-394. See also E.P. Thompson, *The Making of the English Working Class* (New York: Vintage, 1966), 375-378. Thompson goes as far as to speak of "psychological terrorism" in relation to the Sunday School.

> Beautiful was it to mark how the poorest began to improve in personal
> appearance immediately after they came to our class; how they gradu-
> ally got shoes and one bit of clothing after another, to enable them to
> attend our other meetings, and then to go to church.[13]

Paton found that the "humbler poor", usually mill-workers, who visited his
mission gradually improved their social position, then in an ongoing process,
moved to "more respectable and healthy localities", gradually distributing
themselves all over the city.[14]

Broadly similar patterns can in fact be seen in "The Ward" in 1880s
Toronto. An "ill-used" Irish woman, wife of a "hard-drinking" man,[15] worked
to provide for her young daughter. Gradually the daughter and then the
mother were incorporated into a mission Sunday School. The husband gave
up alcohol, more money was afforded for basic necessities, the family became
prominent in "The Ward", and eventually moved out to better environs.[16]

Though Marguerite Van Die has remained insistent that late Victorian
evangelicalism was a function of the middle classes,[17] there are an accumu-
lating number of studies from Canada and elsewhere that present evidence of

---

[13] John G. Paton, *John G. Paton: Missionary to the New Hebrides, An Autobiography*, Edited
by His Brother (London: Hodder and Stoughton, 1889), 59-60. I owe this reference to
Callum G. Brown, *Religion and Society in Scotland Since 1707* (Edinburgh: Edinburgh
University Press, 1997), 107.

[14] John G. Paton, *John G. Paton: Missionary to the New Hebrides*, 64.

[15] I have taken the wording and situation from Paton, p. 56.

[16] There does exist an account of such a city missionary to "The Ward" during the 1880s,
Jonathan Goforth, but it is a second-hand account written by his wife decades later. A farm
boy from Thorndale Ontario, Goforth, while studying at Knox College, visited prisoners at
the Don Jail each Sunday morning; his weekdays were regularly spent visiting the "slums" as
a city missionary, much like Paton. Excerpts from a letter from the Canadian author, Charles
R. Gordon (Ralph Connor) recount Goforth's sallies into The Ward. The letter appears to
have been written in the 1930s. See Rosalind Goforth, *Goforth of China* (Grand Rapids:
Zondervan, 1937), 32-35.

[17] See especially Marguerite Van Die, ""The Marks of a Genuine Revival": Religion, Social
Change, Gender, and Community in Mid-Victorian Brantford, Ontario," *The Canadian
Historical Review* 79, no. 3 (September 1998): 524-563. Van Die heavily references Doris
O'Dell, "The Class Character of Church Participation in Late Nineteenth-Century Belleville"
(PhD diss., Queen's University, 1990).

solid working class involvement in the movement.[18] The overall percentage of the population attending churches in Toronto strongly suggests that there were large numbers of the working classes regularly in attendance. The 1891 Canada Census listed over 23,000 industrial jobs in the city with the bulk of these jobs of the skilled and labouring classifications. That nineteenth-century churches and Sunday Schools were middle-class enclaves is a statistical impossibility.[19]

Salvation Army activity resulted in heavy working class participation in BEP worship. Census Sunday in 1888 saw 10,000 attending Salvationist citadels for worship. While many who attended Army "barracks" were middle-class, it is apparent from mainstream commentary on the movement that large numbers of poor were being "rescued". The *Telegram* reporter writing on the 1888 census at the height of the Army's popularity attributes its low financial revenue to the fact it is "universally conceded that this body of religionists

---

[18] Studies that emphasize heavy working class participation in the BEP movement include Nancy Christie and Michael Gauvreau, *Christian Churches and Their Peoples, 1840-1965*, 77-80; Kenneth L. Draper, "A People's Religion: P.W. Philpott and the Hamilton Christian Workers' Church," *Social History* xxxvi, no. 71 (May 2003): 99-122; Edward Smith, "Working Class Anglicans: Religion and Identity in Victorian and Edwardian Hamilton, Ontario," *Social History* xxxvi, no. 71 (May 2003): 123-144; Nancy Christie, ""On the threshold of manhood": Working-Class Religion and Domesticity in Victorian Britain and Canada," *Social History* xxxvi, no. 71 (May 2003): 145-175. For strong working class evangelical involvement in England at mid-century see Murray Watts, *The Dissenters* 2, 558-564, 596-598. See also Callum Brown, *The Death of Christian Britain*, 156, 163. In line with recent British studies, John Stenhouse, writing on the BEP movement in Dunedin, demonstrates empirically that virtually all congregations were dominated by the working classes, particularly when it is kept in mind that the majority of attenders were women. John Stenhouse, "Christianity, Gender and the Working Class in Southern Dunedin", pp. 18-44.

[19] The Toronto city population in 1891 was 144,000. In the city there were 17,000 males over 16 years with industrial jobs and over 7,000 women with industrial jobs. There were 27,000 families in the city with an average size of 5.3 members. In addition there were many laboring class adults that did not have "industrial" jobs but rather were domestic servants for example. Given these numbers, a large majority of Toronto's population was working class and with over 40% attendance on a single Sunday, then it follows that the majority of BEP church attendance could not have been "middle-class", particularly when it is kept in mind that BEP attendance was disproportionately women and children.
See *Census of Canada, 1890-1891*, vol.1(Ottawa: Government of Canada, 1893), 174, 370; *Census of Canada, 1890-1891*, vol. III (Ottawa: Government of Canada, 1894), 384.

deals almost exclusively with the poorer classes of the city."[20] The sort of thing they found attractive is evident in the uniforms and parades of the Army and the enthusiastic choreographed display of BEP 'religion' evinced. A scathing description of the Army in Toronto is provided by C. Pelham Mulvany, *M.A., M.D.*, a one-time Anglican clergyman:

> Bang! whang! bang! goes the wretched band, the tawdry banners flaunt, the ignoble finery of a parody on military parade defiles through Queen Street. One feels inclined, as he sees those unintellectual faces, those lugubrious looking women, those hysterical girls, that congeries of possibly reclaimed hoodlum, harlot, and humbug, to quote poor Alexander Smith's too soon forgotten verses:
> "In the street the tide of being, how it surges, how it rolls! God! what base, ignoble faces! God! what bodies wanting souls."[21]

The movement's demotic face, and how it might be viewed, is nowhere more evident.[22]

Elements of the labour movement could also see BEP discourse and activity as tawdry. In the *Trip Hammer*, the employee journal of the Massey Manufacturing Company, the Army is chastised for its religious services that featured "hand clapping and the body swaying and the dancing" while its seeking to rehabilitate "several thousand abandoned women" would "pour out upon the unoffending a deluge of vice and crime" and little more.[23] The critique of the Salvation Army by the *Hammer* may have been driven by a perceived threat to working class culture that was centred in the tavern. But whatever its cause, it pointed to an influence that was growing and increasing.

The coming of the Salvation Army was the radical edge of BEP growth

---

[20] *Evening Telegram*, December 22, 1888: 6.

[21] C. Pelham Mulvany, *Toronto: Past and Present. A Handbook of the City* (Toronto: W.E. Caiger, 1884), 184. Also see the entry for Mulvany in *Dictionary of Canadian Biography*.

[22] C. Pelham Mulvany, *Toronto: Past and Present*, 147.

[23] *Trip Hammer* 1, no. 8 (September 1885): 107-108. See also *Trip Hammer* 1, no. 10 (November 1885): 132-133.

in general and was the vehicle of a powerful BEP discourse in the closing portion of the Victorian era. The often raw religious emotion of its worship practices, as criticized by the *Hammer*, that featured the banging of tambourines and drums, accompanied by the "swaying" of bodies and the clapping, gave it real appeal. Evangelical religion, whether in the Presbyterian hymnody of Mackenzie King or in the choruses that were accompanied by Salvation Army bands, had a powerful attraction for the Toronto evangelical believer who represented a wide range of occupational classes.[24] There was also strong BEP reach outside strict institutionalized religion. Praying at home, and singing hymns at home were important.[25]

Certainly the early Methodists were predominately poor yet by the late Canadian Victorian period, according to Van Die, Canadian Methodists were predominately "middle class".[26] At minimum, considerable uncertainty remains in this claim. Given the conclusions of Thompson with regard to Methodism, one could draw lines between Methodism and a developing middle class assuming that it originated from at least, the skilled working class. Likewise, the phenomenon of the Salvation Army, a late Victorian off-shoot of Methodism that spanned the Empire, is relevant here as it was very much a working class movement. While Thompson is writing in a British context, the British religious census data, as shown previously, is congruent with that of the Ontario population justifying the term, BEP. The Ontario population was overwhelmingly derived from the British Isles and reflected

---

[24] For an excellent discussion of the issues surrounding religious experience and historical interpretation, with an emphasis on women, see Phyllis Mack, *Heart Religion in the British Enlightenment: Gender and Emotion in Early Methodism* (Cambridge University Press, 2008).

[25] Hugh McLeod, *Religion and the Working Class in Nineteenth-Century Britain*, (London: Macmillan, 1984), 14, 22-23. In addition, Bible-reading was pervasive in large swaths of British Victorian society from Methodists to Anglican to Unitarians and even to agnostics and atheists. See Timothy Larsen, *A People of One Book: The Bible and the Victorians* (Oxford: Oxford University Press, 2011). See also E.P. Thompson, *The Making of the English Working Class*, 332-415.

[26] Marguerite Van Die, "The Marks of a Genuine Revival": 524-563. But note that Methodists were considerably underrepresented in Parliament in Ottawa.
See Richard Allen, *The View from Murney Tower: Salem Bland, the Late Victorian Controversies, and the Search for a New Christianity*, Book One, *Salem Bland: A Canadian Odyssey* (Toronto: University of Toronto Press, 2008), 275.

the demographics of Britain.

If the poor and members of the working class were attracted to the BEP community, so also were certain ethnic minorities. In the 1901 Canadian Families Project 5% census sample, 10 men of Chinese ancestry were listed in Toronto. Of these, 7 are listed as Methodist, 1 as Presbyterian, 1 as Christian, and 1 has a blank space in the religion column. All are identified as being able to read and write. This is highly significant in that 80% are linked identified with denominations that were strongly BEP.[27] This demonstrates the intensity with which BEP ideology was diffused. The fact also points to the even greater force BEP ideology would be likely to have on native English speakers and inhabitants with British roots.

5.2 BEP Take-Up and a Hypothetical Mechanism for Constraining Violence

It is at this point that the thesis of this study concerning a decline in interpersonal violence connects with the argument that the various discourses of British Protestant evangelicalism shaped churchgoing habits and value orientation. At the heart of BEP ethics was a rejection of violence that had earlier in the century been associated with slavery, duelling, cock-fighting, and prize-fighting. The association of males and drinking was in BEP teaching connected with violence and crimes of all types and especially with wife-beating and was to be utterly condemned. The effect this teaching had on actual behavior was, this thesis argues, dramatic in the extreme.

By 1880, the BEP movement had grown at the grassroots to such an extent that it had developed a non-centralized but strong infrastructure and, had become a dominant social force in the city. This highly visible infrastructure can be measured in rates of growth, whether in numbers of buildings or attendees, of the Methodist and Baptist expressions of religious belief as well as in the evangelical wings of the Presbyterian and Anglican denominations. By 1890, Toronto church and associational budgets exceeded $1 million, at a

---

[27] See the SPSS 1901 database at the Canadian Families Project: web.uvic.ca/hrd/cfp/ Given the 5% sample, one can estimate that there were 100 Chinese residents of Toronto in 1901. An 1882 *Globe* article estimated that there were 21 males living in the city and that 16 of them were taking English classes at the YMCA. *Globe*, October 23, 1882: 8.

time when the budget for the Province of Ontario was less than, $4 million.[28] Furthermore, considerable BEP political capital had been amassed. Both the federal and provincial Liberal Party were controlled by BEP political leaders, and the Toronto mayoralty was in BEP hands for much of the period from 1880 to 1900. In summary, Toronto's evangelicals possessed the machine and personnel needed to significantly shape Toronto's cultural norms by the later nineteenth century.

An important part of the mechanism for constraining aberrant male behaviour is described by J.M. Cameron, longtime minister of East Toronto Presbyterian Church. In a column entitled "Church and Poor", outlining the various responses of city churches located in "poorer districts", Cameron was interviewed and asked by a *Globe* reporter whether the lack of "proper clothing" kept people from coming to church. Cameron responded that he thought not but nonetheless opined that "as soon as you get them to come to church regularly quite a change for the better is evident in their personal appearance." When asked to account for this change he responded:

> Well, when they originally leave off going to church they almost invariably fall into bad habits and spend their earnings in drink, etc.: and when they begin to go to church regularly again, they give up these bad habits and get into better ways again. If they are properly noticed in the church and get into work, they rapidly regain their self-respect and feel that their manhood is not lost.

The reporter recounted how Cameron had begun the church as a mission without a single member in a predominately poor area of the city. Cameron, much like Paton in Glasgow, was able to build the church up through house-to-house visitation of poor people. He found that "one or two visits would not avail much, but that continuing visits were usually successful." Concerning the church's work in providing material relief to the poor he mentions "the

---

[28] For 1891, total expenditures by the Province of Ontario were $3.9 million. See Ontario Legislative Assembly, *Ontario Sessional Papers* xxiii—part v (Toronto: Queen's Printer, 1891), 301. See APPENDIX B for the financial details of Toronto churches during the period.

ladies who worked with me" suggesting, when this text is read across the grain, that a considerable part of the visiting was done by women.[29]

Again and again, there is evidence of the influence of women at the heart of the BEP discourse of anti-violence. Over the course of the century, women had gained a considerable "space" within public life in an expanding industrial Toronto.[30] Especially within the temperance movement and its associated voluntary organizations, women had enormous, still under-studied, influence.[31] Leonard Tilley,[32] speaking at the International Temperance Convention in Saratoga, New York, recalled how the words of his mother "had a great power with him". It was in "the influence of the gentler sex upon the rising generation" that "we may hope on and hope ever, resolving to battle

[29] *Globe*, November 12, 1888: 8. Also see the biographical sketch of Cameron in G. Mercer Adam, *Toronto, Old and New: A Memorial Volume* (Toronto: The Mail Printing Company, 1891), 87-88. Cameron, a one-time Royal Engineer, was active with Howland in temperance work, and turned down an offer of the nomination to run for a Liberal seat in Ottawa. In preliminary work with the 1901 Canada census, one sees on the occupations of officers in Cameron's church that several of the officers were working class or low paid clerical workers. For example, James J. Cowan, an elder in the church in 1896, was a teamster making $500 per year in 1901 and in 1911 had become a grocer with annual earnings of $1000. Interestingly he had become a Baptist by 1911. For the list of officers see J. Ross Robertson, *Landmarks of Toronto,* Fourth Series, 294-299.

[30] This is of course not to say that women did not possess a "space" in earlier periods. However in an industrializing city such as Toronto, women's gaining the vote as well as leadership positions in visible and formal associations were novel.

[31] Certainly the historiography on women during this time period is abundant. However there is a lack of personal writing by women working "on the ground" in the Toronto BEP churches and associations for the period under study. There appears to be no equivalent source that comes near to matching the richness of the Mackenzie King diaries. Mariana Valverde, *The Age of Light, Soap, and Water* relies heavily upon newspaper and journal articles, reports, retrospective biographies and secondary sources as does Jan Noel in *Canada Dry.* The Salvation Army *War Cry* does contain short, contemporary autobiographical articles. The diaries of Elizabeth Smith do show significant BEP take-up in the life of a young teacher and medical student. However Smith was not an activist at this point and her life had not intersected with Toronto. Elizabeth Smith, '*A Woman with a Purpose': The Diaries of Elizabeth Smith, 1872-1884* ed. Veronica Strong-Boag (Toronto: University of Toronto Press, 1980). See also Marguerite Van Die, *Religion, Family, and Community in Victorian Canada: The Colbys of Carrollcroft* (Montreal and Kingston: McGill-Queens's University Press, 2005).

[32] Tilley's and Howland's wives were sisters. Both were leaders in the Dominion Alliance. See Gregory S. Kealey, *Toronto Workers Respond to Industrial Capitalism*, 15-18.

to the end." While the rhetoric may seem heavy and sentimental, it reflects a profound religious and social revolution whose impact is reflected in the words of Tilley's speech and in the details of year-end reports of dozens of BEP voluntary societies in late Victorian Toronto.

Central to these concerns of women was the reality of the household situation on an industrial frontier. Large numbers of males shared similar religious concerns but it was women who provided the bulk of the personnel that allowed the BEP "machine" to function and to spread the rhetoric and values of the BEP moral code.

5.3 The Shaping of Male Behaviour: Introduction

Following Robert Muchembled, male aggression is a biological reality but it is also shaped by culture; this variable factor can be described as plasticity. Since the early modern period, European norms increasingly blunted a violence based on honour codes that included the usual male-on-male violence as well as a less physical violence directed at women in the context of hierarchical relations. Over time homicide became taboo and Western culture became obsessively controlling with respect to an interpersonal violence that previously had been commonplace. The behaviour management of young males was key. The Northern Protestant "factory" proved most adept at morally shaping young males of marriageable age. These young males had previously been often even encouraged in violent ways. When disciplined with strong moral codes they adapted with a high degree of plasticity such that not only did homicide largely disappear, but also robbery and sexual assault dramatically declined.[33]

In the British context the control of young males involved a "moral package". The Protestant ascetic ethic, which had been absorbed in the BEP movement, increasingly included honesty, thrift, and regular participation in church life, temperance with respect to alcohol, the eschewal of "rough" activity, and the confinement of sexual activity to marriage. In response to this moral regime in settings that were still highly communal, British rates of

---

[33] Muchembled, *History of Violence*, 40

interpersonal violence plummeted over the course of the nineteenth century and continued at low levels well into the twentieth century. My initial work on the frequency of violence in late Victorian Toronto, as indicated by homicide rates, confirms that this decline was duplicated in Toronto.[34] While a moral and religious revolution may not be enough to entirely explain this new and peaceful phenomenon, it becomes a factor needing consideration in the setting of the Victorian city with its web of associations and daily newspapers.[35]

5.3.1 The Diary of a Young BEP Activist: Ideology and Behaviour

In the fall of 1891 an enthusiastic young man of 16 years from Berlin, Ontario arrived in Toronto to study at University College. Immediately gaining the nickname "Rex", he threw himself into a frenzy of activities. The pranks he engaged in would hardly have granted him pious credentials but beneath the exterior, there was a conventional Presbyterianism infused with an evangelical seriousness. William Lyon Mackenzie King is an important BEP indicator of the ways in which BEP ideology acted in the thinking of at least some young people in the Toronto area. Being young and possessing remarkable talents, he is a protean subject with the energy, intellectual capacity, and people skills to encounter a range of urban experiences. He also displays the discipline to record his interpretation of them at the end of the day. The diary demonstrates some of the dynamics of the BEP movement in Toronto, how BEP discourse might shape a young man's thought, and how this thought might be converted into action within a variety of BEP associational and communication networks. Over time, King's beliefs meshed with inner piety and outward expression. There is no other comparable source relating to these

---

[34] See William D. Reimer, *A Depressing Story? Homicide Rates In Late Victorian Toronto* (master's thesis, University of British Columbia, 2006). Note that in my database, a homicide-suicide for January 4, 1890 did not take place in Toronto and was listed in error. Another case of manslaughter involving an assault that took place near Gravenhurst, Ontario resulted in the death of John Scott in the Toronto General Hospital. I have not counted this event as a Toronto homicide in the above calculations although it remains in my database. See APPENDIX A below for my revised database.

[35] On the importance of towns and cities, in combination with religion and morality, in the control of violence see Robert Muchembled, *History of Violence*, 223-225.

matters for the Toronto of this time period. Furthermore, the strict keeping of a diary highlights a Weberian emphasis that both created and bequeathed an important document.[36]

We are privy to this inner BEP world of a young man because of the penchant for self-examination BEP ideology encouraged. With the start of his third year of university, King began a daily diary in which he made entries for almost 60 years that amounted to 50,000 pages. In the first sentence the author states that the diary should be a "<u>true and faithful account</u>". He would be "ashamed to even one day have nothing worthy of its showing" and that the diary would demonstrate "how the author sought to <u>improve his time</u>."[37]

In the fall of 1893 King's evangelical faith seemed to intensify. On October 15 he wrote, "My present thoughts suggest that there is no life like a christian's. I am going to ask to know more of Christ and try to live a better Life. For soon we find that the world is false, Christ is always true. 'Things are not what they seem.'" King's inner piety sent him to church two times a Sunday and then out into the world of BEP activism, often on several days and nights a week.

"Thoughts of entering the ministry" were frequently present in King's mind as he became immersed in BEP associational activity in the fall of 1893. Each Sunday morning saw King visiting the Victoria Sick Children's Hospital and leading a "service" before church. These visits continued over the course of his entire time in Toronto.[38]

Ever present in the midst of his activities was a deep consciousness of his own sin. His inner sense of self fluctuated between religious euphoria and feelings of religious inadequacy. On Christmas Sunday, 1893, King visited Sick Kids' where he led a service for a ward of "22 girls". After, in his room and with a "bad cold", he sang hymns, wrote a long letter to one of his "girls", and then had time to return to the hospital for more visits before retiring. Back at the residence he entered in his diary, "I cried a little to myself tonight. This is

---

[36] Again, Weber emphasized the Calvinist habit of keeping a personal diary. Max Weber, *The Protestant Ethic and the Spirit of Capitalism*, 76-77.

[37] *Diaries of William Lyon Mackenzie King*, September 6, 1893.

[38] For example King makes frequent reference to Irene Shields, listed in the 1891 census as 13 years of age and living with two older siblings, and visits her later in the Asylum where

the first Sunday I have missed church for a long time. May next Xmas eve find me a true and better child of God."[39]

The next Sunday, New Year's Eve, in what was to be his pattern, King looked back over the year. As the bells rang in the New Year he ended with the last words of the hymn, "Thy way not mine oh Lord." He recounted a year that was "black with sins" but also had "many bright and happy hours" and he had been brought "closer to Christ". Although he had also won the coveted Blake Scholarship it was a description of his Christian growth that he closed his diary with:

> "The end of the year to me has been better than the beginning." I have decided I may say <sic> to become a Minister of the Gospel of Christ. I have been the means of drawing some souls nearer to Christ and have received a letter from a little girl [see above footnote] worth more to me than any I possess. I feel that I am Christ's forever. May these things always be.[40]

In the following hour King composed a hymn that reflected the inward experience that drove his outward activism:

> "One sweetly solemn thought
> Comes to us o'er and o'er
> I am nearer home today-today
> Than I've ever been before"

> "Nearer my Father's House
> Where the many mansions be
> Nearer the Great white throne
> Nearer the crystal sea"

---

she was being treated for morphine use. See multiple entries including November 9, 1893; April 15, 1894; October 3, 1894.

[39] Sunday, December 24, 1893. The quotation marks here are present in the typed diary.

[40] Sunday, December 31, 1893.

"Nearer the bounds of Life
Where we lay our burdens down
Nearer leaving the cross
Nearer gaining a crown"

"Father be near me when my feet
Are slipping o'er the brink
For may be I am nearer Home
Nearer today than perhaps I think"

W.L.M.K.
Jan. 1ˢᵗ 1894, about 1 A.M.[41]

Saturated in sentiment, BEP hymnody can easily be dismissed as the product of an insulated existence. However, in the case of nineteenth-century BEP activists, exposure to death was a constant. Certainly the sight of death at Sick Kid's was frequent for King.

Turning down a scholarship to study at the University of Chicago, King decided instead to stay in Toronto to article in his father's law practice. At the same time he became a newspaper reporter, briefly with the *News*, and then with the *Globe* where he was employed for ten months. Assigned to the Police Court by the *Globe*, King also reported on a range of topics including sermons, the activities of BEP charitable associations, and municipal politics. By checking between his diary and the newspaper it is possible to identify many of his reports in the *Globe*. While I did not seek to systematically track all of his articles, a sampling allows one to see how a *Globe* writer could inject BEP ideology into newspaper copy making the newspaper—already an instrument of propagation for BEP ideology—even more of an influence in that field.[42]

King's decision to spend time reporting was deliberate; it would, he thought, be preparatory for his now anticipated, religiously-motivated, career

---

[41] Sunday, December 31, 1893.

[42] It appears that much of his court reporting appeared in the evening edition of the *Globe* (the on-line and microfilm versions are the morning edition) and this was no doubt driven by the need for same-day coverage as dailies became more numerous and competitive.

in social welfare work. Though his first day in Police Court, led him to remark that "there was a very long list [of cases] this morning and the air was frightful. I was thoroughly disgusted when I got through,"[43] the next day saw him view matters in a quite different way:

> I will find this a good plan to see the shadowy side of life, looking at everything from an economic standpoint. I will derive great benefit for my after work. I fully intend to make academic work my profession and am taking Journalism as an extra year of practical experience in the great school of life.[44]

King was observing suffering firsthand, and his diary entries allow the interpreter to see his immediate reactions. Following the practice of reporters visiting victims in their homes in the immediate aftermath of tragedy, King visited the home of a mother who had reportedly smothered her child. While he agreed with the inquest conclusion that the death was accidental, he did not mention that the woman had been drinking because she seemed "respectable" and had promised to refrain from alcohol in the future. Faith in moral worthiness of an individual trumped any desire to make a scandal of the woman's negligence.[45]

Later in November on Thanksgiving weekend, King manifested another kind of moral concern; he must, he wrote, save money[46] and "not let it fall through my hands."

> I must become a better christian I am not at all satisfied with the hypocritical life I am leading before I begin to pray for others I must be sure that my petitions for myself are heard,—that I have a right to intercede

---

[43] November 4, 1895.

[44] November 5, 1885. Note that in entries in both 1893 and 1894, King had expressed the desire to enter the "ministry". See above. His vocational goals were in flux and changing.

[45] October 28, 1885.

[46] Here is a classic Weberian emphasis on thrift and the need for the individual to save money.

with so merciful a Father.[47]

His BEP consciousness of personal sin constantly threw up questions about his inner life and propelled him on a new set of strivings while at the same time checking his behaviour.

On the occasion of the visit of Edward Booth, Commandant of the Salvation Army in Canada and son of founders William and Catherine Booth, King wrote a 1,400 word article on the Army in Toronto. Along with a group of "leading citizens", King accompanied the Booth entourage, visiting Army facilities including a home for "fallen" women, shelters for men and women, and a children's home. In keeping with BEP discourse, King made reference to the metrics of the Army efforts: the women's shelter had housed a total of 2,500 women, over the course of a year for a night, while the men's facility had "slept" 24,500 with 42,000 meals served. At the children's home, when the command was given to "Fire a volley", the group of visitors was startled by a "chorus" of "Amens" from the home's young residents. King concluded that:

> Those who had the good fortune to take a look yesterday into the work done by the Salvation Army in this city will never forget the revelation of practical Christianity which was afforded them, nor will they be less likely to remember the perfect system of organization and discipline which exhibited itself at every turn; perhaps, too, they will not be unmindful of the many evidences of the power of Christian love in the rebuilding and purifying the shattered lives and bodies of the so-called "under strata of society."[48]

The Army was consistent with King's BEP sensibilities emphasizing a practical, disciplined Christianity that sought to incorporate the poor and the "fallen" into the larger community. It also shows BEP machinery at work and

---

[47] November 24, 1885.
[48] *Globe*, June 5, 1896: 4.

operating strongly enough to accomplish substantial tasks.

King was visibly impressed by the example of the Army:

> Felt much inspired after day's outing. On coming home I was talking
> to myself and demonstrating with my left hand. I was not conscious of
> it until a young lady at a street corner called out "Keep at it old fellow".
> Then I laughed at myself. I felt a better man after my trip with these
> people & was greatly impressed by their work.[49]

Still inspired, King made a return visit to Salvation Army headquarters. After conversing with an officer, he again left "much impressed".[50] On the 11th he took in an Army event when he went to hear Mrs. Booth speak.[51] Three nights later he attended a Sunday evening service at Cooke's Presbyterian on Queen Street, and while listening to the service, decided to withdraw an application for a fellowship at the university and to move to Chicago.

> While listening to [Mr. Winchester] I made up my mind to withdraw
> my appl'n. from Toronto & to go to Chicago & here my heart will be
> drawn, nearer to God & the poor. After going to Globe I came home
> wrote letter to registrar mailed it & then wrote out some of my reasons.
> The chief was a voice which kept telling me so to act,—I believe the
> voice of God, who has his work for me to do.[52]

In hearing this "call" King conformed to a standard BEP paradigm. Others by the thousands went into "dark" urban places of Toronto in practical works of service and evangelism. There is an intense BEP drive that, very much part of the BEP "package", goes far beyond mere "constraints" and "protocols". Its influence on King was clear:

[49] June 4, 1896.
[50] June 5, 1896.
[51] June 11, 1896.
[52] June 14, 1896.

I believe that in Chicago my love for the masses will deepen, I will be thrown more on myself, character will develop more, my real hidden nature will reveal itself better, I can get out of old ruts & break off from old & indifferent habits & become more zealous. I believe I can be drawn closer to God there. Away from home my thoughts will turn more constantly to Him who watches over those we love, alone in the world to some extent, I will seek the more for Him who is a friend to all men. Having only myself to look into to see what I really am, I will be led to reflect more, to think more & to act more.

O my God that knoweth all things, grant that I am reasoning aright, grant that my thoughts are but a vision of a great reality, grant that my prayers be heard & my desires known where good accomplished.[53]

Here were displayed a deep inner scrutinizing and a yearning for personal piety that fitted with the BEP emphasis on the unity of all humanity. Again, as was his pattern, King made his recent encounter with the Salvation Army combine with his ongoing BEP values to provide the impetus for his moving to Chicago, to Hull House and the University of Chicago, and then on to Harvard.

The King diary is a remarkable window into the mind of a young BEP male. It shows a young male adopting, and acting in terms of, BEP ideology. It also shows others such as Lizzie Harvie, doing the same. Its value is immense. It provides a deep account of the shaping of a young BEP male mind with numerous entries that touch on humanitarian and non-violent impulses.

[53] June 14, 1896.

6

THE TAKE-UP OF BEP IDEAS: BEP REACTION TO ACCOUNTS OF VIOLENCE IN LATE VICTORIAN TORONTO

By 1880 a near universal literacy had taken hold in Toronto in line with BEP literacy regimes, as outlined previously, and following Weberian pathways that had seen mass literacy first in Prussia, Netherlands, and Great Britain.[1] Multiple daily Toronto newspapers circulated discourse on violent events taking place both locally and abroad. Reporting displayed evidence of BEP ideas but in turn reinforced BEP moral outlooks and played an important role in the ongoing decline of interpersonal violence in Toronto. This hypothesis follows Steven Pinker in his argument that literacy is the most likely candidate in the "exogenous change" that was critical for the inflation of the "empathy circle."[2]

Overview

Chapter Six, Part 1 presents a selection of homicide cases from Ontario during the last two decades of the nineteenth century. Condemned prisoners were embraced by the BEP community, confession and repentance were elicited, and clemency appeals were made on their behalf. An increased aversion to capital punishment was set within an ongoing, BEP-inspired, trajectory of prison reform. There was a concern with rehabilitation rather than simply punishment.

---

[1] See for example David Vincent, *The Rise of Mass Literacy*, 8-26.

[2] Pinker is of course referring to the ongoing and broader spread of literacy over centuries in Western contexts. Steven Pinker, *Better Angels of Our Nature*, 174-177. Here again, I do not see a sharp disjuncture between BEP values and humanitarian values. In BEP Toronto the only group with the personnel to spread humanitarian values was the BEP movement.

Chapter Six, Part 2 uses daily newspaper reports to demonstrate the measure in which Canadian behavior was contrasted with images of American violence, lynching, persistence of slavery in various parts of the world, cruel punishments, and violence against minorities, particularly in the form of pogroms. Existing Canadian dispositions towards relatively non-violent behavior were reinforced.

6.1.1 Fratricide On Bathurst Street

On a March night in 1896 Brothers John (Jack) and Frank Finlay found themselves walking home along Queen Street West. They had already stopped for drinks at the McHenery Hotel, and after crossing Spadina Avenue they entered Cameron House for more.[3] Having spent the evening drilling at the Armoury as a member of the Governor General's Body Guard, 28-year-old Jack was decked out in military uniform with sword and scabbard at his side.[4] Though married, with an eight-year-old daughter, he was separated from his wife Maggie as the result of a court protective order, probably the result of more than one appearance before Toronto Police Magistrate Colonel George Taylor Denison and a conviction as a "wife-beater".[5] He was currently residing above a livery stable on Strachan Avenue where he was employed.[6]

The 26-year-old brother, Frank, on good terms with Jack, had attended the drill as a spectator. A husband, father and jeweller by trade, he was currently working as a coachman for a wealthy woman because of "the slackness of [his regular] work".[7] The two left Cameron House at about 11 p.m. and headed

---

[3] *World*, March 28, 1896: 2.

[4] *World*, March 26, 1896: 3.

[5] *Daily Mail & Empire*, March 26, 1896: 6; *World*, March 26, 1896: 3. The *Globe* reported that Jack's wife had procured an "order of protection or separation" from "the Magistrate" in the context of an additional mention of appearing before "Magistrate Denison". *Daily Mail and Empire*, March 26, 1881: 6. The handwritten court reports on the Finlay case are microfilms and are virtually illegible. One could also consult Toronto Archives to check the criminal roster for the time for possible additional information.

[6] *Daily Mail & Empire*, March 26, 1896: 6.

[7] *World*, March 26, 1896: 3.

up Bathurst Street.[8]

Fuelled by alcohol,[9] their conversation became increasingly animated. One of them was heard to shout, "Shut up and give somebody else a show."[10] Possibly because of something that Jack said to him about his (Jack's) wife,[11] Frank began punching Jack in the face. Jack pulled his sword out of its scabbard and began waving it at Frank. At some point a younger brother, Armand, joined the two. Yelling to some gathering onlookers and hoping to have assistance in breaking up the altercation, he called out, "Is there no gentlemen in the crowd?" No one responded.[12]

Somehow, Armand was able to wrestle the sword away from Jack. As the scuffle continued, Jack cried, "Stop and I'll let go." He then struck Frank on the right ear several times. Frank fell to the sidewalk with a cry and slipped into unconsciousness. Armand rushed to Frank's side and "remarked", "You have killed my brother."[13]

A Police Constable came on the scene and assisted the two brothers in carrying Frank to his home while someone ran to get a neighbourhood doctor. Upon arriving at Frank's domicile on nearby Robinson Street, the doctor examined the victim and pronounced the injury "not serious". Frank's wife and Jack together sat up the night with him. The doctor—Dr. Watson by name— returned the next morning, saw that bloody liquid was oozing from the ear, and promptly had Frank admitted to the Toronto General Hospital. Despite the best efforts of the doctors, he died in the early afternoon without having ever fully regained consciousness.[14]

---

[8] This was the neighbourhood where the family members resided in at least four households. The various addresses are listed in the above reports. In the Canada Census for 1891 and 1901 the members of the family are all listed as Methodists except for the mother (deceased sometime prior to the killing) who was Baptist.

[9] *World*, March 28, 1896: 2; *Daily Mail & Empire*, March 26, 1896: 6.

[10] *World*, March 26, 1896: 3.

[11] The *Globe* reported that it was "probable" that the discussion centred on Jack's separation from his wife. *Globe* March 26, 1881: 2.

[12] *Globe*, April 1, 1896: 2.

[13] *Daily Mail & Empire*, March 26, 1896: 6

[14] *Globe*, April 1, 1896: 2.

Next day, March 27, Jack attended the inquest at Police Station 3, accompanied by his father, Samuel, a 53-year-old Scottish iron moulder. Jack, who had a blackened eye and cuts to the nose, "wept bitterly."[15] The medical examination found that Frank had suffered a skull fracture, possibly because of his "exceedingly thin skull".[16] It also noted that the lethal "stroke was not delivered with felonious intent."

Appearing before Magistrate George Denison on April 1, Jack was nonetheless charged with murder and remanded for one week. Both father and son were deeply "affected".[17] On April 8th Jack was committed for trial at the Assizes, though Denison stated that he personally felt that that the charge should not be stronger than one of manslaughter.

On April 27 the Spring Assizes opened with J.K. Kerr leading on behalf of the Crown. Kerr, a board member of several BEP voluntary associations, was also churchwarden at St. James's Cathedral and the brother-in-law of Samuel and Edward Blake. The *Globe* reported on the case as follows:

In the case of the Queen v John Finlay for manslaughter "no bill"[18] was returned. This is the case in which two brothers, John & Frank Finlay, quarrelled on their way home from drill, the quarrel resulting in Frank Finlay's death from a blow from his brother's scabbard. John showed himself terribly distressed over the consequences of his blow, and a medical examination showed the skull to have been abnormally thin.[19]

The Frank Finlay homicide is illustrative at multiple levels for the purposes of this study. First, it is an example of frequently occurring male-on-male interpersonal violence. Across time and cultures homicide is an act committed

[15] *Globe*, April 1, 1896: 2; *World*, April, 1: 4.

[16] *Globe*, April 9, 1896: 12; March 28, 1896: 28.

[17] Mother Elizabeth had in recent years passed away.

[18] This indicates that there was no indictment. An indictment would be termed a "true bill".

[19] *Globe*, April 29, 1896: 10. The above narrative was pieced together from the following reports: *Globe*, March 26, 1896: 2; March 27: 10; March 28: 28; April 1: 2; April 9: 12; April 28:10; April 29: 10; *World*, March 26, 1896: 3; March 28: 2; April 1: 4; *Daily Mail & Empire*, March 26, 1896: 6; April 2: 6. Also see Canada Census 1891, 1901, 1911.

overwhelmingly by males. Various twentieth-century studies have found that when comparing male-male to female-female homicide across a variety of cultures from Asia to Africa to the Americas, the male proportion, with one exception, varied from 91.6% to 100%.[20] Examination of homicides committed by men involving non-relatives show the average holding steady at 95% across the Western world for 450 years, even as women were becoming increasingly involved in the social conditions producing it.[21]

In the case of Toronto, during the years 1880-1899, there were 45 homicides recorded where the assailant can be identified. Of these, 41 (91.1%) were committed by males. Of the 41 victims killed by males, 31 were themselves male. Only one female was killed by another female.[22]

The second reason that the Finlay homicide is important for this study is the alcohol factor. The evidence presented at the inquest by PC Newton was that "the deceased smelled strongly of liquor."[23] This increased its significance for BEP-observers.

The third factor giving the case importance is its relationship to BEP communal norms. Detailed reference in newspaper reports to the two brothers' family circumstances, conditions of living, and values constitutes an implied commentary on the good and the bad in peoples' lives. One account has Jack "weeping bitterly" at the inquest while another states that he was accompanied by his father, Samuel, and that both were "much affected." It was reported

---

[20] M. Daly and M. Wilson, *Homicide* (New York: Aldine de Gruyter, 1988), 146-148. The one outlier was Denmark with a proportion of 85.3% male. The total number of studies was 35.

[21] Randolph Roth, *American Homicide* (Cambridge, MA: Harvard University Press, 2009), 16.

[22] When one examines same-sex only homicides the male proportion of this type is thus 97%. (The calculation here is 31 divided by 32 equals 97%.) I have excluded cases of infanticide and cases of homicide involving the death of a woman while undergoing an abortion. See APPENDIX A for a listing of Toronto homicides that I have identified using newspapers and official sources. The 97% male same-sex proportion is very close to the 94.4% in the Canadian study cited by Daly and Wilson covering the years 1974-1983 that examined 3,140 homicides. See Daly and Wilson, *Homicide*, 147. Over time, male behaviour had been increasingly the focus of the justice system as courts sought to redefine masculinity. In Britain from the late nineteenth to the early twentieth-century the percentage of women tried at Old Bailey fell from 45% to 12%. Clive Emsley, *Crime and Society in England, 1750-1900*, 2nd ed. (London: Longman, 1996), 152.

[23] *World*, March 28, 1896: 2.

that "John showed himself terribly distressed" at the Assizes. Extenuating circumstances were stressed. A BEP Crown attorney was involved. Jack in the end was released with the tacit approval of a representative sample of a religious culture; no public outcry of injustice ensued.[24]

The fourth element has to do with the role of medical treatment. Frank might have survived with modern care.[25] Eric Monkkonen has argued that 50% of homicide victims at the middle of the nineteenth century might have survived if turn of the twenty-first century medicine had been present; Eisner concurs with this judgment.[26] This is an important question within the literature on the history of violence, and I will return to it later in the chapter.

Lastly, the killing of Frank Finlay is an event of a kind that was becoming relatively rare in late Victorian Toronto, something that itself relates directly to the increasing influence of BEP ideas: two Methodist males involving themselves in a drunken brawl is, statistically, a not very common event in the Toronto of this time period.[27]

6.1.2 BEP Penal Reform

The shooting death of Edward De Coursier by his brother, Robert,[28] in

---

[24] One can contrast John Finlay with George Bennett, the unemployed former *Globe* employee who under the influence of alcohol, brandished a revolver, scuffled with George Brown and in the process delivered a flesh wound that caused death by an infection a month later. The Roman Catholic Bennett, reputed to be living with a woman that he had not married, was one of only three men to be hung in the Don Jail during the period under study. Obviously the person that Bennett shot mattered deeply and one could also postulate that one's "moral standing" did not assist him in gaining clemency.

[25] See for example Anthony R. Harris, Stephen H. Thomas, Gene A. Fischer, and David J. Hirsch, "Murder and Medicine: The Lethality of Criminal Assault, 1960-1999," *Homicide Studies* 6, no. 2 (May 2002): 126-166.

[26] Eric Monkkenon, "New Standards for Historical Homicide Research," *Crime, Histoire et Societe—Crime, History and Society* 5, no. 2 (2001): 7-26; Manuel Eisner, "What Causes Large-scale Variation in Homicide Rates?" (working paper, July 2012): 1-25. www.crim.cam. ac.uk/people/academic_research/manuel_eisner/large_scale-variation.pdf, accessed May 22, 2013. This paper has been published in Hans-Henning Kortum and Jurgen Heinze, eds. *Aggression in Humans and Other Primates* (Berlin: De Gruyter, 2012).

[27] In APPENDIX A I have detailed records of homicide for the period 1880-1899 for Toronto from 1880-1899.

[28] Coincidentally, Robert was a member of the Governor General's Body Guard as was John Finlay.

BEP REACTION TO ACCOUNTS OF VIOLENCE

September 1879, produced an entirely different outcome from that yielded by the Frank Finlay fratricide; it nonetheless also shows the presence and influence of BEP ideas. Firstly, the language used to report the crime, trial, and interval leading up to the date of execution is laced with religious rhetoric. Secondly, reactions of various participants in the case illustrate the religious constraints that a broadly BEP culture attempted to place on individuals. Finally, the posture of the jury and the various efforts made to obtain clemency for De Coursier are suggestive of BEP-inspired resistance to capital punishment and the rejection of violence in general.

The setting of the De Coursier crime was the main street of the "pretty little village" of Lambton Mills. Located on the eastern bank of the Humber River, six miles west of Toronto, the village derived its name from the mills owned by the William P. Howland family. Early one morning, Robert waited three hours outside his brother's place of work with shotgun in hand and ammunition pouch slung over his shoulder. Guns were nothing unusual for the locale, and when asked if he was going to be shooting rooks, Robert responded that he was after "bigger game". Brother Edward finally appeared at noon, outside his main street place of employment in a wagon shop, and Robert rose to meet him. Firing the first barrel of his shotgun into the unsuspecting Edward, Robert then ran over to the prone, face-down body of his moaning brother, and, at close range, discharged the second barrel.

As Robert walked away from the scene he reached into his pouch, withdrew a container, and drank from its contents. Continuing on he went into his house, proceeded up the stairs, and, shortly after, was found frothing at the mouth as the result of ingesting hydrocyanic acid. A doctor was summoned by one of the several men who had followed him to his house, and he was revived.[29]

A new, well-oiled, and loaded revolver was discovered in Robert's pocket along with a "dirty" bag full of thirty-five cartridges. News reports gave details of the guns and ammunition, but nothing unusual was noted with respect

---

[29] *Mail*, September 27, 1879:6; September 29, 1879; *Globe*, September 27, 1879:5; September 29, 1879.

to the fact that Robert was carrying a shotgun on the main street of town; it was assumed that he was "going out for a day's shooting." Nothing surprising was seen in Robert's possession of these arms. The only oddity noted was the fact that Robert tried to poison himself as opposed to using the revolver.[30]

At the trial the prosecution attempted to link Robert's carrying of firearms to premeditation; the defence mustered neighbours who testified that there was nothing unusual about Robert carrying a gun around town.[31] Guns, including revolvers and ammunition for them, were readily available in late nineteenth-century Ontario.

BEP sensitivities are present in several dimensions of the case. Initial reports—mistaken, as it turned out—disapprovingly identified the source of the shot Robert purchased as Mr. Ware, "a tavern-keeper". Subsequently a correction was made to the effect that Ware was not a "tavern-keeper".

In addition, Edward and Robert were initially described by the *Globe* as both "being the worse of liquor".[32] By contrast, their brother Henry was described in model BEP terms. He was "an orderly, respectable, religious young fellow" who eschewed "the unseemly quarrels his brothers engaged in". It was rumoured that "because of the dark shadow" that had clouded his life he now intended to leave the area so that he could "live down his family's disgrace."[33] BEP influence permeated the language of the initial reporting and the subsequent trial, whether in the Conservative *Mail* or the Liberal *Globe*. The ostensible reason behind the fratricide was initially given as that of a feud over the "pittance" of property that their father had left the brothers. However in the following days it became apparent that the conflict also involved the brothers' relationship to a "young woman", Mary Mills. At the trial she testified that Robert had first "kept company" with her and that she believed he would marry her. While Robert was away, Edward "seduced her"

---

[30] *Globe*, September 27, 1879: 5.

[31] It was reported that two weeks prior to the death, Robert had been away for a week's vacation of "gunning". *Mail*, September 29, 1879.

[32] *Globe*, September 27, 1879: 5.

[33] *Mail*, September 29, 1879. Henry is not found in the subsequent three censuses either as De Coursier or with the original family name of Coursey.

under a promise of eventual marriage.

When Mills became pregnant her father had threatened to sue Edward, prompting him to request that Robert collude with him to misstate his property holdings in an effort to avoid a costly settlement. In the witness stand Mary Mills, identified at the top of the article as 'The Inevitable "Woman"', disclosed that Edward had confided to her that he had seduced her out of "spite" as he knew Robert intended to marry her. Sin, questionable moral behavior, and violation of BEP norms, seemed plain.[34]

Perhaps because of the moral issues involved, the defence mounted an "unsound mind" defence on behalf of De Coursier. Because the father had committed suicide some years before by,—perhaps coincidentally, ingesting "prussic acid"— one Dr. Berryman was called to give expert testimony. Berryman had examined the prisoner on two occasions, on the first finding De Coursier's "pupils very much dilated, the scalp hot, and the pulse running up to 100." On a second occasion, there were found "other symptoms" leading to the conclusion that there was "irritation of the brain". Later examinations found De Coursier to be "insane". Referring to the "family history" of "a suicidal tendency", and even though admitting that De Coursier knew the "difference between right and wrong", the defence argued that his mind was diseased and did not allow him to "restrain his impulse to commit a wrong action." Witnesses, moreover, unanimously vouched for his "good character".[35]

The jury's members, after being reminded by the Crown that they had a responsibility to both "their God" and to the "fabric of society in which they lived", retired late in the afternoon and deliberated into the evening for three hours. When they reassembled, the foreman informed the judge that the jury could not reach a decision; furthermore there was "no prospect" of agreement. This proved, however, an exaggeration; after being asked to retire again they finally reached a verdict of guilty of murder with a "strong recommendation to mercy." When asked on what grounds this recommendation was made, the foreman replied that it was because of De Coursier's "previous

[34] Concerning the "seduction" see *Mail*, September 27, 1879: 6; *Globe*, April 28, 1890: 10.
[35] *Globe*, April 28, 1890: 10.

good character." The judge, Thomas Galt, refused the recommendation, put on his "black cap", and, visibly moved, sentenced De Coursier to death; no hope "whatever" was offered to the condemned.[36]

The newspaper reporting of the homicide and trial is steeped in religious language. While British law had always been inextricably linked to religion, the De Coursier case demonstrates the increasing sway of BEP rhetoric. The preliminary, though mistaken, association of alcohol with the two feuding brothers was part of this. The *Mail* wrote of, "The Hand of Cain".[37] Newspaper reports drew attention to the prominent place in the De Coursier home of a large red Bible at the top of a bookcase.[38]

In the lead-up to the appointed day of execution, June 16, 1880, the religious dimensions of the case continued to be apparent. The alleged seduction of Mary Mills by Edward De Coursier gained greater prominence in the media.[39] The April 1880 trial highlighted both the Mary Mills seduction and the child born outside of marriage. Mills testified that Edward had informed her that the seduction was to "spite" Robert who he knew had intended to marry Mills.[40] BEP concerns were especially evident in the petitions on behalf of De Coursier that came in from numerous localities. So great was the pressure that the Department of Justice asked Judge Galt for his views on the jury's "recommendation to mercy".[41] Galt replied that the only grounds for mercy was De Coursier's "good character", and that, in effect, this was insufficient.[42]

In an internal memo dated May 29 from the Acting Minister of Justice

[36] *Globe*, April 28, 1890: 10.

[37] *Mail*, September 27, 1879: 6.

[38] *Mail*, September 29, 1879. It was reported that De Coursier went on to quote the biblical King David in some fashion that could not be remembered.

[39] *Mail*, September 29, 1879: 2.

[40] *Globe*, April 28, 1880: 10.

[41] The urgency behind the telegram can be seen in its wording. A reply was requested with the wording, originally stated, "at your earliest convenience" being struck out and replaced by "as early as possible". Letters in Capital Case Files, Robert William Decoursier, RG 13, vol. 1417 file 142A; 1880, Department of Justice (Canada), Library and Archives Canada, Ottawa.

[42] Galt went on to become Sir Thomas Galt and later served as Chief Justice. He was an

BEP REACTION TO ACCOUNTS OF VIOLENCE

A. Campbell, reference was made to "thousands" of signatures on behalf of De Coursier. Department of Justice archival files include additional petitions received after this date. Although Department documents show that by June 1 a decision had already been made that the "law be allowed to take its course", pressure—some of it from important places—continued to be brought to bear.

On June 10 the arch conservative D'Alton McCarthy, MP from Barrie, sent a letter to the Department along with a fresh petition that was "influentially signed." Making a reference to a long June 8 editorial on behalf of the condemned in the *London Advertiser*, McCarthy showed that he felt the political heat.[43] On June 8 the *Mail* had made an editorial about-face on De Coursier, arguing for reconsideration by the "Executive" with respect to the decision to allow the law "to be carried out." While the editor still acknowledged that the crime had been "foul" and "premeditated", he now argued in emphatically BEP term:

> But it is said, with what truth we do not know, that since the trial matters have been brought to light showing that the prisoner received terrible provocation from the murdered man. The story of the girl to whom, it is alleged, the prisoner was engaged and who was seduced by the deceased, has been printed; and if it be true, certainly it cannot be said that the condemned murdered his brother wantonly and without cause. In matters of this kind, it is not for the press to presume to advise the Executive, but we do think, that, if it has not been already done, this girl's statement should be thoroughly examined. If it can be shown that the deceased committed this unpardonable sin against the prisoner, the crime will have been relieved of some portion of its horrible colouring; and it will be for the Executive to consider whether they will be justified in the public interest in granting the prayer of the petition for commutation.[44]

Anglican, according to the 1881 Canada Census.

[43] Letter in Capital Case Files, Robert William Decoursier, RG 13.

[44] *Mail*, June 8, 1880: 2.

The *Globe* responded with its own editorial the next day, echoing the *Mail*, and declaring that Robert had been "basely betrayed" and that he was the "injured party in the family". In the end though it drew back; granting clemency would "put a premium on lynch law" and would not act as a deterrent.[45]

BEP rhetoric and dispositions also governed the direct handling of De Coursier himself. The evangelical Anglican William Rainsford and the more conventional Anglican, John Langtry, were the clergy appointed to be "spiritual advisers" to De Coursier, with, according to the *Globe*, De Coursier speaking freely to them.[46] The newspaper reports suggested that Rainsford took an active role in the attempt to gain clemency for the condemned, even travelling to Ottawa in an effort to gain a reprieve.[47] It was Rainsford who received the message on June 14 from the Minister of Justice that the Executive "had not been induced" to alter their decision.

More than once De Coursier had stated that he would "cheat" the gallows. On June 16 the *Globe* announced that the condemned man had indeed done so, having, despite a round-the-clock guard, ingested "prussic acid". The whole case points to a growing public empathy with accused criminals that reflects BEP concerns.

In the period of the 1870s fully 70% of death sentences were commuted.[48] This high rate of commutation during the 1870s calls for a closer examination. The years immediately after Confederation, through the 1870s, included significant numbers of death sentences for convictions that were not

[45] *Globe*, June 9, 1880: 4.

[46] *Globe*, June 2, 1880: 6.

[47] *Globe*, June 8, 1880: 6. The *Globe* compared the De Coursier suicide with that of the Condemned William Greenwood in 1864. See *Globe*, June 16, 1880: 3. The detailed reporting of testimony of Greenwood's BEP Anglican spiritual adviser, Rev. Sanson, gives unique insight into the nature of the long conversations that ministers had with condemned prisoners. See *Globe*, February 24, 1864: 2.

[48] On commutations during the 1870s see Carolyn Strange, "The Lottery of Death: Capital Punishment in Canada, 1867-1976," *Manitoba Law Journal* 23, 3 (1995): 594-619. See especially footnote 54 on p. 613. It is unclear whether Strange is attempting to provide an explanation for the high commutation rate of the 1870s or merely noting it. There were of course variations over time but Strange's key point is that the commutation rates for both Liberal and Conservative governments were virtually identical.

for murder. Piracy, treason, rape, attempted murder, and even three cases of burglary in PEI in 1876 were all convictions for which the judge had donned the death cap. But after 1867, all such death-sentences were routinely overturned except for the case of Louis Riel in 1885.[49]

For the purposes of this study, the period of the 1870s is important in that it is the "high-water" mark of BEP influence at the level of the federal government. During the decade from 1873-1878, the Baptist Alexander Mackenzie served as Prime Minister while the BEP Anglican, Edward Blake, served as Justice Minister from 1875-1878. If a BEP humanitarian discourse had the power to sway decision-making, then the researcher should find evidence of changes in commutation rates during this time period. It is during this decade that both Samuel Blake and his brother Edward became involved in the Prisoners' Aid Society in Toronto. Even if Edward did not have the same level of involvement with the Society, due to time spent living in Ottawa, considerable time in Toronto afforded him interaction with his brother.

Using the Department of Justice register of persons sentenced to death, it is relatively easy, if tedious, to disaggregate the capital convictions for murder from those not involving murder. When this is done startling results obtain. If one divides the broad period *politically* by Prime Minister, excluding the transitional election years, then there are three periods to compare: the Macdonald years of 1867-1872, the Mackenzie years of 1874-1877, and the Macdonald years of 1879-1881.[50] For the 1874-1877 Mackenzie years, there

---

[49] Death sentences imposed by military tribunals are not included in the Department of Justice register.

[50] For comparative purposes I included the Macdonald years in the 1860s and the period of 1878 to 1881 in order to create somewhat equitable comparative periods both before and after the Mackenzie administration, as while as an upper date that included the De Coursier case and ending in the election year of 1882. While not identifying political variations in rates of commutation, F. Murray Greenwood and Beverley Boissery mention correspondence in which Alexander Mackenzie wrote John A. Macdonald pleading in vain for the life of an accused to be spared. F. Murray Greenwood and Beverley Boissery, *Uncertain Justice: Canadian Women and Capital Punishment, 1754-1953* (Toronto: Dundurn Press, 2000), 156, 177. In a study of capital cases in British Columbia from 1872-1880, Jonathan Swainger ignores the wide variation in commutation rates between the Macdonald and Mackenzie ministries. Jonathan Swainger, "A Distant Edge of Authority: Capital Punishment and the Prerogative of Mercy in British Columbia, 1872-1880" in *Essays in the History of Canadian Law*, vol. 6,

were 39 capital murders and of these 28 were commuted, yielding a commutation rate of 72%. The Macdonald years from 1867-1872 and 1879-1881 saw 60 capital cases involving murder and only 23 commutations for a total commutation rate of 38%. If the Macdonald years are examined separately the resulting rates are remarkably consistent, with 13 of 33 commuted in the first period for 39% and 10 of 27 in the second or 37%. The Macdonald years are in stark contrast to the Mackenzie years with respect to commutation rates. Plainly, the conventional assumption that both political parties commuted sentences at the same rates during this period is wildly off mark.[51] One can hypothesize that BEP thinking, influential among important Liberal leaders, was in play here.

A potentially important—and quite different—development pointing to the influence of BEP ideology has to do with penal reform. There is no doubt of a marked coincidence between plunging rates of violence and penal reform.[52] By 1880 there already was a long tradition of penal reform in the stream of British evangelicalism. It is from this tradition that one finds, for example, the roots of the Toronto chapter of the Prisoners' Aid Association in which Samuel Blake and William Howland played such prominent roles. By 1775 evangelicals in Britain had become active in penal reform, first with a

---

British Columbia and the Yukon, ed. Hamar Foster and John McLaren (Toronto: University of Toronto Press for the Osgoode Society for Canadian Legal History, 1995), 204-241.

[51] Strange is reliant for statistics on Guy Favreau, *Capital Punishment: Material Relating to Its Purpose and Value* (Ottawa: Queen's Printer, 1965). A recent work on capital punishment in Canada makes no mention of political differences with respect to commutation of death sentences. It does however mention John Diefenbaker's visceral distaste for capital punishment motivated by his former work as a criminal lawyer. Certainly the move towards abolition was part of a much broader impulse, but the St. Laurent commutation rates, immediately before the election of Diefenbaker, were in sharp contrast. See Ken Leyton-Brown, *The Practice of Execution in Canada* (Vancouver: UBC Press, 2010), 35. Leyton-Brown contends that Diefenbaker was lined up against the other members of his cabinet on the death penalty. No mention is made of Diefenbaker's religious upbringing. Diefenbaker was raised in a BEP household and describes his pious BEP upbringing in his memoirs. He lived from ages 5-8 years just outside of Toronto. His father, a teacher, forbade him from fighting. Both his parents had a "deep hatred of war", although not pacifists. See John G. Diefenbaker, *One Canada: The Crusading Years, 1895-1956* Toronto: Macmillan, 1975), 1-18.

[52] Of course Toronto's BEP penal reform movement borrowed extensively from penal developments in Britain and the United States.

focus on jails and prisons, and then with gains in political power through legislative agitation. Prominent evangelicals involved in penal reform included John Howard, William Wilberforce, Elizabeth Fry, and her brother-in-law, the parliamentarian Thomas Fowell Buxton.

While the Utilitarians, most prominently Jeremy Betham, were also active in penal reform, evangelicals worked alongside them and according to a recent study by Richard Follett, provided the foot soldiers and the passion needed for reform. Follett argues that in recent historiography, evangelical penal reform has wrongly been subsumed under the figure of Jeremy Bentham and that the movement possessed an intensity "many shades brighter than the dim picture of penal reform" in the writings of Foucault, Michael Ignatieff, or Victor Gatrell.[53]

In Canada it is more difficult to take in the landscape of nineteenth-century penal reform. Like the accumulated layers of grime on an old portrait, the figures on the canvas are difficult to discern. Prior to the 1880s, in a colonial context with multiple provincial centres, there was not a Bentham, Fry, a Howard, or a Buxton. The figure of George Brown, who had a brief, albeit combative, role as a critic of Upper Canada penitentiaries at mid-century, is, however, discernible in the portrait.

Brown's views of justice were shaped by a BEP ideology laden with a mix

---

[53] Richard R. Follett, *Evangelicalism, Penal Theory and the Politics of Criminal Law Reform in England, 1808-30* (Houndmills, Hampshire: Palgrave, 2001), viii-ix. Follett was first attracted to this "brighter shade" by a letter written by Buxton to his wife. After visiting Newgate Prison in 1817, he was overcome with sadness by the sight of four young men who were to be hung the following week. At a crossroads between a conventional career in business or a more difficult path of "service", he wrote after witnessing the wrenching prison scene that he desired to do something, such that "life may not pass quite uselessly—but that in some shape or other I may assist in checking and diminishing crime and its consequent misery". Continuing, he wrote that on this more difficult path, "I might become a real soldier of Christ, I may feel that I have no business on earth but to do his will & to walk in his ways—& I may direct every energy I have to the service of others." From an archival letter quoted by Richard R. Follett, *Evangelicalism, Penal Theory*, viii. (Here Buxton's language is very similar to the diary of the young Mackenzie King.) Of course Buxton went on to a parliamentary career as an abolitionist and social reformer. For the origins of evangelical penal reform, including the career of John Howard, see Laurie Throness, *A Protestant Purgatory: Theological Origins of the Penitentiary Act, 1779* (Aldershot, Hampshire: Ashgate, 2008).

of abolitionist and generally humanitarian outlooks that was imported directly from the British Isles. Both he and his fellow Scottish immigrant friend, Alexander Mackenzie, carried their particular ideology into the parliamentary halls of Ottawa via the popular votes of an ascendant BEP movement.

6.1.3 "They Had Abused Me Up There Like A Dog": The Hanging of Robert Neil

Within the BEP movement, at the grassroots associational level, one can identify clear indications of BEP influence on behaviour. Both in the De Coursier appeal process and, as well as we will now see, in the Robert Neil appeal process led by Howland, one can track a reforming spirit that percolated upwards and was a force to be reckoned with, even in Ottawa. Indeed, the BEP reforming spirit had an arguably important role in the establishment of a Mackenzie administration.[54] The high commutation rate of the Mackenzie government serves as a key marker of a commitment to criminal reform; perhaps even the De Coursier appeal would have been successful had it been directed to a Mackenzie cabinet.[55]

The portrait of Howland has become distorted with the passage of time. In current Canadian historiography he has become an icon of the "purity" crusade that was strictly fixated upon vice and prohibition.[56] In reality Howland took on a wide range of humanitarian causes over the course of almost three decades and was indefatigable in his voluntary pursuits. One of these included the Prisoners' Aid Society.

Dominated by Anglican BEP laymen, the names of the executive of the Prisoners' Aid Society in 1888 (and virtually every year over a span of two decades) reflect the sons of elite families who attended St. James' Cathedral. The

---

[54] Mackenzie, a strict Baptist, was heavily dependent on rural and small-town BEP Ontario.

[55] The memory of earlier BEP reformers is conjured by the place name of Buxton, Ontario or the designation Shaftesbury Hall. Fascinatingly, the one-hundredth anniversary of John Howard's death was commemorated in the *Globe* by an illustrated article in excess of a full page at the precise time that the Prisoners' Aid Society was lobbying for a Commission on Prisons. *Globe*, April 5: 2-3.

[56] Desmond Morton is an exception, although from an earlier generation of historians. See especially Desmond Morton, "Mayor Howland: The Man Who Made Toronto Good", *York Pioneer* (Toronto), 75, no. 2 (1980): 23-30.

president was almost invariably Samuel Blake, while vice-presidents included Howland, Edward Blake, John Hodgins, and Clark Gamble. On March 2, the President brought an "earnest and practical" matter before the group.[57]

Three nights before, Robert Neil, a young Irish immigrant convicted of murdering a Central Prison guard, had been hanged at the Toronto Gaol. Howland and his colleague, William Gooderham, as well as the Methodist minister, Hugh Johnston, were present with Neil until the end. Probably because Howland and Gooderham were known as compassionate and prominent citizens who regularly visited prisoners, Neil had chosen them as his spiritual advisers rather than the prison chaplain.[58]

By following the case files in the Records of the Department of Justice and reporting in the *Globe*, one can see ideology shaping the activism of an association of BEP men working on behalf of a prisoner condemned by the state.[59] One also catches a glimpse of a BEP cluster of individuals attempting to reform an individual prisoner "inwardly", by bringing about a religious "change of heart". The case illustrates how faith and belief worked in a capital case, at least in one in which youth and mitigating circumstances were factors; it also shows how fully BEP ideology was a shaping element in Torontonians' thinking.

Neil was convicted on January 28, 1888 for the stabbing death of Central Prison guard John Rutledge on the 13th of the same month and was sentenced to hang on February 28th. The sentence set off a frenzy of letters from friends and supporters. Howland, who had been visiting Neil for "some time past", published "an open letter" in the Toronto newspapers on February 21st. Addressed to J.S.D. Thompson, Minister of Justice, its original had been accompanied by a handwritten note explaining "the circumstances justify[ing the hope] that public opinion may have some weight." In the letter Howland argues for clemency because the "boy" was only eighteen, and had "since the age of ten years

---

[57] *Globe*, March 2, 1888:8. On the same page of the *Globe* there is mention of a confession given by Robert Neil to Howland and Gooderham.

[58] *Globe*, Feb. 21, 1888:8; Feb. 29, 1888: 8.

[59] Although a "state" act, the death penalty had deep communal dimensions that ran from the coroner's jury, to the grand jury, to the assize jury, to public opinion and of course to the friends and family of both victim and accused.

of age...been a waif associating with vagabonds and criminals." "He has not in all that time had the influence of a respectable woman." Howland then argued, in keeping with the philosophy of the Prisoners' Aid Society, that any under-age, orphaned boy, who had consorted with criminals should be protected and "should not... be held accountable for his actions to the same extent that others of fuller age or more suitable surroundings are held." Instead, a boy in such circumstances should be placed in an environment where he can mature into "a law-abiding and self-sustaining citizen of the state."

With respect to religion Howland wrote that although Neil had not yet made a religious "profession", he had "awakened" from a "death-like state" and come to realize "the wickedness of the act". He "has become patient, accessible, and kindly" and "full...of real regret." In a forcefully written conclusion, Howland wrote that, in treating Neil as he was now being treated, "Justice might as well slaughter a sheep". Additional correspondence on behalf of Neil was sent from clergymen in Canada and Ireland, from a former boarding house landlady in Toronto, from the foreman of the jury who convicted him, and from the law firm that defended him pro bono. Several "letters to the editor" pled Neil's cause.

In response to Howland's "open letter", Warden James Massie of Central Prison prepared a five-page legal size typed document for the Minister. In it Massie outlined previous violent behaviour on Neil's part as well as the reasons for a flogging that he had received. Massie then took issue with some details of Howland's letter, arguing in particular, that Neil was older than Howland had indicated, being 20-22 years of age.

The appeal discussion in Ottawa appears to have revolved around Neil's "sanity" and the fact that Howland had some of his facts wrong (it did turn out, for example, that Howland had been in error on the age question: Neil was nineteen at the time of the murder rather than eighteen). A letter from Neil's six sisters in Ireland pointing to the fact that Neil's two first cousins were "mentally defective" was considered. The final decision was, nonetheless, "that the law be allowed to take its course."[60]

---

[60] All of the above are contained in RG 13, vol. 1424, file 222A; 1888, Department of Justice (Canada), Library and Archives Canada, Ottawa. In the Central Prison Register, Neil is listed

BEP REACTION TO ACCOUNTS OF VIOLENCE

On execution day, Gooderham, Howland and Johnston, who "stuck to the unfortunate man in his trouble", counselled, prayed, and sang with him in his cell, and then accompanied him to the gallows. In his last words Neil stated haltingly that he never intended to kill Rutledge but that, "They had abused me up there like a dog." He proclaimed his sorrow for the guard and "for his wife and kids." Johnston read from his Bible, knelt and prayed, and then, while Neil recited with him the Lord's Prayer, the act was done.

The *Globe* reporter, under the sub-heading "An Affecting Scene at the gallows", had composed a salvation narrative that, no doubt, was recounted in hushed tones at the meeting of the Prisoners' Aid Society two days later. In the appeal to the Justice Department, there are also several marks of the current BEP influence. Mention was made of the lack of proper female influence, the need to remove "waifs" from criminal associations, and the fact that "rough" and "criminal" behaviour was influenced by one's surroundings. The use of a broad public appeal through the mass media of the daily newspaper was itself a sign of BEP approaches and methods.[61]

Increasingly, capital punishment was under question in some BEP quarters. In 1891 the *Evangelical Churchman*, the BEP voice of Samuel Blake, William Howland and company, responded to the reports of several executions in New York in a condemnatory manner. Arguing that capital punishment was perhaps permissible in more primitive states such as biblical Israel, the *Evangelical Churchman* declared that:

> …in civilized and Christian lands, after eighteen centuries of Christian teaching, something more Christlike should be done with a criminal than to kill him. Surely it is not necessary for self-preservation that the state should inflict the death penalty;…The very obloquy visited

---

as prisoner #8697, committed as Robert Neil, alias John Wilson, July 8, 1887 until July 4, 1889 for a conviction of larceny. His age was listed as 18 years, his health as "good", weight 152 pounds, height 5'7", and discharged into the hands of Sherriff Mowat, January 4, 1888.

[61] *Globe*, Jan. 29, 1888: 8. During this period several hangings were conducted using an experimental weight and pulley method rather than a trap-door. In 1890, after the execution of Thomas Kane, the populist *Toronto World* railed against the "jerking" method of hanging labelling it as not "Christian" as it tended to prolong death. *Toronto World*, February 13, 1890: 1,2.

185

on executioner is a virtual admission by the state that something more Christian should be attempted with prisoners. The problem is, indeed, a most difficult one, but is worthy the most serious consideration of all philanthropists—of all, indeed who wish to see Christ's Kingdom more widely and completely established upon earth before the Lord comes.[62]

Howland was not alone in his opposition to Neil's capital sentence and had some support from the Prisoners' Aid Society prior to submitting his letter for publication. Even though Neil was executed, opinion against capital punishment was building, BEP influence was being felt, both by citizens and by agents of the state. Behaviour, both public and private, was changing.

6.1.4 "Some Say it Thundered": The Hanging of Peg Leg Brown

The case of Marion "Mahdie" Brown details BEP prison reform efforts that, although common fare, were rarely recorded, a capital case being an exception. The case, involving the killing of a police officer, had provoked much public revulsion; nevertheless, a BEP group of individuals befriended Brown and appealed for clemency. All this reflects a growing rejection of state violence and a strong reaction against violence in general. BEP ideas are shown to be active, in play, and influential.

In June of 1898, a railway watchman in London was assaulted at dusk in by a "peg legged", "mulatto tramp". An hour later, a police constable was shot dead while pursuing the fugitive. In the darkness no one witnessed the actual shooting, and the suspect managed to flee. By July 10 fifteen "pegleg tramps" that matched the description had been arrested in the area from Montreal to Minnesota.[63]

---

[62] *Evangelical Churchman*, "Reports of Executions," (August 20, 1891), 187. As quoted by Rodney G. Sawatsky, *"Looking For That Blessed Hope": The Roots of Fundamentalism in Canada* (PhD diss. University of Toronto, 1985), 249. At mid-century, a young Joseph Sheard, later to be a mayor and a prominent Toronto architectect, refused on principle to build the gallows of Toronto's second jail. See Eric Arthur, *Toronto: No Mean City* 3rd ed., rev. Stephen A. Otto (Toronto: University of Toronto, 1986), 47. The 1871 Canada Census lists Sheard as a Primitive Methodist.

[63] *Globe*, July 11, 1898: 1.

In October Marian Brown, a 25 year-old Texan cowboy and prison escapee, was apprehended in Yakima in the Washington Territories, spirited to Victoria, British Columbia, and then sent by train to London to stand trial. Newspapers across the country followed the story. At Union Station in Toronto a *Globe* reporter caught a glimpse of Brown as he changed trains. In racially charged language he was described as:

[A] light-coloured mulatto of medium built but thickset and evidently a very powerful man. He has a full, round face with large, black, glistening eyes, which roved uneasily around on the people who crowded in on the car and gazed on the suspected murder as they would on a caged animal.[64]

A full-length portrait of the suspect accompanied the story at a time when newspaper illustrations were rare. The story had been widely circulated by the time Brown's trial took place in London the following March.

Lasting seven days, the trial hinged on the validity of circumstantial evidence. Brown's defence counsel Patrick McPhillips argued that none of the numerous witnesses could place Brown at the scene of the murder; in the dark, the light sleeves of the assailant's shirt and the dark uniform of the police officer were all that could be discerned. Furthermore, McPhillips argued, the jurors had read the details of the case as reported in newspaper accounts. Critically, the defense also insisted, the combined testimony of witnesses was a "tangled mess of statements unworthy of credence."[65]

The jury delivered a guilty verdict. The presiding judge had made it clear that Brown's defense was not to be taken seriously; comment on newspaper-prejudice was especially to be dismissed. In "an age of newspaper enterprise and universal education" it was to be expected that "every matter of importance came to the notice of the intelligent man" and unless such a man entered the witness box with "a bias pronounced and set", it should "be easy for him to forget" a previous knowledge gained of the case through

[64] *Globe*, October 17, 1898: 17.
[65] *Globe*, March 29, 1889: 8.

the newspaper.[66] Brown's history moreover, was against him: as the judge put it, speaking to him, "Your antecedents are bad. They show that you are a member of the criminal class."[67] Execution was set for May 16, 1899.

McPhillips, convinced that an injustice had been done, worked on behalf of the condemned in order to secure a reprieve or a new trial. A petition was circulated and signed by more than 40 lawyers who believed Brown innocent or the trial had been flawed. Rev. Dr. Robert Johnston, a minister at St. Andrew's Presbyterian, interested himself in the case, became the chief activist on behalf of Brown. Initially he was of the opinion that Brown, though he must have fired the critical shot, did so out of "sudden fear or passion" and thus should not have been convicted of premeditated murder.[68] Later, he seems to have concluded that Brown was in fact innocent.

The key event in Johnston's activity on Brown's behalf was a trip to Ottawa to appeal to the Governor General, Lord Minto. Minto, having listened "earnestly" to his pleas, "thought it wise not to interfere with the decision of his advisers." An attempted meeting between Johnston and Prime Minister Laurier was unsuccessful.

Returning early to London on the day of Brown's scheduled execution, Johnston addressed the Governor General and the Justice Minister, David Mills[69] through the reporters who were gathered in the gaol kitchen:

> I wish to make a protest against the over-straining of British justice in the case of this man, against whom the crime of murder, as described by any statute in the British law has not been proved. In attending him this

---

[66] *Globe*, March 30, 1899: 5. This underscores the vaunted place of the newspaper in late Victorian Canada.

[67] *Globe*, March 30, 1899: 5.

[68] From *The London Free Press*, April 11, 1899 as summarized by Karen Allen, http://lstar-education.com/Marion_Brown.htm, accessed January 12, 2013.

[69] Mills was apparently a Methodist but does not appear to have been active in BEP associations. See his entry in *Dictionary of Canadian Biography*. While the [Toronto] *Evening Star* did not cover the Brown hanging they did include a one-line editorial comment on it with no caption: "The habit of clemency to murderers does not seem to have been acquired by Hon David Mills." *Evening Star*, May 17, 1899: 4.

morning I look upon him not as the subject of justice but as the victim of persecution, and his execution as the culmination of cruelty and not the administration of British law. Strong and unrelenting justice will be required at the hands of those who are responsible for his death.[70]

After finishing his statement, Johnston joined the largely BEP-connected group of supporters in Brown's cell. Minutes later the prison governor and two turnkeys entered, signaling that it was time to go. Brown "welcomed" them and continued with his devotions. The group in attendance then broke into the devotional song, heard even by the reporters waiting outside in the courtyard, "This is My Story, This is My Song."[71]

Brown then shook hands with all present including the hangman. The execution party, and the spiritual advisers, set out for the gallows, the peg leg clopping "cheerily".[72] Brown mounted the eight steps of the gallows "as sturdily as if on parade".[73] As the black cap was placed on his head a light rain started. Johnston recited the Lord's Prayer and Brown cried out, "If it be pleasing to Thee, O Lord, have mercy on my soul." At the words "Deliver us from evil" the door was sprung. Immediately a bolt of lightning flashed, thunder followed, and amidst this backdrop of tragic drama, Johnston raised his arm to the sky and cried out, "God forgive us, and forgive this country."[74]

---

[70] *Globe*, May 18, 1899: 7.

[71] *Globe*, March 30, 1899: 5. See also *The London Free Press*, April 11, 1899 as summarized by Karen Allen, http://lstar-education.com/Marion_Brown.htm, accessed January 12, 2013. On the attempted Laurier meeting see John Lisowski, "Murderers Who Were Hanged— Marion "Peg-Leg" Brown," *Middlesex Law Association Newsletter* 17 (December 2010): 17. See also the October and November issues of the newsletter for previous installments of the story. For a brief discussion of the Brown trial from the angle of race see Barrington Walker, *Race on Trial: Black Defendants in Ontario's Criminal Courts, 1858-1958* (Toronto: University of Toronto Press, 2010) 76-79.

[72] *Mail and Empire*, May 18, 1899: 5.

[73] *Globe*, May 18, 1899: 7.

[74] *Globe*, May 18, 1899: 7. *Mail and Empire* and the *Daily Free Press* reported the lightning and thunder while interestingly the *Globe* did not. While only about 20 persons witnessed the execution, several reporters were present. Johnston, when asked later about a private confession, replied that he believed that Brown "had opened his heart freely and fully with regard to the crime, and I say again that he was as innocent of murder as the birds that fly."

Sheriff Cameron had requested that the bell of St. Paul's Cathedral toll on the hour of execution. The bell remained silent.[75]

Marion Brown's cell was a microcosm of what had become the Ontario BEP world. In his final hours at least eleven church members, five of whom were women, ministered to Brown. Of this group, seven were Salvation Army, one a Baptist, one Presbyterian, and two Methodist. Their presence shows how marked BEP concern to actively support values of truth-seeking, compassion, empathy, and forgiveness had become.

Important, too, was the interdenominational activity in protest against the verdict. The Rev. Dr. Johnston, the Presbyterian minister, Patrick McPhillips, the Roman Catholic defence lawyer, and Bishop Baldwin, the BEP-Anglican prelate, formed a cohesive group in support of redress.

Generally Anglican and Roman Catholic clergy and laity[76] were not participants in capital case protests, with the exception of Patrick McPhillips. Neither the Catholic nor the non-BEP Anglican groups seem to have brought an ideology of improvement and protest to the politics of Toronto, and both tended to side with the Tory political establishment.[77] Though late nineteenth-century BEP activists were not uniformly opposed to capital

---

The following month after the hanging there was an Associated Press dispatch that a prisoner in Chicago, a William Bryan, had confessed to the killing of the London police constable Toohey. I was unable to find any follow-up report, and there are no mentions of this in the summaries that have been compiled on the Marion Brown case. See *Globe*, June 14, 1899: 10.

[75] See John Lisowski, "Murderers Who Were Hanged—Marion "Peg-Leg" Brown," *Middlesex Law Association Newsletter* 17, (December 2010): 17. The Diocese of Huron was a BEP bastion. Maurice S. Baldwin, nephew of A.A. Baldwin, was bishop at the time. Baldwin's signature is clearly evident on an 1880 petition, from Montreal, to the Minister of Justice "praying for a commutation in the case of Robert Decoursier". Petition in Capital Case Files, Robert William Decoursier, RG 13, vol. 1417 file 142A; 1880, Department of Justice (Canada), Library and Archives Canada, Ottawa.

[76] However, BEP-Anglicans did and these included the laymen William H. Howland and Samuel Blake and the clergyman William Rainsford as seen earlier. In the Brown case Bishop Baldwin refused to ring church bells after execution. It should be pointed out that Roman Catholic priests and Anglican clergy regularly visited prisoners. For the case of George Bennett, convicted murderer of George Brown, see *Globe*, July 24, 1880: 5. See also John Ross Robertson, *Landmarks of Toronto*, Third Series, 266-269.

[77] But it should be pointed out that Roman Catholic priests and Anglican clergy regularly visited prisoners.

punishment,[78] those who were were vigorous and insistent. However, in practice, it seems those who were, were vigorous and insistent. In the Neil, De Coursier, and Kane [79] capital cases, BEP reform activists lobbied for commutation of the sentence while Catholics seem to have played no such role in the case of the Roman Catholic, George Bennett.[80] There was much BEP public opposition to capital punishment,[81] and a willingness to critique the

[78] Henry O'Brien argued, for example, that capital punishment acted as a deterrent and that there were scriptural divine commands in favour of its ongoing relevance. O'Brien was a close associate of Howland and was a Conservative, unlike many key BEP activists who were Liberal. O'Brien was responding to other Christians who were using religious arguments in favour of abolition. See a newspaper clipping from the *Mail and Empire* dated Saturday, January 1925. Also in the same file is a clipping from a letter written by O'Brien to the *Mail and Empire*, October 13, 1926, that argues against Prohibition and in favour of "temperance" on the basis of the "Book of Holy Writ" and in the "footsteps" of the Archbishop of Canterbury. See Henry O'Brien Papers, S 154, Box 2, Articles and Clippings about the O'Brien family, 1875-1943, Baldwin Room, Toronto Reference Library.

[79] Kane was convicted of beating to death his sister-in-law, with whom he had been living with following the death of his brother. Up until the day before his execution, he insisted he was Protestant although the clergy visiting him suspected that he was not. On the day before his execution Kane declared that he was a Roman Catholic. He was immediately visited by three priests. Two returned at 5 a.m. to celebrate mass with him, and Kane remarked on the deep compassion shown to him. *Toronto Mail*, February 13, 1890: 6; *Toronto World*, February 12, 1890:1; February 13, 1890: 1; *Globe*, February 13, 1880: 8. Vigorous efforts were made by what appear to be BEP activists who circulated petitions and wrote letters on Kane's behalf. The argument for clemency was that the conviction should have been for manslaughter as Kane was drunk at the time of the beating death. An obviously distraught James A. Macdonald, the defence counsel for Kane, led a vigorous campaign on his behalf and travelled to Ottawa in an attempt to meet with the Minister of Justice. Justice Street, who sentenced Kane and noted the recommendation in a letter dated February 1, 1890, seems to back the recommendation of mercy. The entire jury signed a petition for clemency. Macdonald also wrote a long letter, dated in February, in favour of mercy, and ended it with a flourish of religious language. Macdonald was a Methodist according to the 1891 Canada Census. See Capital Case Files, Thomas Kane, RG 13, vol. 1426 file 237A; 1890, Department of Justice (Canada), Library and Archives Canada, Ottawa.

[80] *Globe*, July 24, 1880: 5. Although it did not help that a person of George Brown's stature had been the victim.

[81] This functional opposition can also be seen in the Toronto death of John Varcoe who was shot in his home by two burglars in November, 1899. Varcoe lived for a number of hours, was conscious, and was subjected to his two assailants being brought to his deathbed by the police for purposes of identification. Fully conscious and in agony, Varcoe implied that the two were his attackers, but turned away, refused to positively identify them, and instead pled that mercy be shown them, even though one of them "cursed" him. Varcoe was

state that was part of a trajectory of BEP inspired penal reform and gives an important measure of the extent to which BEP ideology was actively at work in the community.

6.1.5 The 1891 Ontario Prison Commission

By 1890 a flurry of BEP penal reform efforts were underway. The relationship between penal reform and declining levels of violence in a culture is indeterminate. Nevertheless, both then and now, theories have existed that posit prisons as being "schools" for violence and crime. According to these theories the separation of young offenders from "hardened" criminals prevents crime and violence and allows for rehabilitation. Furthermore, penal reform, whether increasingly restricted capital or corporal punishments, reflects a growing cultural aversion towards harsh penalties in general. Hence, according to this line of reasoning, a culture with increased restraints on interpersonal violence will produce fewer acts of violence while more moderate sentencing produces fewer habitual violent offenders. This perspective on penal reform is solidly backed up by the fact that incarceration rates in Ontario fell sharply during the period under study as did all categories of criminal offences and especially those against the person and against public order and the peace.[82]

BEP penal reformist efforts, and particularly those of the Prisoners' Aid

---

a "prominent" member of the BEP Cooke's Presbyterian Church. One of the gunmen later died of a bullet wound sustained in a gun battle with police during the course of the burglary while the other, Henry Williams, was executed in April, 1900, despite a recommendation of mercy by the jury. *Globe*, November 10, 1899: 12. George Brown, although an advocate of the death penalty, apparently did not "condemn" his attacker according to the sermon at his funeral. *Globe*, May 17:6. The empathy that is shown in both these examples is very difficult for the historian to quantify but is significant when seen in the context of my following argument that there is a decline in "honour" killing. The *Globe* in 1890 noted a marked resistance to capital punishment over the past 25 years and predicted that it would eventually be abolished. *Globe*, May 12, 1890: 4. In this it was prescient and during this time period only a religious humanism can account for it as opposed to a "secular" variant.

[82] See Peter Oliver, *"Terror to Evildoers"*, 368-380. Crimes against the person dropped sharply during the 1890s so the sharp drop in incarcerations is not merely a function of relaxing the penalties for drunkenness.

Association (PAA),[83] culminated in the *Report of the Commissioners Appointed to Enquire into the Prison and Reformatory System of Ontario, 1891*.[84] The bulk of the 800-page report consists of transcripts of testimony on crime, criminals, and the prison system from the perspectives of police, judicial, government and prison officials, and reformers. A survey of the prison system in Britain and the U.S. was also undertaken and the testimony of numerous prison and reformatory officials in the United States was included.

Among the six Toronto reformers interviewed by the Commission, five were prominent BEP activists.[85] The emphasis of the six was on the social and environmental causes of crime as opposed to causes that accented personal choice. This was true especially in the case of the young offenders who were twenty years of age and under. The testimony featured associations that were attempting to prevent children and youth from falling into lives of crime or being dependent on the House of Industry that provided shelter for the indigent and the transient who were often viewed as contributing to a criminal "class".[86]

---

[83] Howland chaired the Prison Reform Conference of 1889, which was formative for the Commission of 1891. The Prison Reform Conference of 1891, also chaired by Howland, reinforced the findings of the Commission, which in turn mirrored the resolutions of the 1889 Conference. The commissioners were prominent delegates at the 1891 Conference. While the conferences were driven by BEP concerns and dominated by BEP delegates, there was a lone Roman Catholic delegate who opened the 1891 Conference in prayer. See *Report of the Prison Reform Conference, Held in Toronto November 27, 1891* (Toronto: Prisoners' Aid Association of Canada, 1891). For a summary of these developments see Peter Oliver, *Terror to Evil Doers*, 486-499. The Irish Catholic Benevolent Union spoke out on behalf of abused Catholic prisoners and advocated legal counsel for them in the context of charges brought in 1885 against James Massie, Warden of Central Prison. *Globe*, June 17, 1885: 6.

[84] *Report of the Commissioners Appointed to Enquire into the Prison and Reformatory System of Ontario, 1891* (Toronto: Government of Ontario, 1891).

[85] The sixth was Goldwin Smith, who served as a trustee of the House of Industry along with Howland. That the two could serve on the same board, after taking opposite sides in several municipal elections, is of note. The testimony of Smith generally chimed with the other five, although Smith downplays the role of alcohol as a primary cause of crime and instead refers to low wages, unemployment and "suffering" as often causal; issues that were also emphasized by the other five members.

[86] For the British response to "juvenile delinquency" and its context see Pamela Horn, *Young Offenders: Juvenile Delinquency, 1700-2000* (Chelford: Amberley Publishing, 2010). Canadian developments in laws and justice policies concerning juveniles were heavily influenced by the British experience as well as the American. Canadians both defined themselves

In the *Report*, ex-mayor Howland can be seen as a driving force behind penal reform. He was accorded deference by the commission and contributed more than eight pages of testimony. He argued that it was a "horrid practice" to place "drunkards" in gaol with criminals. Likewise not to intervene in the lives of young delinquents, and to place them on trial in adult court, was "a scandalous thing" likely to set a child on the path of a "criminal career". In keeping with BEP opposition to theorizing on the racial or hereditary causes of crime, Howland rejected such reasoning, pointing to the success of many poor Irish immigrants as proof that it did not work.[87]

Detective William Stark, testifying before the Prison Commission, went against the grain of testimony when he advocated bringing children before the magistrate in the Toronto Police Court. Stark outlined how in the period from the previous July through October there had been 213 males convicted of various offences, including housebreaking and shopbreaking. Of these, 73 were between the ages of seven and fifteen years of age with three being aged seven. He attributed juvenile crimes to a lack of adult supervision, poorly enforced truancy laws, and the fact that the laws only mandated 100 school days per year. In referring to the group of young "criminals", Stark explained that four-fifths were the children of "respectable mechanics" and "industrious people who have lost control of them." This kind of parent, he testified, had a "wholesome dread" of the court and "exposure" in the press when children went awry. Juvenile crime was on the upswing and needed to be addressed.[88]

The final recommendations of the Commission were a contradiction of the current penal policy of the day and an affirmation of the PAA agenda. The concluding words boldly stated that "The neglect of its duties by the State and by society in all its other forms of organization, is largely responsible for the prevalence of vice and crime."[89] The most lasting influence Howland and the

---

against the United States but also borrowed *from* their neighbour.

[87] *Report of the Commissioners*, 689-697.

[88] *Report of the Commissioners*, 715-723.

[89] From the Ontario Prison Commission Report, 44, as quoted in Peter Oliver, *Terror to*

PAA had was the Children's Protection Act of 1893 enacted by the Ontario government. A blend of American and British ideas and practice, it was also picked up in aspects of the Canadian Criminal Code of 1893.[90] But by the year's end, Howland was dead. Canada had lost a public figure with an insatiable drive for a prison reform that was wedded to a personal humanitarianism. It did not gain another.

The relation between penal reforms and any decline in interpersonal violence is complex. At the baseline there is clearly a trajectory of reform over time, both in Britain and in Canada with Canadian reformers importing ideas from Britain but also incorporating penal theories from the U.S. by direct observation, as seen in the 1891 Ontario Commission. Evangelicals were deeply involved in penal reform in Britain, while in Ontario they dominated the penal reform as seen in Children's Protection Act of 1893.

The distance from the Halifax of 1751, which saw the hanging of two house-breakers,[91] to the Toronto of 1880-1899, when a total of only four individuals were hanged, is much longer than the miles or years separating the events.[92] The involvement of evangelicals in penal reform, both at the legislative level and in the "trenches" as seen in the capital narratives examined above, is ever-present in nineteenth-century Ontario and shows BEP ideology to have been formative. Ideology and penal reform legislation interacted in an urban nexus. Reform impulses, encoded in law, combined for increasing and new restraints on a variety of violent behaviours ranging from cock fights to baby farms to violence to animals to wife-beating to male-on-male violence motivated by "honour".

Evil-Doers, 489. For the PAA response to the Report see *Prison Reform* (Toronto: Prisoners' Aid Association, 1894?). The PAA drive for the Commission can be seen in an earlier pamphlet also entitled *Prison Reform* (Toronto: Prisoners' Aid Association, 1889).

[90] Henri E. Taschereau, *The Criminal Code of the Dominion of Canada, As Amended in 1893* (Toronto: Carswell, 1893), 7-8.

[91] D. Owen Carrigan, *Crime and Punishment in Canada: A History* (Toronto: McClelland and Stewart, 1991), 302.

[92] Other physical punishments were also within memory. William Lyon Mackenzie as mayor once had an "old woman" placed in stocks. *Globe*, November 30, 1883: 7.

6.2 Toronto On the Curve

Historians Carolyn Strange,[93] Constance Backhouse,[94] Karen Dubinsky,[95]

[93] Carolyn Strange, *Toronto's Girl Problem: The Perils and Pleasures of the City, 1880-1930* (Toronto: University of Toronto Press, 1995). Strange focuses on the "delights" and "dangers" in the experience of Toronto's single wage-earning women. For some, prostitution was chosen for various reasons; criminal case files involving prostitution are examined as well as the varying arrest rates over time as the Toronto Police Department selectively enforced moral laws and codes. Strange narrowly defines the mandate of Toronto's "Morality Department", instituted by Howland, as entirely involved in the enforcement of laws concerning alcohol and prostitution. Howland is introduced in a one-dimensional manner. Strange repeatedly alludes to only 20 lines of Howland's testimony out of more than 500 lines (although this testimony includes a wider discussion than simply working women) of his testimony before the *Royal Commission on Labour and Capital* while his sole contribution with respect to penal reform, according to Strange, was a policy of "removal" from homes so as to "nip minor's 'evil tendencies' in the bud". See pp. 17, 34-38, 45-46, 55, 93, 131. Contra Strange see for example the case of ten-year-old James Kimber, "A Distressing Case", *Globe*, November 13, 1880. However Strange is quite effective in her use of criminal cases to show the ongoing challenges of adjustment facing single working women and the agency that they employed for coping in an urbanizing Toronto. See especially the 1893 trial of Clara Ford for the murder of Frank Westwood, pp. 78-83. But an over-reliance on the details of criminal case files and the lack of sustained interaction with data on levels of violence causes one to question the relative level of "danger". Still, her references to "danger" are often playful.

[94] Constance Backhouse, *Colour-Coded: A Legal History of Racism in Canada, 1900-1950* (Toronto: University of Toronto Press, 1999). Beginning with the "colour-coded" 1901 census, Backhouse sheds considerable light on the racialized boundaries of turn-of-the-century Toronto, dispelling any myths of "the ideology of racelessness" with respect to Canadian historiography and the way that "race" has functioned in the Canadian legal system. Backhouse touches on the development of social Darwinism and "scientific" studies of physiognomy but does not consider any countervailing tendencies in the BEP tradition of monogenesis. See for example Daniel Wilson, "On the Supposed Prevalence of One Cranial Type Throughout the American Aborigines," in *Edinburgh Philosophical Society Journal*, New Series (January 1858), text-fiche, p. 31, CIHM 63246. Likewise in her study of women and the law in the nineteenth century, and their vulnerability before it, Backhouse places the "wife-beater" newspaper discourse in context but seems to imply a general stasis over time with no real change until the 1970s. Constance Backhouse, *Petticoats and Prejudice: Women and Law in Nineteenth-Century Canada* (Toronto: Canadian Scholars' Press and Women's Press: 1991), esp. 167-199.

[95] Karen Dubinsky, *Improper Advances: Rape and Heterosexual Conflict in Ontario, 1880-1929* (Chicago: University of Chicago Press, 1993). An examination of 400 cases involving complaints to the police of sexual assault. While *Improper Advances* is a study of sexual violence against women in rural southern Ontario and Northern Ontario, there is a wider focus that overlaps with Toronto. Dubinsky rightly focuses on patriarchy as materially based power and seems to imply that rape and violence are constants over time. I am arguing that violence

and Keith Walden[96] have emphasized danger, deception, violence, disorder, and racist "colour-coding" in late nineteenth-century Toronto and its hinterland as determinants of social behaviour. They share a common methodology which makes extensive use of criminal cases and emphasizes the reality and the frequency of crime.

The angle of vision is extremely narrow and skewed. It involves a quite narrow definition of "morality". Generally, the four confine their discussion to issues of sexuality, alcohol, and race; matters of "rough" male behaviour, adequate education and food for children, the development of public hospitals, and the protection of animals are all overlooked.[97]

Much of the rather narrowly conceived argument developed by the four comes from C.S. Clark's *Of Toronto the Good* (1898).[98] A journeyman newspaper reporter, Clark is an enigmatic and shadowy individual who was not captured in any of the censuses. He claimed to have lived in Ottawa, Buffalo, Montreal, and "different American cities".[99] He was an observer of urban

---

in general, including sexual violence, varies across time and culture.

[96] Keith Walden, *Becoming Modern in Toronto: The Industrial Exhibition and the Shaping of a Victorian Culture* (Toronto: University of Toronto Press, 1997). A cultural history of the founding of the Toronto Industrial Exhibition whose purpose is to explore "how certain cultural dispositions formed around an institution." Walden sees the occasion of the Exhibition as producing "exceptional levels of crime and disorder" (p. 53) but, using newspaper reports, is hard-pressed to recount events of actual violence. Arrest rates for what were usually petty crime and drunkenness seem to be only marginally higher (e.g. in 1898 there were a total of 440 charges in Police court for the 13 days of the Exhibition while for the same period the previous month there were 357 and while for 1899 there was a reversal with 453 versus 479 charges for the previous month, p. 66). But Walden's study gives a fascinating look into attempts to order life (often successfully) around a particular event in a late nineteenth-century culture.

[97] In addition to the earlier references see Keith Walden, "Toronto Society Response to Celebrity Performers, 1887-1914," *Canadian Historical Review* 89, no. 3 (September 2008): 375; Constance Backhouse, "Nineteenth Century Prostitution Law: Reflections of a Discriminatory Society," *Histoire Sociale-Social History* 18, no. 36 (novembre-November 1985): 392-393; Carolyn Strange, "Sin or Salvation? Protecting Toronto's Working Girls," *The Beaver* 77, no. 3 (June 1997): 8.

[98] Clark is widely cited in Canadian historiography for the period. For example, see J.M. Bumsted, *The Peoples of Canada: A Post Confederation History* Second Ed. (Toronto: Oxford University Press, 2004), 76, 81, 164. Bumsted includes Clark on a timeline of key events and people in urban Canada and excerpts a page of Clark's book.

[99] C.S. Clark, *Of Toronto the Good*, 26.

activity, with an eye to puncturing the pristine image that Toronto sought to project to the outside world.

Clark's object no doubt was to sell books, and in that line he sought to titillate without running afoul of the Attorney General. In Clark's racy narratives the sexual agency of young workingwomen was operating in new ways spreading throughout the city a casual prostitution in contrast to the kind found in traditional "bawdy" houses. Clark was an open advocate of a regulated prostitution.[100]

Highly critical of the police, and in particular the Morality Squad, Clark was eager to point out cases of police brutality and incompetence, as well as a prevalence of crime that Clark illustrated with newspaper accounts and police statistics published by Chief Constable "Grassett" [sic] himself. In sharp contrast to the picture of Toronto presented by delegates to both "the Social Purity Congress" in Baltimore[101] and the world convention of the "Women's"

[100] C.S. Clark, *Of Toronto the Good*, 87.

[101] Clark does accurately refer to a National Purity Conference held in Baltimore in 1895 but distorts the one Canadian report in the published proceedings. The Canadian speaker, Rev. C.W. Watch, readily admits that there is prostitution in Toronto but that "there is not a known house of ill fame that can keep its establishment open as such." Rather, known prostitutes "gravitate between the court room, jail and street". Aaron Powell, *The National Purity Conference: Its Papers, Addresses, Portraits* (New York: National Purity Alliance, 1896), 277. Clark reports Watch as saying that there is not a "known house of prostitution" thus greatly exaggerating what Watch actually said and making it sound like a claim that there was no prostitution in Toronto. C.S. Clark, *Of Toronto the Good*, 117. It should be pointed out that the "purity" agenda in Canada included advocacy of greater penalties against sexual assault including that of rape within marriage, prize fighting, baby farming, and the abuse of children and animals. See Aaron Powell, *The National Purity Conference*, 437-451. Less circumspect in the 1897 conference in Toronto, delegate J.J. Maclaren, Q.C. did give a triumphalist purity address in which he stated "that—speaking broadly, we have no slums, no tenements, as the words are understood in your large cities, no immigrant population, so that many of the problems that are perplexing you…are to us unknown." Maclaren extolled the high percentage of church-goers as shown in a recent church census, voluntary associations funded by both province and city, and strict alcohol licensing laws which had succeeded, over the course of the 1890s, in drastically lowering incarceration rates. While Maclaren believed that the "home was the essential unit of Christian civilization", it was the duty of the state to intervene in order to protect children in situations of "vice and crime". State regulation of child employment and "baby farming" had been instituted. It is possible that Clark conflated aspects of the two conferences. See J.J. Maclaren, "Moral Reform in Ontario: An Encouraging Outlook" in *Twenty-Fourth National Conference of Charities* [Social Work]: *Official Proceedings of the Annual*

[sic] Christian Temperance Union held in Toronto, Clark argued that all was not as portrayed in the gritty reality of Toronto, the City of Churches.

His view was insistently anti-BEP. He presents a puritanical, strong-arm Toronto that had no empathy and charity. His interpreters follow the same course. *Of Toronto the Good* has, however, been given far more weight by them than it can carry.[102]

While Clark makes use of official statistics that can be verified, most of his observations are questionable. His recounting of an 1882 homicide serves as an example. In the actual event, Constable John Albert shot and killed seventeen year-old Andrew Young while Young and some companions were boating on Grenadier Pond in High Park, just west of Toronto. Albert had been called to the scene, and, in the course of his efforts to persuade the young men to leave the area, grabbed Young by the shoulder. Words were exchanged, and Young was shot at close range, dying within minutes. Albert was convicted of murder, with a recommendation of mercy, and was sentenced to be hanged. The sentence was later commuted, and he was committed to penitentiary.[103]

According to Clark, the little "lads" (Young was 17 and one of his companions was 24) were playing near "one of the wharves". The arrest of a policeman was found by Clark to be a "peculiarity". The rigorous efforts on Albert's behalf by defence counsel were seen by Clark as exceptional. The charge on which he was convicted was identified as "manslaughter" when in fact it was murder with the full agreement of the judge.[104] Errors of misrepresentation abound. Clark is not reliable. A picture of late nineteenth-century Toronto derived

---

Meeting, 1897, ed. Elizabeth Burrows (Boston: Geo. H. Ellis), 1898.

[102] Maria Valverde argues that Clark exaggerates the number of brothels in Toronto; arrest records do not support his claims. Maria Valverde, *The Age of Light, Soap, and Water: Moral Reform In English Canada, 1885-1925*, 2nd ed. (Toronto: University of Toronto Press, 2008), 82, 183 n. 16. Constance Backhouse labels Clark an "eccentric author" but does not critically evaluate him as a source in her writings. See Constance Backhouse, "Nineteenth-Century Canadian Prostitution Law", 392. Carolyn Strange makes the most frequent references to Clark in several writings, but hers are generally uncritical readings. See Carolyn Strange, *Toronto's Girl Problem*, 9, 15, 90, 93-97, 100, 106-107, 115, 118-124 (there is an implied critique here), 163-165, 182, 210.

[103] *Globe*, July 24, 1882: 1,8; October 13, 1882: 5.

[104] C.S. Clark, *Of Toronto the Good*, 23.

from him is misleading in the extreme. To the extent that the four historians rely on him, they are to be questioned. Other sources offer much more helpful information.[105]

By 1890 some astute observers were recognizing that crime was falling in both Canada and Britain. In the month after Howland's death, *The Globe* published the Toronto Chief Constable's annual report on crime in Toronto. In it the Chief Constable wrote that it was a "matter for sincere congratulations that murder, the darkest crime of all, has almost disappeared from the records."[106] In 1899, after a decade of extremely low homicide numbers, Grasett he could sound an even more triumphant note:

> Once more the Police Department of Toronto is able to report a material decrease in serious crime at a time when the population is increasing rapidly. The record in the case of murder especially is one that fills the breast of police officials all over America with envy. There is no community of the size of Toronto on the continent where the only murders during the entire year were committed by two persons of unsound mind.[107]

[105] It is fascinating to note that Clark provided the Conservatives with the "treasonous" pamphlet by Edward Farrer, editorial writer of the *Globe*, which advocated annexation; it was this pamphlet that helped John A. Macdonald win the 1891 election. Christopher Pennington, *The Destiny of Canada: Macdonald, Laurier, and the Election of 1891* (Toronto: Allen Lane, 2011), 127-129, 201-202. Pennington does not connect Clark with *Of Toronto the Good*, and the previously mentioned writers do not mention Clark as being a pivotal figure in the 1891 election. Perhaps Pennington recently made this discovery based on the letters that he mentions from Clark to Goldwin Smith.

[106] The *Globe*, January 29, 1894, p. 3. The lone "murder" for the year was due to the death of a woman who died after undergoing an abortion.

[107] *Globe*, February 2, 1899: 7. For a similar report by Grasett see *Globe*, February 16, 1895: 8. "[O]ur city has not altogether forfeited the claim to the title of Toronto the Good. There is no other city in America of equal population that has but one case of murder to charge up against the past year...and the tendency is steadily in the direction of a decrease in murderous assaults." But in Grasett's report for 1895 he was forced to admit that murders were up. Ingeniously he argues that the majority of premeditated murders were "committed by aliens and cannot be charged against the people of Toronto." *Globe*, January 23, 1896: 6. Two of the murders were indeed committed by an American briefly in the city, who was later convicted in the U.S. of multiple murders. Nonetheless homicides had declined over the course of the decade in Toronto. On the American serial killer, H.H. Holmes, see Erik Larson, *The*

The social world of Toronto in the 1890s was vastly different from the York of 1800,[108] in ways that go far beyond simply the physical size of the city.

A principal indicator of what was happening was the change in incarceration rates for crimes against the person. The published figures show a steady drop, from 52.1 per 100,000 to 41.2 in 1890 and then a fall to 29.3 in 1899.[109] Committals to Central Prison were declining from 3,600 in the period 1886-1890, to 3,300 in 1891-1895, and to 3,100 during the period from 1896-1900. Interpersonal violence as measured by convictions was clearly on the decrease.[110]

Despite the apparent drop in the Nineties of crimes against the person, including violent offences, a rhetoric of crime can be detected in the daily newspapers. Crime reporting in the Toronto dailies possessed a highly moralistic form that reflected the ideology of British evangelical Protestants and reinforced it with daily illustrations of the consequences of intemperate behaviour. Even a casual reading of Toronto's daily newspapers makes apparent that Late Victorian culture attached importance to relatively minor offences. Newspaper court reports regularly featured stories of individuals convicted of minor offences ranging, for example, from clothes being stolen from a clothesline to a pair of gloves being shoplifted from a dry goods store. The name of the individual was given, even in the case of minors, no doubt a source of shame for many families and individuals.

Reports of physical violence received extended coverage. The caption, "wife-beater", was often included in a headline. Behaviour was seen as being open to

---

Devil in the White City: Murder, Magic, and Madness at the Fair That Changed America (New York: Crown Books, 2003).

[108] Toronto was named York until 1834 when it became "Toronto City" and then "Toronto" in 1837. For a report on the drop in crime in Britain by James Massie, Warden of Central Prison, see *Report of the Commissioners*, 767-776.

[109] See Peter Oliver, *Terror to Evildoers*, 371-373. Although crimes against the person in the whole of Canada dropped during this period, they did not drop at the steep rate seen in Ontario. See *Canada Yearbook 1900* (Ottawa: Government of Canada, 1900), 581.

[110] Helen Boritch has shown that arrests for violent crimes decreased in the 1890s. Helen Boritch, *The Making of Toronto the Good: The Organizing of Policing and Production of Arrests, 1859-1955* (PhD diss. University of Toronto, 1985), 208-255. These decreases took place at a time when population continued to grow.

shaping by what was viewed as the potentially shaming effect of having one's name printed in multiple daily newspapers in association with the epithet. The police magistrate constantly excoriated males appearing in court for assaulting wives, and repeat offenders were often "sent down" to Central Prison. The reports reported messages from pulpits and lecterns against "rough" male behaviour that was often occasioned by the consumption of alcohol present in, or making their way into, the community more generally.

By 1880 this "wife-beater" discourse, perhaps occasioned by an increase in page counts, was quite prominent in the *Globe*; the behaviour which it recorded was viewed as a scourge of crisis proportions. Representative headlines and sub-headings include the following: "Wife Beater",[111] "Wife Beaters",[112] "A Wife Beater",[113] "A Wife Beater Fined",[114] "Assaults",[115] "Assaults",[116] "A Wife-Beater",[117] and "Three Wife Beaters".[118] With the expansion of the page count, descriptions of assaults became much more graphic. For example, a

[111] *Globe*, March 17, 1880: 4. John Locke beat and threatened the life of his wife Mary.

[112] *Globe*, March 18, 1880: 4. In this case three men were convicted of assaulting and "illusing" their wives. The editorial comment concerns the fact that for some men this was a recurring event and the writer raises the oft-stated complaint that there should be a more severe "punishment" than what the magistrate generally "inflicted". This complaint increased over time and would have influenced public if not the judges' opinion.

[113] *Globe*, April 1, 1890: 1. Michael Bergen was arrested for beating his wife and even after the arrest "struck her twice, she having unfortunately ventured within his reach."

[114] *Globe*, May 6, 1880: 6. Michael O'Brien was fined $3.

[115] *Globe*, June 22, 1880: 5. Charles Gallagher was accused of assaulting his wife with a chair, but the complainant did not appear and he was discharged.

[116] *Globe*, June 24, 1880: 4. In this report there are gross variations. John Orchard on remand for assaulting wife Mary was discharged. John Flood was fined $1 or 6 days for assaulting Mary Ryan (he claimed the complaint was "out of spite") but W.J. Smith was fined $20 or 60 days for an assault in a business office and furthermore was bound over by $500 to keep the peace. The accused then made an "unparliamentary remark" and was fined a further $3.

[117] *Globe*, August 12, 1880: 6. In the case of John Oliver, "a sinister looking man in oleaginous garb", his wife was willing to testify concerning his ongoing abuse. John Baxter J.P. let the accused know how much he "despised" him and fined him $10 or 60 days of hard labour. Leaving the dock Oliver gave his wife a "most significant glance", "betokening no extreme affection" for her.

[118] *Globe*, June 29, 1880: 8. In this case the magistrate handed out fines of $10 or 30 days in two cases. A third, David Walsh, was sent to the Central for 30 days with no option after hitting his wife with a ginger beer bottle and then threatening a doctor who had treated her.

particularly brutal description of an assault by Robert Harrison on his wife Rebecca appeared in the newspaper in April, 1881. The accused was fined $100 or 30 days and required to post two $100 sureties to "keep the peace" for two years.[119]

During the 1880s there were increasing calls for the lash to be used on wife-beaters. A *Globe* editorial in 1888 brought attention to the frequency of wife-beaters appearing in court. It called for penalties to be increased and for judges to use the outer limits of the law in sentencing. However it stopped short of advocating the lash for wife-beaters.[120] But in 1890 the *Globe* supported the use of the lash in cases that involved the sexual assault of young girls. Although there were BEP penal reformers who advocated the lash as a replacement for incarceration, with its risk of contamination by contact with habitual criminals, there was also a BEP discourse employed against its use.[121] Towards the end of the century, court-imposed flogging seems to have diminished.[122]

By 1899 a much-expanded *Globe* was able to point to a culture that

[119] *Globe*, April 7, 1881: 4.

[120] *Globe*, May 21, 1888: 4. But by 1890 the lash was being used against men convicted of assaulting young girls. The editorial position of the *Globe* was in support of the use of the lash in these cases. *Globe*, August 8, 1890: 4. For reporting on the use of the lash for example see *Globe*, July 21, 1888: 10; July 15, 1889: 8; September 8, 1890: 8; January 23, 1891: 8. In an examination of penalties for 'wife-beating" over the first few months of 1890, it appears that magistrates were making more frequent use of court orders of protection. Fines or alternatively prison terms seem to be heightened albeit based on impressionistic analysis. See *Globe*, January 7, 1890: 5; March 4: 8; March 6: 10; March 20: 10; April 4: 8; April 22:8; April 25: 8; April 26: 20; May 1: 8. Assaults on children carried heavier penalties. For example, Ellen McFarlane received ten days in jail for throwing "her little boy against a bedstead" severely cutting his head. April 9, 1890: 8. By 1890 police court reporting became more concise and sporadic in the *Globe*, and by 1899 is not a regular feature. The same is true of the *Toronto World* and the *Empire and Mail*. Convictions had fallen over the 1890s, but the decline in the details of court reporting I would attribute to broad cultural shifts of an unknown nature. Certainly long stories on sensational crimes and trials remained.

[121] See a letter to the *Globe*, August 27, 1890: 8. "Justice", the writer, terms the floggings "degrading", "torture", "barbarous", bespeaking Russia more than Canada and "a reproach to our civilization and to our religion." For a response from "A Woman" advocating more extreme measures than flogging, see *Globe*, August 30, 1890: 10.

[122] However as late as 1899 a Grand Jury advocated flogging for both habitual drunkards and wide-beaters. *Evening Star*, May 19, 1899: 1.

took an increasingly serious view of male violence directed at women and children. In common with the situation in England, as described by Martin Wiener, Toronto placed increasing discursive constraints on the violence of males particularly of the kind directed towards women.[123] Within this discourse in Toronto, there was a tension as to whether or not to impose harsh physical punishment. But in the end an increasingly humanitarian response and a rejection of physical violence in BEP-influenced Toronto meant that the resort to court-ordered use of the lash did not prevail with respect to "wife-beating".[124] The lash did, however, continue to be used for males convicted of sexual assault against women and children.

The mass media nature of the daily newspaper, combined with almost universal literacy, turned the Victorian newspaper into a "billy club" that gained entrance to both the home and the place of leisure. By 1891 combined Toronto daily newspaper circulation exceeded 200,000, giving enormous coverage for "court report" columns. In a communal and religious culture, the public naming of individuals had an important shaming effect.

6.3 The Roots of "The Peaceful Canadian"

Through the daily newspaper, Canadians constructed "peaceful" identities for themselves by reading accounts of violence in the U.S. and overseas and then contrasting these images with evolving and increasingly moralistic Canadian ones. This process was fused with religious conceptions, combined with the vaunting of Canada as an integral part of the British Empire. This image of the "peaceful Canadian" overlapped but was not coterminous with an ideology of British Empire. The idea of Canada as a haven for non-English-speaking European refugees began to be imprinted in the identities of Canadians, and although linked to centralized Canadian immigration

---

[123] Martin J. Wiener, *Men of Blood*. Clive Emsley argues in a similar, if more cautious, fashion in Clive Emsley, *Hard Men: The English and Violence Since 1750* (London: Hambledon and London, 2005).

[124] From one angle these developments could be viewed as simply a function of an increasingly regulated society under the influence of reform movements from Britain and the U.S. But from another angle, these reform movements were heavily permeated by evangelical Protestant ideas. In the Ontario context, BEP actors dominated penal reform movements.

policies, gives evidence of definitions of a local, empathetic "space" that began to affect understandings of the nation at large. The evolution of a "peaceful Canadian image" can be tracked, in some of its early phases, by examining the reporting in Toronto newspapers of select overseas events during the period under study.

6.3.1 Why Dreyfus Mattered Then: BEP Responses to Anti-Semitism and Pogroms

Reports of violence toward overseas ethnic minorities were frequent in Toronto's newspapers during the 1880s and 1890s. Beginning in 1880, there were stories of anti-Jewish persecutions in Russia and of anti-Semitism in Germany.[125] Similar reports followed from Hungary.[126] More serious reports of pogroms in Russia and Poland became frequent. Front-page stories in 1882 described a number of massacres in detail in the *Globe*. In Britain there was widespread outrage, led by philo-Semitic evangelicals who agitated on behalf of allowing refugees to emigrate. Between 1881 and 1905 an estimated 750,000 mainly working-class Jews emigrated, with 600,000 travelling to the U.S. and 100,000 to Britain.[127] Canada had received approximately 10,000 Jewish refugees by 1900.[128] Toronto's Jewish population stood at 500 in 1881 and 1,425 in 1891, rose to 3,000 by 1901, and then grew rapidly to reach 31,000 in 1921.[129]

While ostensibly Jewish immigrants were required to settle west of Ontario to help populate the Canadian North West, in reality it was accepted that they would populate urban centres. In Toronto the vast majority made their new homes in the Ward. The fact that over 10,000 Jews journeyed to Canada and 100,000 to England points to a broadly philo-Semitic element in BEP discourse. The late Victorian emigration of Jews to Canada and to Britain was

[125] *Globe*, January 12, 1881: 4. On the Dreyfus affair see Louis Begley, *Why the Dreyfus Affair Matters* (New Haven: Yale University Press, 2009).
[126] *Globe*, July 1, 1882: 1.
[127] Donald M. Lewis, *The Origins of Christian Zionism: Lord Shaftesbury and Evangelical Support for a Jewish Homeland* (Cambridge: Cambridge University Press, 2009), 223-226.
[128] Gerald Tulchinsky, *Canada's Jews: A People's Journey* (Toronto: University of Toronto Press, 2008), 75.
[129] J.M.S. Careless, *Toronto to 1918*, 201.

possible, in part, because of the relatively hospitable environment that BEP discourse hoped to create.[130]

A humanitarian, philo-Semitic outlook is quite evident on the front page of the *Globe* during the 1880s. By 1882, pogroms in Poland and Russia had placed the Russian government on the defensive in the face of withering British criticism from a range of religious communities.[131] The issue took on a highly religious tone with the Archbishop of Canterbury, the Catholic Cardinal Manning, the BEP reformer Lord Shaftesbury, and the London preacher, Charles Spurgeon, all becoming involved in the protest movement.[132] In London the Lord Mayor's Jewish Relief fund had already raised 35,000 pounds.[133]

BEP humanitarianism in Toronto is evident in a letter to the editor of the *Globe* in response to coverage of the pogroms that followed the assassination of Czar Alexander in 1881:

APPEAL FOR HELP TO PERSECUTED JEWS

Sir, —I have learned through your columns and other sources of the frightful injustice and cruelty inflicted on the Jews in Russia. Viewing the matter simply in the light of a large number of our fellow beings of the human-family suffering indescribable hardships, even to starvation, it appears to me that all who possess any measure of human sympathy and kindness, living in this highly favoured land of plenty, and where no such brutal outrages as these poor people have been subjected to would be permitted for one moment, should contribute to relieve their special

---

[130] The "Atlantic boom" had immense implications even for Europe's hinterlands, with religion playing a key role in the formation of North Atlantic networks. With respect to a similar migratory event in an earlier period, Bernard Bailyn poses the question of why 100,000 German Protestants, of a total of 500,000 who fled the Palatinate, left for a hazardous trip to the Americas when they could have gone to nearby Prussia. Clearly religious ideology has greatly influenced migratory destinations. See Bernard Bailyn, *Atlantic History: Concept and Contours* (Cambridge, MA: Harvard University Press, 2005), 36-38.

[131] However, it was the BEP quarter that drove the philo-Semitic agenda for decades. See especially Donald M. Lewis, *The Origins of Christian Zionism*.

[132] *Globe*, February 2, 1882: 2.

[133] *Globe*, February 8, 1882: 1.

wants and assist them from departing from under such a barbarous people and from under such an unjust Government, and thus manifest thankfulness to the Giver of all Good that we are happily freed from the endurance of such calamities and the inclination to indulge in such odious crimes as those poor helpless people have suffered from. This help is urged from consideration of the common brotherhood of man. But the careful student of God's Word and the enlightened Christian may well may be influenced by higher motives and more cogent reasons to render help to Jewish people in a time of calamity. They belong to the same nation as God's friend Abraham, as Moses the law-giver, as David the most sublime among the poets; as Isaiah, Daniel, John and an illustrious line of inspired prophets; as the Apostles Paul, Peter, and others who persevered through every difficulty and danger that we Gentiles might be delivered from the bondage of idolatry and superstition in this life and have glorious prospects in the life to come; as Jesus, the Son of God, the King of Israel, the Redeemer of Mankind. I refer also to the fact that they are of the same nationality as multitudes of the greatest names in this present age among statesmen, musicians, philosophers, historians, and financiers. It would seem from what we learn that it is because they have more talent, industry, and economy, and are therefore more successful as business men, that some of the barbarous people among the Russians and Germans have been excited to the acts of cruelty toward them of which we have heard.

But, to be practical, I suggest that one or more of our respected Jewish fellow-citizens should make it known that contributions will be received by them for the purposes above indicated.

I shall be happy to contribute fifty dollars.

Yours, &c.,

CHRISTIAN HUMANITY.

February 7, 1882.[134]

---

[134] *Globe*, February 10, 1893: 3.

On display in the above letter are classic BEP outlooks and doctrines. Espousing monogenesis in terms of human origins, this deep-seated belief is extended to fit the contexts increased communications had created. Beliefs concerning human beings made in the "Image of God" encompass beings far removed from Canada. Railways and steamships, the products of industrialization, allow for the migration of Jewish refugees over vast distances. The telegraph has widened the field of protest. A BEP apparatus takes on a new cause. A novel mechanism involving material aid is hinted at; the idea of a "relief fund", a concept that evangelicals built on throughout the remainder of the century, emerges. Jews in Toronto are referred to as "fellow-citizens". Canada is presented as a kind of 'haven'.

The next day a letter in response appeared. Issuing from an organization, newly dubbed as the Anglo-Jewish Association, and signed by its president, Mark Samuel, and two other executive members, it acknowledged "the noble, philanthropic, and truly Christian sentiments" the 'Christian Humanity' letter had expressed. Some measure of Christian-Jewish cooperation and solidarity was clearly present. A kind of comprehensive, cross-religious citizenry was in existence. Anti-Semitism may still have remained an element in Canadian culture, but its presence was qualified.[135]

Over the decades of the 1880s and the 1890s, pogroms involving rapes and massacres of Jews in Poland and Russia continued to receive BEP-inflected news coverage. Mass journalism and a humanitarian ideology put entire groups of people in a new light.[136] The newspaper also served as a fund-raising instrument for BEP-influenced causes: Russo-Jewish Relief Fund, for example.[137] By the 1890s relief-fund-columns this was expanded beyond Russian Jewish relief to assistance for other groups.

[135] *Globe*, February 11, 1882: 16. Mark Samuel is listed in the 1881 Canada Census as an English-born merchant while Emanuel Samuel is a Quebec-born merchant of German ethnicity. The other signatory to the letter, Alfred D. Benjamin, is not listed in the census and is possibly a newcomer. See also *Globe*, March 4, 1882: 14; May 24, 1882: 6; January 25, 1883: 6; June 23, 1887: 8.

[136] See for example *Globe*, February 21, 1882: 2; April 20, 1882: 2; 26:1; May 22, 1882: 1; July 1, 1882; June 25, 1884: 1; July 3, 1896: 1.

[137] See for example, *Globe*, March 4, 1882: 14; March 18: 14.

BEP REACTION TO ACCOUNTS OF VIOLENCE

Reaction to the celebrated Dreyfus case in France was similarly influenced by BEP thinking. One letter to the editor of the *Globe* declared that "the English people of both Continents" had been shocked by the news of the second court martial of the "innocent martyr" and called for a boycott of the upcoming World's Fair in Paris. After the court's decision the *Globe* published a full page on the affair and also devoted more than one-half of the front page to it.[138] The case, said the *Globe*, was an "outrage", a violation of a sense of justice "that had been strengthened and consolidated by years of Christian civilization".[139]

Atrocities committed against Armenians were also being reported in Canadian newspapers, and in similar language. "MASSACRES, Horrible Accounts of Turkish Cruelty, BUTCHERY OF ARMENIANS, Helpless Women and Children Slaughtered. SHAMEFUL ATTROCITIES" were occurring. Babies were reported to have been killed; blood was reported to have flowed from the doors of churches.[140] Calls were made for immediate British intervention in Turkey[141] in the face of a perceived lack of decisive action from the Central Powers.[142]

A special meeting of the Evangelical Alliance, held at the Bond Street Congregational Church, and chaired by Samuel Blake, drew up a resolution that was sent to the Evangelical Alliance in London. It demanded a thorough investigation of the massacres; it also demanded that action be taken by Europe and America to prevent their reoccurrence. It was now time, as a young Armenian McMaster Hall seminary student put it, to go beyond looking on from the sidelines in "heartless apathy"; Canadians must stop "turn[ing] a deaf ear to the cries of this helpless and oppressed race." "Britain", as Blake reminded the meeting, "had always sympathized with the oppressed

---

[138] *Globe*, September 12, 1899: 1, 10.

[139] *Globe*, September 12, 1899: 2. The quote is from Nova Scotia Attorney-General James Wilberforce Longley, and reflects the stance of the *Globe*. September 12, 1899: 2.

[140] *Globe*, November 17, 1894: 13. Note that this was the first page of the news portion of the Saturday paper, with the first section being the weekly features supplement.

[141] *Globe*, January 17, 1895: 2.

[142] *Globe*, December 17, 1894: 1; January 18, 1895: 8.

in any part of the world", and Canada should now follow suit.[143]

Regular newspaper coverage of the ongoing "outrage" showed how concerned the Toronto public was. Detailed reports were given of the British response.[144] Careful, village-by-village accounts of death and destruction were published. "Christendom" was reproached for its neglect of the Armenian people. "Armies" of "unpartisan" volunteers to provide for and to "inspire", "feed and clothe" the "victims" were called for.[145]

George Grant, concerned at the lack of action in support of the Armenians concerning the tragedy,[146] wrote to the *Globe* asking that a relief fund be formed on behalf of Armenian victims. Mentioning that there were several Queen's University graduates working in the affected areas, and vouching for their integrity, he appended a letter from one of them, Rev. R. Chambers, a former minister in Whitby, Ontario. The letter urged financial support for the victims and underscored the appeal by making reference to a mass killing in which, Chambers estimated, 50,000 people had been "butchered".[147]

Reportage steadily kept attention on the cause. The *Globe* editorialized on "The Shame of Christendom". American relief efforts were lauded. Clara Barton of the American Red Cross was singled out; her work demonstrated to the "bestial Turk what resolute womanhood, enfranchised from the western

[143] *Globe*, January 18, 1895: 8.

[144] *Globe*, August 19, 1895: 5.

[145] *Globe*, November 28, 1885: 1-2.

[146] Reporting showed increasing pessimism about any action being taken. One eyewitness writer complained bitterly that people were only interested in receiving news of the latest massacre in time for the "breakfast table" and that the "European powers are playing a farcical representation around the graves of a Christian people." *Globe*, December 30, 1885: 1. *Globe*, February 11, 1882: 16. By December there were reports that one-half million were dead or near death as a result of starvation. *Globe*, December 9, 1895: 3. The Toronto branch of the Evangelical Alliance continued to discuss and to urge for action on behalf of the Armenians. *Globe*, December 16, 1885: 10; January, 10, 1896: 10. On December 28, readers opened the Saturday features section, and after viewing a portrait of the Trinity Medical College Banquet Committee, were confronted by a large, graphic drawing, taken from a photograph, of dozens of dead Armenians awaiting burial and surrounded by chatting Turkish soldiers. *Globe*, December 28, 1895: 2.

[147] *Globe*, January 29, 1886: 9. For a report from another Canadian missionary in the Armenian area of Turkey see *Globe*, March 28, 1896: 12.

world with honor and liberty, can do." The editorial urged support for George Grant's plea to establish a fund for Armenian relief.[148]

The first donor list appeared in the pages of the *Globe* in March. Of the donating churches 17 were Presbyterian, 5 were Methodist, 1 was Baptist, 1 was Congregational, 1 was Anglican, and 1 was United Brethren.[149]

The following year, with the outbreak of catastrophic famine in India, BEP institutions took similar action with the establishment of an India Famine Fund.[150] The newspaper, combined with the telegraph, had brought a human calamity to the Toronto breakfast table or shop floor, and readers and organizations alike responded.[151]

[148] *Globe*, February 10, 1896: 10.

[149] *Globe*, March 5, 1896: 12; March 17, 1896; June 16, 1896: 12. While the individual controlling the collection, Dr. Walter Geikie, was Presbyterian, the *Globe* did not identify him as such and merely printed his mailing address. Geikie taught at the University of Toronto medical school. While I found four relief fund lists, there was reference to at least five. However the Church of England Woman's Auxiliary voted that their "extra cent-a-day self-denial money" for the month, the significant amount of $64", go towards Armenia relief. *Globe*, March 14, 1896: 20. Also, a Grimsby town hall meeting on Armenia raised $100. *Globe*, March 14, 1896: 15. On March 26th Geikie is reported to have sent a sixth bank draft for $1,250 for Armenian relief from Ontario donors. *Globe*, March 26, 1896: 12. Significantly Geikie was the son of the Presbyterian Rev. Adam Archibald Geikie, who was a founding committee member of the Anti-Slavery Association of Canada.

[150] See for example: *Globe*, February 12, 1897: 12; February 13: 28; March 4, 1897: 12; April 12: 10; April 15: 12 (The March 4 and April 15 lists were almost entirely donations from Presbyterian churches. The relief drive seems to have been organized primarily by Rev. Dr. Warden of the Canadian Presbyterian Church, with the cooperation of several banks and the *Globe*). For the initial efforts to organize a relief fund in England see *Globe*, January 13, 1897: 1. At the end of 1899, missionary reports from India spoke of the deaths of 1000-1500 daily in one area alone. Both Canadian missionaries and newspaper readings were being confronted by indescribable horror, a portent of the century to come. *Globe*, December 29, 1899: 10.

[151] Other overseas clusters of violent events portrayed in newspapers include: Turkish slaughter of Bulgarians (*Globe*, May 3, 1880: 1); an anti-Chinese pogrom in Peru leaving 80 dead (*Globe*, April 7, 1881: 2); riots in China (*Globe*, November 11, 1884: 1); massacre of Christians in China (*Globe*, November 6, 1886: 10); a description of executions in Bulgaria (*Globe*, May 28, 1887); an eyewitness account of a mass scene of torture and execution in Canton where "human beings" were slaughtered "like pigs" (*Globe*, July 27, 1889: 7); the torture and butchery of prisoners during a civil war in Haiti (*Globe*, August 7, 1889: 1); Japanese killings of Chinese (*Globe*, January 8, 1895: 1); sectarian riots in India (*Globe*, September 4, 1895: 1); a reported killing of 25,000 Muslims by pillaging Greek troops

6.3.2 "The Daily Lynching Report"

Reports on violence in North America also indicate the degree to which BEP ideas were influencing reactions to it. In what the *Globe* once christened "The Daily Lynching Report",[152] it gave BEP-inflected accounts of various examples of that outrage. Deeply disturbing images of the American South and West were no doubt etched in readers' minds. On a number of occasions burnings at the stake were described in detail.[153]

Duels from both overseas and in the American South were regularly reported. These ranged from South Carolina to Texas, Russia, Hungary, Vienna, and Paris. A prurient flavour characterized the descriptions; sexual rivalries or wives who had been slighted were featured.[154] BEP moralizing was much in evidence.

Narratives of anti-Semitic pogroms, the massacre of Armenians, and reports of lynching and duels all combined to indicate the presence of BEP ideology. The cementing of the image of Canada as a non-violent haven for the persecuted and abased undoubtedly had origins in this period, regardless of how closely it corresponds with "reality". The need to define oneself as not being a "barbarian" was internalized in the behaviour of the residents of Toronto including those who were recent immigrants.[155] These internal

---

(*Globe*, February 23: 1); execution by beheading of rioters in Korea (*Globe*, July 1, 1899: 12); widespread rioting in Italy (*Globe*, March 6, 1896: 1). For a study of how written accounts of "oriental" tortures have functioned in the Western imagination see Timothy Brook, Jerome Bourgon, and Gregory Blue, *Death by a Thousand Cuts* (Cambridge, MA: Harvard University Press, 2008).

[152] *Globe*, August 15, 1894: 1. Two Blacks were lynched in Lauraville, Florida and the heading reads, "The Daily Lynching".

[153] See for example a report from New Orleans, *Globe*, December 31, 1885: 1; from Paris, Texas, *Globe*, February 2, 1893: 2. For other lynching see *Globe*, February 21, 1881: 3; March 31, 1891: 13; April 16, 1881: 1; August 1, 1893; August 2, 1893; August 10, 1896; May 13, 1897: 1; August 11, 1898. I made no attempt to do a comprehensive search for lynching. This is a sampling. In one year alone there had been 37 lynching to date. *Globe*, September 26, 1884: 1. Many of those hung in the Western U.S. were whites.

[154] *Globe*, June 4, 1880: 1; June 1, 1883: 1, 2; August 13, 1883: 8; October 23, 1883: 1; August 2, 1890: 2; January 2, 1891: 1; June 7, 1880: 2. I have made no attempt to be comprehensive in this listing.

[155] For a stream of nineteenth-century Canadian thought that saw Canada as a "haven for

restraints were much influenced by a BEP ideology that allowed for new expressions of human empathy and are evident in the written texts that have been highlighted in this chapter. An important shaping force was at work.

6.4 Reducing Interpersonal Violence in Late Nineteenth-Century Toronto

Interpersonal exchanges in late nineteenth-century Toronto were increasingly controlled by BEP protocols. These prescribed proper deportment whether on a streetcar or in a department store. Increased constraints were placed on activity deemed to be criminal, ranging from petty larceny to public drunkenness to common assault. The gross underrepresentation of prisoners with BEP affiliations in Central Prison demonstrate these constraints in play. Let us now turn to how these mechanisms worked.

By the 1880s, BEP power was increasingly evident at the municipal, provincial and federal levels and was positioned to supply the leverage to pass legislation that touched on all aspects of culture including the regulation of alcohol, education, the social "safety net", and the penal system. Males were being more and more effectively regulated through this BEP web of cultural influence; this can be seen, very dramatically, through the examination of homicide rates earlier in this study.

The fact that prison committals declined across denominations in the 1890s can be attributed to a non-violent discourse being spread in a "contagion" fashion. Toronto culture as a whole had adapted to urbanization and industrialization in non-violent ways. This adaptation of course reaches back in time, but within the BEP disciplining process I propose that non-violence was heightened in three ways.

First, British evangelical Protestantism was a communal movement. Earlier in this chapter, I used the example of Rev. J.M. Cameron to describe

---

the oppressed", see Allan Smith, *Canada- An American Nation? Essays on Continentalism, Identity, and the Canadian Frame of Mind*, (Montreal and Kingston: McGill-Queen's University Press, 1994), 32-36. Exactly how these "myths" were incorporated into Canadian identities is complex. However, the capacity of Canadian culture to "settle" immigrant populations in the coming decades without widespread race riots and pogroms must have roots in the period under discussion. Canada was part of a region that for well over a century participated in the largest migration in history, of peoples from a periphery to a centre.

a process whereby males were socialized into the church and thereby were able to leave their drinking and spending habits behind, replacing them with regular employment and an accompanying self-esteem. Within this process Cameron mentioned the work of the "ladies" in visiting households, while on another occasion he spoke of their work on temperance reform.[156] William H. Howland's rise to power demonstrates not only the presence of a strong BEP political discourse that included an alcohol regulatory agenda that was adopted. This broad process involving the activism of both BEP men and women undoubtedly disciplined male behaviour in general by increasingly removing males from the tavern and placing them in the church, religious and other associations, and within families. Interpersonal violence became less likely.

Secondly, males in BEP Toronto came under increased constraints and were forced into church contexts in order to pursue marriage, at a time when single women disproportionately participated in church life and followed religious protocols.[157] Even when not religiously active, high percentages of males remained exposed to church teaching through religious women. BEP discourse in particular reduced the overall use of alcohol in Toronto and thereby strengthened household economies. By 1894 eligible women voted overwhelmingly for the prohibition of alcohol.[158] Males were increasingly

---

[156] *Globe*, November 12, 1888: 8.

[157] For material on the example of a young migrant to the city, Frank Roberts, see Nancy Christie, *Christian Churches and Their Peoples*, 88; Nancy Christie, "Young Men and the Creation of Civic Christianity in Urban Methodist Churches, 1880-1914" *Journal of the Canadian Historical Association*, 17, No. 1 (2006): 79-106.

[158] Women "led the charge" in the Prohibition campaign. For example, in the 1894 Toronto plebiscite on Prohibition, 72% of women voted in favour of Prohibition as compared to 57% of the total vote that was favour of Prohibition. The women's vote was distinguished by a blue ballot while it was yellow for men. Of course, only a minority of women could vote. *Globe*, January 2, 1894: 2. The total 1894 vote saw 85% of eligible women vote in favour of prohibition. See Ruth E. Spence, *Prohibition in Canada: A Memorial to Francis Stephen Spence* (Toronto: Ontario Branch of the Dominion Alliance, 1919), 211. There is a wealth of current research that links the abuse of alcohol with increased interpersonal violence. See Brad J. Bushman, "Effects of Alcohol on Human Aggression: Validity of Proposed Explanations," *Recent Developments in Alcoholism*, vol. 13, *Alcohol and Violence*, ed., Mark Galanter (New York: Kluwere, 1997), 227-243; B.J. Bushman and H.M. Cooper, "Effects

tied to women and children and disciplined by the mix of marriage and religion. Interpersonal violence decreased. Women gained a greater measure of power, with their concerns increasingly driving the familial agenda. BEP communities exhibited high levels of literacy.[159] In the process the new entrepreneurial networks in which BEP working class males became involved gave them increased access to better job possibilities and worked for the benefit of household economies.[160] I tentatively argue that this familial configuration

---

of Alcohol on Human Aggression: An Integrative Research Review," *Psychological Bulletin* 107, 3 (May, 1990): 341-354. It is argued that alcohol indirectly increases physical aggression in the context of "provocations, frustrations, and aggressive cues". They argue that the "crowded, noisy, smoky, and provocative environments" of bars explain the all too common "barroom brawls". The authors' conclusion was that one way to produce a "kinder, gentler society" would be to simply consume less alcohol. BEP reformers of all stripes, prohibitionist or not, would have agreed with this conclusion on the basis of their observations. Recent studies have also shown that control of outlets selling alcohol leads to less consumption when compared to locations with deregulated sales outlets. For example, excessive alcohol consumption was responsible for 79,000 deaths in the U.S. during 2001. See Carla Alexia Campbell, Robert A. Hahn, Randy Elder, et al, "The Task Force on Community Preventative Services," *American Journal of Preventive Medicine* 37, no. 6 (December 2009): 556-559. Gavin Dingwall, *Alcohol and Crime* (Cullompton, Devon: Willan Publishing, 2006); Robert Nash Parker with Linda-Anne Rebhun, *Alcohol and Homicide: A Deadly Combination of Two American Traditions* (Albany: State University of New York Press, 1990); M. Lehti and J. Kivivuori, "Alcohol-related Violence as an Explanation for the Difference Between Homicide Rates in Finland and the Other Nordic Countries," *Nordisk alcohol-och narkoticatidskrift* 22, English Supplement (2005): 7-24. Additional research argues that the regulation of alcohol diminishes the incidence of violence in line with the thesis of this study of nineteenth-century Toronto. See W.A. Pridemore and T.H. Grubesic, "Alcohol Outlets and Community Levels of Interpersonal Violence: Spatial Density, Type of Outlet, and Seriousness of Assault" *Journal of Research in Crime and Delinquency* 50, no. 1 (February 2013): 132-159; Robert Nash Parker, "Alcohol and Violence: Connections, Evidence and Possibilities for Prevention" *Journal of Psychoactive Drugs* 36, sup. 2 (2004): 157-163.

[159] Current research links literacy with lower levels of homicide on both a macro-level and an individual level. See for example Andrew Stickley and William A. Pridemore, "The Social-Structural Correlates of Homicide in Late-Tsarist Russia," *British Journal of Criminology* 47, no. 1 (January 2007): 80-99.

[160] For example, the YMCA sought to find job placements for young men. The Prisoners' Aid Association also sought work for released prisoners. Undoubtedly most BEP work networks would have been informal. Valverde accepts that male "purity" reinforced the capitalist ethic, allowing for familial economic gains. She is, however, ambivalent about the extent that "purity" was shaped by the agendas of women. Mariana Valverde, *The Age of Light*, 29-33. In the second edition of her monograph, Valverde acknowledges that temperance should have held a much larger place in her thought (p. 12). Paul E. Johnson argues that evangelical

was to hold for decades both in Toronto, but also across a wider swath of Canadian culture.

Finally, Steven Pinker, following Wilson and Daly, has posited that in the limiting of sexual partners, violence decreases as the result of fewer sexual rivalries.[161] For Canada, W. Peter Ward has provided evidence of this increased limiting of sexual partners in an examination of a cluster of church parish registers in Eastern Ontario for the first half of the nineteenth century. These registers show "illegitimacy" rates of 1-3%. Ward estimates that even accounting for "concealed bastardy", the "illegitimate" birth rates in English Canada never would have exceeded 5% throughout the nineteenth century and most likely were in the 2-4% range. If this is correct, then Canada had lower rates of "illegitimacy" than most of Western Europe, with only Ireland having a lower rate. In England and Wales the rates fluctuated from 6% early in the nineteenth century to 4% later in the century.[162] Ward elsewhere argues

---

working class converts in Rochester, New York during the revivalist movements of the 1830s and 1840s gained economic credentials that allowed them to economically better their families. See Paul E. Johnson, *A Shopkeeper's Millennium: Society and Revivals in Rochester, New York, 1815-1837* (New York: Hill and Wang, 1978), 116-128. This change was brought about by the temperance society, the Sunday School, and the revival (p. 6). Johnson argues that "pious housewives", impacted by revivalism, gained a "new kind of moral authority", brought about the conversions of males, and that household became "inappropriate places in which to get drunk" (pp. 55-61, 108).

[161] Steven Pinker, *Better Angels of Our Nature*, 105-116. Pinker quotes Wilson and Daly frequently, including, on page 105, where his longer discussion of men, sexuality, self-control and the influence of marriage on violent male behavior is heavily dependent on them. Wilson and Daly, *Homicide*, 137-155, 174-303. "Monogamy" in this context refers to the cultural practice of having one sexual partner. It need not necessarily entail lifelong sexual partnership.

[162] W. Peter Ward, "Unwed Motherhood in Nineteenth-Century English Canada," *Historical Papers*, 1981, 34-55. Ward's data, based on birth records, indicates that approximately 10% of Canadian brides, for the period 1800-1878, were pregnant when married. Given that only 2% of births were outside of marriage, and it needs to be remembered that the child born prior to a marriage was deemed a bastard even if the mother subsequently married the father, then these data seem to clearly show the compulsion of a couple to marry following pregnancy. See pp. 38-39. See also Peter Laslett, Karla Oosterveen and Richard M. Smith, eds., *Bastardy and its Comparative History: Studies in the History of Illegitimacy and Marital Nonconformism in Britain, France, Germany, Sweden, North America, Jamaica and Japan* (Cambridge: Harvard University Press, 1980), esp. 19-29. More recent British studies have not changed this picture. "Illegitimacy" in England and Wales rose steadily during the

that it was women and children, the most economically vulnerable, who profited the most from the general respect that society afforded marriage.[163] By 1921 official out-of-marriage births stood at 2%. This is clear evidence that pre-nuptial conceptions were "legitimized" by subsequent marriage.[164] In an age of less reliable contraception, these rates point to sexual partnerships that were generally restricted to marriage, and if Pinker is correct, lower levels of interpersonal violence were in part a result of fewer sexual rivalries; increased monogamy resulted in decreased violence.

These factors, acting in combination with a BEP disciplining process, lowered specific kinds of interpersonal violence within the BEP community. Furthermore, through the BEP "machine", new cultural norms were produced in Toronto, which acted on all parts of the whole. Ultimately, dense social relationships were produced in all sectors of society, with relatively strong household economies spread throughout the city. These reciprocal networks enabled the expression of high levels of empathy.[165] Over the coming decades

---

seventeenth century, peeked at about 7% in 1850 and then dropped steadily such that it was under 4% at the beginning of World War II. See Alysa Levine, Thomas Nutt and Samantha Williams, eds., *Illegitimacy in Britain, 1700-1920* (London: Palgrave Macmillan, 2005), 5-8. The Canadian data seem to be slightly lower for the later nineteenth century but are virtually identical with England and Wales in 1940. The steepest drop in England is in the period 1880-1900 with the lowest point circa 1900, precisely when BEP ideology was most prevalent in both Canada and England and Wales.

[163] W. Peter Ward, *Courtship, Love, and Marriage in Nineteenth-Century English Canada* (Montreal and Kingston: McGill-Queen's University Press, 1991), 49.

[164] M.C. Urquhart and K.A.H. Buckley, *Historical Statistics of Canada* (Toronto: Macmillan Company, 1965), 38. The Canadian rate (Quebec excluded from 1921-1925) rose very slowly from 2.0 in 1921, to 4.0 in 1942, and to 4.3 in 1960. These are very low rates historically. If there were vagaries in the classifying of births one would expect fluctuations, but with the exception for the end of the War figures (1943, 4.1%; 1944, 4.2%; 1945, 4.5%; 1946, 4.1%; 1947, 4.0%; 1948, 4.3%; 1949; 4.0%), the figures through the 1950s held stable from 3.9%-4.2%.

[165] In addition to Robert Putnam see also Richard Wilkinson and Kate Pickett, *The Spirit Level: Why Greater Equality Makes Society Stronger* (New York: Bloomsbury Press, 2009). But for a critique of social capital theorizing see Barbara Arneil, *Diverse Communities: The Problem with Social Capital* (Cambridge: Cambridge University Press, 2006). While Constance Backhouse and others have documented the systematic discrimination against ethnic and cultural minorities within communities such as Toronto, I argue that it was the formation of social capital that over time provided "space" for the "other". This had earlier

this communal, economically responsible, family-focussed social order was to prove highly adept at reproducing a largely non-violent culture. The critical importance of a "moral individualism" in the decline of interpersonal violence has gained clarity.[166]

been demonstrated in the abolition of slavery, a novel and religious development.

[166] Manuel Eisner, "Long-Term Historical Trends in Violent Crime," 112-113. Likewise Gorski emphasizes the "ethical behavior of individual believers" as a driving force behind a revolutionary social change. See Philip S. Gorski, *The Disciplinary Revolution*, 170-172.

7

THE TAKE-UP OF BEP IDEAS: QUANTIFYING HOMICIDE AND INTERPERSONAL VIOLENCE IN LATE NINETEENTH-CENTURY TORONTO

Overview

Homicide rates declined sharply in Toronto during the period from 1880 to 1900 and this decline was due to the increasing dominance of a British evangelical Protestant (BEP) religious expression that brought about changes in "civility", including increased constraints upon interpersonal violence.

This tentative conclusion was brought about by a two-stage process. In the first-stage, I followed the British findings of Gatrell, Emsley, and Weiner, as outlined in Chapter One that found homicide declining in Victorian Britain. Using both official data and newspaper reports I calculated both murder and homicide rates for the period from 1880 to 1900. For the period of 1880-1889 my calculation was 2.6 homicides per 100,000 per year and dropping to 1.5 per 100,000 per year for 1890-1899. These are extremely low rates and consistent with declining homicide rates in Britain during the same period.

In the second stage, I follow the Darroch/Soltow thesis that one can gain access to the "conduct and deportment" of populations in the past by accessing prison records. This examination confirmed the Darroch/Soltow finding that the more evangelical groups were severely underrepresented and even after socio-economic factors are accounted for, there remains a stubborn religious dimension to the data. Central Prison Register records over 10,000 committals as the result of convictions for indictable offences from 1874-1889. Over 2,500 of these are men who listed Toronto as their place of residence. By examining the nature of these men's offences, I was able to isolate convictions that involved physical violence. By examining the personal information provided—this included religious affiliation, occupation, and judgments concerning literacy and the prisoner's use of alcohol—I was able to group prisoners accordingly to their association with various groups. This allowed me to conclude that involvement with BEP beliefs lowered levels of male interpersonal violence in Toronto during the later decades of the nineteenth century; a connection between behavior and ideology seems clear. Furthermore, these finding confirm Weberian theorizing that the asceticism of Protestant "sects" morally shaped their communities and surrounding culture.

Introduction

There are undoubtedly multiple pathways to cultural configurations marked by low levels of interpersonal violence.[1] Gurr, Eisner, Muchembled, and others have demonstrated that homicide rates plummeted over much of Europe from the medieval era through the nineteenth century. While this general phenomenon has been firmly established, the reasons for this remain in the realm of hypothesis. I will argue that in the last two decades of the nineteenth century, in the midst of this broad decline, Toronto's homicide rate took a particularly steep downward turn. This sharp dip within a long decline is also mirrored in English homicide statistics for the same period and so far has not recurred either in England or in Canada.[2]

This Victorian downturn in violence begs historical investigation. That violence would decrease in the midst of increasing affluence is contrary to late twentieth-century historical and criminological orthodoxies; from 1960-1990, for example, increased crime and violence tended to accompany increased affluence. As outlined in Chapter One, Robert Muchembled and Manuel Eisner, perhaps the premier interpreters of the U-shaped curve of violence, have hypothesized that the decline came about through a moralistic

---

[1] How "interpersonal violence" is defined is important, and I address this below.

[2] V.A.C. Gatrell, Bruce Lenman, and Geoffrey Parker, eds., *Crime and the Law*, 342. The British homicide rate with slight variation remained from approximately 1.4 to 2 per 100,000 between 1860 and 1888. From 1891 it did not exceed 1.1 per 100,000. But note that 2 per 100,000 is already an extremely low rate compared to any culture across time for which recorded data exists. See the data in the appendix in Dane Archer and Rosemary Gartner, *Violence and Crime in Cross-National Perspective* (New Haven: Yale University Press, 1984).

and religious reshaping of male behaviour. Muchembled has seen the banning of male violence from both the public and private spheres as possible because of the "extreme plasticity of civilizations".[3] This plasticity of culture, particularly in a city, allows for moral regimes whereby the prohibition against male interpersonal violence becomes an "obsession".[4] Both Muchembled and Eisner have cited the need for additional studies that would look at how a moral individualism was shaped at the local level.[5] This study has attempted to do so from within the culture of late nineteenth-century Toronto. I now turn to the "take-up" of BEP ideas as evidenced in first, the decline of violence within the broader Toronto culture and then second, the disproportional decline of violence within the BEP denominations.

7.1 Toronto Homicide Rates: 1880-1890

Homicide is the most easily measured violent crime;[6] homicide becomes a good measure of interpersonal violence in a culture. From the aggregate homicide cases from this time period, murder convictions can be examined by using the National Archives of Canada publication, *Persons Sentenced to Death in Canada, 1867-1976: An Inventory of Case Files in the Records of the Department of Justice* RG13.

Murder conviction rates in Toronto for the period 1867-1940 were as follows:

---

[3] Robert Muchembled, *A History of Violence*, 303. By "extreme plasticity" Muchembled is arguing that violence is capable of being controlled by culture and that there are large variations in violence across cultures and time.

[4] Robert Muchembled, *A History of Violence*, 4, 223.

[5] Manuel Eisner, "Long-Term Historical Trends in Violent Crime," 112-113. Robert Muchembled, *A History of Violence*, 2, 211, 223. Here Muchembled emphasizes the moral shaping of young males that takes place in urban environments in conjunction with the "political, moral, religious, or economic explanations" of declines in violence (p. 223).

[6] Armed bank robberies that were highly visible and always the subject of sensational news reports would also be an easily measured violent crime, of a sort, although in Toronto in the period under examination, they are almost non-existent. One could thus calculate rates of armed bank robberies to get a measure of a particular act of violence across time. The fact that armed bank robbery was an almost non-existent crime, and that a bank robbery homicide did not occur in the period of study, is supportive of my thesis. But see January 29, 1893: 1; January 30, 1893: 8 for an example of a bank robbery.

Table 7.1 Murder convictions in Toronto, 1867-1940

Period	Rate of Convictions Per 100,000	Number	Population Average	Census[7] Count	Year
1867-1870	0.00	0	50,457	44,821	1861
1871-1880	0.56	4	71,253	56,092	1871
1881-1890	0.35	4	115,219	86,415	1881
1891-1900	0.07	1	150,061	144,023	1891
1901-1910	0.21	6	182,069	156,098	1901
1911-1920	0.33	7	251,552	208,040	1911
1921-1930	0.08	4	463,136	295,064	1921
1931-1940	0.10	7	649,332	631,207	1931
				667,457	1941

There was a discernible dip in interpersonal violence in Toronto beginning around 1880; extremely low rates of violence continued well into the twentieth century.[8]

The decline could, to be sure, attributed to an increasing hesitancy of juries to convict on a capital charge. While acknowledging the force of this objection, I would counter that there is enough of a pattern in the above data to posit that the key element is the fact that homicides *deemed to be murder* were of sharply declining frequency.

The remainder of this discussion will therefore concern homicides put in

[7] These are original calculations and are not reproduced from other published work. Through 1921 these are the actual census counts in the census year and are unadjusted to account for expanded city boundaries in subsequent years. See *Canada Census* for each year.

[8] However the identification of the vast majority of knifing, gunshot, and beating deaths did not change over time. Arguably the identification of the cause of death in poisonings, victims found in the water, and apparent suicides did improve with time. Establishing rates is dependent on a legal apparatus including a legal bureaucracy and widespread literacy as seen in the ready availability of newspapers. These ingredients are all present in Victorian Toronto, along with an interest in the details of crime on the part of the general public. No doubt various forms of violence against the person can vary independently of homicide over time and across cultures.

this category whether there was a conviction or not. The Canadian Criminal Code of Canada as amended in 1893 defined murder and manslaughter as follows:

> 227. Culpable homicide is murder in each of the following cases: (a) If the offender means to cause the death of the person killed. (b) If the person means to cause to the person killed any bodily injury which is known to the offender to be likely to cause death; and is reckless whether death ensues or not; (c) If the offender means to cause death or, being so reckless as aforesaid, means to cause such bodily injury as aforesaid to one person, and by accident or mistake kills another person, though he does not mean to hurt the person killed. [Here murder is further defined.] 229. Culpable homicide, which would otherwise be murder, may be reduced to manslaughter if the person who causes death does so in the heat of passion caused by sudden provocation. [Here manslaughter is further defined.][9]

In practice there was a blurring between the categories of murder and manslaughter depending on the dynamics of the jury, the status of the accused, and a range of other factors. Peter Spierenburg has argued, in the context of the history of homicide in the Netherlands, that the historian cannot easily separate murder from manslaughter but should rather combine the two to arrive at a "homicide rate".[10] I follow Spierenburg and use the term "homicide rate" rather than the term "murder rate".

Spierenburg approached long-term homicide trends by studying court records and coroners' reports; this allowed him to arrive at a homicide rate. To make his research manageable he restricted his study to Amsterdam. He

[9] Henri Taschereau, *The Criminal Code of the Dominion of Canada As Amended in 1893*, 210-211.
[10] Peter Spierenburg, "Long-term Trends in Homicide: Theoretical Reflections and Dutch Evidence, Fifteenth to Twentieth Centuries" in *The Civilization of Crime: Violence in Town and Country Since the Middle Ages*, ed. Eric Johnson and Eric M. Monkkonen (Urbana: University of Illinois Press, 1996), 69-71.

excluded infanticides, reasoning that they disclose little about a "propensity for aggression and a lot more about shame and desperation."[11] He also counted victims rather than perpetrators and excluded homicide attempts.[12]

Supplementing records of homicides with newspaper accounts can be useful. This is an arduous task, but Ted Robert Gurr argues that it provides more information about offenders, victims, and the context of the crimes than do official sources.[13] This is the approach that I used in an earlier study of homicide in Toronto for the period 1880-1899.[14] The Toronto of this period was well served by newspapers. As a primary "text" the *Globe* was used, with other Toronto newspapers consulted as needed. The details of even petty crime appeared regularly in a range of Toronto dailies.[15]

---

[11] Peter Spierenburg, "Long-term Trends in Homicide," 72. It is also much more difficult to follow reports of infanticide both in both newspapers and in official sources.

[12] Peter Spierenburg, "Long-term Trends in Homicide," 76.

[13] Ted Robert Gurr, "Historical Trends in Violent Crime: Europe and the United States" in *Violence in America*, vol. 1, *The History of Crime*, ed. Ted Robert Gurr (Newbury Park: Sage, 1989), 46. Martin Wiener made extensive use of newspaper accounts in his massive study of violent crime in Victorian England. From 1858 until 1900 Wiener was able to find a reference in the *Times* to virtually every murder trial and in reverse was able to match every conviction listed in the Annual Judicial Statistics with an article in the *Times*. He argues that newspapers supply a wealth of information and that the accounts are generally reliable and written by barristers. Martin J. Wiener, *Men of Blood*, viii. For commendation of Toronto Police Court reporters see George T. Denison, *Recollections of a Police Magistrate* (Toronto: Musson, 1920), 258-260. A young Henry O'Brien, Q.C. was a court reporter at Osgoode Hall from 1866 to 1876, which is suggestive of a tradition in Canada of law reporters with legal training. G. Mercer Adam, *Toronto Old and New*, 97. John Weaver, in a study of crime and the criminal justice system in nineteenth and twentieth-century Hamilton, Ontario, made a "thorough reading of newspapers" looking for homicides. In no instance did he find a homicide in the coroner's inquest book that was not reported in Hamilton's newspapers. John Weaver, *Crimes, Constables, and Courts: Order and Transgression in a Canadian City: 1816-1970* (Montreal and Kingston: McGill-Queen's University Press, 1995), 217, 309 n. 80.

[14] William D. Reimer, *A Depressing Story? Homicide Rates In Late Victorian Toronto* (master's thesis, University of British Columbia 2006), viewed January 14, 2013, https://circle.ubc.ca/handle/2429/18107. In my database a homicide-suicide listed January 4, 1890 did not take place in Toronto and was listed in error. Another case of manslaughter involving an assault that took place near Gravenhurst, Ontario resulted in the death of John Scott in the Toronto General Hospital. I have not counted this event as a Toronto homicide in the above calculations although it remains in my database. See APPENDIX A for my revised database.

[15] On Toronto's newspapers see Paul Rutherford, *A Victorian Authority*.

Cases of homicide in Toronto invariably received reporting in the dailies; coverage of some was enormous.[16] Such reporting also confirms the decline in homicide rates for the two decades of 1880-1899. The period 1880-1889 saw 78 incidents of possible homicide reported, while the period 1890-1899 saw 61 incidents. These include accidental deaths where there was possible negligence and cases of infanticide. The general trend downward for 1890-1899 remains even when homicides involving negligence (as in the case of streetcar deaths), abortions, and infanticides are dropped from consideration.[17] After infanticides and those homicides classed as "accidental"[18] are separated out, there remains a total of 30 cases that I judged as homicides for the first period from 1880-1889.

For the second period, from 1890-1899, my reading yielded a total of 61 cases[19] involving a finding by a coroner's jury of either "murder" or "manslaughter".[20] If one continues to exclude infanticides and accidental deaths then for the period from 1890 through 1899 there were a total of 23 homicides as compared to 30 cases in the 1880s.[21]

---

[16] The trial of James Birchall in Woodstock received multi-page coverage on successive days and included full transcripts as well as interviews with the accused. See *Globe*, September 30, 1891: 1, 7-9 for approximately four full pages in a ten-page issue. Cases involving manslaughter or infanticide often had full column articles and updates on subsequent days. Even for these less sensational cases it is possible to "capture" a case initially and then "recapture" it again after an inquest was conducted, and then again, if a "true bill" was produced, as it travelled on to trial. An additional "recapture" can be obtained in the Chief Constable's Report, although often only as an aggregate statistic. The newspaper coverage included the location of where the body was found, allowing for a determination as to whether the homicide occurred within Toronto or an outlying community. How long a victim lived can often be ascertained from a newspaper account. If a victim lingered for several days, one can on average conclude that he or she would have survived a similar assault today, given advancements in trauma medicine.

[17] See APPENDIX A.

[18] "Accidental" deaths include industrial and vehicular deaths, deaths of infants and children as the result of neglect, deaths as the result of the use of Christian Science methods for the treatment of illness, and deaths to women as the result of undergoing an abortion.

[19] In two cases there was a double homicide and in one a triple.

[20] In two cases where the juries could not agree on a finding, I categorized them "murder" as the facts seemed obvious that there was a homicide of some type.

[21] For cross-checking purposes, I consulted at Toronto Archives the annual report of the Chief Constable in the *City Council Minutes* for the years 1881-1900, where the homicides

When calculations are made on a per capita basis, the drop in homicides for the second period appears even steeper. The rate for the 1880s appears as 2.6 per 100,000 per year. For the 1890s it drops to 1.5 per 100,000—very low indices relative to other Western countries in the same approximate time period.[22]

An analysis of the individual homicides themselves is revealing. As pointed out earlier, there were no sectarian killings or lynching in Toronto in the late nineteenth century. There do not appear to be "clan-like" homicides due to ongoing feuds. Neither was there a daughter killed by a "dishonoured" father. No homicide was reported to have been that of a homicide-sexual assault case.[23] There was no one killed during the commission of an armed bank robbery, although there was one victim during an armed burglary.[24] All this suggests strongly that constraints were at work. The lack of homicides in the above-mentioned categories, in an urban area during a two-decade period, points to acceptance of fundamental cultural prohibitions of certain types of violent activity. There is *prima facie* evidence for this thesis's argument that the presence and circulation of BEP beliefs was having effects.

When one looks at the gender categories of homicide, one finds that male

---

for the previous year are listed. It is difficult to match precisely the numbers for a given year with newspaper reports since individual cases are not listed, but totals appear to be consistent with each other for each of the years.

[22] This is a tentative assertion, in that the date of the earliest central government statistics varied. The English, Dutch, and Canadian figures include 1900. The Belgium figures begin in 1909, those for Norway in 1903, while New Zealand's begin in 1920. In addition some of the above data include all known homicides, while for others the rates are based on convictions only. Obviously the later would be an undercount. See the data in the appendix in Dane Archer and Rosemary Gartner, *Violence and Crime in Cross-National Perspective* (New Haven: Yale University Press, 1984). It needs to be emphasized that emergency medicine was primitive.

[23] "Victorian" Canada crime reporting was very explicit with respect to the crime scene and the details of the victim's body. See for example the only murder-suicide, *Globe*, March 25, 1895: 2. Sexual assaults were regularly reported including the name of the attacker and the victim although the details of the assault were censored. For an editorial defence of the way in which Canadian newspapers report sensational news without including salacious details of a "corrupting" nature, in contrast to some papers in the U.S., see an editorial entitled "News and Morality" in the *Globe*, July 27, 1885: 4.

[24] Eisner argues that an important area for future research involves subtypes of homicide including those that are robbery-related killings. Manuel Eisner, "Long-Term Historical Trends," 132.

on male homicide is the most common:

Male on Male-	25 homicides. Of these 6 involved handguns and 3 knives as the weapon.
Male on Male Group Violence-	3 homicides. One involved a cricket game, while the other two possibly involved "gang-like" activity.
Male on Female-	12 homicides. One involved a knife as the weapon. Male and Female on Male- 1 homicide.
Male and Female on Female-	1 homicide.
Male and Female on Child-	2 homicides.
Female on Female-	1 homicide. Took place at the asylum. Not guilty by reason of insanity.
Female on Male-	2 homicides. One involved a handgun as the weapon and the other poison.
Unknown Person on Female-	3 homicides.
Unknown Person on Child-	1 homicide.
Unknown Person on Male-	1 homicide.

Males were involved as perpetrators in 45 of 53 homicides, women in 7 (although only 3 that were strictly female on male), and persons unknown in 5. Of 12 male on female homicides, 4 involved husbands killing wives. The two female on male cases, and the male and female on male case, involved wives killing husbands or participating in such action. In all, of 53 homicides, spouses were involved in only 7.

With husbands killing wives accounting for only 4 of the homicide cases, wife-killing rates appear to be relatively low; this suggests that constraints on violent male behaviour were operating and that they were having some effect. Wife-beating, to be sure, continued—and may even have increased,[25] but the relatively low incidence of wife-killing suggests at least some modification in what the culture legitimated—a conclusion in line with the findings of Clive Emsley and Martin Wiener in their studies of male violence in late Victorian English culture, and with those of Helen Boritch and John Hagan in their examination of policing in Toronto during the same period.[26]

The fact that there was only one homicide-suicide (it involved a male killing his female partner and then himself) provides further support for the conclusion that males were responding to tighter constraints on interpersonal violence during the last two decades of the century. With this single occurrence yielding a homicide-suicide rate for the period of 0.038 per 100,000, we see an extremely low rate.[27]

---

[25] It appears that the reporting of wife-beating increased and it is possible that this reflects increased violence directed against wives and women in general. However, if constraints against wife-beating were increasing, then reports of violence against women could have increased due to an increased intolerance of such violence. I would argue that the latter is the case.

[26] Clive Emsley, *Hard Men: The English and Violence Since 1750* (London: Hambledon and London, 2005), highlights the multitude of data that point to a drop in violence that extends over the later nineteenth century and well into the twentieth; it includes a cautious nod toward the importance of Victorian ideals about the English "gentleman" who was controlled and restrained and did not beat his wife. Martin J. Wiener, *Men of Blood: Violence, Manliness and Criminal Justice in Victorian England* (Cambridge: Cambridge University Press, 2004), persuasively demonstrates that male violence, during the Victorian period, was increasingly an issue for English society. Although such violence provoked conflicting responses, the net result was there were increasing constraints placed on the violence of males, and in particular that directed towards women. Helen Boritch and John Hagan. "Crime and the Changing Forms of Class Control: Policing Public Order in "Toronto the Good," 1859-1955," *Social Forces* 66, 2 (1987), 307-335, argues that policing in Toronto was a form of selective class control. The study affirms that violent crime declined over the last decades of the nineteenth century, and argues that there was an overall decline in arrest rates. Boritch and Hagan do not calculate homicide rates for Toronto.

[27] The percentage of homicides that were homicide-suicides is also a drastically low 1.9%. In contrast, Rosemary Gartner and Bill McCarthy calculated the rate of homicide-suicide for Toronto from 1900-1990 at 0.17 per 100,000 and homicide-suicides as a percentage of homicides at 9%. Rosemary Gartner and Bill McCarthy, "Homicide-Suicide in Four North American Cities" in *Histories of Suicide: International Perspectives on Self Destruction in the Modern World*, ed. John Weaver and David Wright (Toronto: University of Toronto Press,

Male on female homicides did increase in the 1890s, rising to 8 from 1890 to 1899 as compared to 4 for the decade 1880 to 1899. Equally, however, there were 3 women killed in the 1880s by persons unknown as compared to 1 in the 1890s; since one can reasonably conjecture that these killings were by male perpetrators, one can posit a decline there. Moreover, women as victims accounted for 27.8% of the homicides in the two decades together; this figure is significantly lower than the 36% average for Canada during the years 1921-1990[28] and suggests that tighter constraints on male violence, and particularly violence directed at women, were operating in late nineteenth-century Toronto.

Handguns were readily available in Toronto. They could be legally purchased by any individual age sixteen or older.[29] But they rarely appear in

---

2009), 289. For the period of 1900-1990 in the four cities, Seattle had a homicide rate of 7.34 per 100,000, a homicide-suicide rate of .72, and a homicide-suicide percentage of homicides of 9%; Buffalo was 6.97, .30, and 5%; Vancouver was 3.79, .26, and 6%; while Toronto was lowest at 1.62, .17, and 9%. An interesting calculation would be the rates from 1900-1959 and then 1960-1990, because of the sharp increases in homicide beginning in the 1960s.

[28] See Rosemary Gartner, "Homicide in Canada" in Jeffrey Ian Ross, ed., *Violence in Canada: Sociopolitical Perspectives* (Toronto: Oxford University Press, 1995), 200. Interestingly, male victimization rates as a percentage rose in Canada in the 1970s with the sharp increase in homicide, as it did generally in Europe. See Rosemary Gartner, "Homicide in Canada", 200. Pieter Spierenburg, *A History of Murder: Personal Violence in Europe from the Middle Ages to the Present* (Polity: Cambridge, UK, 2008), 212.

[29] Henri Taschereau, *The Criminal Code of the Dominion of Canada*, 66. This law also applied to ammunition. The seller was required to record the name of the buyer and the make of the gun. In addition concealed weapons were prohibited except with special authorization. Laws concerning handguns originated in BEP quarters. In 1878 Edward Blake sponsored a federal law that regulated handguns in urban settings. While this law was passed in the context of the fear of Fenian sectarian violence, it was extended indefinitely despite there being very little violent use of handguns. The legislation reflects a BEP obsession with violence. For a fascinating essay on the law designed to control the carrying of firearms in the face of potential sectarian violence see Susan W.S. Binnie, "The Blake Act of 1878" in Louis A. Knafla and Susan W.S. Binnie, *Law, Society, and the State: Essays in Modern Legal History* (Toronto: University of Toronto Press, 2005), 215-242. The law was enacted by the Liberal Edward Blake, despite there being no evidence of riot deaths due to firearms and no popular clamour for their control. Even with the popularity of carrying revolvers, the riots were remarkably controlled with respect to firearms. The Liberal Alexander Mackenzie experienced "overwhelming anxiety" when on one occasion he reluctantly called out the troops, which was not normal practice for the Liberals. Blake and Alexander Mackenzie supported handgun legislation while John A. Macdonald led the opposition against it. Gladstone was

cases of physical assault. I counted only six homicides as a result of a gunshot wound during the period 1880-1889 and only two cases in the period 1890-1899.[30] Again, one can argue that constraints on interpersonal violence in the culture of Toronto prevented their widespread use against human beings. Handguns were inconsequential because of a particular culture.[31] The thesis

---

unable to have similar legislation passed in England. Increasingly handguns were associated with young urban males who were increasingly carrying cheap revolvers in order to demonstrate their "manliness", even against women. Drunken males in particular were seen to be prone to using handguns. Blake had previously opposed firearms legislation introduced by the Macdonald government. R. Blake Brown, "'Pistol Fever': Regulating Revolvers in Late-Nineteenth-Century Canada", *Journal of the Canadian Historical Association*, n.s., 20:1 (2009), 117-120, 124-127, 130-132,134-135; R. Blake Brown, *Arming and Disarming: A History of Gun Control in Canada* (Toronto: Osgoode Society, University of Toronto Press, 2012), 61-80. Total gun imports rose rapidly in the last two decades of the century. See also an editorial in the *Globe*, in the aftermath of George Brown's death that asked for a consideration of a law that would provide a mandatory prison sentence for those convicted of unlawfully carrying a concealed handgun. *Globe*, May 27, 1880: 4. On the easy availability of cheap handguns see for example an ad for the Toronto, Church Street gun dealer, Charles Stark, who advertises fifty models of revolvers starting at $1. *Globe*, August 26, 1882: 5.

[30] Here one can speculate on the British tradition of a "fair" fight. According to this line of reasoning the use of guns and knives in a fight would not be "fair". In addition to the 6 gunshot homicides I counted only 4 homicides where the weapon was a knife in the period 1880-1899. See also John E. Archer, *The Monster Evil: Policing and Violence in Victorian Liverpool*, 83-85.

[31] It was not illegal to *possess* a handgun under the age of sixteen years. See R. Blake Brown, "'Pistol Fever': Regulating Revolvers in Late-Nineteenth-Century Canada", 107-138. My argument at this point should not be construed as an anti-gun control argument. (I am an advocate of strict gun controls.) For examples of the use of handguns see ~~Globe~~ *Globe*, June 6, 1880: 6; January 15, 1890: 4; April 9, 1890: 8; March 18, 1897: 12; April 8, 1891: 1. See the latter for a reference to a "small boy with a pistol habit" who accidentally wounded a friend. For evidence of the easy availability of handguns through department mail order catalogues see Timothy Eaton Company, *The 1901 Editions of the T. Eaton Co. Limited Catalogues for Spring & Summer Fall & Winter* (Toronto: Stoddart, reprinted 1970), 140. See also R. Blake Brown, "Pistol Fever", 107-138. While there may have been some improvement in the medical care of puncture wounds, including those as the result of gunshots and knives, I would argue that significant advances in trauma medicine did not take place until the later part of the twentieth-century. These make the low levels of homicide in late nineteenth-century Toronto all the more remarkable. See Anthony R. Harris, Stephen H. Thomas, Gene A. Fischer, and David J. Hirsch, "Murder and Medicine: The Lethality of Criminal Assault, 1960-1999" in *Homicide Studies* 6, no. 2 (May 2002): 128-166. The authors argue that annual decreases in the lethality of violent assaults, in the period of the study, were 2.5-4.5%. Some of this drop could be due to the increased reporting of lethal attacks, but the drop is consistent with annual drops of 3%

of this study provides the reason why they were not a factor. In summary, my homicide rate calculations point unmistakably to a cultural condition of low rates of interpersonal violence in late nineteenth-century Toronto. These calculations are original to this study.

The baseline then, for this thesis, is an extremely low homicide rate in Toronto by the end of the nineteenth-century regardless of the causes of this low rate. Accounting for the cause of low rates of homicide is fraught with difficulty. In seeking to access the "conduct" and "deportment" of Ontario residents in the 1870s, Gordon Darroch and Lee Soltow sourced prison records in order to find whether or not there were "variations in denominational conformity of personal conduct."[32] While they expected to find in prisons an overrepresentation of Irish born and Roman Catholics because of a disadvantaged class position, it was "a good deal more surprising" to find the overrepresentation of Anglicans among prison populations. They conclude:

> Moreover, by comparison, the underrepresentation of the more evangelical groups is very marked. Particularly noticeable is the fact Baptists and members of the more evangelical groups and members of other denominations and sects were thoroughly underrepresented among inmates. Class and economic position are intertwined with cultural predispositions in these data, but the striking break between the two diocesan and the more evangelical groups remains.[33]

---

to more than 16% in mortality involving general traumatic injury (such as in those sustained in automobile accidents) for the same period. In other words trauma medicine, in the period of 1960-1999, underwent a revolution in the treatment of injuries in general including those caused by interpersonal violence and hence greatly impacted homicide rates for the period. An example of the advances in Victorian medicine and the prevalence of revolvers can be seen in the introduction of the X-ray machine at Toronto General Hospital in 1896, when a fifteen-year-old boy accidentally shot himself while loading a revolver. The bullet was located eight inches from the entrance wound and would have been difficult to find apart from the X-ray. *Globe*, July 13, 1896: 10. Of course, I am not arguing that medical advances had significantly lowered homicide rates in 1900.

[32] Gordon Darroch and Lee Soltow, *Property and Inequality in Victorian Ontario*, 109.

[33] Gordon Darroch and Lee Soltow, *Property and Inequality in Victorian Ontario*, 109.

In keeping with Weber, Darroch and Soltow found that groups with the "strongest Protestant sectarian roots" were most represented among both Ontario teachers and students and were most likely to "foster middle-class standards of family life, social respectability, and self-discipline."[34] John Weaver predicted that Darroch and Soltow might provoke "a fusion of religion, cultural, and social history" on the part of Ontario historians. Two decades later, the response has been nil with respect to the study of religion and crime.[35]

The discussion by Darroch and Soltow on the denominational variations among populations of prisoners in 1870s Ontario was very brief and summarized in the space of one page. Although their preliminary conclusion that religion causally trumped economic status in accounting for the denominational variations in prison population, they do not present economic, birthplace, or occupational data on Ontario prisoners. In pursuing the Eisner hypothesis on the importance of moral individualism in accounting for declines in interpersonal violence, and following Darroch and Soltow, it appears that an analysis of a large prison population holds promise as "a way into" the personal conduct of a culture.

7.2 An Analysis of the Central Prison Population and the Influence of Religious Denominational Affiliation

Previous pages have examined the relationship between violence and cultural constraint by looking at Toronto as a whole. In the next section I will examine a marginal population confined by the walls of Central Prison. It, like the city itself, was defined by age, gender, marital status, occupation, birthplace, and, importantly for this study, denominational affiliation. I will argue, based on analysis of the prison population, that males heavily exposed to BEP discourse were much less likely to become residents of Central Prison, whether for drunkenness, violent assault, or any other type of behaviour. I

---

[34] Gordon Darroch and Lee Soltow, *Property and Inequality in Victorian Ontario*, 97. For analysis of Weber and Protestant "sects" see Peter Ghosh, *Max Weber and the Protestant Ethic: Twin Histories* (Oxford: Oxford University Press, 2014), 339-386.

[35] John Weaver, "Review of Property and Inequality in Victorian Ontario," 88.

will also argue that correlations between religious affiliation and behavior account for the disparity the numbers of different religious groups incarcerated. Finally, I will argue that the broad BEP culture of Toronto caused a decline of committals to Central Prison in general.

7.2.1 The Relevance of the 1901 Canadian Families Project

Any analysis of the demographics of Central Prison is reliant upon provincial census data for comparative purposes. While the Darroch/Soltow study was reliant on census samples that were manually generated, and the Oliver study was restricted to published official data, the present study has been able to make use of the digitized Canadian Families Project 5% sample of the 1901 Canada Census for comparisons between the Central Prison population and the general population.[36] Furthermore, the computerized sample allows for disaggregation of data pertaining to Toronto and especially religious categories with an ease that was not possible at the time of the above studies.

That BEP discourse was having a general impact can be followed by tracking changes in religious identifications through data from federal decennial censuses. In the 1842 census of Upper Canada, 16.7% of inhabitants were listed as having "no religion". By 1871 this classification had dropped to 1.2% and in the period under study in Toronto to less than 1%. Note also that there are very few individuals who identify themselves simply as "Protestant". This is an indicator that the vast majority of people had very specific formal religious identities, such as "Anglican" or "Roman Catholic", even if they were not "practicing" Christians.

Using the Canada Families Project 5% sample of the 1901 Canada Census, I calculated the religious affiliations for the city of Toronto as follows:

Table 7.2 Grand totals by religious affiliation in Toronto, 1901

	5% Sample		Projection to 100%	Actual 1901 Census Count	
Baptist	445	5.5%	8,900	8,148	5.2%

[36] See the SPSS 1901 database at the Canadian Families Project: web.uvic.ca/hrd/cfp/.

	5% Sample		Projection to 100%	Actual 1901 Census Count	
Church of England	2299	28.2%	45,980	46,442	29.8%
Methodist	1755	21.5%	35,100	35,130	22.5%
Presbyterian	1695	20.8%	33,900	30,812	19.7%
Roman Catholic	1200	14.7%	24,000	23,699	15.2%
Other	756	9.3%	15,120	11,867	7.6%
	8,150		163,000	156,098 [37]	

Note that this is a 5% sample and is generally consistent with the Toronto city population of 158,000 as given in the 1901 Census. One would predict a population of 163,000 from the sample totals (see above); presumably the difference is due to the fact that dwellings were sampled instead of individuals, a decision made by the Canadian Families Project in an effort to best represent the residents of larger dwellings such as hospitals and rooming houses. For

[37] See *Fourth Census Of Canada, 1901*, vol. 1, *Population*, (Ottawa: Government of Canada, 1902) 4, 383-384. The literature on Toronto's history presents conflicting data on Toronto's population. J.M.S. Careless repeatedly seems to confuse original census counts with "revised" counts listed in the next census. It does appear that the original census count of 156,000 for 1901 was revised to 208,000 as listed in the 1911 census volume for comparative purposes. However, the change is due to the retrospective addition to the 1901 counts of areas annexed after 1901. Naturally, it was deemed desirable to include the 1901 counts of these annexed areas in order to compare with the count of the same bounded areas of the 1911 census. J.M.S Careless presumes that the religious counts vary widely from the total population counts when in reality they are identical. See J.M.S. Careless, *Toronto to 1918*, 200-203, 208 n. 2. The above comments are not in reference to the accuracy of the census counts, but rather to the retrospective harmonizing of the results of the two censuses, with regard to population only, as originally published. The numbers on "Religion" were not retrospectively adjusted. To be more specific, in 1901 the population count was 156,000 and the religion count agrees at 156,000. However, after the 1911 census the listed population for the 1901 census was changed from 156,000 to 208,000 to adjust for the 1901 census count of those areas that were annexed between 1901 and 1911. The religion data was not retrospectively adjusted and hence it appeared to Careless that there was a part of the population that did not participate in the religion portion of the census; the difference between 156,000 and 208,000. These counts are important for the calculation of homicide rates. I am using the lower figure as the most accurate which has the effect of increasing the homicide rate for the period under study. If I had used the higher and adjusted census population figures, the homicide rates would have decreased by 21%.

comparative purposes across denomination I will use the actual census percentages, while for computer analysis the Canadian Families database is required.

One might posit that the size of the Methodist group was simply a function of immigration from England. However, when one selects the Toronto data from the 1901 census samples and conducts an analysis cross-tabulating for "religion" and "birthplace", the following results are obtained:

Table 7.3 Birthplace by denominational affiliation for the Toronto population, 1901

Denomination						Birthplace											
	n	Can%	n	Eng %	n	Ire%	n	Ont%	n	Scot%	n	USA%	n	Other%	Total
Bap	7	1.5%	97	22%	8	1.8%	307	70%	9	2%	12	2.5%	5	1%	445
CE	93	4%	515	22.5%	139	6%	1444	63%	19	1%	52	2%	37	1.5%	2299
Meth	42	2.5%	203	11.5%	51	3%	1361	77.5%	19	1%	46	2.5%	33	2%	1755
Pres	38	2%	64	4%	123	7%	1215	71.5%	194	11.5%	46	2.5%	15	1%	1695
RC	103	8.5%	44	3.5%	166	14%	766	64%	9	1%	47	4%	65	5.5%	1200
Other	49	6.5%	76	10%	12	1.5%	438	58%	18	2%	38	5%	125	16.5%	756
Totals	332	4.1%	999	12.3%	499	6.1%	5531	67.9%	268	3.3%	241	3%	280	3.4%	8150

The three denominations that most closely represent BEP ideology, the Baptists, Methodists, and Presbyterians, are all distinguished by the highest levels of Canadian-born adherents. The Methodist percentage, at 77.5 % Canadian-born, is significantly higher than all other denominations. This suggests that their powerful growth during the last three decades of the century was due more to their exposure to an internal, Toronto-based BEP discourse than to any effect religious discourse from Great Britain may have had.[38]

7.2.2 The Great Blue Book: Central Register 1, Comparisons, 1874-1889

[38] It needs to be emphasized that Methodism was even stronger in Toronto's hinterland. By 1901, Methodism was Ontario's largest denomination at 31% of the population. Evangelicalism also remained a dominant religious force in both Great Britain and the US. However, the argument here is that the development of BEP ideology in the urban setting of Toronto produced a multi-faceted social movement that succeeded in shaping the economic, political, and moral dimensions of Toronto and its surrounding hinterland.

Measuring approximately three feet in breadth when open and two feet in height, the Central Prison register possesses the weight, heft, and gravitas appropriate to an instrument of a Victorian institution that was known as "a terror to evildoers." With some thirty columns spread across both pages, giving personal details of each prisoner, the register presents the researcher with a wide variety of data sets.

Opening in 1874 in Toronto on Strachan Avenue near King Street West, Central Prison was designed to provide relief from the overcrowding in the province's jails. The prison possessed 336 cells and could accommodate 445 prisoners. Terms ranged from fourteen days to two years minus a day.

The prison represents the largest pool of Toronto residents convicted of violent crimes and experiencing incarceration and is the obvious source for data on violent male behavior during the late nineteenth-century. For the years 1874-1900 a total of 17,500 prisoners were committed with 2,200 of these having been convicted of a crime against the person.[39] Volume 1 of the register covers the years 1874-1889; over one-quarter were listed as Toronto residents and it is reasonable to project a similar percentage of Toronto residents for the entire period.

7.2.3 Methodology: Expanding the Darroch/Soltow and Oliver Studies

Volume 1 of the prison register lists in chronological order the record of 10,281 committals. I focused on prisoners who were listed as residents of Toronto. In most cases their convictions took place before the magistrate in the Toronto Police Court or before a judge in the County Assizes. A total of 2,800 convicted Toronto residents were entered into a SPSS[40] database. This total represents 27.2% of all Central Prison committals. Variables used include the prisoner number, the given name, location of the court where

---

[39] Peter Oliver, *Terror to Evil-Doers*, 413.

[40] SPSS (Software Package for the Social Sciences) is a software package for statistical analysis. Entries are made into a database that is viewed as a spreadsheet with the rows representing individual prisoners and the columns representing characteristics such as birthplace, age, religious affiliation, criminal offence convicted of, etc. Descriptive statistics are readily available that include frequencies and cross-tabulations. For a brief time from 2009-2010 the software product was known as PASW (Predictive Analytics Software) before reverting to SPSS.

convicted, location of residence, country of birth, occupation, the judgment as to "temperate" or "intemperate" and the ability to read and write, marital status, religious affiliation, the nature of the criminal offence, and the age of the prisoner. I did not enter an additional nineteen categories that included colour of hair, complexion, weight, and length of sentence, all of which have less relevance to this study.[41] While one could argue that only the category of religion is relevant to this study, religion and how it relates to literacy, temperate or intemperate, birthplace, marital status, occupation, and criminal offence are key questions. Each of these categories are of great relevance to the wider study of the history of interpersonal violence. For example, Darroch and Soltow follow a Weberian line of argument that views the emphasis that Protestant "sects" placed on literacy as critical for the moral ordering of a Victorian Ontario culture.[42] Steven Pinker also holds that the spread of mass literacy was a key mechanism for declining rates of violence even if he does not emphasize the importance of religion.[43]

The entering of all 2,800 prisoners committed from 1874-1889, listed as Toronto residents, into my database allows for a wealth of cross-tabulations that were not available to the Darroch/Soltow and Oliver studies. These two studies relied on official published data for the general Central Prison population as a whole and do not "drill down" to isolate out Toronto residents. I followed Peter Oliver's statistical profile of the general Central Prison population including the categories of occupation, offences committed, birthplace, literacy, religion, marital status, and drinking habits. I was then able to readily compare the general Central Prison population to those prisoners who were listed as Toronto residents. Furthermore, using the 1901 Canadian Family Studies Project and the decennial Canada Census, I was able to make comparisons between the general Toronto population and that portion of the

---

[41] I received permission to examine the second volume of the register that runs from 1889-1912 (and hence overlapped with privacy restrictions), but this permission was granted towards the end of this study and I have not had time to analyze these additional data.

[42] Gordon Darroch and Lee Soltow, *Property and Inequality in Victorian Ontario*, 49, 135, 145.

[43] Steven Pinker, *Better Angels*, 172-176, 666. See similarly Gregory Clark, *A Farewell to Alms: A Brief Economic History of the World* (Princeton: Princeton University Press, 2007), 166, 175-181.

Central Prison population listed as Toronto residents.

Studies on Ontario prison populations by Gordon Darroch and Lee Soltow, and by Peter Oliver, found that Baptists, Methodists, and Presbyterians were significantly underrepresented while Roman Catholics and Anglicans were almost equally over-represented. My results show that with respect to Baptists and Methodists, this phenomenon is heightened among prisoners listed as residents of Toronto and continues with Presbyterians; Anglicans remain overrepresented and Roman Catholics extremely overrepresented. The denominational affiliation data for Toronto prisoners are as follows:

Table 7.4 Frequency of denominational affiliation for Toronto prisoners in Central Prison, 1874-1889

	Baptist	C of E	Meth	Pres	RC	Other or None	Total
Number	41	1114	179	257	1159	50	2800
% of Total	1.5%	39.8%	6.4%	9.2%	41.5%	1.8%	
% Toronto Population[44]	4.5%	34%	21%	18%	16.5%	6%	
% Central divided by % Toronto	0.3	1.17	0.3	0.51	2.5	0.3	

Here we see Baptists and Methodists extremely underrepresented, Presbyterians present at one-half their level of representation in the general population, Anglicans overrepresented, and Roman Catholics extremely overrepresented.

[44] These are the figures for the general Toronto population, using the average figures from the 1881 and 1891 Canada Census counts.

Table 7.5 Frequency of denominational affiliation for Toronto prisoners in Central Prison, 1874-1889, as compared to the general Central Prison population, 1880-1900

	Baptist	CE	Meth	Pres	RC	Other or None	Total
Toronto CP Prisoners % of Total	1.5%	39.8%	6.4%	9.2%	41.5%	1.8%	100
General CP Prisoners % of Total[45]	3.2%	31.7%	15.4%	12.4%	34.6%	2.7%	100

The above sets of data are consistent with the findings of Oliver and those of Darroch and Soltow and show unmistakably that there is a relationship between religion and committal rates to Central Prison. In the case of prisoners listed as residents of Toronto, there is, however, a pronounced heightening of this effect. There is a BEP gradient that is far steeper than that identified in the Oliver and Darroch/Soltow studies. Baptists and Methodists are even more underrepresented among Toronto prisoners than the general prison population, Presbyterians are somewhat underrepresented, while Anglicans and Roman Catholics are pronouncedly overrepresented.[46]

Given that Darroch and Soltow do not present data on the socio-economic status of prisoners but simply present their conclusion, I examined the data with relation to birthplace, occupation, temperance, marital status, and education in an effort to ascertain whether religion simply coincides with and/or masks another variable. Each of these variables are of relevance to the study of crime and violence regardless of any conclusion with respect to causality.

[45] Peter Oliver, *Terror to Evil-Doers*, 449. Oliver has used data from the *Journals of the Legislative Assembly of the Province of Canada*, "Annual Reports of the Inspectors of the Provincial Penitentiary". See Peter Oliver, *Terror to Evil-Doers*, 525 n. 35.

[46] Note that the general Central Prison population includes Toronto prisoners. If the Toronto prisoners were removed from the general figures, this BEP effect would be further heightened.

The results of the calculation on the frequency of birthplace of Toronto prisoners are as follows:

Table 7.6 Frequency of birthplace for Toronto prisoners in Central Prison by birthplace and denomination, 1874-1889

	Can	Eng	Ire	Scot	USA	Other	Total
Number	1330	546	594	136	138	56	2800
% Central Prison Population	47.5%	19.5%	21.2%	4.9%	4.9%	2%	100%
% Toronto General Population[47]	64.7%	15.8%	9.2%	4.4%	0.5%	5.3%	
	93162	22801	13252	6347	799	7662	144023

The upper part of the table is birthplace of the general population of Central Prison versus the general population of Toronto. Below is birthplace of Toronto prisoners only by denominational affiliation.

Birthplace by Denomination Central Prison Toronto Residents	Can	Eng	Ire	Scot	USA	Other	Total
Baptist	19	4	1	1	15	1	41
%	46.5%	10%	2%	2%	36.5%	2%	
CE	446	441	167	12	37	12	1115
	40%	39.5%	15%	1%	3.5%	1%	
Meth	113	31	9	2	22	2	179
	63%	17.5%	5%	1%	12.5%	1%	
Pres	98	8	30	107	10	5	258
	38%	3%	11.5%	41.5%	4%	2%	
RC	641	56	382	13	49	18	1159
	55.5%	5%	33%	1%	4%	1.5%	
Other	14	9	5	1	6	13	48
	29%	19%	10.5%	2%	12.5%	27%	
Grand Total Toronto CP Prisoners							2800

[47] These are the figures for the general Toronto population, using the average figures from the 1881 Canada Census counts. Note: The top of the table compares the general Central

So far as birthplace is concerned, these data show foreign-born prisoners in general significantly overrepresented. In particular, English-born Anglicans and Irish-born Catholic prisoners are in this category while American-born prisoners are overrepresented among all denominations and extremely so among Baptists. Next to Methodists, Catholics are most likely to be born in Canada. The comparison between Presbyterians and Methodists is significant. Methodists are much more likely to be Canadian-born than Presbyterians, but Presbyterians are slightly less likely to be born in Canada than Anglicans. Yet incarceration rates are much higher for Anglicans; hence, denominational affiliation at Central Prison cannot be explained simply as a function of place-of-birth across the board.[48]

Prison population with the Toronto general population. The bottom portion of the table compares the Central Prison Toronto residential prisoners by denominational affiliation.

[48] At this point it is helpful to examine the meagre statistics on denominational affiliation that exist for England and Wales, and Scotland for prisoners. The fact that there are similar rates of overrepresentation and underrepresentation for both Britain and Canada suggests common cultural processes and linkages. Only two official lists were published and these appeared in the House of Commons Parliamentary Papers in 1866 and 1906. The more detailed and complete 1906 list is as follows:

Table 7.7 Denominational affiliation of prisoners in England, Scotland and Wales, 1906

England and Wales	Number	%	Scotland	Number	%
Church of England	16,089	74.5%		146	5.1%
Roman Catholic	4,397	27.3%		981	34.3%
Judaism	257	1.2%		5	0.2%
Methodist	469	2.2%			
Congregationalist	53	0.2%			
Presbyterian	79	0.4%		1,724	60.3%
Baptist	132	0.6%			
Unitarian	11	0.005%			
Quaker	1	0%			
Plymouth Brethren	1	0%			
Lutheran	19	0.01%		1	0%
Other or None	72	0.3%			
	21,580			2,857	

Parliamentary Papers 1906, vol. 99, *Prisons (Religious Creed of Prisoners)* (London: The House

The data for marital status are as follows:

Table 7.8 Frequency of birthplace and marital status for Toronto prisoners in Central Prison, 1874-1889

Country	Can	Eng	Ire	Scot	USA	Other	Total
Single or	1041	369	388	75	107	29	2009
Widowed	78%	67%	65%	55%	78%	56%	72%
Married	290	180	206	61	31	23	791
	22%	33%	35%	45%	22%	34%	28%

Table 7.9 Frequency of denominational affiliation and marital status for Toronto prisoners in Central Prison, 1874-1889

Denomination	Meth	CE	RC	Pres	Bap	Other	Total
Single or Widowed	117	771	891	164	30	36	2009
	65%	69%	77%	64%	73%	78%	71%
Married	62	343	268	93	11	14	791
	35%	31%	23%	36%	27%	22%	29%

The prison population had a preponderance of unmarried men. This is consistent with general findings that unmarried males are more likely to engage in criminal activity than their married counterparts. The fact does not however,

---

of Commons, 1906), 1-4. While there are no census data on religious affiliation in Britain, in 1851 an estimated 60% of the population would have identified as Anglican and about 4% as Roman Catholic, increasing to 5% by 1900. In parallel with the data for Central Prison, in British prisons Anglicans are overrepresented, Roman Catholics extremely overrepresented, while Protestant Nonconformists are drastically underrepresented. There is no breakdown by religion according to type of criminal offence. For the British denominational statistical patterns see Hugh McLeod, *Religion and Society in England*, 11-13; Robert Currie, Alan D. Gilbert, Lee Horsley, *Churches and Churchgoing: Patterns of Church Growth in the British Isles Since 1700* (Oxford: Oxford University Press, 1978). Significantly, Hugh McLeod demonstrates that there were large numbers of Nonconformist working class through the end of the century while a predominately middle-class Methodism was a twentieth-century development. Hugh McLeod, *Religion and Irreligion in Victorian England* (Bangor: Headstart History, 1993), 30-36. See also Hugh McLeod, *Religion and the Working Class in Nineteenth-Century Britain* (Cambridge: Economic History Society, 1984). While there were high levels of anti-Catholicism in British society, historically Protestant Nonconformists had experienced significant social discrimination making the degrees of their under-representation in British prisons surprising.

suggest that this variable had any special relationship to a person's involvement with such activity.

Analysis of literacy, an important dimension of the Darroch/Soltow study, for both birthplace and denominational affiliation yields:

Table 7.10 Frequency of birthplace and literacy for Toronto prisoners in Central Prison, 1874-1889

Birthplace	Can	Eng	Ire	Scot	USA	Other	Total
Read and Write	1041	474	448	123	114	40	2240
	78%	86%	75%	91%	82%	75%	80%
Neither R or W	289	75	146	12	25	13	560
Or R Only	22%	14%	25%	9%	18%	25%	20%

Table 7.11 Frequency of denominational affiliation and literacy for Toronto prisoners in Central Prison, 1874-1889

Denomination	Meth	CE	RC	Pres	Bap	Other	Total
Read and Write	158	950	828	232	33	39	2240
	88%	85%	71%	90%	79%	81%	80%
Neither R or W	21	166	331	25	8	9	560
Or R Only	12%	15%	29%	10%	21%	9%	20%

Literacy is present at relatively high levels for the entire Toronto culture; it especially marks those prisoners identifying with BEP denominations.

Baptists have a lower rate of literacy than the average for Toronto prisoners. However, 36.5% of Toronto prisoners were born in the U.S. as opposed to only 0.5% of the general Toronto population. (Methodist prisoners are closest to Baptists but with only 12.5% U.S. born, and then it drops to 4% U.S. born for Presbyterians and Catholics.) When U.S. born Baptists deemed not to be able to both read and write[49] are deducted from the aggregate, then only 1 non-U.S. born Baptist could neither read nor write. Thus 24 of 25 Baptists, born

---

[49] Here "both read and write" refers to the ability to read and write as opposed to "read only" or "none". I am judging those who "read only" to be illiterate. One could of course break the category down further by measuring the percentages for a given group that "read only" or "none".

in Canada, Britain, Ireland, and Europe, were judged capable of both reading and writing. In other words, 7 of the 8 Baptists judged not capable of reading and writing, were born in the U.S. Fully 96% of non-U.S. born Baptists were deemed to be able to read and write. This group of Baptist prisoners had higher levels of literacy than the average rate of the general Toronto population (see below), levels virtually identical with the highest rates for the city. This is significant in the extreme and points to a powerful literacy discourse within a BEP religious minority and is consistent with the findings of Darroch and Soltow on religion, education and literacy.[50] The link between literacy and declining interpersonal violence will be evaluated later in the chapter.

When one conducts a cross-tabulation between religion and the ability to write using the 1901 census sample of Toronto residents, the following results are obtained:

Table 7.12 The Frequency of denominational affiliation and literacy for Toronto in the 1901 census sample

Denomination	Bap	CE	Meth	Pres	RC	Other	Total
Can Write	387	2056	1538	1547	1010	513	7051
Cannot Write	10	105	42	50	84	110	401
% Can Write	97.5%	95%	97%	97%	93%	92%	94.5%

The general levels of literacy in turn-of-the-century Toronto are, on the surface, astounding.[51] These levels were achieved in a predominately working class culture.[52] Even the prison population exhibited very high literacy levels.

[50] Of the 15 U.S.-born Baptists, 8 were not judged capable of reading and writing. Of these 15, 10 are recorded as being African American. Of these 10, 8 could not write. In contrast, only 1 African Canadian could not write. These data point to the legacy of slavery in the U.S. Of the African Canadians, only 1 was judged not able to write. While African Canadians remained on the margins of Toronto society, their higher rates of writing suggests at least a degree of increased opportunity in Canada for persons of African ancestry. See also Gordon Darroch and Lee Soltow, *Property and Inequality in Victorian Ontario*, 141-144. One might be tempted to hive off African American Baptists from the 'Baptist' category but African Canadian Baptists generally share the same 'Baptist' roots.

[51] There are of course multiple levels of writing ability.

[52] On the vibrant reading culture of the British working class, no doubt influential in

The overall uniformity of the results is consistent with a strong religious sub-group emphasis on literacy and with the thesis that a particular religious ideology, one that emphasizes the need to read religious texts, underlies this literacy phenomenon receives significant support.

The category of "Temperate" gives the following:

Table 7.13 Frequency of "Temperate" by birthplace and denominational affiliation for Toronto prisoners in Central Prison, 1874-1889[53]

Number	US	Eng	Can	Scot	Ire	Other	Total
Temperate	28	105	215	11	41	11	411
	20%	19%	16%	8%	7%	14.5%	14.5%
Intemperate	111	443	1114	125	553	41	2387
	80%	81%	84%	92%	93%	85.5%	85.5%
Denomination	**Bap**	**CE**	**Meth**	**Pres**	**RC**	**Other**	**Total**
Temperate	15	180	35	37	134	14	411
	36.5%	16%	19.5%	14.5%	11.5%	22%	14.5%
Intemperate	26	935	144	220	1025	50	2387
	63.5%	84%	80.5%	85.5%	88.5%	78%	85.5%

Although few in number, Baptists clearly had a very high rate of temperance. Likewise, Methodists had almost identical rates of temperance and both denominations, along with the "Other" category, had the lowest conviction rates for assault (see below). Those prisoners born in Canada, the US, and England had relatively high temperance rates while those born in Scotland and Ireland have the lowest rates.[54] No doubt these rates reflect socio-reli-

---

Canada through vehicles such as the mechanics' institutes, see Jonathan Rose, *The Intellectual Life of the British Working Classes* (New Haven: Yale University Press, 2001).

[53] I did not count the handful of instances where the appropriate box was blank, illegible, or the box was mistaken for another category.

[54] Fortunately Warden James Massie had occasion to comment directly on how it was ascertained whether a prisoner was "temperate" or "intemperate." In Royal Commission testimony when asked how this was elicited, he stated that, "if a man says he is intemperate, we accept that. If he says that he takes a glass occasionally, we put him under the head of temperate."

gious attitudes towards alcohol and are in line with the Weberian virtue of sobriety that was a characteristic of the Protestant "sects".

7.2.4 Analysis of Rates of Assault Convictions for Toronto Prisoners of Central Prison by Birthplace and Denomination, 1874-1889

Large numbers of prisoners, prior to the late 1880s, were committed to prison for vagrancy and drunkenness[55] while the largest category of criminal offence committed by prisoners at Central Prison was for larceny.[56] For historical reasons, and because it was considered premeditated, property crime often resulted in longer sentences than physical assault which was usually viewed as a crime of passion.

For the purposes of this study, which focuses on physical violence, crimes involving physical assault have been separated out in the following analysis.[57]

Massie further expanded on this: "Of course, the Deputy Warden and the Surgeon have more to do with that than I have, because they register it directly; but they have never intimated to me that any declined to answer straightforwardly the questions put to them." *Report of the Royal Commission on the Liquor Traffic: Minutes of Evidence*, volume iv-part ii, *Province of Ontario* (Ottawa: S.E. Dawson, 1895), 1051. While this testimony should not be accepted at face value, and no doubt prison officials made personal judgments about responses, it does give background to the handwriting that is uniform for sometimes years at a time. By the varying percentage results according to temperance within a religious affiliation, it is obvious that prisoners were not categorized on strictly the basis of denomination. Presbyterians, for example, had the second lowest rate of "Temperate". This is supplemented by a description of the registration of the convicted murderer, James Birchall, in 1890 in the Woodstock Ontario gaol. Newspaper reporters were present as he was registered by Gaoler John Cameron. He was registered as "J.R. Birchall, gentleman by profession, aged 25, born in England and belonging to the Church of England." When asked if he were married he replied, "Yes." "Are you temperate or intemperate?" asked Mr. Cameron. This seemed to puzzle him for a second, and when the question was put in another form, "Do you take a 'nip' occasionally?" he understood and replied, "Yes when I can get it." He is entered as intemperate." (The inside quotation marks are as printed in the paper.) *Globe*, March 14, 1890: 2.

[55] During the first 10 years of the prison, the offences vagrancy and drunkenness accounted for 30-35% of committals to Central Prison. See Peter Oliver, *Terror to Evil-Doers*, 413.

[56] For the years 1874-1899, larceny continuously accounted for more than one-third of all committals reaching as high as 45% for the years 1876-1880. See Peter Oliver, *Terror to Evil-Doers*, 413.

[57] Often crimes labelled "disorderly" or "drunkenness" did involve physical violence but there is no way to identify these instances from the prison register. One would need to examine the details of the circumstances of each conviction using newspaper court reports. I have

Using the prison register column that specifies the prisoner's offence, I have identified for Toronto residents at Central Prison the following: all instances of common assault, aggravated assault, assault and robbery, assaulting a constable or "peace" officer, assault with intent to kill, felonious wounding, indecent assault, intent to rape, malicious wounding, manslaughter, shooting, stabbing, and variations of the above offences involving physical assault.

The frequency of physical assault by birthplace for Toronto prisoners breaks down as follows:

Table 7.14 Frequency of physical assault convictions by birthplace for Toronto prisoners in Central Prison, 1874-1889

Birthplace	US	Eng	Can	Scot	Ire	Other	Total
Numbers Physical Assault	14	48	191	13	68	10	344
% Physical Assault[58] Within Birthplace	10%	9%	14.5%	9.5%	11.5%	18%	12.5%
Non-Physical Assault Offences[59]	124	498	1139	123	526	46	2456

A number of initial observations can be made on the above data. Physical assaults make up a small percentage of the offences.[60] Of the nationalities represented, English-born and Scottish-born prisoners committed a significantly lower percentage of physical assaults. Canadian-born prisoners accounted for an elevated percentage of physical assaults. The "Other"[61] category included the highest percentage of physical assaults although the actual number (10) of assaults was small.

---

done this for a span of time in 1881, the census year. See below.

[58] The percentage calculation is within the birthplace grouping and is the number of violent offences divided by the total offences.

[59] The difference between total offences within a birthplace group minus physical offences.

[60] However often convictions for drunkenness and disorderly conduct involved physical violence.

[61] This group is made up of Congregationalists, Unitarians, Jews, those with a blank in the religion column of the register, and those with an illegible entry.

It should be emphasized that the "% Physical Assault" (both in the tables above and below) is a measure of the rate of physical assault within a group. The actual numbers of physical assaults varies dramatically across religious groupings. The following is a comparison of the rates of physical assault by religious affiliation, using census data for the general population of Toronto:

Table 7.15 Frequency of physical assault convictions by denominational affiliation for Toronto prisoners in Central Prison, 1874-1889

Denomination	Bap	CE	Meth	Pres	RC	Other	Total
% Physical Assault	4	125	22	32	159	2	344
% Physical Assault Within Denomination[62]	10%	11%	12%	12.5%	14%	4%	12%
Non-Physical Off.	37	990	157	226	1000	46	2456
% Total Assaults Across Denominations[63]	1%	36.5%	6.5%	9.5%	46%	0.5%	100%
% Toronto Population[64]	4.5%	34%	21%	18%	16.5%	6%	100%
% Central Assault divided by % Toronto Population	0.22	1.07	0.31	0.53	2.8	0.08	

The "assault" category concerns prisoners convicted of physical assault and is the most relevant to this study. Baptists and Methodists are severely underrepresented, with Presbyterians significantly underrepresented, whether within the general prison population or among those convicted of physical assaults. Anglicans are slightly overrepresented among the Toronto resident prison population. Roman Catholics are extremely overrepresented, with a heightened effect when those with convictions for physical assaults are isolated out. Toronto Catholics make up a disproportionate number of Catholic prisoners

[62] The percentage calculation is within the denominational grouping and is the number of violent offences divided by the total offences.

[63] The percentage calculation of total physical assaults across all denominations.

[64] These are the figures for the general Toronto population, using the average figures from the 1881 and 1891 Canada Census counts.

as compared to the Ontario hinterland, while Toronto Anglicans are under-represented as compared to Anglicans from the rest of Ontario.

Issues involving socio-economics, discrimination on the basis of religion and ethnicity, and the marginalizing of a population of transients who at the time were variously labelled "criminals", "tramps", and "vagrants" may have played a part in producing these results.[65] In taking into account these considerations, I examine the occupations of prisoners by religion as recorded in the Central Prison register. Specifically I focus on the occupation of "Labourer", the classification under which 40.5% of Central Prison's Toronto population was recorded in the register.

For purposes of comparison, I give the denominational ratios for the entire Central Prison population regardless of conviction offence:

% Central Population divided by % Ontario[66]	Bap	CE	Meth	Pres	RC	Other
	0.6	1.8	0.5	0.57	2.05	0.36

Table 7.16 Frequency of the occupation of "Labourer" as sorted by denominational affiliation for Toronto prisoners in Central Prison, 1874-1889

Denomination	Bap	CE	Meth	Pres	RC	Other	Total
# of Labourers in Central Prison[67]	19	416	68	61	566	13	1143
% Labourers in Denominational Group in CP[68]	46.5%	37.5%	40%	23.5%	49%	26%	41%
Denomination	Bap	CE	Meth	Pres	RC	Other	Total

[65] For reporting that describes the population of Central Prison as being from a "very low strata of society" see *Globe*, September 20, 1881: 10. See also December 5, 1881: 7; February 7, 1882: 5; March 19, 1885: 3.

[66] These figures were calculated using Central Prison population data covering the years 1880-1900, while the Ontario denominational percentages are derived from the 1891 Canada Census. See Peter Oliver, *Terror to Evil-Doers*, 449.

[67] The number of labourers in Central Prison listed as residents of Toronto.

[68] This line is a straight percentage calculation by denominational affiliation of the 2800 prisoners who are listed as residents of Toronto.

% Total Labourers in General Toronto Population[69]	3%	31%	15.5%	17%	30%	3.5%	100
% Toronto by Denomination[70]	4.5%	34%	21%	18%	16.5%	6%	100
% of Labourers Divided by % Toronto Pop.[71]	0.66	0.91	0.74	0.95	1.82	0.58	

Again, a BEP gradient is present in the above data. Baptists and Methodists had lower percentages of labourers while Presbyterians had significantly lower percentages. Presbyterian artisans were no doubt regarded as valuable workers within the prison industries by court and prison officials, and one can hypothesize that judges and magistrates committed Presbyterian artisans disproportionately to Central Prison.[72] Roman Catholics were more likely to be labourers.

Within Toronto's general population, Roman Catholics were disproportionately labourers. However, Presbyterian males were slightly more likely to be labourers than Anglicans. This is highly significant for a hypothesis that would see rates of incarceration as a function of rates of skills or lack of them.

One can make denominational comparisons from several angles at this point. Anglicans had 1.4 times the percentage of labourers in the general Toronto population as compared to Baptists and Methodists but had almost 4 times the rate of assault convictions among Toronto prisoners in Central

[69] These figures were generated from the 1901 census sample published by the Canadian Families Project.

[70] These percentage calculations are for the general Toronto population and are an average of the 1881 and 1891 Canada Census data on denominational affiliation.

[71] This figure is arrived at by dividing the denominational percentage of Toronto labourers by the denominational percentage of the general population. A figure of less than 1 is a measure of the underrepresentation of labourers while over 1 is a measure of overrepresentation of labourers for a denomination.

[72] For the industrial dimension of Central Prison and the transferal there of prisoners with job skills to further these industrial ends see Peter Oliver, *Terror to Evil-Doers*, 405-409.

Prison. Presbyterians had slightly higher rates of labourers as compared to Anglicans but had half the rate of assault convictions. Roman Catholics had almost triple the rate of assault convictions among Toronto prisoners as compared to Anglicans and double the rate of labourers in the general Toronto population.

While one can hypothesize that there is a strong relationship between Catholic committals for assault and the large numbers of poor Catholic labourers among the general population, the data make the relationship much more problematic among the Protestant denominations. Presbyterians, with a slightly higher percentage of labourers than the Anglicans, had a 50% lower assault committal rate to Central Prison than did the Anglicans. While Baptists and Methodists did have slightly lower percentages of labourers among the general population than Anglicans, both Baptists and Methodists had a vastly lower assault conviction committal rates than Anglicans.

These data point to a cultural explanation that follows a BEP gradient; Baptists and Methodists have assault conviction committal rates of approximately one-quarter that of Anglicans and one-half that of Presbyterians. The Baptist and Methodist denominations were clearly BEP, while Presbyterians were heavily influenced by BEP principles. However, since the BEP influence in late nineteenth-century Toronto cut across all sectors of the Toronto population, the entire culture experienced a severe lowering in rates of interpersonal violence that lasted well into the twentieth century.

7.2.5 Probing the Newspaper and Census Data

Previously in this study, it has been shown that the growth of Baptist, Methodist, and Presbyterian church buildings and budgets corresponded closely to the numerical growth of these denominations as reflected in Canada Census manuscripts. That source is also relevant to the questions posed by the population of a Central Prison that contained a disproportionate number of labourers with lower levels of literacy, high rates of recidivism,[73] and immi-

---

[73] Peter Oliver calculated that 30.1% of Central Prison prisoners had been imprisoned at least once before. Peter Oliver, *Terror to Evil-Doers*, 418.

grant origins. Using it in that connection, however, requires the researcher to take a harder look at it. Because the census theoretically records the place of dwelling of each Toronto resident on the day of the census, the window for matching the records contained in the Central Prison register with those it contains is quite narrow. The 1881 Census is the only census that overlaps with the first volume of the Central Prison register which runs from 1874-1889.

The procedure I used for attempting to match the census data with individual prisoner data was as follows. Given that the 1881 census took place on April 4, I examined the prison register for Toronto residents who were convicted before and after this date, beginning with the first entries in January, running past April 4, and continuing to the middle of August. These records included 118 names, of which I could distinguish the surnames of 112.[74] Of these I found reasonably strong matches in the 1881 on-line Canada Census site for 52. Undoubtedly there are more; these, however, are not recoverable due to illegibility in writing of surnames, data entry errors in the digitization of the census, the frequent use of aliases by prisoners, and the transient patterns of large numbers of labouring males.

On what basis did the prison registrar record that a prisoner was a "resident" of Toronto? This is not defined and was no doubt quickly decided by a clerk of the court or even an arresting officer. Documentation would then have been passed on to the prison office, along with committal warrants. At frequent intervals the register records a prisoner as a resident, for example, of Hamilton or Kingston even though he was convicted in a Toronto court. This is evidence that some care was taken to determine a prisoner's place of residence.[75] With Toronto located on well-developed railway lines, Toronto residents frequently travelled to U.S. cities such as Cleveland, Cincinnati, Detroit and Chicago. Journeys in the other direction also occurred; the register

[74] While it is easy to distinguish the handwriting of a given name, it is often difficult to do so with a surname. Hence only given names were used on the database. The signifiers for birthplace, gender, race, denomination, marital status, and education are very discernible.

[75] My computer analysis excludes residents of other localities, even though I included all prisoners convicted in Toronto on the larger database.

records numerous instances of U.S. residents being arrested in Ontario cities. The further one travels in the register away from April 4, either before or after, the less likelihood there is of "capturing" the prisoner in the census. Thus an initial match of close to 50% of a run of the register, spanning an eight-month period, does, however, suggest a high degree of accuracy in the census. For example, a prisoner convicted in August could easily have been in Great Britain on the census day in April and hence absent from the census manuscript.

Examination of court reporting in Toronto daily newspapers helps with the picture.[76] Additional names can be captured. For example, a John "Reilley" appeared in the register on March 19 following a conviction; the *Globe* makes mention of a John "Riley" being convicted on March 18 for drunkenness and for stealing a "ladies jacket". The John Reilly listed in the register is a nineteen year old shoemaker convicted of larceny. There is a high probability that the John Reilly listed in the register is the John Riley in the *Globe* police court report. There is, however, no match using either spelling in the April census.

The religious identities of individuals can also be tracked by comparing the prison register with census data. Convergence is high; in only one case does the "religion" category vary in the 52 instances where there are reasonably strong matches between register and census. In that case, one Henry Pearce[77] is listed in the prison register as a 22 year old, single, Congregationalist carpenter, whereas the April census lists a Henry Pearce as a 22 year old, single Baptist carpenter.[78]

Further confirmation of the accuracy of the recording of religious affiliation

---

[76] These newspapers were the *Globe*, *Toronto World*, and *Daily Mail*.

[77] Pearce is listed as #4049 in the Central Prison Register. Pearce was convicted of vagrancy in a London, Ontario court on March 3 and sentenced to six months in Central Prison. Undoubtedly the judge saw this as a means to return an out-of-work carpenter to Toronto. Pearce is categorized as "temperate" in the prison register, which is consistent with "vagrancy" as opposed to "drunkenness".

[78] He could have attended two churches over time, could have been influenced by a Baptist while in prison, the registrar might have assumed that a Congregationalist was essentially a Baptist, etc.

is given by the fact that the prison register is in agreement with information in those instances where a prisoner is recorded as being in prison at the time of the census. In these cases where there were matches between census and register, there was no variation on the religion category.

7.2.6 Summary of the Analysis of the Central Prison Register

The BEP gradient present among Toronto prisoners at Central Prison, one manifest in extremely low levels of incarcerated Baptists, Methodists, and persons characterized as "Other", in significant underrepresentation of Presbyterians, in slight overrepresentations of Anglicans, and in extreme over-representation of Roman Catholic prisoners is clear. Economic factors are also evident, in that Catholic labourers are overrepresented among the general Toronto population by a factor of almost two. Toronto's Catholic population no doubt experienced a degree of economic and religious discrimination.[79] Marginal minorities, in a variety of settings, have also been found to exhibit higher rates of interpersonal violence.[80] The religious variable is, however, the key variable.

Turning to the data on Presbyterians, one finds that they had an almost identical denominational ratio of labourers (even slightly higher at .95 versus .91) as compared to Anglicans, even though the latter had much higher incarceration rates as well as equally higher levels of convictions for assault. To argue that differences here were based on discrimination would be difficult. There remains a stubborn religious dimension to the incarceration of males at Central Prison as the result of convictions for physical assault. Males with a BEP affiliation were much less likely to be convicted of a violent offence and incarcerated in Central Prison than Roman Catholics but also Anglicans.[81]

---

[79] Liberal BEP participants such as Howland and the Blake brothers were anti-Orange Order despite their Irish Protestant backgrounds. Mowat also was anti-Orange. See A. Margaret Evans, *Oliver Mowat* (Toronto: University of Toronto Press, 1992), 121. William J. Smyth seems to be unaware of this anti-Orange BEP flavour. See William J. Smyth, *Toronto, the Belfast of Canada: The Orange Order and the Shaping of Municipal Culture* (Toronto: University of Toronto Press, 2015).

[80] Manuel Eisner, "What Causes Large-scale Variation in Homicide Rates?": 14-25.

[81] This also applies to penitentiaries and prisons for Ontario during the same period,

The data point towards the take-up of a stricter ethic within BEP communities and follows Weberian theory. Though, in consequence, discrimination—against Catholics notably—no doubt played a role, personal, BEP-induced behavioural constraints were the critical thing.

Reinforced by BEP rhetoric, the identity of Toronto's residents had been transformed in an associational, communal process that in turn fed back to reinforce the rhetoric. Across the population of Toronto, male behaviour had undergone deep changes as BEP ideology manifested itself in increased investments of social capital, dense webs of human interaction, and empathy being expressed in new ways.

7.2.7 Where in Hell Are the Baptists?

Small religious minorities that included most visibly Baptists, but also Congregationalists, Plymouth Brethren, Jews, Salvationists, Quakers, and Unitarians, were noticeable in the Central Prison register by their near absence. The registrar did know of the denominational niche that each represented, because from time to time most do appear in the register. Together the Baptists and the "Other" category accounted for 10.5% of Toronto's population.[82] Unlike Baptists within the general population of Toronto, the Toronto Baptist population in Central Prison was 47% American-born. If the Baptist number is disaggregated so that the American-born are removed, then the representation of this 10.5% of the population becomes startlingly low at Central Prison and, indeed, verges on the non-existent.[83] While

---

although the data are not disaggregated for Toronto. Note that crimes against property and crimes against "public morals and decency" had little change and no doubt fluctuated with the interaction between law and culture. However crimes against "public order and peace" did drop significantly over the period but not at the rate of crimes against the person. See Peter Oliver, *Terror to Evil-Doers*, 372-373.

[82] Baptists and Congregationalists on their own made up 7% of Toronto's population and reflect a solidly BEP ideology.

[83] To disaggregate would not be normal procedure, but the American-born population of Toronto was only 0.5% according to census data and 3.9% of the Central Prison population in general. Methodists with a prisoner population of 12.4% American-born had the second largest number, and then it dropped to only 4% American-born for the Anglican prisoner population.

Congregationalists, Quakers, and Unitarians were solidly middle, business, and professional class by occupation, the same cannot be said uniformly of Baptists, Jews, Plymouth Brethren and Salvationists. Many of this 10.5% group would have been on the cultural margins of Toronto, and a good number would have been poor.[84]

Within these groups, religious strictures on everyday male behaviour would have been ever-present. These tight strictures are evident in low committal rates to Central Prison. Though this category represented 10.5% of Toronto's population, it accounted for only 3.3% of the prisoners from Toronto. Persons in it committed only 3 of 288 assaults, or 1%. It is difficult to provide an explanation other than that male behaviour was substantially modified as the result of the working of religious ideology.

It may seem possible that Baptists as a whole were simply a self-selecting group who shared characteristics, whether economic or sociobiological, that made it unlikely that a member might be incarcerated. With Baptists representing only about 5% of Toronto's population this seems plausible. However, at least 50% of the 'Other' religious category that comprised 10% of the total population is Baptist-like in polity and beliefs. Thus the Baptist-like are at least 10% of the population. Add in the Methodists, the largest Ontario denomination and accounting for 22% of Toronto's population, who differ little from Baptists in terms of incarceration rates and violent convictions and are solidly BEP, and the number becomes 32% of Toronto's population. Add in perhaps a majority of the Presbyterians as essentially BEP in beliefs (and significantly underrepresented in Central Prison) and a sizeable percentage of Anglicans who are evangelicals, then suddenly the number of Toronto residents with BEP identities is greater than 50%. The BEP continuum in Central Prison between Baptist and Presbyterian is relatively close in terms of underrepresentation. Given that Toronto is essentially a BEP culture, as will be demonstrated later in the thesis, the self-selection factor appears smaller

---

[84] See Livio Di Matteo, "The Effect of Religious Denomination on Wealth: Who Were the Truly Blessed?" *Social Science History*, 31, no. 3 (Fall 2007): 299-341. In a study of nineteenth-century probate records based on census data for Hamilton and Thunder Bay, Di Matteo argues that Methodists and Baptists had the lowest levels of wealth.

and socialization much larger.[85]

In summary, the denominational data on crime as reflected in multiple data sets from Central Prison, strongly confirm the conclusion of Darroch and Soltow that there was a stubborn religious dimension to personal conduct and deportment in Ontario during the second half of the nineteenth-century. When Toronto prisoners are isolated out and violent offences disaggregated, this religious dimension is heightened along BEP and Weberian lines with prisoners who are listed as belonging to the more evangelical denominations being much less represented.

7.3 Interpretation

The above data sets support the thesis that there is a relationship between declining rates of interpersonal violence in late nineteenth-century Toronto and the prevalence of a British evangelical Protestantism.

First, the data on incarceration with respect to gender shows that from 1869-1902, men were incarcerated at a rate of 8 to 2 over women.[86] Furthermore, males were the perpetrators in 85% of Toronto homicides from 1880-1899.

Second, with respect to marital status, single males were incarcerated at Central Prison, from 1880-1900, at a rate of 7 to 3 as compared to married prisoners, irrespective of a conviction for either a violent offence or a non-violent one.

Third, Anglicans were incarcerated at Central Prison for violent offences at a rate of almost 8 to 2 as compared to Baptists,[87] 7 to 2 as compared to Methodists, and 2 to 1 as compared to Presbyterians.

---

[85] Baptists and Methodists had disproportionately more women than men. Thus the percentage of males in the general Toronto population is slightly less than the total population percentage for these two denominations; i.e. in 1901 Toronto's Methodists made up 22.5% of the population but male Methodists made up only 20.9% of the adult male population. Even when an adjustment is made for this variation, and the variation differs over the course of 1881-1901, there is no significant difference in the above calculations.

[86] See Peter Oliver, *"Terror to Evil-Doers"*, 371. During this period 262,640 men were incarcerated in Ontario gaols versus 51,775 women.

[87] If American-born Baptists are disaggregated out because of huge overrepresentation among Baptists, then this ratio becomes wildly higher.

Several observations can be made. The tight correlation between male singleness and incarceration as well as maleness and incarceration suggests a causal nexus in both cases.[88] The difference between single males and married males fits with the explanation put forward in this study that "rough" male behaviour is disciplined within the institution of marriage.

When one moves to the relationship between denominational affiliation and incarceration for a violent offence, it is difficult to argue that discrimination against Anglicans on the basis of religion was the cause of Anglicans being imprisoned for violent offences at rates much higher than those for Baptists and Methodists. A class factor may, however, have been present; Baptists and Methodists did have lower rates of labourers in the general population of Toronto as compared to Anglicans. One could make a case that class position affected propensities towards violence, though this would be difficult to do.

This difficulty can be demonstrated when one compares the incarceration rates for violent offences of Anglicans as compared to Presbyterians. We have seen that this ratio stands at 2 to 1 despite Presbyterians having a higher percentage of single males in the Toronto general population than Anglicans did and a higher percentage of males classed as "labourers".

Thus the argument that incarceration rates for violence follows a BEP ideological gradient continues to be persuasive. Baptists and Methodists, the two major denominations most marked by BEP ideology, have the lowest rates of incarceration for violent offences. Presbyterians, also heavily marked by BEP ideology, and having higher percentages of their number in the labouring class than Anglicans (and significantly higher than Baptists and Methodists), nonetheless have incarceration rates for violent offences that are one-half the rate of Anglican males.

Within the population of Central Prison, foreign-born prisoners are overrepresented, but this variable does not explain incarceration rates across

<hr/>

[88] In deploying a deductive method to test the thesis, I have demonstrated that BEP religious identities correlated tightly with very low rates of committal to Central Prison for all offences but especially for assault. Although reliant on correlation, there is a covalence that gives strength to the argument of this study.

denominations. With respect to marital status, single males outnumber those married by a 7 to 3 margin. This overrepresentation of single males holds true across the range of ages of prisoners. Denominationally, Roman Catholic prisoners are especially overrepresented, with an almost 8 to 2 ratio of single to married men; marital status of prisoners by itself does not, however, explain the overall denominational breakdown.

Literacy rates among prisoners are depressed as compared to the Toronto general population. This is especially true for Roman Catholic prisoners and Baptist prisoners born in the U.S. Within Toronto's general population, Baptists, Presbyterians, and Methodists have the highest levels of literacy, despite the presence of relatively high levels of "labourers" among Presbyterians. This is very significant and points to a relationship between BEP discourse and literacy. Similarly, Baptists and Methodists had the highest percentages of prisoners judged temperate, with Baptists having by far the highest levels; again, a BEP connection seems indicated.

The key measurement in favour of denominational affiliation as being the explaining variable in the analysis of Toronto prisoners in Central Prison is the data on physical assault as highlighted at the beginning of this section. The extremely low percentages of Baptist, Methodist, and Presbyterian prisoners convicted of assault does not vary from the percentages convicted of non-physical offences and even decreases slightly for Baptist prisoners. If one group of prisoners convicted of vagrancy or drunkenness were being singled out in a discriminatory fashion, one would expect the denominational percentages to move closer for more serious offences. This is not the case, and that is the strongest indicator of a disciplining process being imposed on BEP males through BEP ideology. In this I concur with Darroch and Soltow's earlier analysis on the denominational affiliation of Ontario prisons, that "Class and economic position are intertwined with cultural predispositions in these data but the striking break between the two diocesan and the more evangelical groups remains."[89] The importance that Weber laid upon evan-

---

[89] Gordon Darroch and Lee Soltow, *Property and Inequality in Victorian Ontario*, 109.

gelical ascetical traits seems to be justified.[90] Thus, the Central Prison data support the Eisner hypothesis on the importance of moral individualism in the decline of interpersonal violence.

[90] On the moral traits of the Protestant "sects" (that included Baptists and Methodists according to Weber) see especially Max Weber, *From Max Weber*, 302-322.

8

CONCLUSION: A MICRO-FIELD OF STUDY AND WHAT THAT STUDY MEANS

Embodying many of the features that characterize modern society's experience with complex patterns of community life, open to investigation in terms of an extraordinarily rich array of source materials, and offering important opportunities for detailed examinations of the correlations[1] between interpersonal behavior and a distinct, religiously-inflected variety of what Manuel Eisner calls "moral individualism", late nineteenth-century Toronto holds much of value for students of societal history and behavioural change. The localized decline in violence in late nineteenth-century Toronto, descending perhaps to the limits of cultural possibilities, was part of a much broader decline in violence throughout the Western world beginning from approximately the middle ages and extending well into the twentieth century. This study is the first to explicate this Protestant moralizing and disciplining process in relation to interpersonal violence within the context of a largely Protestant city over the course of two decades.

Allowing construction of a solidly-grounded argument for close connections between community order and citizen involvement with a particular world view and sensibility, it points to the need for a major refinement in what has become our prevalent understanding of the linkages between personal deportment and prescribed moral norms. The view that citizen rectitude and

---

[1] On correlation see Thomas J. Archdeacon, *Correlation and Regression Analysis: A Historian's Guide* (Madison: University of Wisconsin Press, 1994), esp. 245-247. See also Pat Hudson, *History by Numbers: An Introduction to Quantitative Approaches* (London: Arnold: 2000), esp. 36-40, 181-187. For a helpful discussion of causation see Richard J. Evans, *In Defence of History*, new ed. (London: Granta Publications, 2000), 129-160. Both deductive and inductive arguments have been used. This covalence gives strength to the argument.

responsibility are—in at least some circumstances—features shaped by more than functional adjustment to the tensions growing social complexity yields or increased citizen exposure to generalized, secular prescriptions and injunctions is sharply reinforced. Support for an understanding of that rectitude and responsibility as elements produced by situation-specific conditions and influences is enhanced. The religiously-motivated drive to regulate the use of alcohol, on a nineteenth-century urban frontier, gains new notice. The sense—held by Eisner himself—that appreciation of behaviour's roots and origins is best advanced by careful, and ultimately comparative, examination of varying types of situation and circumstance receives strong augmentation and significant new weight. The case for a particular type of religious belief as a critical factor in the production of low levels of interpersonal violence is particularly assisted and given new strength. The continued serviceability of the Weber thesis concerning the disciplining influence of Protestant "sects" appears obvious.

A good deal follows on a second front too. In providing documentation that allows women's role in the articulation and entrenchment of normative standards and community codes to come forward in detailed, visible ways, Toronto permits a vital—but often only imperfectly perceived—society-shaping force to appear with a markedly telling clearness and a sharply evident form. The overwhelming support of Ontario women in favour of the prohibition of alcohol gains resonance. The "lost cause" of Prohibition is cast in sharper relief. Narrative concerning a critical structuring element has unusually distinct lineaments and a strong, defining frame. Account and representation are strongly founded and firmly based. More than inferential reasoning, or reading sources against the grain, or the frequently ambiguous results speculative thinking gives is in play. Reporting of action proceeds on the basis of direct, comprehensive testimony and decisively indicated ground. Influences are very obviously apparent and very plainly in view.

In no domain does Toronto's salience appear more clearly than that concerned with religion's place in Canadian life at large. Already enforcing claims that—even in an age of encroaching secularizing and modernizing change—religion remained important to the Canadian scene (one thinks of Marguerite

CONCLUSION

Van Die's referencing of the city's religious links as factors strengthening argument for "the important role of religious beliefs, practices, and institutions in the transformation from a pre-industrial to a modern society.")[2] Toronto can now be understood as providing such enforcement on an even greater scale. Depiction of Toronto as a locus of the sort of heavily-institutionalized, deeply-entrenched, palpably behavior-shaping religious influences with which this study is occupied positions it as a still more significant pillar of the case for religion in Canadian life than it has previously thought to be.[3] Critical additional backing is accorded the claim that religion didn't simply slow the progress of secularizing/modernizing trends but was sufficiently strongly in place to ensure that it would figure as "a prominent voice…in Canadian society until the 1960s."[4] A centrally important interpretive stance finds a potent new ally and a forceful new friend.

Made possible by the existence of extensive and revealing data sets, reinforcing both major and minor shifts in perspective, and clearing new pathways as well as broadening out old, the study of Toronto offers considerable benefits on multiple fronts. Enriching understanding not only of a particular community but also of the nation in which it is situated, providing an extended sense of the conditions that shape behavior and give to its cast, and delivering an elaborated picture of social processes and functions too, this study extends comprehension as it re-moulds its form. Issues are clearer and more fully fleshed out. Explication has added texture and wider reach to a pivotal period in the history of violence in Canada.

Limitations

The finding that the Baptists, Methodists, and the "Other" category included in their number significant numbers of working class precludes a

---

[2] Marguerite Van Die, "Protestants, the Liberal State, and the Practice of Politics: Revisiting R.J. Fleming and the 1890s Toronto Streetcar Controversy", *Journal of the Canadian Historical Association* New Series 24, no. 1 (2013): 92.

[3] For a summary view of that case see Richard Allen, *The View from Murney Tower*, xv-xxxviii.

[4] Marguerite Van Die, "Protestants, the Liberal State, and the Practice of Politics", 92.

strict separation of Baptists, Methodists, and "Other" from Anglicans and Roman Catholics on the basis of class. Presbyterians and Anglicans had similar numbers of males classed as "labourers" in their numbers according to the Canadian Families Project 1901 sample but had significantly lower representation in Central Prison of prisoners convicted of violent offences. However, Roman Catholics living in BEP Toronto did have significantly higher percentages of labourers in their community suggesting that their members could have faced discrimination based on religion and possibly birthplace. The discrimination factor remains an unknown. Broader issues connected to religious affiliation and occupation also remain unknown. Within the general Toronto population, Presbyterians were slightly more likely to be classed by a census enumerator as a labourer than were Anglicans but Anglicans had significantly higher rates of incarceration for violent offences. This significant difference would need to be explained if one reaches for economic causal theory. Questions do remain about spatial localities within Toronto and related inequalities. But the rejoinder that takes an ideological line of reasoning would be that males in stronger networks, and possessing cultural tools such as literacy,[5] would have increased job and housing opportunities. BEP Protestants, with more participatory church leadership structures, had denser social networks than Anglicans and Roman Catholics. In a colonial setting, BEP church structures and polities allowed for the rapid planting of new churches as compared to the more hierarchical Anglican and Roman Catholic churches. These denser networks enabled more scrutiny of male behaviour, in harmony with an ascetic Protestant ethic that placed great emphasis on self-control. This social capital advantage, even according to Pinker, would produce lower levels of male interpersonal violence.

Quantitative sources always have limitations. Analysis of the Central Prison register allows only an angled, skewed, and squinted glance into the interstices of Toronto culture. But names in the register are the product of

---

[5] Current research links literacy with lower levels of homicide on both a macro-level and an individual level. See for example Andrew Stickley and William A. Pridemore, "The Social-Structural Correlates of Homicide in Late-Tsarist Russia," *British Journal of Criminology* 47, no. 1 (January 2007): 80-99.

innumerable urban interactions and the judgments of a culture on the nature of these interactions. The use of the 1901 Canada Census sample for calculations concerning literacy, marital status, and birthplace for the general population of Toronto does generally follow the contours of the earlier 1881 and 1891 censuses. Full digital encoding of the 1881 and 1891 censuses would be of great value to historical researchers.

A "temperance" evaluation of the general Toronto population by religious affiliation is of course impossible but greater analysis of the published individual votes for the 1878 Duncan Act referendum, in combination with religious affiliations, could yield patterns with respect to the public attitudes towards alcohol of qualified voters. The role of Mowat and his use of BEP ideology, even if avoiding the prohibition controversy, to enable his 24 successive years as Premier, would be promising study.

Moving Forward

It is anticipated that additional analysis of the heights and weights of prisoners, according to religious denomination could be conducted on the register of the Central Prison. This would have the potential to add a further measure of economic equality across denominational lines, a promising research path that has yet to be explored.[6] In addition, comparative work on individual prisoner lists in Britain could be used. Even though regular summary reports on the religious makeup of Britain's prisons were not regularly compiled, there are religious categories in some individual nineteenth-century prison registers.[7]

Summing Up

The larger argument of this thesis is that for a significant period of time, a religious culture in Late Victorian Toronto produced a relative peacefulness across a variety of class, religious and increasingly ethnic distinctions. This

---

[6] See for example Robert W. Fogel, *Explaining Long-Term Trends in Health and Longevity* (New York: Cambridge University Press, 2012).

[7] See: http://www.genguide.co.uk/source/criminal-registers-criminals/214/ Accessed April 22, 2014.

peaceful image of Toronto was perpetuated in a variety of ways, ironically leaving the city with the tag, "Toronto the Good"; ironical in that the phrase was originally a derogatory epithet that had its origins in the Toronto Police Department's efforts to control vice. When a culture achieves a homicide rate of less than 2 per 100,000 without the heavy hand of a police state, this is an event of significance. This decline of interpersonal violence allowed for new spaces for human interaction. Religious discourse mattered in late nineteenth-century Toronto.

Bibliography

Archival Sources

Central Prison Register, Vol. 1, 1874-1889, RG 20-55-1, Barcode D360801. Archives of Ontario, Toronto, Ontario.

City Council Minutes, 1881-1900, City of Toronto, Toronto Archives.

Gadoury, Lorraine, and Antonio Lechasseur. *Persons Sentenced to Death in Canada, 1867-1976: An Inventory of Case Files in the Records of the Department of Justice* RG13. Government Archives Division, National Archives of Canada, 1992.

Henry O'Brien Papers, S 154, Box 2, Articles and Clippings about the O'Brien family, 1875-1943. Baldwin Room, Toronto Reference Library, Toronto.

King, William Lyon Mackenzie King. *Diaries of William Lyon Mackenzie King*, MG26-J13. Archives Canada, Ottawa, Ontario. http://www.collectionscanada. gc.ca/databases/king/index-e.html.

Letters in Capital Case Files, Robert William Decoursier, RG 13, vol. 1417, file 142A; 1880, Department of Justice (Canada), Library and Archives Canada, Ottawa.

Letters in Capital Case Files, Thomas Kane, RG 13, vol. 1426 file 237A; 1890, Department of Justice (Canada), Library and Archives Canada, Ottawa.

Letters in Capital Case Files, Robert Neil, RG 13, vol. 1424, file 222A; 1888, Department of Justice (Canada), Library and Archives Canada, Ottawa.

Newspapers (with years researched)

Christian Guardian, 1880-1900
Globe, 1850-1900
Mail and Empire, 1895-1900
Telegram, 1880-1900
Toronto Empire, 1887-1895
Toronto Life, 1888
Toronto Mail, 1880-1895
Toronto Star, 1892-1900
Toronto World
Trip Hammer, 1885

Printed Primary Sources

Annual Report of the Inspector of the Public Schools of the City of Toronto for the Year Ending December 31, 1880. Toronto: Patterson and Company, 1881.

Canada Yearbook 1900. Ottawa: Government of Canada, 1900.

Fourth Census of Canada, 1901, Vol. 1, *Population*. Ottawa: Government of Canada, 1902.

Prison Reform. Toronto: Prisoners' Aid Association, 1889.

Report of the Prison Reform Conference, Held in Toronto November 27, 1891. Toronto: Prisoners' Aid Association of Canada, 1891.

Report of the Commissioners/Ontario. Royal Commission Appointed to Enquire into Certain Charges Against the Warden of Central Prison and the Management of Said Prison. Toronto: Legislative Assembly of Ontario, 1886.

Report of the Royal Commission on the Liquor Traffic: Minutes of Evidence, Volume IV-Part II, *Province of Ontario*. Ottawa: S.E. Dawson, 1895.

The Coffee Public-House News and Temperance Hotel Journal. London, November 1, 1883.

The Yeas and Nays Polled in the Dunkin Act Campaign in Toronto, Carefully Prepared With the Official Returns, With Introductory Remarks and Extracts of Speeches Delivered During the Campaign. Toronto: Leader Stream Job Printing Office, 1877.

Adam, G. Mercer. *Toronto, Old and New: Historical, Descriptive and Pictorial*. Toronto: The Mail Printing Company, 1891.

Birks, T.R. *First Principles of Moral Science: A Course of Lectures*. London: Macmillan, 1873.

_____. *The Victory of Divine Goodness*. London, Oxford, and Cambridge: Rivingtons, 1867.

Blake, Samuel H. *Our Faulty Gaol System*. Toronto: Methodist Magazine and Review, 1897.

_____. *The Call of the Red Man*. Toronto: Bryant Press, 1908.

_____. *The Young Men of Canada: A Lecture*. Toronto: B.J. Hill, 1876.

Brown, Peter. *The Fame and Glory of England Vindicated Being an Answer To "The Gory and Shame of England." By Veritas*. New York and London: Wiley and Putman, 1842.

Burrows, Elizabeth, ed. *Twenty-Fourth National Conference of Charities* [Social Work]: *Official Proceedings of the Annual Meeting, 1897*. Boston: Geo. H. Ellis, 1898.

Carlyle, Thomas. *The Edinburgh Review* (June 1829): 442-443.

BIBLIOGRAPHY

Clark, C.S. *Of Toronto the Good: The Queen City as it is: A Social Study*. Toronto and Montreal: The Toronto Publishing Company, 1898.

Clarke, Edward, and William Roaf. *By-laws of the city of Toronto*. Toronto: Rowsell, 1890.

Cruikshank, E.A. ed. *The Correspondence of Lieut. Governor John Graves Simcoe*. Vol. 1 and 2. Toronto: Ontario Historical Society, 1923.

Denison, George T. *Recollections of a Police Magistrate*. Toronto: Musson, 1920.

Dewart, Edward Hartley, et al. *Centennial of Canadian Methodism*. Toronto: William Briggs, 1891.

Dewart, Edward Hartley. *Selections From Canadian Poets*. Montreal: John Lovell, 1864.

_____. *Songs of Life*. Toronto: Dudley and Burns, Printer, 1869.

Dickens, Charles. *Oliver Twist*. London: HarperCollins, 2010.

Diefenbaker, John G. *One Canada: The Crusading Years, 1895-1956*. Toronto: Macmillan, 1975.

Doran, George H. *Chronicles of Barabbas, 1884-1934*. Toronto: George J. McLeod, 1935.

Durant, Charles. *Reminiscences of Charles Durant, Barrister*. Toronto: Hunter, Rose, 1897.

Durkheim, Emile, trans. by John A. Spaulding and George Simpson. *Suicide: A Study in Sociology*. New York: Free Press, 1951.

Ferguson, John. *Social Purity*. Toronto: Toronto YMCA, 1891.

Globe. *Constitution and Bye-Laws of the Anti-Slavery Society of Canada*. Toronto: Globe Office, 1851.

Goforth, Rosalind. *Goforth of China*. Grand Rapids: Zondervan, 1937.

Grant, George Munro. *Ocean to Ocean: Sanford Fleming's Expedition Through Canada in 1872*. Toronto: James Campbell, 1873.

Henning, Thomas. *Slavery In the Churches, Religious Societies, Etc*. Toronto: Globe Book and Job Office, 1856.

Hodgins, J. George, ed. *Aims and Objects of the Toronto Humane Society*. Toronto: William Briggs, 1888.

Kelso, J.J. *Early History of the Humane and Children's Aid Movement, 1886-1893*. Toronto: L.K. Cameron, 1911.

Mackenzie, Alexander. *The Life and Speeches of George Brown*. Toronto: Globe Printing Company, 1882.

McCurdy, J.F., ed. *Life and Work of D.J. Macdonnell*. Toronto: William Briggs, 1897.

Morgan, Henry J. *The Canadian Men and Women of the Time*. Toronto: William Briggs, 1912.

Mudie-Smith, Richard. *Religious Life in London*. London: Hodder, 1904.

Mulvany, C. Pelham. *Toronto: Past and Present, A Handbook of the City*. Toronto: W.E. Caiger, 1884.

O'Brien, William. *Evening Memories*. Dublin: Maunsel, 1920.

Paton, John G. *John G. Paton: Missionary to the New Hebrides, An Autobiography*. Edited by His Brother. London: Hodder and Stoughton, 1889.

Pierce, Lorne, ed. *The Chronicle of a Century: The Record of One Hundred Years of Progress in the Publishing Concerns of the Methodist, Presbyterian and Congregational Churches in Canada*. Toronto: Ryerson Press, 1929.

Powell, Aaron. *The National Purity Conference: Its Papers, Addresses, Portraits*. New York: National Purity Alliance, 1896.

Robertson, J. Ross. *Robertson's Landmarks of Toronto: A Collection of Historical Sketches of the Town of York From 1792 until 1837 and of Toronto from 1834 to 1904 Also Nearly Three Hundred Engravings of the Churches of Toronto Embracing the Picture of every Church Obtainable from 1800-1904*, Fourth Series. Toronto: Telegram, 1904.

Spence, Ruth E. *Prohibition in Canada: A Memorial to Francis Stephen Spence*. Toronto: Ontario Branch of the Dominion Alliance, 1919.

Taschereau, Henri E. *The Criminal Code of the Dominion of Canada, As Amended in 1893*. Toronto: Carswell, 1893.

Taylor, Conyngham Crawford. *Toronto Called Back*. Toronto: William Briggs, 1892.

Timothy Eaton Company. *The 1901 Editions of the T. Eaton Co. Limited Catalogues for Spring & Summer Fall & Winter*. Toronto: Stoddart, reprinted 1970.

Ward, Samuel Ringgold. *Autobiography of a Fugitive Negro*. New York: Arno Press and the New York Times, 1968.

Weber, Max. *From Max Weber: Essays in Sociology*. Translated by H.H. Gerth and C. Wright Mills. New York: Oxford University Press, 1958.

_____. *The Protestant Ethic and the Spirit of Capitalism*. Translated by Talcott Parsons. New York: Charles Scribner, 1958.

Webster, Edward, A.H. Dymond, and Henry Mayhew, *Three Papers on Capital Punishment*. London: Society for Promoting an Amendment of the Law, 1856.

Willis, Michael. *Pulpit Discourses, Expository and Practical and College Addresses, etc.*

BIBLIOGRAPHY

London: Nisbet, 1873. Text-fiche, CIHM 14855.

Wilson, Daniel. "On the Supposed Prevalence of One Cranial Type Throughout the American Aborigines," in *Edinburgh Philosophical Society Journal*, New Series, Jan., 1858. Text-fiche, CIHM 63246.

Wooley, John G. and William E. Johnson, *Temperance Progress in the Century*. London, Toronto, Philadelphia: Linscott Publishing, 1903.

Young Men's Christian Associations (Toronto, Ont.) *Shaftesbury Hall Weekly Bulletin* 1-6 (1880-1885).

Theses and Dissertations

Boritch, Helen. "The Making of Toronto the Good: The Organizing of Policing and Production of Arrests, 1859-1955." PhD diss., University of Toronto, 1985.

Draper, Kenneth L. "Religion Worthy of a Free People: Religious Practices and Discourses in London, Ontario, 1870-1890." PhD diss., McMaster University, 2000.

Hanlon, Peter. "Moral Order and the Influence of Social Christianity in an Industrial City, 1890-1899: A Local Profile of the Protestant Lay Leaders of Three Hamilton Churches: Centenary Methodist, Central Presbyterian, and Christ's Church Cathedral." Master's Thesis, McMaster University, 1984.

O'Dell, Doris. "The Class Character of Church Participation in Late Nineteenth-Century Belleville." PhD diss., Queen's University, 1990.

Reimer, William D. "A Depressing Story? Homicide Rates in Late Victorian Toronto." Master's thesis, University of British Columbia, 2006.

Sawatsky, Rodney G. "Looking For That Blessed Hope": The Roots of Fundamentalism in Canada." PhD diss. University of Toronto, 1985.

Smith, Allan C. L. "The Imported Image: American Publications and American Ideas in the Evolution of the English Canadian Mind, 1820-1900." PhD diss., University of Toronto, 1972.

Secondary Sources

Adler, Jeffrey S. *First in Violence, Deepest in Dirt: Homicide in Chicago, 1875-1920*. Cambridge, MA: Harvard University Press, 2006.

Andrews, William L. and Henry Louis Gates Jr. *Slave Narratives*. New York: Library of America, 2002.

Akerlof, George A., Janet L. Yellen, and Michael L. Katz, "An Analysis of Out-of-Wedlock Childbearing in the United States". *The Quarterly Journal of Economics* 111, no. 2 (May, 1996): 277-317.

Allen, Richard. *The Social Passion: Religion and Social Reform in Canada, 1914-1928*. Toronto: University of Toronto Press, 1971.

_____. *The View from Murney Tower: Salem Bland, the Late Victorian Controversies, and the Search for a New Christianity*, Book One, *Salem Bland: A Canadian Odyssey*. Toronto: University of Toronto Press, 2008.

Appiah, Kwame Anthony. *The Honor Code: How Moral Revolutions Happen*. New York: Norton, 2011.

Archdeacon, Thomas J. *Correlation and Regression Analysis: A Historian's Guide*. Madison: University of Wisconsin Press, 1994.

Archer, Dane and Rosemary Gartner. *Violence and Crime in Cross-National Perspective*. New Haven: Yale University Press, 1984.

Archer, John E. *The Monster Evil: Policing and Violence in Victorian Liverpool*. University of Liverpool Press, 2011.

_____. "The Violence We Have Lost? Body Counts, Historians and Interpersonal Violence in England" *Memoria y Civilizacion* 2 (1999): 171-190.

Armstrong, Christopher and H.V. Nelles. *The Revenge of the Methodist Bicycle Company: Sunday Streetcars and Municipal Reform in Toronto, 1888-1897*. Toronto: Peter Martin Associates, 1977.

Arthur, Eric. *Toronto: No Mean City* 3rd ed., Revised by Stephen A. Otto. Toronto: University of Toronto, 1986.

Ash, Marinell and Elizabeth Hulse ed. *Thinking with Both Hands: Sir Daniel Wilson in the Old World and the New*. Toronto: University of Toronto Press, 1999.

Backhouse, Constance. *Colour-Coded: A Legal History of Racism in Canada, 1900-1950*. Toronto: University of Toronto Press, 1999.

Backhouse, Constance. "Nineteenth Century Prostitution Law: Reflections of a Discriminatory Society". *Histoire Sociale-Social History* 18, no. 36 (novembre-November 1985): 392-393.

Bailyn, Bernard. *Atlantic History: Concept and Contours*. Cambridge, MA: Harvard University Press, 2005.

Baskerville, Peter. *A Silent Revolution? Gender and Wealth in English Canada,*

BIBLIOGRAPHY

1860-1930. Montreal and Kingston: McGill-Queen's University Press, 2008.

Bebbington, David. *Evangelicalism in Modern Britain: A History from the 1730s to the 1980s*. London: Routledge, 1989.

———. *The Dominance of Evangelicalism: The Age of Spurgeon and Moody*. Downers Grove, IL: Intervarsity Press, 2005.

Begley, Louis. *Why the Dreyfus Affair Matters*. New Haven: Yale University Press, 2009.

Bennett, Paul W. ""Turning 'Bad Boys' into 'Good Citizens'": The Reforming Impulse of Toronto's Industrial Schools Movement, 1883 to the 1920s." *Ontario History* LXXVIII, No. 3 (September 1986): 209-232.

Berger, Carl. *The Sense of Power: Studies in the Ideas of Canadian Imperialism, 1867-1914*. Toronto: University of Toronto Press, 1970.

Berger, Carl. *The Writing of Canadian History: Aspects of English-Canadian Historical Writing, 1900-1970*. Toronto: Oxford University Press, 1976.

Birmingham, Lucy, and David McNeill. *Strong in the Rain: Surviving Japan's Earthquake, Tsunami, and Fukushima Nuclear Disaster*. New York: Palgrave Macmillan, 2012.

Birrell, A.J. "D.I.K. Rine and the Gospel Temperance Movement in Canada." *Canadian Historical Review* 58, no. 1 (1977): 23-44.

Bliss, Michael. *Plague: A Story of Smallpox in Montreal*. Toronto: Harper Collins, 1992.

Bolt, Christine and Seymour Drescher. *Anti-Slavery, Religion and Reform: Essays in Memory of Roger Anstey*. Folkestone, Kent: Wm Dawson and Sons, 1980.

Boritch, Helen and John Hagen. "Crime and the Changing Forms of Class Control: Policing Public Order in "Toronto the Good," 1859-1955." *Social Forces* 66, no. 2 (1987): 307-335.

Bradley, Ian. *Call to Seriousness: The Evangelical Impact on the Victorians*. New York: Macmillan, 1976.

Brook, Timothy, Jerome Bourgon, and Gregory Blue, *Death by a Thousand Cuts*. Cambridge, MA: Harvard University Press, 2008.

Brown, Callum G. *The Death of Christian Britain: Understanding Secularisation, 1800-2000*, London: Routledge, 2001.

———. *Religion and Society in Scotland since 1707*.Edinburgh: Edinburgh University Press, 1997.

Brown, Desmond H. *The Genesis of the Criminal Code of 1892*. Toronto: Osgoode Society, University of Toronto Press, 1989.

R. Blake Brown, *Arming and Disarming: A History of Gun Control in Canada* (Toronto: Osgoode Society, University of Toronto Press, 2012

_____. Brown, R. Blake, "'Pistol Fever': Regulating Revolvers in Late-Nineteenth-Century Canada." *Journal of the Canadian Historical Association* 20, no. 1 (2009): 107-138.

Browning, Christopher. *Ordinary Men: Reserve Battalion 101 and the Final Solution in Poland*. Rev. ed. New York: Harper Collins, 1998.

Brusco, Elisabeth E. *The Reformation of Machismo: Evangelical Conversion and Gender in Columbia*. Austin: University of Texas, 1995.

Buhrmann, Andrea D. and Stefanie Ernst, eds. *Care or Control of the Self? Michel Foucault, Norbert Elias, and the Subject in the 21st Century*. Newcastle: Cambridge Scholars' Press, 2010.

Bumsted, J.M. *A History of the Peoples of Canada*. Toronto: Oxford University Press, 2003.

_____ *The Peoples of Canada: A Post Confederation History* Second Ed. Toronto: Oxford University Press, 2004.

Bushman, B.J., and H.M. Cooper. "Effects of Alcohol on Human Aggression: An Integrative Research Review." *Psychological Bulletin* 107, no. 3 (May 1990): 341-354.

Campbell, Carla Alexia, Robert A. Hahn, et al. "The Task Force on Community Preventative Services." *American Journal of Preventive Medicine*, 37, no. 6 (2009): 556-559.

Careless, J.M.S. *Brown of the Globe*. 2 vols. Toronto: Macmillan, 1959. 1963.

_____. "Mid-Victorian Liberalism in Central Canadian Newspapers, 1850-67." *Canadian Historical Review* XXXI, no. 3 (September 1950): 221-236.

Careless, J.M.S. "Somewhat Narrow Horizons", *Historical Papers* 1968: 1-10.

_____*Toronto to 1918: an Illustrated History*. Toronto: James Lorimer, 1984.

Carrigan, D. Owen. *Crime and Punishment in Canada: A History*. Toronto: McClelland and Stewart, 1991.

Caulfield, Jon. "The Growth of the Industrial City and Inner Toronto's Vanished Church Buildings." *Urban History Review/Revue d'histoire urbaine* 23, no. 2 (March 1995 mars): 3-43.

Childs, Craig. *House of Rain: Tracking a Vanished Civilization Across the American*

BIBLIOGRAPHY

Southwest. New York: Little, Brown, and Company, 2007.

Christie, Nancy and Michael Gauvreau. *Christian Churches and Their Peoples, 1840-1965*. Toronto: University of Toronto Press, 2010.

_____. "Modalities of Social Authority: Suggesting an Interface for Religious and Social History", *Histoire sociale / Social History* 36, no. 71 (Mai-May, 2003): 1-30.

Christie, Nancy ed. *Households of Faith: Family, Gender, and Community in Canada, 1760-1969*. Montreal and Kingston: McGill-Queen's University Press, 2002.

_____. ""On the threshold of manhood": Working-Class Religion and Domesticity in Victorian Britain and Canada. *Social History* 36, no. 71 (May 2003): 145-175.

Clark, Gregory. *A Farewell to Alms: A Brief Economic History of the World*. Princeton: Princeton University Press, 2007.

Clark, S.D. *Church and Sect in Canada*. Toronto: University of Toronto Press, 1948.

Clark, S.D. *The Developing Canadian Community*, Second ed. Toronto: University of Toronto Press, 1968.

Clarke, Alison. "Churchgoing in New Zealand, 1874-1926, a re-evaluation." Unpublished paper with accompanying slides presented at the New Zealand Historical Association Conference, Hamilton, November 2011.

Clarke, Brian P. *Piety and Nationalism: Lay Voluntary Association and the Creation of an Irish-Catholic Community in Toronto: 1850-1895*. Montreal and Kingston: McGill-Queen's University Press, 1993.

Cockburn, J.S. ed. *Crime in England, 1550-1800*. Princeton: Princeton University Press, 1977.

Cockburn, J.S. "Patterns of Violence in English Society: Homicide in Kent, 1560-1985," *Past and Present* 130, no. 1, (1991): 70-106.

Colley, Linda. *Britons: Forging the Nation, 1707-1837*. 2nd ed. New Haven: Yale University Press, 2005.

Constant, Jean-Francoise, and Michel Ducharme. *Liberalism and Hegemony: Debating the Canadian Liberal Revolution*. Toronto: University of Toronto Press, 2009.

Cook, Ramsay, et al eds. *Dictionary of Canadian Biography*, Vol. 1-15. Toronto: University of Toronto Press, 1966-2005.

Craig, E. ed. *Routledge Encyclopedia of Philosophy*. Vol. 4. London: Routledge, 1998.

Creighton, Philip. "Lizzie Creighton," *York Pioneer* 98 (2003): 53-60.

Crouse, Eric R. *Revival in the City: The Impact of American Evangelists in Canada, 1884-1914*. Montreal and Kingston: McGill-Queens University Press, 2005.

Cunliffe, Barry. *Europe Between the Oceans: 9000 BC-AD 1000*. New Haven: Yale University Press, 2008.

Curtis, Bruce. *The Politics of Population: State Formation, Statistics, and the Census of Canada, 1840-1875*. Toronto: University of Toronto Press, 2001.

Currie, Robert, Alan Gilbert, and Lee Horsley. *Churches and Church-Goers*. Oxford: Oxford University Press, 1977.

Daly, M. and M. Wilson. *Homicide*. New York: Aldine de Gruyter, 1988.

Darroch, Gordon, and Lee Soltow. *Property and Inequality in Victorian Ontario: Structural Patterns and Cultural Communities in the 1871 Census*. Toronto: University of Toronto Press, 1994.

Davidoff, Lenore and Catherine Hall. *Family Fortunes: Men and Women of the English Middle Class, 1780-1850*. Chicago: University of Chicago Press, 1987.

Davies, Christie. *The Strange Death of Moral Britain*. New York: Transaction Publications, 2004.

Di Matteo, Livio. "Effect of Religious Denomination on Wealth: Who Were the Truly Blessed?" *Social Sciences History* 31:3 (Fall 2007): 299-341.

Dingwall, Gavin. *Alcohol and Crime*. Cullompton, Devon: Willan Publishing, 2006.

Draper, Kenneth L. "A People's Religion: P.W. Philpott and the Hamilton Christian Workers' Church". *Social History* 36, no. 71 (May 2003): 99-122.

Drescher, Seymour. *Abolition: A History of Slavery and Antislavery*. Cambridge: Cambridge University Press, 2009.

_____. *Econocide: British Slavery in the Era of Abolition*. Pittsburg: University of Pittsburg Press, 1977.

Dubinsky, Karen. *Improper Advances: Rape and Heterosexual Conflict in Ontario, 1880-1929*. Chicago: University of Chicago Press, 1993.

Eisner, Manuel. "Long-Term Historical Trends in Violent Crime." *Crime and Justice: A Review of Research* 30 (2003): 83-142.

_____. "What Causes Large-scale Variation in Homicide Rates?" (working paper, July 2012): 1-25. www.crim.cam.ac.uk/people/academic_research/manuel_eisner/large_scale-variation.pdf, accessed May 22, 2013.

BIBLIOGRAPHY

Eisner, Manuel and Amy E. Nivette, "Does Low Legitimacy Cause Crime? A Review of the Evidence." In *Legitimacy and Criminal Justice: An International Exploration*, edited by Justin Tankebe and and Alison Liebling, 308-325. Oxford: Oxford University Press, 2014.

Elias, Norbert. *The Civilizing Process*. Oxford: Blackwell Publishing, 1994.

Emmerichs, Mary Beth. "Getting Away With Murder? Homicide and the Coroners in Nineteenth-Century London." *Social Science History* 25, no. 1 (March 1, 2001): 93-100.

Emsley, Clive. *Crime and Society in England, 1750-1900*. 2nd ed. London: Longman, 1996.

_____. *Hard Men: The English and Violence Since 1750*. London: Hambledon and London, 2005.

Esberey, Joy E. *Knight of the Holy Spirit: A Study of William Lyon Mackenzie King*. Toronto: University of Toronto Press, 1980.

Evans, A. Margaret. *Oliver Mowat* . Toronto: University of Toronto Press, 1992.

Evans, Richard J. *In Defence of History*, New ed. London: Granta Publications, 2000.

Favreau, Guy. *Capital Punishment: Material Relating to Its Purpose and Value*. Ottawa: Queen's Printer, 1965.

Ferdinand, Theodore N. "The Criminal Patterns of Boston since 1849." *American Journal of Sociology* 73 (July 1967): 688-698.

Ferry, Darren. *Uniting in Measures of Common Good: The Construction of Liberal Identities in Central Canada*. Montreal and Kingston: McGill-Queen's University Press, 2008.

Fogel, Robert W. *Explaining Long-Term Trends in Health and Longevity*. New York: Cambridge University Press, 2012.

Follett, Richard R. *Evangelicalism, Penal Theory and the Politics of Criminal Law Reform in England, 1808-30*. Houndmills, Hampshire: Palgrave, 2001.

Foster, George E. *The Canada Temperance Manual and Prohibitionist's Handbook*. Toronto: Hunter, Rose, and Co., 1881.

Foster, Hamar, and John McLaren, ed. *Essays in the History of Canadian Law*. Vol. 6, *British Columbia and the Yukon*. Toronto: University of Toronto Press for the Osgoode Society for Canadian Legal History, 1995.

Foster, Hamar, Benjamin L. Berger, and A.R. Buck. *The Grand Experiment: Law and Legal Culture in British Settler Society*. Vancouver: UBC Press, 2008.

Fryer, Mary Beacock, and Christopher Dracott. *John Graves Simcoe, 1752-1806: A Biography*. Toronto: Dundurn Press, 1998.

Fukayama, Francis. *The Origins of Political Order: From Prehuman Times to the French Revolution*. New York: Farrar, Straus and Giroux, 2011.

Galanter, Mark, ed. *Recent Developments in Alcoholism. Vol. 13, Alcohol and Violence*. New York: Kluwere, 1997.

Gat, Azar. *War in Human Civilization*. Oxford: Oxford University Press, 2006.

Gatrell, V.A.C., Bruce Lenman, and Geoffrey Parker. *Crime and the Law: The Social History of Crime in Western Europe since 1500*. London: Europa Publications, 1980.

Gauvreau, Michael. "Reluctant Voluntaries: Peter and George Brown; The Scottish Disruption and the Politics of Church and State in Canada." *The Journal of Religious History* 25, No. 2 (June 2001): 134-157.

Gauvreau, Michael and Ollivier Hubert, eds. *The Churches and Social Order in Nineteenth-and Twentieth-Century Canada*. Montreal and Kingston: McGill Queen's University Press, 2006.

Gartner, Rosemary, and B. McCarthy. "20th Century Trends in Homicide Followed by Suicide in Four North American Cities." *Historical Studies in Suicide*, edited by John Weaver and David Wright. Toronto: University of Toronto Press, 2008.

Ghosh, Peter. *Max Weber and the Protestant Ethic: Twin Histories*. Oxford: Oxford University Press, 2014.

Glaeser, Edward. *Triumph of the City: How Our Greatest Invention Makes Us Richer, Smarter, Greener, Healthier, and Happier*. New York: Penguin, 2011.

Goody, Jack. *The Theft of History*. Cambridge: Cambridge University Press, 2006.

Gorski, Philip S. *The Disciplinary Revolution: Calvinism and the Rise of the State in Early Modern Europe*. Chicago: University of Chicago Press, 2003.

Gorski, Philip S. "Recovered Goods: Durkheimian Sociology as Virtue Ethics" in *The Post-Secular in Question: Religion in Contemporary Society*, edited by Philip S. Gorski. New York: New York University Press, 2012).

Graham, Hugh Davis, and Ted Robert Gurr, eds. *Violence in America: Historical and Comparative Perspectives*. Rev. ed. Beverley Hills: Sage Publications, 1979.

Graham, John R. "The Haven, 1878-1930: A Toronto Charity's Transition from a Religious to a Professional Ethos." *Histoire sociale-Social History* 25, no. 50 (novembre-November 1992): 283-306.

Graham, John R. "William Lyon Mackenzie King, Elizabeth Harvie, and Edna: A prostitute rescuing initiative in late Victorian Toronto." *The Canadian Journal of Human Sexuality* 8, no.1 (Spring 1999): 47-60.

Gramsci, Antonio, edited by David Forgacs. *The Antonio Gramsci Reader: Selected Writings, 1916-1935*. London: Lawrence and Wishart, 1999.

Grant, John Webster. *A Profusion of Spires: Religion in Nineteenth-Century Ontario*. Toronto: University of Toronto Press, 1988.

Gray, John. "Delusions of Peace." *Prospect* (September 21, 2011), accessed Aug. 30, 2013, http://www.prospectmagazine.co.uk/magazine/john-gray-steven-pinker-violence-review/#.UiEmQT8ph3s.

_____. *Straw Dogs*. New York: Farrar, Straus and Giroux, 2007.

Greenwood, F. Murray, and Beverley Boissery. *Uncertain Justice: Canadian Women and Capital Punishment, 1754-1953*. Toronto: Dundurn Press, 2000.

Gross, Jan T. *Neighbors: The Destruction of the Jewish Community in Jedwabne, Poland*. Princeton: Princeton University Press, 2001.

Gurr, Ted Robert ed. *Violence in America*. Vol. 1, *The History of Crime*. Newbury Park: Sage Publishing, 1989.

Gurr, Ted Robert , Peter N. Grabosky, and Richard C. Hula. *The Politics of Crime and Conflict: A Comparative History of Four Cities*. Beverly Hills: Sage Publications, 1977.

Gwowski, Peter. *The Morningside Years*. Toronto: McClelland and Stewart, 1997.

Gwowski, Peter. *The Private Voice: A Journal of Reflections*. Toronto: McClelland and Stewart, 1988.

Gzowski, Peter. "What's It Like to Have a Famous (But Forgotten) Ancestor" *Maclean's Magazine* (May, 1959).

Hackett Fischer, David. *Albion's Seed: Four British Folkways in America*. Oxford: Oxford University Press, 1989.

Hallowell, Gerald, ed. *Oxford Companion to Canadian History*. Toronto: Oxford University Press, 2006.

Harris, Anthony R., Stephen H. Thomas, Gene A. Fischer, and David J. Hirsch, "Murder and Medicine: The Lethality of Criminal Assault, 1960-1999." *Homicide Studies* 6, no. 2 (May 2002): 126-166.

Harrison, Brian. *Drink and the Victorians: The Temperance Question in England, 1815-1872*. 2nd ed. Staffordshire: Keele University Press, 1994.

Haughen, Gary A. and Victor Boutros, *The Locust Effect: Why the End of Poverty Requires the End of Violence*. New York: Oxford University Press, 2014.

Hay, Douglas, Peter Linebaugh, John G. Rule, E.P. Thompson, and Cal Winslow, eds. *Albion's Tree: Crime and Society in Eighteenth Century England*. London: Allen Lane, 1975.

Hazell, Alastair. *The Last Slave Market* (London: Constable, 2011.

Hemingway, Ernest. *Ernest Hemingway Selected Letters*. Edited by Carlos Baker. New York: Scribner, 2003.

Hempton, David. *Methodism: Empire of the Spirit*. New Haven: Yale University Press, 2005.

Heron, Craig. *Booze: A Distilled History*. Toronto: Between the Lines, 2003.

Hill, Michael. *A Sociological Yearbook of Religion in Britain*, 6. London: SCM Press, 1973.

Hilton, Boyd. *The Age of Atonement: The Influence of Evangelicalism on Social and Economic Thought, 1795-1865*. Oxford: Clarendon Press, 1988.

_____. *A Mad Bad and Dangerous People? England, 1783-1846*. Oxford: Oxford University Press, 2006.

Himmelfarb, Gertrude. *The De-Moralization of Society: From Victorian Virtues to Modern Values*. New York: Vintage, 1994.

_____. *The Roads to Modernity: The British, French, and American Enlightenments*. New York: Knopf, 2004.

Hogeveen, Brian. "Accounting for Violence at the Victoria Industrial School." *Histoire Social/Social History* 43, no. 82 (May 2009): 147-176.

Horn, Pamela. *Young Offenders: Juvenile Delinquency, 1700-2000*. Chelford: Amberley Publishing, 2010.

Howe, Daniel Walker. *What Hath God Wrought: The Transformation of America, 1815-1848*. New York: Oxford University Press, 2007.

Hudson, Pat. *History by Numbers: An Introduction to Quantitative Approaches*. London: Arnold: 2000.

Hunt, Alan. *Governing Morals: A Social History of Moral Regulation*. Cambridge: Cambridge University Press, 1999.

BIBLIOGRAPHY

Hunt, Tristram. *Building Jerusalem: The Rise and Fall of the Victorian City*. New York: Metropolitan Books, 2005.

Ignatieff, Michael. *True Patriot Love: Four Generations in Search of Canada*. Toronto: Viking, 2009.

Jackson, Hugh. "Churchgoing in Nineteenth-Century New Zealand." *New Zealand Journal of History*, 17 (1983), 43-59.

Johansen, Per Ole. "The Norwegian Alcohol Prohibition; A Failure". *Journal of Scandinavian Studies in Criminology and Crime Prevention* 14, no. s1 (2013): 46-63.

Johansen, Peter. "For Better, Higher and Nobler Things." *Journalism History* 27, no. 3 (Fall 2001): 94-105.

Johnson, Eric, and Eric M. Monkkonen, eds. *The Civilization of Crime: Violence in Town and Country Since the Middle Ages*. Urbana: University of Illinois Press, 1996.

Johnson, J.K. *Becoming Prominent: Regional Leadership in Upper Canada, 1791-1841*. Montreal and Kingston: McGill-Queen's University Press, 1989.

Johnson, Paul E. *A Shopkeeper's Millennium: Society and Revivals in Rochester, New York, 1815-1837*. New York: Hill and Wang, 1978.

Jones, David J.V. *Crime in Nineteenth-Century Wales*. Cardiff: University of Wales Press, 1992.

Judt, Tony. "What Have We Learned if Anything?" *New York Review of Books* (May 1, 2008), viewed on-line, June 1, 2013, http://www.nybooks.com/articles/archives/2008/may/01/what-have-we-learned-if-anything/?pagination=false.

Kaestle, Carl F. et al. *Literacy in the United States: Readers and Reading Since 1880*. New Haven: Yale University Press, 1991.

Katz, Michael B., and Paul H. Mattingly. *Education and Social Change: Themes from Ontario's Past*. New York: New York University Press, 1975.

Kealey, Gregory S. *Toronto Workers Respond to Industrial Capitalism, 1867-1892*. Toronto: University of Toronto Press, 1980.

Kearney, Hugh. *The British Isles: A History of Four Nations*. Cambridge: Cambridge University Press, 1989.

Keeley, Lawrence. *War Before Civilization: The Myth of the Peaceful Savage*. New York: Oxford University Press, 1996.

Kidd, Colin. *The Forging of the Races: Race and Scripture in the Protestant Atlantic*

World, 1600-2000. Cambridge: Cambridge University Press, 2006.

Knafla, Louis A., and Susan W.S. Binnie. *Law, Society, and the State: Essays in Modern Legal History.* Toronto: University of Toronto Press, 2005.

Kortum, Hans-Henning, and Jurgen Heinze, eds. *Aggression in Humans and Other Primates.* Berlin: De Gruyter, 2012.

Lane, Roger. *Policing the City: Boston, 1822-1885.* Cambridge: Harvard University Press, 1967.

Larsen, Timothy. *A People of One Book: The Bible and the Victorians.* Oxford: Oxford University Press, 2011.

Larson, Erik. *The Devil in the White City: Murder, Magic, and Madness at the Fair That Changed America.* New York: Crown Books, 2003.

Laslett, Peter, Karla Oosterveen and Richard M. Smith, eds. *Bastardy and its Comparative History: Studies in the History of Illegitimacy and Marital Nonconformism in Britain, France, Germany, Sweden, North America, Jamaica and Japan.* Cambridge: Harvard University Press, 1980.

Lears, T.J. Jackson. "The Concept of Cultural Hegemony: Problems and Possibilities." *American Historical Review* 90 (June 1985): 567-593.

LeBlanc, Steven A., and Katherine Register. *Constant Battles: The Myth of the Peaceful Noble Savage.* New York: St. Martin's Press, 2003.

Lehti, M., and J. Kivivuori. "Alcohol-related Violence as an Explanation for the Difference Between Homicide Rates in Finland and the Other Nordic Countries," *Nordisk alcohol-och narkoticatidskrift* 22, English Supplement (2005): 7-24.

Levine, Allan. *King: William Lyon Mackenzie King, A Life Guided by the Hand of Destiny.* Vancouver and Toronto: Douglas and McIntyre, 2011.

Levine, Alysa, Thomas Nutt and Samantha Williams, eds. *Illegitimacy in Britain, 1700-1920.* London: Palgrave Macmillan, 2005.

Levitan, Kathrin. *A Cultural History of the British Census: Envisioning the Multitude in the Nineteenth Century.* New York: Palgrave Macmillan, 2011.

Lewis, Donald M. *The Origins of Christian Zionism: Lord Shaftesbury and Evangelical Support for a Jewish Homeland.* Cambridge: Cambridge University Press, 2009.

Leyton-Brown, Ken. *The Practice of Execution in Canada.* Vancouver: UBC Press, 2010.

Lisowski, John. "Murderers Who Were Hanged--Marion "Peg-Leg" Brown". *Middlesex Law Association Newsletter* (December 2010).

BIBLIOGRAPHY

Mack, Phyllis. *Heart Religion in the British Enlightenment: Gender and Emotion in Early Methodism*. Cambridge: Cambridge University Press, 2008.

Magrill, Barry. *A Commerce of Taste: Church Architecture in Canada, 1867-1914*. Montreal and Kingston: McGill-Queen's University Press, 2012.

Maguire, Mike, Rod Morgan, and Robert Reiner, eds. *Oxford Handbook of Criminology* Oxford: Oxford University Press, 2007.

Malesevic, Sinisa, and Mark Haugaard, eds. *Ernest Gellner and Contemporary Social Thought*. Cambridge: Cambridge University Press, 2007.

Marks, Lynne. *Revivals and Roller Rinks: Religion, Leisure and Identity in Late-Nineteenth-Century Small-Town Ontario*. Toronto: University of Toronto Press, 1996.

Martin, David. *Pentecostalism: The World Their Parish*. Oxford: Blackwell Publishing, 2002.

Masters, D.C. *The Rise of Toronto, 1550-1890*. Toronto: University of Toronto Press, 1947.

McGowan, Mark G. *The Waning of the Green: Catholics, the Irish, and Identity in Toronto, 1887-1922*. Montreal and Kingston: McGill-Queen's University Press, 1999.

McKay, Ian. "The Liberal Order Framework: A Prospectus for a Reconnaissance of Canadian History" in *Canadian Historical Review*, 81 (2000): 620-621.

McLeod, Hugh. *Religion and Society in England, 1850-1914*. New York: St. Martin's Press, 1996.

_____. *Religion and the Working Class in Nineteenth-Century Britain*. London: Macmillan, 1984.

McNairn, Jeffrey L. *The Capacity to Judge: Public Opinion and Deliberative Democracy in Upper Canada, 1791-1854*. Toronto: University of Toronto Press, 2000.

Monkkonen, Eric H. *Murder in New York City*. Berkeley: University of California Press, 2001.

Montigny, Edgar-Andre, and Lori Chambers, eds. *Ontario Since Confederation: A Reader*. Toronto: University of Toronto Press, 2000.

Morris, N., and M. Tonry, eds. *Crime and Justice: An Annual Review of Research*, Vol. 3. Chicago: University of Chicago Press, 1981.

Morton, Desmond. *Mayor Howland: The Citizens' Candidate*. Toronto: Hakkert, 1973.

_____. "Mayor Howland: The Man Who Made Toronto Good". *York Pioneer* 75, no. 2 (Fall 1980): 23-30.

Morton, W.L., ed. *The Shield of Achilles*. Toronto: University of Toronto Press, 1968.

Moyles, R.G. *The Blood and Fire in Canada: A History of the Salvation Army in the Dominion, 1882-1976*. Toronto: Peter Martin Associates, 1977.

Muchembled, Robert. *A History of Violence: From the End of the Middle Ages to the Present*. Cambridge: Polity, 2012.

Murphy, Terrence, and Roberto Perin, eds. *A Concise History of Christianity in Canada*. Toronto: Oxford University Press, 1996.

Newsome, David. *The Parting of Friends: The Wilberforces and Henry Manning*. Cambridge, MA: Harvard University Press, 1966.

Nivette, Amy E. "Cross National Predictors of Crime: A Meta Analysis." *Homicide Studies* 15, no. 2 (2011): 103-131

_____. "Violence in Non-State Societies: A Review." *British Journal of Criminology* 51, no. 3 (2011): 578-598.

Noel, Jan. *Canada Dry: Temperance Crusades Before Confederation*. Toronto: University of Toronto Press, 1995.

Noll, Mark. "George Rawlyk(1935-1995): His Life and Work." Recorded Aug. 3, 2000 (tape 3016 D pt. 1), Regent College. Cassette.

Nolland, Lisa Severine, and Clyde Binfield. *A Victorian Feminist Christian: Josephine Butler, the Prostitutes and God*. Carlisle: Paternoster Publishing, 2004.

Oliver, Peter. *The Conventional Man: The Diaries of Ontario Chief Justice Robert A. Harrison, 1856-1878*. Toronto: Osgoode Society, University of Toronto Press, 2003.

Owen, David. *English Philanthropy, 1660-1960*. Cambridge: Harvard University Press, 1964.

Parker, Robert Nash, with Linda-Anne Rebhun. *Alcohol and Homicide: A Deadly Combination of Two American Traditions*. Albany: State University of New York Press, 1990.

Parker, Robert Nash. "Alcohol and Violence: Connections, Evidence and Possibilities for Prevention." *Journal of Psychoactive Drugs* 36, sup. 2 (2004): 157-163.

Pearson, William H. *Recollections and Records of Toronto of Old: With Reference to Brantford, Kingston, and Other Canadian Towns*. Toronto: William Briggs, 1914.

Pennington, Jonathan. *The Destiny of Canada: Macdonald, Laurier, and the Election of 1891*. Toronto: Penguin, 2011.

Philips, David. *Crime and Authority in Victorian England: The Black Country,*

BIBLIOGRAPHY

1835-1860. London: Croom Helm, 1977.

Phillips, Jim, Roy McMurtry, and John T. Saywell. *Essays in the History of Canadian Law, Volume 10, A Tribute to Peter Oliver*. Toronto: University of Toronto Press, 2008.

Pinker, Steven. *The Better Angels of Our Nature: Why Violence Has Declined*. New York: Viking, 2011.

_____. *How the Mind Works*. New York: W.W. Norton, 1997.

Pinker, Steven. *The Stuff of Thought: Language as a Window Into Human Nature*. New York: Viking Press, 2007.

Porter, Andrew, ed. *Oxford History of the British Empire*, Vol. 3, *The Nineteenth Century*. Oxford: Oxford University Press, 1999.

Pridemore, W.A., and T.H. Grubesic. "Alcohol Outlets and Community Levels of Interpersonal Violence: Spatial Density, Type of Outlet, and Seriousness of Assault." *Journal of Research in Crime and Delinquency* 50, no. 1 (February 2013): 132-159.

Prochaska, Frank. *Christianity and Social Services in Modern Britain*. Oxford: Oxford University Press, 2006.

_____. *The Voluntary Impulse: Philanthropy in Modern Britain*. London: Faber and Faber, 1988.

_____. *Women and Philanthropy in Nineteenth-Century England*. Oxford: Oxford University Press, 1980.

Pue, W. Wesley, and Barry Wright ed. *Law and Society: Issues in Legal History*. Ottawa: Carleton University Press, 1988.

Pue, W. Wesley, and David Sugarman. *Lawyers and Vampires: Cultural Histories of Legal Professions*. Oxford and Portland, OR: Hart Publishing, 2003.

Putnam, Robert. *Bowling Alone: The Collapse and Revival of American Community*. New York: Simon and Schuster, 2000.

_____. *Democracies in Flux: The Evolution of Social Capital in Contemporary Society*. New York: Oxford University Press, 2002.

Rawlyk, George A., ed. *The Canadian Protestant Experience, 1760-1990*. Burlington, ON: Welch Publishing, 1990.

Reynolds, Lindsay. *Footprints: The Beginnings of The Christian and Missionary Alliance in Canada*. Toronto: Christian and Missionary Alliance in Canada, 1981.

Rice, Duncan. *The Scots Abolitionists, 1833-1861*. Baton Rouge: LSU Press, 1981.

Ripley, C. Peter, ed. *The Black Abolitionist Papers*. Vol. II, *Canada, 1830-1865*. Chapel Hill: University of North Carolina Press, 1986.

Rose, Jonathan. *The Intellectual Life of the British Working Classes*. New Haven: Yale University Press, 2001.

Ross, Jeffrey Ian, ed. *Violence in Canada: Sociopolitical Perspectives*. Toronto: Oxford University Press, 1995.

Roth, Randolph. *American Homicide*. Cambridge, MA: Harvard University Press, 2009.

Ruff, Julius R. *Violence in Early Modern Europe, 1500-1800*. Cambridge: Cambridge University Press, 2001.

Rutherford, Paul. *A Victorian Authority: The Daily Press in Late Nineteenth-Century Canada*. Toronto: University of Toronto Press, 1982.

Ryrie, Alec. *Being Protestant in Reformation England*. Oxford: Oxford University Press, 2013.

Sager, Eric. "The Transformation of the Canadian Domestic Servant, 1871-1931". *Social Science History* 31, no. 4 (Winter 2007): 509-537.

Saul, John Ralston. *A Fair Country: Telling Truths About Canada*. Toronto: Viking, 2008.

Schull, Joseph. *Edward Blake*. Vol. 1, *Man of the Other Way (1833-1881)*. Toronto: Macmillan, 1975.

Scott, James C. *Seeing Like a State: How Certain Schemes to Improve the Social Condition Have Failed*. New Haven: Yale University Press, 1999.

Semple, Neil. *The Lord's Dominion: The History of Canadian Methodism*. Montreal and Kingston: McGill-Queen's University Press, 1996.

Sewell, William H. Jr. *Logics of History: Social Theory and Social Transformation* Chicago: University of Chicago Press, 2005.

Sharpe, J.A. "Debate: The History of Violence in England: Some Observations." *Past and Present* 108, no. 1 (1985): 205-215.

Smith, Allan. *Canada-An American Nation? Essays on Continentalism, Identity, and the Canadian Frame of Mind*. Montreal and Kingston: McGill-Queen's University Press, 1994.

Smith, Edward. "Working Class Anglicans: Religion and Identity in Victorian and Edwardian Hamilton, Ontario in *Social History* 36, no. 71 (May 2003): 123-144.

Smith, Elizabeth. *'A Woman with a Purpose': The Diaries of Elizabeth Smith, 1872-1884*. Edited by Veronica Strong-Boag. Toronto: University of Toronto Press, 1980.

BIBLIOGRAPHY

Smyth, William J. *Toronto, the Belfast of Canada: The Orange Order and the Shaping of Municipal Culture*. Toronto: University of Toronto Press, 2015.

Spierenburg, Pieter. *A History of Murder: Personal Violence in Europe from the Middle Ages to the Present*. Cambridge: Polity, 2008.

Spierenburg, Petrus. "Punishment, Power, and History: Foucault and Elias." *Social Science History* 28, no. 4 (Winter 2004): 607-636.

Stenhouse, John. "Christianity, Gender, and the Working Class in Southern Dunedin, 1880-1940." *Journal of Religious History* 30, no. 1 (February 2006): 18-44.

Stacey, C.P. *A Very Double Life: The Private World of Mackenzie King*. Toronto: Macmillan, 1976.

Stickley, Andrew, and William A. Pridemore, "The Social-Structural Correlates of Homicide in Late-Tsarist Russia." *British Journal of Criminology* 47, no. 1 (January 2007): 80-99.

Stiller, Brian. *From the Tower of Babylon to Parliament Hill: Being a Christian in Canada Today*. Toronto: Harper Collins, 1997.

Stone, Lawrence. "Interpersonal Violence in English Society, 1300-1980." *Past and Present* 101, (1983), 22-33.

_____. "A Rejoinder." *Past and Present* 108, no. 1 (1985): 216-224.

Stouffer, Allen P. *The Light of Nature and the Law of God: Antislavery in Ontario 1833-1877*. Montreal and Kingston: McGill Queen's University Press, 1992.

Strange, Carolyn. *Imposing Goodness: Crime and Justice in "Toronto the Good", 1793-1953*. Toronto: Law Society of Upper Canada, 1991.

_____. "Sin or Salvation? Protecting Toronto's Working Girls". *The Beaver* 77 (June-July 1997): 8-13.

_____. "The Lottery of Death: Capital Punishment in Canada, 1867-1976", *Manitoba Law Journal* 23, no. 3 (1995): 594-619.

_____. "The Undercurrents of Penal Culture: Punishment of the Body in Mid-Twentieth-Century Canada." *Law and History Review* 19, No. 2 (Summer 2001): 343-385.

_____. *Toronto's Girl Problem: The Perils and Pleasures of the City, 1880-1930*. Toronto: University of Toronto Press, 1995.

Stubbs, Todd Russell. *Visions of the Common Good: Britishness, Citizenship, and the Public Sphere in Nineteenth-Century Toronto*. PhD diss., University of Toronto, 2007.

Sussman, Herbert. "Machine Dreams: The Culture of Technology." *Victorian Literature and Culture* 28, no. 1 (2000): 197-204.

_____. *Victorian Technology: Technology, Innovation and the Rise of the Machine.* Santa Barbara: Praeger, 2009.

Swainson, Donald. Oliver *Mowat's Ontario.* Toronto: Macmillan, 1972.

Taylor, Howard. "Rationing Crime: The Political Economy of Criminal Statistics Since the 1850s." *Economic History Review* 51, no. 3 (1998): 569-590.

Taylor, Tim. "Ambushed by the Grotesque: Archaeology, Slavery, and the Third Paradigm." In *Warfare, Violence, and Slavery in Pre-History*, edited by M.P. Pearson and I.J.N. Thorpe. Oxford: Archaeopress Press, 2005, 225-233.

Thomas, Keith. "The Rise of the Fork." *New York Review of Books* (May 9, 1978): 28-31.

Thompson, E.P. *Customs in Common.* London: Penguin, 1991.

_____. *The Making of the English Working Class.* New York: Vintage, 1966.

Thomson, Dale C. *Alexander Mackenzie: Clear Grit.* Toronto: Macmillan, 1960.

Thompson, F.M.L. *Cambridge Social History of Britain, 1750-1950*, Vol. 3, *Social Agencies and Institutions.* Cambridge: Cambridge University Press, 1990.

Throness, Laurie. *A Protestant Purgatory: Theological Origins of the Penitentiary Act, 1779.* Aldershot, Hampshire: Ashgate, 2008.

Tulchinsky, Gerald. *Canada's Jews: A People's Journey.* Toronto: University of Toronto Press, 2008.

Urquhart, M.C., and K.A.H. Buckley. *Historical Statistics of Canada.* Toronto: Macmillan Company, 1965.

Valverde, Maria. *The Age of Light, Soap, and Water: Moral Reform In English Canada, 1885-1925.* New ed. Toronto: University of Toronto Press, 2008.

Van Die, Marguerite. *Religion, Family, and Community in Victorian Canada: The Colbys of Carrollcroft.* Montreal and Kingston: McGill-Queens's University Press, 2005.

_____. ""The Marks of a Genuine Revival": Religion, Social Change, Gender, and Community in Mid-Victorian Brantford, Ontario". *Canadian Historical Review* 79, 3 (September 1998): 524-563.

_____. "Protestants, the Liberal State, and the Practice of Politics: Revisiting R.J. Fleming and the 1890s Toronto Streetcar Controversy". *Journal of the Canadian Historical Association* New Series 24, no. 1 (2013): 89-129.

Vincent, David. *The Rise of Mass Literacy: Reading and Writing in Modern Europe.*

BIBLIOGRAPHY

Cambridge: Polity, 2000.

Walden, Keith. *Becoming Modern in Toronto: The Industrial Exhibition and the Shaping of a Victorian Culture.* Toronto: University of Toronto Press, 1997.

_____. "Toronto Society Response to Celebrity Performers, 1887-1914". *Canadian Historical Review* 89, no. 3, (September 2008): 373-397.

Walker, Barrington. *Race on Trial: Black Defendants in Ontario's Criminal Courts, 1858-1958.* Toronto: University of Toronto Press, 2010.

Ward, W.R. *Christianity Under the Ancien Regime.* Cambridge: Cambridge University Press, 1999.

_____. *Early Evangelicalism: A Global Intellectual History, 1670-1789.* Cambridge: Cambridge University Press, 2006.

Ward, W. Peter. *Courtship, Love, and Marriage in Nineteenth-Century English Canada.* Montreal and Kingston: McGill-Queens University Press, 1991.

_____. "Unwed Motherhood in Nineteenth-Century English Canada." *Historical Papers*, Canadian Historical Association, 16, no. 1 (1981): 34-55.

Watts, Michael. *The Dissenters*, Volume Two, *The Expansion of Evangelical Nonconformity.* Oxford: Oxford University Press, 1995.

Wearmouth, Robert F. *Methodism and the Common people of the Eighteenth Century.* London: Epworth Press, 1945.

Weaver, John. *Crimes, Constables, and Courts: Order and Transgression in a Canadian City: 1816-1970.* Montreal and Kingston: McGill-Queen's University Press, 1995.

Webster, Anthony. *The Debate on the English Empire.* Manchester: Manchester University Press, 2006.

Wiener, Martin J. *Men of Blood: Violence, Manliness and Criminal Justice in Victorian England.* Cambridge: Cambridge University Press, 2004.

Westfall, William. *Two Worlds: The Protestant Culture of Nineteenth-Century Ontario.* Kingston and Montreal: McGill-Queen's University Press, 1989.

Wilkinson, Richard, and Kate Pickett. *The Spirit Level: Why Greater Equality Makes Society Stronger.* New York: Bloomsbury Press, 2009.

Wood, J. Carter. "Criminal Violence in Modern Britain." *History Compass* 4, no. 1, (January 2006): 77.

Appendix A

My own judgment on a case is indicated by: e.g. [Manslaughter]

1880
April 3 Body of an infant found in the rear of a Toronto house. An inquest was held and it was ruled that the infant was born alive and died of neglect. There does not appear to have been any arrests made in the case. (April 2:4; 3:6) [Negligence]

March 26 *Globe* owner George Brown was shot in the leg and died May 9 after gangrene had set in. George Bennett was found guilty of murder and hung. Brown lived for several weeks. (April 3:6; May 10:3, 5; 12:1, 3; July 23:6; 24:5) [Murder]

Sept 12 Jurors in inquest of death of Annie Broxup returned an open verdict of "wilful murder" by person or persons unknown after her body was pulled from the water. (Sept 21:6, 22:15, 24:1, 6) [Murder]

Nov 10 Mary Wheeler was found dead in a house on William St., face down with blood coming from the mouth, and evidence of a blow to the left side of the head. The jury in the inquest ruled that the death was caused by "intemperance and exposure." However, was this a case of homicide that was overlooked because of an "intemperate" lifestyle? A neighbour testified that the sounds of a person being beaten emanated from the house on the night that Wheeler died. (Nov 10:6, 11:6, 12:6) [Homicide]

1881
June 30 Dead infant found in water at Bailey's Coal Dock. (June 30:8)

[Possible Infanticide]

Oct 18 Robert Hozack found dead in a culvert. Probability of foul play. (Nov 10:11) [Possible Homicide]

1882
April 25 Body of a 10-20 day-old infant found at the corner of Adelaide and Charlotte. Ruled that the child had died of neglect. (April 25:10) [Negligence]

May 1 Body of a boy, gone missing the previous October, found drowned in the Don. (May 3:6) [Open Verdict]

July 12 A young man by the name of William Long killed as the result of a fight at the corner of Strange St. and Kingston Road. Long was still alive on July 15. (Aug 2:1,8;3:5; Jan 19:6.) Perhaps the homicide was slightly outside city limits but because of the uncertainty I deemed it a Toronto homicide. Two men, Wise and Phillips, were convicted of manslaughter. Case reopened in 1883. [Manslaughter]

July 23 Constable John Albert shot and killed Andrew Young in High Park, July 23. Albert was convicted of murder but the location was outside Toronto limits. (Sept 22:8; Oct 13:5) [Murder outside city limits]

Aug 25 William Spencer driving a wagon killed a boy George Hammond. Charged with manslaughter and acquitted by a jury. (Aug 25:6; Oct 14:4) [Accidental]

1893
Aug 7 James Marooney was shot and was dead at the scene at the corner of York and Pearl Sts. Charles Andrews was convicted of manslaughter. The jury was unwilling to convict Andrews of murder and the speculation was because he was the father of a child. (Aug 8:1; 11:6,13,14; Oct 27:3; 29:4,6)

APPENDIX A

[Manslaughter]

Aug 22 The body of an infant was found in the bay and it was ruled that death was caused by party or parties unknown. (Aug 22:6) [Infanticide]

1884
April 8 John Hackett was shot in a struggle with Horace Allkins on Jarvis St. Admitted to hospital and died later. Allkins was found not guilty as it could not be proven exactly how Hackett died. (April 10:2; 11:6; 18:6; April 26:14) [Manslaughter]

May 2 John McGuire died May 2 on the Dutch Farm at the Don and Danforth Rd., "near Toronto." Because McGuire had diseased organs the cause was deemed natural. He had complained of being beaten by Charles Heber, was bleeding from the head, and died several hours later. Being on the border I counted this as a Toronto homicide. (May 5:6; 6:5,6) [Manslaughter]

May 24 Samuel Kerr died on Edward St. near Elizabeth St. after a fight on the 24th. Hattle Jeffrey and John Falvey acquitted of murder. (May 26:6; 29:5; June 4:5; 7:13; 10:3; June 30:1,6.) [Manslaughter]

July 13 Charles Martin died several days after a quarrel related to a cricket game on July 13 in a field between Dovercourt Rd. and Lakeview Ave. Charles Thompson and Percy Read were charged with manslaughter but the judge directed the jury to find them not guilty. However it still seems that Martin was beaten to death. (July 15:6; 18:10; Nov 13:6) [Manslaughter]

July 31 Christina Leslie charged with manslaughter in the death of an unknown female infant who died in a "baby farm" establishment in Leslieville within the city limits. She was found not guilty by a jury. (July 31:2; Aug 4:6; 5:6; 6:6; 7:6; 9:10; Oct 30:6; 31:6) [Negligence]

Aug 15 Margaret Ellis was charged in the death of an infant who was found in an outhouse on Teraulay St. The inquest was not able to determine that the child was born alive. (Aug 15:6; Aug 16:10) [Possible Infanticide]

Sept 9   An infant in a baby carriage on a Toronto Island ferry plunged into the water and drowned. Two of the ferry crew, John Quinn and John Carnegie were arrested and charged with manslaughter. (Sept 9:6; 10:3; 14:6) [Accidental]

Oct 24   Lizzie Smith was tried for the murder of an infant whose body was discovered on Edward St. A witness testified to hearing an infant cry and then hearing a splash in an outhouse. Found not guilty as it was not proven that the child was born alive and the accused was described as being of "good character." (Oct 24:6; Nov 1:4) [Infanticide]

Oct 24   George Cliffe, druggist clerk, was tried for manslaughter, in the poisoning death of Jane Frankish who died as the result of being dispensed the wrong drug. He was acquitted. The death occurred in Parkdale, outside the bounds of Toronto at that time. (Oct 24:6) [Accidental]

1885
Feb 28 John Fairbanks died in hospital on March 6, six days later after being assaulted with a weight. Martin Maloney was convicted of manslaughter. Controversial because Maloney was sentenced to only one year. (March 7:14; April 29:6; May 1:6; 5:6) [Manslaughter]

June 16   An infant's body was found near the Northern Elevator. "Found dead." (June 16:6) [Possible Infanticide]

June 26   Body of Maurice Murry found on Barrymore St. in Rosedale outside of city limits. (June 26:6; 29:2) [Suicide]

July 27   John Warden was assaulted, after playing pool in a saloon, at the corner of King and Berkeley Sts. on July 27 and died July 29 as the result of a fractured skull. James Gibson was tried for manslaughter and acquitted. (July 30:6; 31:6; Aug 6:6; 8:4; Oct 30:6; 31:9) [Manslaughter]

Sept 6   A female infant with a woman's handkerchief around its neck was found on a vacant lot at Lumley and Lennox Ave. Mrs. William's claimed that it was born still-born and the judgement by the Coroner's Jury was in her favour. (Sept 3:6; 8:6; 9:36) [Possible Infanticide]

October 8   James Coffey died after being beaten several days before. Edward Emmett had been hemorrhaging from the nose continuously until his death. Emmett was discharged after being put on trial for murder. (Oct 9:6; 10:10; 13:6; 15:6; 16:6; 17:10; 30:6) [Manslaughter]

Oct 26   The body of a newborn male infant was found in a bag in the bay. (Oct 27:6) [Possible Infanticide]

1886
Feb 1   John Crewe and Susan Barton tried for manslaughter in the death of a child who was left alone in the house while the mother was in the yard. The child died a day later. The accused were found "not guilty." However there were multiple signs of abuse on the body of the child including bruises, a broken thigh, and a facial fracture. (Feb 1:8) [Manslaughter]

March 2   The body of a dead infant was found in a box on Charlotte St. There were signs of violence on the body including a broken jaw. (March 2:8) [Infanticide]

March 18   The body of John Cochrane was found in the water at the foot of Berkely St. The death was deemed accidental but Robert Neil confessed to the murder in 1888. (Feb 29:8, 1888; March 2:8, 1888.) [Manslaughter]

April 13   Merle Roche (Maggie Rock) of Wilton St. admitted to killing her infant by throwing it over a fence. There does not appear to have been a trial in the case. (April 12:2; 13:8) [Infanticide]

May 8 Charles Reid was shot and killed while apparently either trying to kill his wife Sarah or while trying to commit suicide. There was an "open" verdict from the Coroner's Jury. (May 8:14; 11:8) [Accidental or Suicide]

June 17 Freddie Bennet was run over and killed by an "express waggon" with a "wilful manslaughter" finding. (June 17:8) [Accidental or Negligence]

June 21 The body of a three month old infant was found on Agnes St. with abrasions on head and having died of exposure. (June 21:8) [Infanticide]

June 23 Minnie Browness age 14 was killed by a stone thrown by 11 year-old William McKetchie on Funston Lane. McKetchie was acquitted of manslaughter. (June 23:8; June 25:1,8) [Accidental]

June 28 A charge against Annie Tonn of concealing birth was dismissed by Col. Denison. (July 10:2; Oct 21:8) [Possible Infanticide]

Aug 12:8 Michael and May McDermott were arrested for an alleged infanticide due to suffocation. They were released from custody. (Aug 12:8; 13:8) [Possible Infanticide]

Aug 2 Caroline Norris died after being kicked ten days previously by William Smith. She later complained of pains in her side. However, because she had been unwell since the previous November, her death was deemed due to "natural causes." (Aug 18:2) [Probable Manslaughter]

Oct 12 Alfred and Catherine Smith were charged in the suffocation death of their infant Albert Nathaniel Smith, on Monroe St., Sept. 27. The mother "overlay" the child and Denison dismissed the charges. (Oct 12:8; 13:10) [Accidental]
Oct 15 Jane Clark, "a frequenter of the Police Court," died mysteriously with

her body being found on the sand at the foot of Scott St. An 'open verdict' was found with a suspicion of "foul play." (Oct 15:2; 16:16; 19:8; see also *Toronto Daily Mail* Oct 19:8)
[Probable Manslaughter]

Nov 2 A body of an infant, believed to have suffocated, was found in a trunk on Strachan Ave. Annie Howley (Alice Halley) was charged but acquitted of concealing birth. (Nov 2:8; Jan 13:8, 1887) [Possible Infanticide]

Nov 18 Charles McCauley was found guilty of manslaughter by the Coronor's Jury in the Borden St. beating death of his father John McCauley, age 60, who was dead at the scene. The father had reportedly been drinking. The case apparently did not proceed to trial. (Nov 18:8; 19:8) [Manslaughter]

1887
Feb 25 The body of an infant with a black mark on the chin was found in Toronto. (Feb 25:8) [Infanticide]

March 7 The body of an infant was found on the CPR tracks at Bathurst St. (March 7:8) [Infanticide]

April 1 William Cocking , two years old, came to death by foul play in the home of Peter and Mrs. Rooks on Jones Ave. There apparently was no trial. (April 1:3) [Manslaughter]

May 13 The body of an infant that had been dead two weeks was found in a trunk in the Albion Hotel and it was presumed suffocated. Fanny and Carry Smith were charged but no bill was found for either infanticide or concealment of death. (May 13:8; June 23: 8; 24:8) [Possible infanticide]

May The body of George Moore was found in shallow water at the foot of Berkeley St. At the time it was reported as a suicide but in 1888 Robert Neil confessed that he was involved in the murder of Morse. (Feb 28:1, 1888;

29:8, 1888; March 2:8, 1888) [Manslaughter]

June 9 Robert Sole threw a stone that hit John Crowe resulting in death and a manslaughter charge. No bill was found for manslaughter. (June 9:8; June 24:8)[Accidental]

Aug 11 The remains of a baby were found in a box by workmen. (Aug 11:8) [Unknown]

Oct 29 John Torrance, a 21 year-old carpenter, died Oct 29 in the Toronto General Hospital of loss of blood after a fight at an eating house on Adelaide St. in which a knife was thrust into his back. Torrance live a number of hours. John Downs was charged with murder but it appears that the case did not proceed. (Oct 31:2; Nov 5:16; 10:8; 14:8) [Manslaughter]

Dec 9 John Fellows an infant died and as a result Elizabeth Fellows was declared insane. (Dec 9:8) [Infanticide]

Dec 21 Eighteen year old Elizabeth Bray died while undergoing an abortion for which John Gamble was convicted of murder with the sentence commuted to life in prison. (Dec 21:8; Feb 2:5; March 2:8) [Accidental]

1888
January 27 Robert Neil was sentenced to death for the murder of Central Jail guard J. Rutledge. (Jan 27:8; Feb 28:1; Feb 29:8; March 2:8) [Murder]

Feb 2 John Gamble was sentenced to death for the murder of Elizabeth Bray who died as the result of undergoing an abortion. The sentence was commuted to life in prison. (Feb 2:5; March 2:8) [Accidental]

Feb 24 An infant's body was found in a valise at Union Station. (Feb 24:8) [Possible infanticide]

APPENDIX A

May 14 Tom Buckley "brutally" beat his partner Bertha Robinson to death on Victoria Lane. She lived for one hour. Both were reported to be intoxicated. (May 15:8; 16:8; Oct 11:8; 12:5; 13:16) [Manslaughter]

May 29 An infant girl was killed by a blow to the head by person(s) unknown. (May 29:8) [Infanticide]

June 14 Eva Harris was charged in the death of an infant found in her room but was acquitted despite "suspicious" circumstances. (June 14:8; 23:1) [Infanticide]

June 21 Grace Allen died as the result of a wound caused by an abortion. (June 21:8) [Accidental]

Oct 13 An inquest was held into the death of an infant found stillborn at Huron and Baldwin. The druggist, doctor, and the father were all acquitted. (Oct 13:16; Nov 28:8; Dec 1:1; 3:5; 11:1; June 27:10; Oct 8:8) [Possible Infanticide]

1889
April 9 An infant was found dead on Toronto Island with a verdict of murder by person(s) unknown. (April 9:8) [Infanticide]

June 16 Katie Dunbar died three months after undergoing an abortion. Death was ruled as due to natural causes. (June 1:16; 3:8; 4:10, 8:1) [Accidental]

June 10 Maggie Flanigan was charged in the death of an infant found on Douro St. and convicted of a misdemeanor. (June 10:2; 27:10; Oct 10:8) [Possible Infanticide]

June 17 A body of a two month old female was found on Dundas St. (June 17: 8) [Possible Infanticide]

July 8 James Smith died at Ronan's Hotel after fighting with Hugh McKay at Beaconsfield and Queen St. Smith was dead at the scene. McKay was acquitted. (July 9:8; 10:4;Oct 5:15; 22:1,8) [Manslaughter]

July 15 John Gilroy and Frank Kane were convicted of manslaughter in the street car death of Harry Flood and were sentenced to one year in Central Jail. (July 15:8; Oct 5:15; Oct 10:8; 24:8; 26:16) [Accidental]

July 19 Barker Potter killed Hector McDonald with a sharpened piece of metal at the Asylum. No blame was attached as Potter was "insane." (July 19:2) [Manslaughter]

Aug 23 The body of an infant with a stone attached was found floating in the Bay. The Coroner's Jury came to a verdict of murder by person(s) unknown. (Aug 23:8; 26:8; 31:20) [Infanticide]

Sept 17 William ("Willie") Ingle, a "boy", died after saying that he had been held down by Patrick ("Patsey") Holland and beaten by another boy. Both doctors who participated in the post-mortem stated that there were no marks of violence on the body, but that death was due to "brain inflammation" as a result of "lack of nourishment." Earlier Ingle had complained about being chased by boys. No charges were laid. The conclusion was that Ingle died "not due to violence but to brain trouble." (Sept 17:10; 20:3) [Manslaughter]

Sept 27 Mike Birtle was shot on Elizabeth St. by Louis Dees and died three weeks later. (Sept 27:1; Oct 14:8; Oct 18:8; 24:8; Jan 15:4, 1890) [Manslaughter]

Oct 15:8 An infant was found dead on Simcoe St. due to exposure. (Oct 15:8) [possible Infanticide]

Nov 8 Mary Ann Hare was killed by Flora McLeod at the Asylum. Death occurred two and one-half hours after the attack as a result of the loss of blood. No conviction charges due to insanity. (Nov 6:8) [Manslaughter]

Oct 14 An infant died of exposure after being left at a doorstep. (Oct 14:8; 15:8) [Accidental]

Nov 18 Mary Kane was beaten to death by Edward Kane on Defoe St. Kane was hung Feb 12, 1890. (Nov 18:8; 19:6; Jan. 15) [Murder]

Nov 27 Henry Leech was killed on Pape Ave. by a streetcar. Thomas Moses, Stewart White, Thomas Edwards, and Edmund Wragge were all charged with manslaughter but there were apparently no convictions. (Nov 27:4) [Accidental]

1890
Jan 10 Jane Speers found strangled in her home. Murder by person unknown. (Jan 10: 13, 16:6, 18:7) [Murder]

Jan 11 A buried child's body was found by workmen. Inquest declared "wilful" murder. (Jan 11, 21:8) [Infanticide]

March 25 John Byron found guilty of manslaughter, by a coroner's jury, for killing John Wade on a train that was headed for Mimico. The victim had attacked the offender. Jury found not guilty. (March 25:8, Oct 16:8) [Manslaughter]

Aug. 22 Thomas Tait, a C.P.R. supervisor, tried for murder in a train death in which a train allegedly approached a crossing too fast. Not guilty. (Aug 22:8, Oct 16:8) [Accidental]

Sept. 22 William Elliott the driver of a wagon that killed John Kellackey charged with murder or manslaughter. The case was discharged. (Sept 22:8; 23:11) [Accidental]

Oct. 6 Infant Samuel Duggan died of a ruptured stomach. Both parents were intoxicated at the time but the case does not appear to have proceeded. (Oct 6:8, 7:8, 8:8) [Infanticide]

Oct. 16 Mrs. Stewart, a Christian Science practitioner, charged with manslaughter after a person in her care died. Not guilty. (Oct 16:8) [Accidental]

Dec. 27 Robert Scarlett, a bar owner, threw James Douglas out a bar. Douglas died 24 hours later. Scarlett acquitted. (Dec 27:17, 29:8) [Manslaughter]

1891
Jan. 9 Peter Shabot continually beat a baby. It is unclear as to whether he was convicted. (Jan 9:3)[Infanticide]

Feb. 16 Jane Harding and Christopher Mcgrain quarrelled. Harding had been in ill health and died some hours later. Mcgrain was remanded on a wilful murder charge but was found not guilty. (Feb 16:8, 17:6, 17:8, 20:8, April 23:8, June 23:8, 26:8) [Manslaughter]

Feb. 28 An infant of Sarah Fox found strangled. Wilful murder found but Fox was released. (Feb 28:18, Mar 2:8, May 19:8) [Infanticide]

April 2 An Orangeville mother left the body of newborn in Toronto because of shame. (April 2:3) [Infanticide]

April 23 Matilda Berry was acquitted of manslaughter by a grand jury after a coroner's jury had found her culpable in the death of the child William Marshall. (April 23:8) [Infanticide]

May 2 Thomas Mills, an invalid, was poisoned by Marion Mills. Released. (May 2:20) [Manslaughter]

July 1 The baby of Annie Stover was found floating in the bay. A charge of wilful murder followed but the crown decided later not to proceed. (July 1:8, 4:20, 8:8, 10:8, Oct 2:8, Jan 7) [Infanticide]

1892
Feb 15 The body of a strangled infant with a wound on the head. Wilful murder by person unknown. (Feb 15:8, 16:8, 18:8) [Infanticide]

May 19 Peter Adams was killed during the demolition of a house. Contractor W.R. Matthewson charged with manslaughter. (May 19:8) [Accidental]

June 9 Richard Walker was killed by James Walsh using a shovel. Charged with manslaughter but no bill was found by the grand jury. (June 9:2, 10:8, Oct 6:8) [Manslaughter]

June 21 Charles Lougheed a Christian Science practitioner was charged with manslaughter but no bill was found by a grand jury. (June 21:8) [Accidental]

Sept 8 Hannah Heron was killed by a streetcar and the motorman was charged with manslaughter. (Sept 8:8) [Accidental]

1893
July 26 A baby found in the bay was determined not to have breathed and the ruling was "found dead." (July 26:8) [Due to the fact that the skull was fractured I have classified as Infanticide]

Nov 4 Lucy Denning's death caused by undergoing an abortion by Dell "Doc" Andrews.
Denning died several days later. Charged with murder and found not guilty in a trial in 1894. (Nov 4:20, 7:8, 8:8, 9:8, 11:8, 22:8, 23:8, Dec 1:8, Jan 12:8, 1894) [Accidental]

(Chief Constable Grasett's annual report confirms that this was the only murder of the year. His report states that it "is a matter for sincere congratu-lations that murder, the darkest crime of all, has almost disappeared from the records." *Globe* Jan 31, 1894.)

1894
March 1   Francis Corrigan was beaten and ejected from a music hall by Thomas Robinson. Corrigan died ten hours later following surgery. Robinson was exonerated by a coroner's jury. (March 1:8, 5:8, 10:20) [Manslaughter]

May 19 Two infants, who had been smothered, were found under a bridge and it was declared wilful murder by persons unknown. (May 19:23) [Infanticide]

September 29   Mrs. Lace, the keeper of a "baby farm", was found guilty of manslaughter in the death of an infant who died in a hospital several days later. Recommendation for mercy. (Sept 29: 13, Nov 17:20, Dec 21:1, 22:15) [Accidental]

Oct 8   Frank Westwood was shot and killed in the doorway of his house. Clara Ford was acquitted of the murder even though she had confessed to detectives that she had killed Westwood after he had previously made unwanted sexual advances towards her. West wood survived for several days in hospital. (Oct 8:8, 10:10, 11:1, 30:10, Nov 13:10, 21:8, 22:2, 23:8, 24:17, 29:1, Dec 1:20, May 1:3, 3:5, 6:5, 1895) [Murder]

1895
Feb 13   Dallas and Harry Hyams were charged with the death of William Wells, two years previous, who had apparently been hit by an elevator weight. They were acquitted by a jury. (Feb 13:8, May 11:11, 13:1, 14:1, 17:1, 21:1, 22:1, 23:1, 24:1, 25:1, Oct 29:10, Nov 5:2, 6:1, 8:2, 9:13, 11:5, 12:5, 14:1,6, 15:3, 2:5, Dec 17:10, Jan 7:3, 1896) [Accidental]

March 7   Arthur Dicks charged with murder in the death of his wife. Discharged. (March 7:2, 8:8, 30:20, May 30:10, Dec 12:5) [Manslaughter]

March 25 John Bell killed Sarah Swallow using a razor and then killed himself. (March 25:2) [Murder]

May 10 Body of new-born found on the railway tracks north of Bloor St. (May 10:1,8) [Infanticide]

June 4 Mrs. Mary Aitkins, an elderly woman, died several days after being assaulted by Frank Smith and William Broom. Convicted of manslaughter by the jury. (June 4:1, Dec 14, 16:5, 18:6) [Manslaughter]

June 26 Charlotte Gosling died several hours after being beaten by Stephen Wright and Mary Ann Clark. (June 26:1,8, 27:10, July 5:8) [Manslaughter]

July 16 The bodies of two children, Alice and Nellie Pietzel were discovered. They were murdered by the stepfather Herman Mudgett, alias H.H. Holmes, on Oct 25, 1894. They were visiting Toronto at the time and were from the U.S. Mudggett was later convicted in the U.S. of multiple murders. (July 16:1, 17:1, 19:8, 22:8, 24:2, 25:1, 27:1, Aug 29:1, April 6:5, 13:4) [Murder]

Oct 7 John Scott was stabbed and killed by fellow-worker John McKenzie in a bar-room fight. Scott died in the hospital sometime later. Both had reportedly been drinking. (Oct 7:8) [Manslaughter]

Nov 4 Percy Beck died while under the care of Mrs. Beer, a practitioner of Christian Science, who was charged with manslaughter. (Nov 4:8, 13:1, Dec 5:5) [Accidental]

1896
Feb 6 James Healey killed John Corrigan with an axe while Corrigan was attempting to break into Healey's house due to a previous quarrel. (Feb 6:1, 7:10, April 27:10) [Manslaughter]

March 26 Frank Finlay was killed by a blow from his brother John Finlay during a quarrel after drinking. The victim lived through the night. Acquitted. (Mar 26:2, April 1:2, May 4:10) [Manslaughter]

April 28 Horse trainer Joe Martin was beaten to death at Woodbine during a robbery. The incident took place April 28th and he died May 3. (May 4:10, July 8:10) [Murder]

May 22 Mrs. Costello was charged with manslaughter as a result of the death of an infant at her "baby farm." The case was dismissed as the baby would have died of other causes. (May 22:1, 29:10) [Accidental]

June 30 Mrs. Beer, the Christian Science practitioner, charged in the death of Adelaide Goodson. (June 30:10) [Accidental]

Aug 19:12 Charles Murray was knocked down in a scuffle, hit his head on the curb, and died the next day. Harry Badgeley and Bert Lyons were charged and as of 1900 were still waiting to go to trial. (Aug 19:12, 20:12, 26:1, Nov 3:10, Oct 13, 1897) [Manslaughter]
Sept 17 At the Howard Lake station the strangled body of an infant was found. (Sep 17:12) [Infanticide]

1897
Oct 19 William Bessey was arrested on a charge of murder after performing an abortion on Jenny Thomas. No bill obtained for murder from the grand jury. Thomas died of "blood-poisoning" one month later on May 30. (Oct 19:1, 22:10, Nov 10:10) [Accidental]

Nov 1 James Hutton stabbed his son John to death after the son had threatened to kill him. Not guilty, acted in self-defence. (Nov 1:1, 10:3, 11:2) [Manslaughter]
Nov 11 Dobbell sentenced for attacking a bailiff with a revolver which was loaded and discharged. I could not find any more information on this

so I assume it was for a "felonious wounding" charge. (Nov 11:2) [Not homicide]

1898
Feb 9 A coroner's jury reached a verdict of manslaughter against Frank Young and William Irwin in the death of Mary Young. No later mention of this case was found so I assume that it did not proceed. I counted it as manslaughter as this was the jury's verdict. (Feb 9:12) [Manslaughter]

Feb 10 Mrs. Malone found guilty of neglect in the starvation death of an infant that was present at her baby farm. (Feb 10:12, 22:12) [Accidental]
Feb 15 Infant found frozen to death. (March 15:12, 16:12) [Infanticide]
May 27 In a hit-and-run accident, Frank Caruso was charged with manslaughter for driving recklessly and killing ten year-old John Jenkins. I am uncertain of the trial outcome. (May 27:12, Nov 10:10) [Accidental]

June 1 Mary McGarvin and Mary Besley were charged with manslaughter in a baby farm death. It appears the case did not proceed. (June 1:7) [Accidental]

Oct 23 Mrs. Charles Burrell killed three young children who were described as "babes" and were buried in the same coffin hence I have tentatively classed the crime as "infanticide." The ages were not given so this case needs further research. Burrell was found not guilty by reason of insanity. (Oct 22:23, 25:9) [Infanticide]

Nov 28 Robert Taggert assaulted his wife with a hammer and she died in hospital a day later. Taggert was judged by the court to be insane. (Nov 28:10, Jan 17:5, 19:7, 21:21) [Manslaughter]

1899
March 2 Mrs. McKane found guilty of negligence in an infant's death of at a baby farm. (March 2:12) [Accidental]

July 31 Patrick Kelly knocked down Mrs. Barbara Billings on July 13 and she died
two weeks later on July 26. The coroner's jury found Kelly guilty of manslaughter. The crown seems not to have proceeded on the case. (July 31:1) [Manslaughter]

Oct 6 The body of a smothered baby was found outside the city limits and a verdict of murder was found by a person unknown. (Oct 6:10, 7:28, 21:28) [Infanticide]

Nov 10 John Varcoe was shot by two burglars, James McIntosh and Henry Williams, and died two days later in hospital. McIntosh also died later of a bullet wound. Williams was hung. (Nov 10:1?, 11:28, 13:3, 16:12, Dec. 1:12) [Murder]

Dec 28 Mrs. James Rogers was killed by a street-trolley and five railway employees and officials were found by a coroner's jury to be guilty of manslaughter. (Dec. 28:12) [Accidental]

Appendix B

TORONTO CHURCHES 1880-1899

Church	Denom-ination	Year Build-ing	Capacity 1890s	Census 82	Census 88	Census 96	Sun-day School Role	Sun Sch Census 88	Annual Giving Circa 1890	Value Building
Trinity	C of Eng	1843	700	207	173	371		300	2,500	40,000
St. James'	C of Eng	1852	1200	1117	535	977		451	17,000	260,000
St. George's	C of Eng	1845	800	540	423	596		250	11,000	30,000
St. Paul's	C of Eng	1842	510	258	212	338		320	3,600	50,000
Holy Trinity	C of Eng	1847	1000	977	573	432		307	10,000	50,000
St. Stephen's	C of Eng	1858	600	500	513	803	650	490	3,500	40,000
St. John's	C of Eng	1860	600	413	300	496	350	350	1,500	18,000
St. Peter's	C of Eng	1866	600	352	314	480	432	350	8,000	35,000
Ch of Redee.	C of Eng	1879	880	320	589	400		280	9,000	55,000
St. Luke's	C of Eng	1870	600	334	340	416		175	7,000	42,000
All Saints	C of Eng	1882	800	967	688	1079		550	8,500	43,000
St. Andrew's	C of Eng	1882	Toronto Island, summer only						350	3,500
St. Bartholomew's	CE	1875	400	136	177	136	200	200	1,000	3,000
Ch of Ascension	CE	1875	900	534	418	297	700	470	10,000	40,000
St. Matthias	C of Eng	1875	350	253	306	190		370	3,500	10,000
St. Thomas	C of Eng	1889	530			771		86	520	23,000
Grace Church	C of Eng	1878	1000	664	300	433	600	400	6,000	25,000
St. Phillip's	C of Eng	1884	750	390	457	606		400	4,150	47,000
St. Mary Mag.	C of Eng	1888	800		107	320	200	100	600	25,000
St. Mary Vir.	C of Eng	1889	350			200	340			14,000
St. Alban's	C of Eng	1887	400		141	236		250	700	80,000
St. Anne's	C of Eng	1862	480	117	137	523		168	1,650	20,000

TORONTO CHURCHES 1880-1899 con't

Church	Denomination	Year Building	Capacity 1890s	Census 82	Census 88	Census 96	Sunday School Role	Sun Sch Census 88	Annual Giving Circa 1890	Value Building
St. Olave's	C of Eng	1887	150		51	27		40	400	2,000
St. Jude's	C of Eng		160			33				
Ch of Messiah	CE	1890	700			264				35,000
St. Cyprian	C of Eng	1892	200			132				
St. Mark's	C of Eng	1877	400		55	483	185	175	2,400	8,000
St. Simon's	C of Eng	1888	750	426	757			175	4,000	26,000
St. Barnabas	C of Eng	1887	120		49	63	200	40	1,000	1,600
Ch of Epiphany	CE	1888	450		151	341		180	1,600	
St. Matthew's	CE	1875	700	77	170	468	400	300	1,000	20,000
St. Martin's	C of Eng	1890	150			85				
St. Margaret's	CE	1890	400			492				12,000
St. Clement's	C of Eng	1889	170			177				3,800
St. John's	C of Eng	1850	350		300	227		30	300	2,500
New St. Andrew's	Pres	1875	1800	1194	591	545		240	27,700	167,500
Knox Church	Pres	1821	1250	1134	771	516	350	440	28,300	Leasehold
Duchess St. Miss.	Pres	1872	250		103		250	180	450	10,000
Old St. Andrew's	Pres	1820	1200	700	638	1066	437	301	22,000	80,000
Cooke's Church	Pres	1857	2500	417	737	2639		250	9,000	60,000
St. James's Square	Pres	1863	1100	830	803	616	325	300	16,700	65,000
St. John's	Pres	1888	425		105	424	392	180	1,900	2,800
Charles St	Pres	1863	1000	400	453		300	280	8,100	20,000
Westminster	Pres	1891	1200			1243	437		11,400	65,000
Erskine	Pres	1879	1100	534	599	763	340	350	7,600	32,000

APPENDIX B

Church	Denomination	Year Building	Capacity 1890s	Census 82	Census 88	Census 96	Sunday School Role	Sun Sch Census 88	Annual Giving Circa 1890	Value Building
Central	Pres	1877	950	664	405	749	200	225	11,000	36,000
College St.	Pres	1873	1200	617	589	862	600	400	8,500	45,200
Reformed	Pres	1882	500		61	73	40	15	500	9,000
Parkdale	Pres	1879	1100		545	1455	400	350	6,500	59,000
Independent	Pres	1877	200	270	226	100	100	125	600	2,000
Bloor St.	Pres	1886	600		383	1127	160	250	12,300	30,000
St. Enoch's	Pres	1889	600			256				27,000
Chalmers	Pres	1877	1100		407			290	13,000	47,000
St. Mark's	Pres	1884	650		203	320	350	350	3,000	16,000
Fern Ave.	Pres	1890	350			115				
Dovercourt	Pres	1890	280			183	200		1,540	
St Paul's	Pres	1889	230			181	200		600	
Bonar	Pres	1890	600			301	504			
Western	Pres	1861	2000	582	503		650	500	5,150	24,000
Ch of the Coven.	Pres	1899					330			13,000
Cowen Ave.	Pres	1895	300			254				
Deer Park	Pres	1881	500		110	196		60	2,000	13,750
East Pres.	Pres	1870	900	531	44	763	500	40	14,100	45,000
Carlaw Ave.	Pres	1873	400			278				
South Side	Pres	1890								10,000
St. Michael's	RC	1848	1800	2600	1796	2200	350			204,000
St. Paul's	RC	1801	1250	1348	693	1742				100,000
St. Mary's	RC	1852	1200	2263	1040	2679				
St. Basil's	RC	1855	450	635	1003	1345				137,000
Our Lady Lour.	RC	1886	380	292	684					45,000
St. Helen's	RC	1867	530	1012		1469	30			12,750

TORONTO CHURCHES 1880-1899 con't

Church	Denom-ination	Year Build-ing	Capacity 1890s	Census 82	Census 88	Census 96	Sun-day School Role	Sun Sch Census 88	Annual Giving Circa 1890	Value Building
St. Patrick's	RC	1861	800	1290	1665	1252	200			21,540
St. Peter's	RC	1872	250			368				
St. Cecilia's	RC	1895	400			409				3,000
Ch of Sac. Heart	RC	1888	500		494	319				
St. Joseph's	RC	1884	600		561	409				25000
Richmond St.	Meth	1845	1200	367						Dis-mantled
Metropolitan	Meth	1870	2500	2106	1088	1011		450	19,500	250,000
Central	Meth	1854	1300		651	1174		350	11,800	80,000
Elm St.	Meth	1855	1680	1564	895	450		400	12,900	50,000
Carlton St.	Meth	1874	1250	663	1072	904	400	350	11,300	70,000
Berkeley St.	Meth	1871	1200	328	709	909		314	5,700	25,000
Sherbourne St.	Meth	1872	1140	830	872	1333		400	16,700	77,000
Bathurst St.	Meth	1860	1400		843	1342	400	300	6,500	37,000
Agnes St.	Meth	1873	1250		915	660	400	160	3,800	26,000
Queen St.	Meth	1864	1500	1137	1291	1569	800	672	10,050	47,000
Yonge St.	Meth	1873	700		295	802	400	250	5,300	30,000
St. Paul's	Meth	1887	1100		384	333	350	260	6,400	40,000
Dunn Ave.	Meth	1889	1600							77,000
Parliament St.	Meth	1871	600	112	450	548	500	175	3,000	15,000
Broadway	Meth	1876	2000		2664				13,700	150,000
Centennial	Meth	1891	450		213					13,000
Woodgreen	Meth	1890	1500	167	599	852		350	2,500	40,000
Perth Ave.	Meth	1889					100			7,000
Clinton St.	Meth	1887	1000		237	450	375	200	3,600	15,000

Church	Denomination	Year Building	Capacity 1890s	Census 82	Census 88	Census 96	Sunday School Role	Sun Sch Census 88	Annual Giving Circa 1890	Value Building
Wesley Church	Meth	1875	1400		585	992	1000	488	7,600	35,000
St. Clare	Meth	1887	350		226	350	230	200	1,750	11,700
Euclid Ave.	Meth	1865	1000		547	800	600	500	6,000	30,000
Epworth	Meth		250			110			1,050	
Gerrard St.	Meth	1880	450	124	242	516	300	210	2,100	7,000
Queen East	Meth	1859	250			107	130	120	950	3,000
Westmoreland	Meth	1883	300			146				
Simpson Ave.	Meth	1890	350			402			1,900	
Trinity	Meth	1889	2000			1136			16,200	130,000
Crawford St.	Meth	1890	800			368	150			13,000
New Richm. St.	Meth	1889	1200		246	498		196	7,500	50,000
King St. E	Meth	1866	600	645	250			150	3,664	7,000
Broadview Free	Meth	1893	100			41				1,800
Jarvis St.	Bapt	1874	2000	659	720	1349		503	14,000	115,000
Chester	Bapt	1886	175			62	120			3,500
Bloor St.	Bapt	1884	1000	462	851			265	6,000	45,000
Dovercourt	Bapt	1887	1000	98	280	476	600	325	2,000	30,000
Immanuel	Bapt	1867	480			263	150			10,500
Alexander	Bapt	1889	600	300	124			150	5,000	43,000
Carleton	Bapt					175				
Tecumseh	Bapt	1887	350		127	292	150	160	1,000	7,000
Beverley St.	Bapt	1880	700	106	203	370	300	300	2,000	19,000
First Ave.	Bapt	1887	550		223	324	500	274	3,000	25,000
Parliament St.	Bapt	1871	800	139	204	544		186	2,000	25,000
First Ave.	Bapt	1880	550		223	324		274	3,000	25,000
College St.	Bapt	1889	950	493	276	516	464	350		56,500
Ossington Ave.	Bapt	1886	350		130	153		120	800	1,600

TORONTO CHURCHES 1880-1899 con't

Church	Denom- ination	Year Build- ing	Capacity 1890s	Census 82	Census 88	Census 96	Sun- day School Role	Sun Sch Census 88	Annual Giving Circa 1890	Value Building
Western	Bapt	1888	250			167	200			
Walmer Rd.	Bapt	1892	1500			846	700			76,600
Sheridan Ave.	Bapt	1888	175			134				
Olivet	Bapt	1890	380				100			8,000
Kenilworth	Bapt	1896	214			110	110			2,200
Eastern Ave.	Bapt	1877					200			
Christie St.	Bapt	1898	350				200			
Century	Bapt	1888								
Baptist (Afri)	Bapt	1827	250	74		48				20,000
Zion	Cong	1883	1100	157	101	120		120	4,700	40,000
Bond St.	Cong	1879	2500	2200	999	1495	240	350	14,900	85,000
Chestnut	Cong							150		
Northern	Cong	1867	700	234	210	335	300	275	6,000	22,000
Olivet	Cong	1876	275		142	224		170	1,723	20,000
Western	Cong	1888	800	233	633	266	200	200	4,000	42,000
Broadview	Cong	1894	350		113	184		340	750	4,200
Parkdale	Cong	1885	300		83	74		85	700	6,000
Bethel	Cong	1889	300							5,500
Bethany	Cong	1893	300		73					6,000
Friend's	Quaker	1878	150		49	106		100	1,000	6,500
Ch of Chr. Bath.	Ch Christ	1892	350		71	75	200	35		9,000
Spadina CC	Ch of Christ		50			47				
Alexander CC	Ch of Christ		200			100				

APPENDIX B

Church	Denom-ination	Year Build-ing	Capacity 1890s	Census 82	Census 88	Census 96	Sun-day School Role	Sun Sch Census 88	Annual Giving Circa 1890	Value Building
Cecil St.	Ch of Christ	1891	600		137	340		85	2,000	27,500
Denison Ave.	Christ. Worker	1890								
College St.	Christ. Worker		100							
Sheridan	Christ. Worker									
Davenport	Christ. Worker									
Great Hall	Salv. Army		2,500		2,215	333			2,291	60,000
Farley Ave.	Salv. Army		1,200		1,432	60			1,597	6,000
Toronto 2	Salv. Army		650		763	109			1,817	18,000
Toronto 3	Salv. Army	1884	800		431	94			1,480	5,000
Toronto 4	Salv. Army		500		566	46			726	20,000
Toronto 5	Salv. Army		600		393	103				4,000
Arthur St.	Salv. Army		250			275				
Eglington	Other		200			133				
Centre St.	Other		150			237				
Christ Ch	Reform. Epis.	1891	350	336	88			60	2,400	20,000
Emmanuel	Reform. Epis.	1897	200			52				
Christian Sc.	Christ. Sci.	1899	700			400				30,000
The Church	The Church	1881	100		27			50	2,000	
Brockton	Ply. Breth.									

TORONTO CHURCHES 1880-1899 con't

Church	Denomination	Year Building	Capacity 1890s	Census 82	Census 88	Census 96	Sunday School Role	Sun Sch Census 88	Annual Giving Circa 1890	Value Building
Spadina	Ply. Breth.									
Elm St.	Disciples Christ									
First Unitarian	Unitarian	1845	600	155	95	113		45	3,000	20,000
Cath. Apo.	Cath. Apostolic		400	106	138	90		30	2,000	10,500
Germ Luth	German Luth	1856	250		87	165	80	75	1,200	6,000
African Meth	Afr Meth Epis	1893								
Syrian Cath	Syrian Cath	1898								
Christad.	Christadelpian	c1860	200		66			20		
Mission Union	Non-denom.	1884	850		147	69		295	4,000	
Assembly	Saints		200		83			50		
Cumberland	Indep.		125		31					
New Jerus.	Elm Sweden.	1887	200		90					
New Jerus.	Park Sweden		160		42					
Seventh Day	Seventh Day		100		31					
Christian 1	Christian		160		105					
Christian 2	Christian		100		91					
Baptist Di	Baptist Di				51					

Church	Denomination	Year Building	Capacity 1890s	Census 82	Census 88	Census 96	Sunday School Role	Sun Sch Census 88	Annual Giving Circa 1890	Value Building
Subtotals										
Church of England			18,950	7,836	7,636	13,838		7,207	120,770	1,064,400
Presbyterian Church			24,285	7,873	8,276	15,025		5,126	211,940	879,250
Roman Catholic Church			8,160	8,428	8,948	12,192				548,290
Methodist Church			32,420	7,398	12,792	20,930		6,495	181,464	1,337,500
Baptist Churches			12,629	1,869	2,972	7,004		2,907	38,800	512,900
Congregational Churches			6,625	2,824	2,281	2,771		1,690	32,773	230,700
Other Churches			12,995	597	7,229	2,947		845	25,511	242,500
Totals			116,064	36,825	50,134	74,707		24,270	611,258	4,815,540

Sources: *Globe*, February 7, 1882: 7; *Evening Telegram*, December 22, 1888: 6; *Evening Telegram*, May 4, 1896.

Church giving was obtained from the following: J. Ross *Robertson's Landmarks of Toronto: A Collection of Historical Sketches of the Town of York From 1792 until 1837 and of Toronto from 1834 to 1904 Also Nearly Three Hundred Engravings of the Churches of Toronto Embracing the Picture of every Church Obtainable from 1800-1904,* Fourth Series (Toronto: Telegram, 1904).

The Robertson book comprises a collection of articles on individual churches that were originally published in the *Telegram* during the 1890s and at the turn of the century. Often, the articles contain figures building capacities, value of the church buildings, and annual giving. Thus, the above table is eclectic and hence not precise. Not all figures were available. Hence there are gaps for some individual churches which renders the totals on the conservative side. The annual giving of the Roman Catholic churches was not published. Some churches were in areas annexed by the City of Toronto and were not included in earlier censuses as they were not yet part of the city and hence were not included in the census. For some of the denominations, data was supplemented by consulting denominational yearbooks. These were as follows:

The Acts and Proceedings of the Sixteenth General Assembly of the Presbyterian Church in Canada, Ottawa, June 11-20, 1890 (Toronto: Press of the Canada Presbyterian), Appendix No. 24, lvi-lix; Rev. William Wye Smith, ed., *The Canadian Congregational Year Book, 1890-90* (Toronto: Congregational Publishing Company, 1890), 23; *Minutes of the Proceedings of the Seventh Session of the Toronto Annual Conference of the Methodist Church* (Toronto: William Briggs, 1890), 38-39; *Minutes of the Proceedings of the Eighth Session of the Toronto Annual Conference of the Methodist Church* (Toronto: William Briggs, 1891), 38-39.

Appendix C

TORONTO AND BRITISH CENSUS DATA INCLUDING THE CHURCH CENSUSES

APP C.1 Evaluating the Nineteenth-Century Census

The Victorian penchant for gathering and publishing statistics was, for example, part of a new mindset that sought to "scientifically" understand a variety of social phenomena, including the religious. The social apparatus needed to conduct the decennial British census was referred to as the "census machinery".[1] Census reports are not, to be sure, absolutely reliable. Bruce Curtis views them as instruments that governments put to use entirely for their own purposes; a "making of things to be taken".[2] They cannot be used by historians to map broad social trends; they were sometimes "corrected" after the fact because of errors made by enumerators. The "protocols" that census administrators used in the final reports are unknown and impossible to reconstruct (at least, says Curtis, for the 1871 Canada census).[3] They can, nonetheless, be useful if deployed with care.

My own use of the Canada Census will be restricted to religious data. Any

---

[1] Kathrin Levitan, *A Cultural History of the British Census: Envisioning the Multitude in the Nineteenth Century* (New York: Palgrave Macmillan, 2011), 26, 32, 36, 37, 88, 151, 156, 166, 188, 200, 251. However there existed a stream of anti-utilitarian thought that balked at the comparison between the social body and the machine. Katherine Levitan, *A Cultural History of the British Census*, 193.

[2] Curtis does emphasize the "messiness" of local dynamics that influence the political centre, and he leaves a place for "ritual and ceremonial" elements. Although he discusses individual census categories in his period of study and the methods utilized in collecting data, nowhere does Curtis, in a 300-page monograph, give an example of a census form. Curtis, in a discussion of the abstract nature of a census, has effectively abstracted the census form itself. In the case of the Montreal 1872 recount, the City Council, who desperately wanted a higher count, could only find a 9% discrepancy that included the growth of the city in those months following the official census. Bruce Curtis, *The Politics of Population: State Formation, Statistics, and the Census of Canada, 1840-1875* (Toronto: University of Toronto Press, 2001), 293-305.

[3] Bruce Curtis, *The Politics of Population*, 314.

census undercount could of course distort our picture of a given denominational grouping, but it is difficult to envision a major change in the religious
profile of the city due to this. For example, in a 10% undercount, Anglicans
might constitute 50% of the undercounted group rather than 36% as in the
published census. This would increase the Anglican percentage of the Toronto
population to 37.25%.[4] But these additional numbers, would not make a
statistically significant change in Toronto's denominational demographics. As
well, the denominational changes from census to census do not suggest wild
swings in denominational percentages. I thus assume that the denominational
census data is functionally reliable for the purposes of this study.

Kathrin Levitan has sharply challenged the view of nineteenth-century
census-taking that sees it as narrowly government-serving. Rather than functioning as a tool of surveillance and social control, Levitan uses her study of
the British Empire (including Canada) to show it as part of a broad cultural
movement that arose out of dialogue among various levels of government,
non-government associations, journalists, and educators including many individuals with an "amateur" interest in statistics. Some saw the census as a useful
mechanism to counter government corruption, while propertied interests
could oppose the census on the fear that it would be used to increase taxes. The
census was prone to being "hijacked" by non-governmental interests. Reform
movements collected data to assert the rights of groups including occupational, gender and religious groups; hence the importance of Levitan for this
study.[5] Ultimately, says Levitan, the portrait of the "imagined" social body
given in the census is much more "complicated" than Curtis suggests.[6]

The British Census certainly helps demonstrate how BEP discourse was

---

[4] The calculation is as follows: The 1881 census count was 144,023 with Anglicans
counted as 46,084 or 36%. The hypothetical 10% undercount would equal 14,402 and if
50% Anglican, there would be an additional 7,201 Anglicans in Toronto. The percentage of
Anglicans for the new total would then be 37.25%. When one examines the census manuscripts, the vast majority of designations regarding religious affiliation are entirely clear. Later
in the thesis I find almost zero variation between religious affiliation in the prison register and
that enumerated in the census manuscript. Curtis only covered the censuses from 1840-1875.

[5] Kathrin Levitan, *A Cultural History of the British Census*, 6-7.

[6] See especially Kathrin Levitan, *A Cultural History of the British Census*, 1-25.

being diffused throughout the empire and especially Canada. Despite its minority status, British Nonconformity, largely consisting of evangelicals, made up the majority of churchgoers in England and Wales on any given Sunday. Attached to churchgoing was a cluster of BEP behavioural protocols that included the eschewal of "rough", violent behaviour on the part of young BEP males. Like the spread of churchgoing, this non-violent behaviour increasingly permeated British society over the course of the century. With—for this study, an important point—communication and emigration, British evangelicalism was channeled from the metropole into English-speaking Canada.

Canada Census data are, not surprisingly, even more relevant. All of Canada's censuses, through 1951, asked respondents their religious affiliations. The continued inclusion of religion in the Canadian Census reflected the powerful position of Nonconformity in Upper Canada, which by 1854 had toppled the religious establishment and disbanded the Clergy Reserves. An ascendant Methodism had by 1881 numerically passed the Anglican Church in Ontario.

In both its demography and its religious makeup, Toronto mirrored the rapidly urbanizing, progressive Protestant Victorian city.[7] On the fringe of Empire, the character of its immigration marked the Toronto of 1891 as a British city, with over 90% of its inhabitants claiming origins in the British Isles. Furthermore it was a Protestant city, with 85% listing a Protestant affiliation.[8] Less than 1% acknowledged no religious affiliation in the 1891 census.

By 1880, the entire Protestant spectrum within Toronto had become coloured by BEP influence. From 1881-1901 the percentage of Anglicans fell 6% and Roman Catholics fell 3%, while the more evangelical denominations grew, with the Methodists gaining 4%, Presbyterians 3%, and Baptists 1%. Even the evangelical faction within the Anglican Church was increasingly powerful. In the following section, I will argue that, by tracking changes in religious identifications throughout the period under study, one can follow

[7] For a recent study of the Victorian city see Tristram Hunt, *Building Jerusalem: The Rise and Fall of the Victorian City* (New York: Metropolitan Books, 2005).

[8] J.M.S. Careless, *Toronto to 1918: An Illustrated History* (Toronto: James Lorimer, 1984), 201-202.

the diffusion of BEP discourse.

The two sets of building blocks for this argument are, first, the results of the federal decennial censuses of 1881, 1891, and 1901. Each of these censuses included the religious affiliation of each family member listed. The second set of building blocks is the results of church censuses conducted by Toronto newspapers in 1882, 1888 and 1892. This latter set of censuses is valuable in that it complements the federal censuses by providing a portrait of actual attendance patterns for each religious affiliation.

In the 1842 census[9] of Upper Canada 16.7% of inhabitants were listed as having "no religion", while by 1871 this classification had dropped to 1.2% and, in the period under study, in Toronto, to less than 1%. There were very few individuals who claimed a self-identity as simply "Protestant". This in itself is an indicator that the vast majority of people had very specific religious identities.

The denominational changes as seen in the Toronto federal census data from 1881 to 1901 are as follows:

Table 1 APP C.1 Denomination Changes in Toronto, 1881-1901

	1881	%	1891	%	1901	%	% Change 1881-1901
C of Eng	30,913	36%	46,084	32%	46,442	30%	50.2%
RC	15,716	18%	21,830	15%	23,699	15%	50.7%
Meth	16,357	19%	32,505	23%	35,130	23%	114.7%
Pres	14,612	17%	27,449	19%	30,812	20%	108.6%
Bap	3,667	4%	6,909	5%	8,148	5%	122.2%
Other	5,150	6%	9,246	6%	11,867	7%	130.4%
Totals	86,415	100%	144,023	100%	156,098	100%	

The Sunday School data yield similar trends to those for church attendance for at least the period from 1880-1888. Culled from newspaper reports and church censuses, they are as follows:

---

[9] While the 1842 census had numerous problems associated with it, the shift from a large group not possessing a specific religious marker to the group's almost extinction in the space of three decades is significant.

Table 2 APP C.1 Sunday School Attendance 1880 and 1888

	1880[10]	1888[11]	% Change
C of Eng	6,064	6909	13.9%
RC	No equivalent Sunday School		
Meth	5,310	7,825	47.4%
Pres	3,519	6,662	89.3%
Bap	2,083	2,828	35.7%
Other	1,093	4,595	320.4%
Totals	19,222	28,819	50 %

The changes in Sunday School enrollment from 1880 to 1888 in the newspaper reports correspond broadly to denominational trends in the popular count of the decennial Canada Census from 1881-1901.[12] Methodists, Presbyterians, Baptists, and other denominations experienced explosive growth, while Anglican and Roman Catholic growth did not match population growth. While a lack of absolute precision certainly exists with respect to census data and religious identities, the overall patterns of religious identity, as laid down in the decennial census, hold up with remarkable consistency when compared to newspaper church censuses or the patterns of voting on temperance and Sunday street car referenda. The pattern of BEP diffusion is also congruent with the 1882, 1888, and 1896 newspaper church census data that will be discussed below.[13]

APP C.2 The Toronto Church Censuses and British Censuses in Comparison

In the aftermath of the demise of the official British church census, British newspapers sporadically filled in the gap by sending out a bevy of reporters and enumerators in an attempt to "capture" the total number of worshippers in a city's churches on a particular Sunday. In 1881-1882, dozens of newspapers in cities and towns in Great Britain conducted such censuses. At

[10] *Globe*, December 10, 1880: 10.

[11] *Evening Telegram*, "The Evening Telegram Church Census", December, 22, 1888: 6.

[12] The Presbyterian Sunday School growth does seem to be an outlier.

[13] The 1901 Canada Census data is clearly inaccurate in the portion of the census that

least 22 follow-up censuses took place in the years 1901-1912, with the most ambitious one conducted in London, England in 1902.[14] In the London census, after accounting for "twicers", only 18.6% of the population attended church on census Sunday. Although overall attendance had declined since the last such event in 1882, Nonconformist attendance had grown.[15]

At least one Canadian newspaper followed the example of the British newspaper church census. The *Globe* canvassed all church services in Toronto on Sunday, February 5, 1882, only a couple of months after the first cluster of British censuses. The *Evening Telegram* followed in 1888 and again in 1896, with additional Toronto church censuses that, combined with the decennial Canada Census data, give historians what is arguably the finest set of historical church attendance data available.[16]

Care must be taken in using these materials. Through an error of analysis in a master's degree thesis, misinformation has crept into the two major studies of religion in nineteenth century Ontario that briefly touch on the topic

---

inventories church buildings. All Protestant buildings were undercounted, while the count of Roman Catholic church buildings is accurate. It appears that small Protestant churches were undercounted and in particular those in the "Other" category. No doubt this was due to the difficulty of accessing church officials in smaller congregations. Furthermore, it appears that the 1901 enumerators included church elementary school students for both Roman Catholic and Anglican categories. While arguably these students should be included, the comparative figures are skewed as compared to the 1880 and 1888 newspaper data, as the Sunday School was not a Roman Catholic institution. The inconsistencies with respect to Sunday School enrollment and church buildings do seem to back the contention of Curtis about the unreliability of census data. However the popular counts, including religious identities, appear to be much more reliable. The general pattern is clear, and there are no abrupt turnarounds like those seen in the 1901 Sunday School census data.

[14] See British Religion in Numbers (BRIN), Appendix 6 and Appendix 9, accessed September 9, 2013, http://www.brin.ac.uk/commentary/drs/appendix6/; http://www.brin.ac.uk/commentary/drs/appendix9/.

[15] Richard Mudie-Smith, *Religious Life in London*, 15-17. One of the participants was quoted as saying, "Wander where we may, there is nowhere a symptom of Baptist decline." Ibid, 289.

[16] For the period after 1851, the national censuses of New Zealand and Australia did include data on religious affiliation. However only the affiliation of the "head" of households was recorded. Although summaries remain, all of the New Zealand manuscripts have been destroyed as well as many of the Australian manuscripts. A census of church attendance does exist for both countries, giving opportunity for comparison to the Canadian church census data.

of the Toronto church censuses.[17] All three studies attribute the 1896 census to the *Globe* and although they mention that the 1882 data is adjusted for "twicers", they fail to mention that the *Evening Telegram* did not make the same adjustment. They thus compare the adjusted 1882 data with the unadjusted 1896 data. Furthermore, they leave out entirely the 1888 census.

The three Toronto newspaper census reports summarize the data as follows:

Table 3 APP C.2 Toronto newspaper census reports, 1882, 1888, 1896

Census Attenders	1882[18] % Attenders		vs % Population	1888[19] % Attenders		vs % Population	1896[20] % Attenders		vs % Population
C of Eng	7,914	20.3%	36%	7,791	15.1%	32%	14,596	17.7%	30%
Bap	1,980	5.1%	4%	3,148	6.1%	5%	6,709	8.1%	5%
Meth	8,779	22.6%	19%	14,058	27.2%	23%	24,412	29.6%	23%
Pres	7,876	20.3%	17%	9,091	17.6%	19%	17,081	20.7%	20%
RC	8,128	20.9%	18%	6,339	12.3%	15%	13,122	15.9%	15%

[17] See Peter Hanlon, "Moral Order and the Influence of Social Christianity in an Industrial City, 1890-1899: A Local Profile of the Protestant Lay Leaders of Three Hamilton Churches: Centenary Methodist, Central Presbyterian, and Christ's Church Cathedral" (master's thesis, McMaster University, 1984), 5-7; by using unadjusted figures from the 1896 census, Christie and Gauvreau conclude that three-quarters of Methodists were in church on a Sunday by 1896. In reality, Methodist attendance was very high but not 75%. Nancy Christie and Michael Gauvreau, *Christian Churches and Their Peoples, 1840-1965* (Toronto: University of Toronto Press, 2010), 72-73; John Webster Grant, *A Profusion of Spires: Religion in Nineteenth-Century Ontario* (Toronto: University of Toronto Press, 1988), 197. I should mention that all three of these works are fine studies and are of relevance to this thesis. The *Globe* did summarize the *Telegram* 1896 census and it evidently was this summary that Hanlon consulted. See *Globe*, May 2, 1896: 4. Brian Clarke does recognize that the 1896 census was conducted by the *Telegram* and that the 1896 data was not adjusted for "twicers". However he errs in making the adjustment such that he concludes that 55% of the Toronto population was in church on census Sunday in 1896 when this should be 41.3% assuming that the Toronto population was 200,000. See Terrence Murphy and Roberto Perin, eds., *A Concise History of Christianity in Canada* (Toronto: Oxford University Press, 1996), 276.

[18] *Globe*, February 7, 1882: 7.

[19] *Evening Telegram*, December 22, 1888: 6.

[20] *Evening Telegram*, May 4, 1896. For a *Globe* summary of the 1896 census see *Globe*, May 5, 1896: 4.

Census	1882 % Attenders			1888 % Attenders			1896 % Attenders		
Attenders	vs % Population			vs % Population			vs % Population		
Other	4,159	10.7%	3.9%	11,201	21.7%	5.8%	6,657	8.1%	5.8%
Totals	38,836			51,628			82,577		
	45% of general pop.			29.5% of general pop.			41.3% of general pop.		

The above numbers are adjusted for "twicers" who attended two services on a Sunday. I have followed the formula used by the *Globe* in 1882, which deducts one-third from the aggregate numbers, and applied this to the *Evening Telegram* census results. This formula closely resembles London congregations that were studied in 1902 for "twicer" attendance.[21] The 'twicer' phenomenon is nonetheless important, for it shows the ability of BEP persuasions to compel followers to attend church more than once on a Sunday.

For comparative purposes the "raw" attendance figures, which include unadjusted attendance figures for all Sunday services, are as follows:

Table 4 APP C.2 Raw attendance figures in the newspaper censuses vs % Toronto population

Census	1882 % Attenders			1888 % Attenders			1896 % Attenders		
Attenders	vs % Population			vs % Population			vs % Population		
C of Eng	11,872	20.4%	36%	11,698	15.1%	32%	21,916	17.7%	30%
Bap	2,971	5.1%	4%	4,727	6.1%	5%	10,074	8.1%	5%
Meth	13,169	22.6%	19%	21,108	27.2%	23%	36,655	29.6%	23%
Pres	11,815	20.3%	17%	13,650	17.6%	19%	25,647	20.7%	20%
RC	12,192	20.9%	18%	9,518	12.3%	15%	19,703	15.9%	5%
Other	6,175	10.6%	3.9%	16,819	21.7%	5.8%	9,996	8%	5.8%
Totals	58,194			77,520			123,991		
	65% of total pop.			44% of total pop.			62% of total pop.		

By dividing the % of total attendees by % of denominational affiliation in

---

[21] See Richard Mudie-Smith, *Religious Life of London*, pp. 1-18. These congregations saw 36% of attendees attending two services and hence he deducted 18% to allow for these

APPENDIX C

the general population, the following ratios are obtained:

Table 5 APP C.2 Percentage of Total Attendees Divided By Percentage Denomination of Total Toronto Population

Census	1882	1888	1896
C of Eng	0.57	0.47	0.59
Bap	1.28	1.22	1.62
Meth	1.19	1.18	1.29
Pres	1.19	0.92	1.04
RC	1.16	0.82	1.06
Other	2.72	3.74	1.38

These data are arresting in several respects. The Weberian emphasis on "belonging" with relation to the Protestant "sects" is evident in the data. They obviously show the much higher attendance ratios for denominations emphasizing BEP perspectives. Weather could, of course, play a role. The *Telegram* census conducted on December 16, 1888 reported that a "drizzling rain" combined with "bad conditions of the streets" conspired to "keep hundreds at home."[22] The general picture is, however, what is important. The 1888 census shows a sharp drop in overall attendance rates as compared to 1882, but in disproportionate ways. Anglican and Roman Catholic attendance rates plummeted, Presbyterian rates decreased slightly, but Baptist and Methodist rates increased significantly. The category of 'Other' surged, largely due to the arrival of the Salvation Army in force. In 1888, at the height of its popularity, census Sunday saw an astounding 10,000 attending the 12 Toronto Salvationist worship locations. Weberian pathways are highlighted in these data.

"twicers". Murray Watts builds a case for one-third "twicers" and I have followed both him and the *Globe* on this. I have adjusted the totals downwards as compared to London in 1902 but this can be justified on the grounds that Toronto had a higher % of "Nonconformists" who were more likely to attend twice. See Murray Watts, *The Dissenters*, vol. two, 671-675.

[22] *Evening Telegram*, December 22, 1888: 6.

329

Appendix D

SAMPLE PAGE FROM THE CENTRAL PRISON DATABASE THAT CONTAINS THE CONDEMNED ROBERT NEIL, PRISONER #8697, SECOND FROM BOTTOM.

CENTRAL3.sav

	NUMBER	First_name	COURT	RESIDENCE	NATIVITY	OCCUPATION	TEMPERATE	MARITAL	RELIGION	EDUCATION
2809	8626	WILLIAM	TORONTO	TORONTO	ENG	LAB	T	S	EPIS	RW
2810	8627	MICHAEL	TORONTO	TORONTO	ENG	SHOEMAKER	T	S	RC	RW
2811	8628	JOHN	TORONTO	TORONTO	CAN	LAB	I	S	PRES	RW
2812	8629	THOMAS	TORONTO	TORONTO	USA	LAB	I	S	RC	RW
2813	8630	THOMAS	TORONTO	TORONTO	CAN	CLERK	I	S	EPIS	RW
2814	8640	JOHN	TORONTO	TORONTO	CAN	LAB	I	S	RC	NONE
2815	8641	WILLIAM	TORONTO	TORONTO	ENG	LAB	I	S	EPIS	RW
2816	8642	JOSEPH	TORONTO	TORONTO	CAN	SILVERSMITH	I	M	METH	RW
2817	8643	JOHN	TORONTO	TORONTO	ENG	LAB	T	S	EPIS	RW
2818	8645	JOHN	LONDON	TORONTO	ENG	LAB	I	S	RC	RW
2819	8650	ELI	TORONTO	TORONTO	USA	BARBER	I	S	BAPT	RW
2820	8651	JOHN	TORONTO	TORONTO	CAN	STEAMFITTER	I	S	EPIS	RW
2821	8652	LEWIS	TORONTO	TORONTO	CAN	WAITER	I	S	RC	RW
2822	8653	DANIEL	TORONTO	TORONTO	CAN	BOLTMAKER	I	S	RC	R
2823	8654	ROBERT	TORONTO	TORONTO	CAN	LAB	I	S	EPIS	RW
2824	8655	EDWARD	TORONTO	TORONTO	CAN	CLERK	I	S	RC	RW
2825	8658	EDWARD	TORONTO	TORONTO	CAN	LAB	I	W	RC	NONE
2826	8659	JOSEPH	TORONTO	TORONTO	CAN	MACHINIST	I	S	EPIS	R
2827	8660	ALEXANDER	TORONTO	TORONTO	IRE	BRICKLAYER	I	M	RC	RW
2828	8661	BENJAMIN	TORONTO	TORONTO	CAN	LAB	I	M	RC	R
2829	8662	JOHN	TORONTO	TORONTO	CAN	LAB	I	S	RC	RW
2830	8663	MICHAEL	TORONTO	TORONTO	IRE	LAB	I	W	RC	RW
2831	8672	JOHN	TORONTO	TORONTO	IRE	LAB	I	S	RC	R
2832	8673	JOHN	TORONTO	TORONTO	IRE	LAB	I	M	RC	NONE
2833	8674	WILLIAM	TORONTO	TORONTO	CAN	LATHER	I	S	EPIS	RW
2834	8675	JOHN	TORONTO	TORONTO	IRE	LAB	I	M	RC	R
2835	8676	MICHAEL	TORRONTO	TORONTO	CAN	BUTCHER	T	S	RC	RW
2836	8677	ARTHUR	TORONTO	TORONTO	ENG	COOK	T	S	EPIS	RW
2837	8678	MICHAEL	TORONTO	TORONTO	IRE	PEDLAR	I	M	EPIS	RW
2838	8679	JOHN	TORONTO	TORONTO	USA	MACHINIST	I	S	RC	RW
2839	8680	THOMAS	TORONTO	TORONTO	CAN	SAILOR	I	M	EPIS	RW
2840	8681	THOMAS	TORONTO	TORONTO	CAN	SHOEMAKER	I	S	RC	NONE
2841	8682	THOMAS	TORONTO	TORONTO	IRE	LAB	I	S	RC	RW
2842	8683	JOSEPH	TORONTO	TORONTO	ENG	GARDINER	I	W	EPIS	RW
2843	8694	JAMES	TORONTO	TORONTO	CAN	LAB	I	S	RC	NONE
2844	8695	WILLIAM	TORONTO	DETROIT	CAN	LAB	I	M	RC	RW
2845	8696	PETER	TORONTO	TORONTO	CAN	STEAMFITTER	I	S	RC	RW
2846	8697	NEIL	TORONTO	TORONTO	IRE	LAB	I	S	EPIS	RW
2847	8698	WILLIAM	TORONTO	TORONTO	CAN	LAB	T	S	EPIS	NONE

CENTRAL3.sav

	TIMES_COMMITTED	OFFENCE	AGE	COMPLEXION	HAIR	EYES	STATURE	HEALTH	WEIGHT_ENTERING
2809		EMBEZZLEMENT	20						
2810		ASS PEACE OFFIC	20						
2811		REFUSE PAY DAM	19						
2812		CARRYING ARMS	57						
2813		DRU	36						
2814		DRU	32						
2815	2	ASS	22						
2816	1	LAR	27						
2817	1	LAR	50						
2818	1	VAG	42						
2819	4	LAR	27	COLOUR					
2820	2	DRU	28						
2821	3	DRU	23						
2822	2	DRU	24						
2823	1	ASS	22						
2824	1	EXPOSING PERSON	27						
2825	3	DRU	41						
2826	7	DRU	27						
2827	1	DRU	37						
2828	1	DRU	31						
2829	1	DRU	39						
2830	1	DRU	59						
2831	1	FELONIOUS WOUND	24						
2832	2	INDECENT ASS	26						
2833	1	FELONIOUS WOUND	21						
2834	5	LAR	65						
2835	1	ROBBERY	19						
2836	2	FORGERY	21						
2837	6	DRU	51						
2838	1	DRU	23						
2839	4	DRU	55						
2840	1	LAR	18						
2841	2	LAR	37						
2842	5	LAR	65						
2843	1	DRU	33						
2844	1	LAR	24						
2845	1	DRU	33						
2846	2	LAR	18						
2847	2	LAR	18						

Index of Topics

discursive Christianity and evangelical
protocols, 44-45, 54-63, 150-151,
213-218, 262-263
male behaviour 44, 51-63
Social Gospel, 78-80, 89, 90, 92, 105

Interpersonal Violence:
decline of, 1-25, 28-30, 260-261
decline in Britain, 7-13, 16-17, 26-27
decline in Canada, 19, 30-32
decline in Toronto, 22-25, 40, 45, 70-
71, 155-159, 200-204, 213-218,
221-222, 225-232
decline in Wales, 27
defined, 34-35
handguns, 7, 62, 172-174, 229-230
male-on-male, 54-55, 155, 170-172,
195, 226-227
medicine 169, 172
murder-suicide, 228
sports, violence in, 61, 82-83
narratives of, 167-218
towards animals, 61, 63-63, 68
towards children, 62-63, 204, 225,
227
towards women, 68, 155, 168, 171,
202-204, 227-229
U-shaped curve of, 9-14, 21, 196,
220

Monogamy, marriage, sexuality and pre-
nuptial births, 27, 29-30, 52, 56-61,
158, 197-198, 214-216
"Moral individualism" hypothesis, 5-6,
14-16, 17, 21, 26, 30, 35, 53-54, 81-
82, 91, 158-166, 167, 218, 220-221,
232, 237, 259-262

Social capital, 6-7, 217

Take-up of BEP ideology, 31, 40, 145-
166, 186, 213-218, 221, 255

Toronto:
BEP ideology, 35, 46-50

birthplaces of prominent ministers,
48-49
census data, 99-100, 146-150, 155,
233-235, 251-254, 264, 321-329
church buildings, 96-97
church budgets, 147-148, 155-156
church growth, 88-89, 95, 99-101,
116, 145-149, 153-154, 156, 235,
242, 251, 323-329
Coffee House Association, 82, 107,
122-123, 133
"City of Churches", 52, 70-72, 109-
110
decline of interpersonal violence, 22-
25, 40, 45, 70-71, 155-159, 200-
204, 213-218, 221-222, 225-232
homicide rates, 220-232, 266
newspaper church census data, 98,
146-150, 152, 201-202321-329
newspapers, 52-53, 109-112, 162-
166, 167-168, 204, 224-225,
251-253
religious demography, 99-100
Sunday Schools, 31, 98-99, 145,
149-150

Voluntary associations, 39, 45, 64-66,
74-77, 91, 100-108, 114, 117, 121,
123-124, 158, 162, 164-165

Weberian pathways and Protestant
asceticism, 5-7, 21, 23, 54-55, 62, 82,
98, 100, 158, 160, 167, 220, 232,
237, 255, 259-260, 264

Index of Names

INDEX OF NAMES

INDEX OF NAMES

Afterword

Revisiting Toronto the Good had its origins at the Vancouver Folk Festival in the summer of 1999. On a blazing hot summer afternoon I stopped by the slam poetry venue to hear the poet, Bud Osborn, the Downtown East Side social activist whom I had heard read poetry at Regent College in the past. During the reading of his poem "Amazingly Alive" Bud broke into a staccato refrain:

> shout f@$# this north american culture of death
> f@$# this north american culture of death
> f@$# this north american culture of death
> f@$# this north american culture of death…

While my ears were not offended, I did ponder his take on North America as Dorcas and I climbed the Point Grey hill and made our way home on that hot afternoon. Why had my grandparents undertaken that long ocean voyage to Canada those many years ago? To be sure, my paternal grandfather, Henry Genders, was shipped off to the colonies from Birmingham England, through Ellis Island, and on to Hamilton, Ontario at the tender age of nine to live with his aunt. He married Hazel Wilson, my maternal grandmother, also an immigrant from England, who tragically died of an infection at the age of 29. But Henry made a go of it in his adopted country, successfully raising a family and running a small, market garden farm.

My paternal grandfather, Gerhard Reimer, arrived with his family of ten in 1926 and settled briefly in Winnipeg before moving on to Leamington, Ontario. He died of pneumonia in 1931 leaving behind my grandmother Gertrude and their seven children. Gertrude, who remembered the visit of the tsar to her village in Ukraine as a child, and lived to receive a congratulatory letter from Brian Mulroney on her 100th birthday, was one of the first "alien" mothers to receive widow's benefits from the Ontario government.

She became a great fan of the British monarchy and when Mackenzie King visited Kitchener one day in the 1940s, she went to City Park and personally thanked him for Canada's generous social programs.

Grandfather Gerhard, a farmer and Mennonite minister, had experienced the worst of the Russian Revolution and fled towards a better field. His children and their descendants were the beneficiaries of his wisdom and foresight. Gerhard would have scoffed at academics who have theorized that he was one of those "sheep-skinned" farmers from Ukraine and parts East that were hoodwinked into emigrating to Canada in order to populate the Canadian West. No. He knew, from coreligionists and family that had settled before him, that Canada was a *good* place.

Chris Friedrichs, one of my former professors, contends that one of the most neglected archives is the one that is nearest; that is the "archive that is between the ears". I am a product of the baby boom and grew up in Toronto's hinterland. Post War Toronto was a haven for migrants who represented an amazing variety of cultures and knew exactly what they were doing in their quest for a peaceful place to build their homes.

These were my thoughts on our walk home from the Folk Festival in 2000. They motivated me to continue an exploration of these themes at the graduate level in the UBC history department. This study grew out of my doctoral studies and is my effort to explain what underlies the attraction that migrants across the decades have for Toronto. Yes, the issues are complex but this complexity should not obscure the overall portrait of a Toronto that has "worked" for everyday people and continues to do so.

Acknowledgements

This book has been a journey that has taken 15 years. I am dependent on the thought and writings of scores of scholars. Most immediately, I am indebted to my supervisors Allan Smith and Wes Pue, both professors at the University of British Columbia. Allan supervised my work for 13 years. He is a superb scholar with the widest range of historical knowledge of any historian that I know. His editorial skills were honed by his tenure as Editor of

AFTERWORD

BC Studies that lasted 13 years. I was the beneficiary of his skills throughout this study.

Wes Pue is a legal historian with a razor-sharp mind. Wes served as a reader for my Master's thesis and then signed up to both co-supervise my studies and be the "professor of record" on Allan's retirement. I enormously benefited from the questions he asked about my assumptions, my use of language, and my logic; all of this was done with wit and humour. Thank-you Allan and Wes.

Tamara Myers, Michel Ducharme, and Robert Menzies also served on my dissertation committee and gave incisive feedback and helped shape my argument in beneficial ways. I also had the privilege of serving as a TA for Tamara, Tina Loo and Bob Macdonald. Sitting in class with these professors was an education in itself. It was an enjoyable and fascinating experience to return to the university undergraduate classroom after 30 years!

Paul Kraus and Thorold Burnham served on my comprehensive examining committee and prepared my exam on the topic of Atlantic Slavery and Abolition while Allan and Wes prepared my exam on Atlantic History. The requirement of being familiar with 100 books for each topic was stretching but memorable and formative! Once again, my hat is off to these professors.

All of my course professors were without exception generous towards this older student who often expressed contrarian ideas. Peter Ward and Diane Newell gave detailed responses to my Toronto project at the Master's thesis level. George Egerton was a source of very helpful advice in the department and read and commented on my thesis at several stages.

Not least have I learned from other seminar participants. David Meola gave detailed critique of my writing in the history PhD research seminar. Adam Coombs very kindly made copies of several files for me at Library and Archives Canada. Numerous archivists assisted me at Toronto Archives, Ontario Archives, and Toronto Public Library. The librarians at UBC Library were always generous with their help.

Working at Regent College, a private institution on the campus of UBC, has allowed for friendships and acquaintance with a range of scholars. Historians who have encouraged me along the way include Beverley Boissery,

Rob Clements, Bruce Hindmarsh, Don Lewis, Mark Noll, Iwan Russell-Jones, Axel Schober, John Stenhouse, John Toews, Marguerite Van Die, Sarah Williams, and David Wood. Several kindly commented on portions of my thesis. Other scholars who have regularly given words of encouragement include Terry Anderson, Gary Hewitt, Jim Houston, David Ley, David MacDonald, Wendy Noble, John Owen, Sven Soderlund, Clement Tong, Rikk Watts, and Jonathan Wilson. The list could go on.

Kathy Gillin and Murray Maisey were enormously helpful with copy editing as well as asking perceptive questions about material that needed clarifying. Caroline Ahn and Robert Hand expertly prepared the text for publication. Joe Lee used his special skills in the electronic formatting of the text. Rebecca Pruitt is the resident Bookstore whiz on all things grammatical and the fine details of Word.

I am blessed with friends who have cheered me on from the sidelines. I never would have finished without them. Where do I start?…Rob Alloway, Kim Boldt (my colleague who put up with my flex hours), Ian and Naomi Elliot, Rod Flannigan, Charles Gibson, Harvey Guest, Phil Hill, Will and Norah Johnston, Jon and Cathy Losee, Hari Malvaiganam, Marian Marinescu, George and Donna Marlatte, Read Marlatte, Tim McCarthy, Jean Nordlund, Edward and Susan Norman, Gunnar Olavsson, Chris Parkman and Sarah Walker, Eugene and Jan Peterson, Peter Quek, Nigel Todd, Paul and Kathy Wagler, Dick Williams, Weldon Wong, Shuxin Zhou…I could go on and have no doubt forgotten somebody important! You know who you are. My church home group has listened to progress reports and kept me in their prayers: Martin and Colleen Barlow, Tim Carter and Susan Kennedy Carter, Manfred Fleishmann, and Bronwyn Smyth.

Without my family who or where would I be? My mother Verna and late father Bill loved us unconditionally. I still see my father's big smile waiting there for me at Pearson Airport. My siblings Janet, Philip and Carol along with their spouses Paul, Sandra, and Randy have always rooted for me and I love to be in their company along with our nieces and nephews. Brothers-in-law Jack Garber and Peter Peer and my late sister-in-law Mary Peer have always wanted updates on the writing. My sons Andrew and Jonathan and daughter (in-law) Thea have supported me, even when I have been on Pluto…how can one formulate the words…Dorcas, you have provided love and encouragement all along this journey.

I am grateful to my Creator and Redeemer from whom all blessings flow.

CPSIA information can be obtained at www.ICGtesting.com
Printed in the USA
LVOW11s0027190316

479838LV00002B/31/P